LUFTWAFFE

LUFTWAFFE

Williamson Murray

London
GEORGE ALLEN & UNWIN
Sydney

George Allen & Unwin (Publishers) Ltd
40 Museum Street, London WC1A 1LU, UK

George Allen & Unwin (Publishers) Ltd
Park Lane, Hemel Hempstead, Herts HP2 4TE, UK

George Allen & Unwin Australia Pty Ltd
8 Napier Road, North Sydney, NSW 2060, Australia

George Allen & Unwin with the
Port Nicholson Press
PO Box 11–838 Wellington, New Zealand

This edition first published in 1985

ISBN 0 04 923080 8

Printed in Great Britain by
Butler and Tanner Ltd, Frome

Contents

Acknowledgments

In a work of this nature, it is not surprising that many people played a considerable role in advising me as I began and conducted my research. The strengths of this book reflect their help; its weaknesses, my failings. In particular, I would like to thank Professor Philip Flammer of Brigham Young University who introduced me to the Air War College and played a major role in developing my interest in doing a study of the *Luftwaffe*.

At the Air University, Colonel Thomas Fabyanic, founder of the Airpower Research Institute (ARI), deserves special mention for his generous support of this project as does the current Director of the Institute, Colonel Kenneth Alnwick. Without the wholehearted support of Major General David Gray, former Commandant of the Air War College, this study could not have been conducted. I would also like to thank the following individuals at the Air War College for their help and guidance: Colonel Donald Frizzell, Lieutenant Colonels Donald Baucom, David MacIssac, David Lupton, and James True; and my colleagues in the ARI, Dr. David Mets and Dr. Kenneth Werrell. My special thanks to John Schenk and Dorothy McCluskie of the ARI for their thorough and detailed editorial assistance. I would also be remiss if I were not to express my thanks to those who helped with the typing of this manuscript and with arrangements for my travels: especially Edna Davis, Jo Ann Perdue, Mary Schenk, Betty Brown, and Norma Todd. I must thank Rose McCall for the excellent graphics and Alan Carter for designing the cover. In the academic world, my colleagues Professors I. B. Holley and Hans Gatzke deserve thanks for their help and advice. At the Ohio State University, Kenneth Watman and Bruce Nardulli were especially helpful in reviewing the content of the final manuscript. I should also like to thank Harry Fletcher for his considerable help in guiding me through the archives at the Albert F. Simpson Historical Research Center. In addition, I received substantial assistance while working abroad in European archives. In Great Britain, Group Captain "Tony" Mason afforded me access to critical materials in the RAF Staff College archives; "J. P." McDonald guided me through the materials available in the Public Record Office (PRO) from his post in the Air Historical Branch; and "Freddie" Lambert and Suzanne Marsh provided invaluable research assistance. I must also thank Professors Paul Kennedy, John Gooch, Brian Bond, and Richard Overy for their help as well as friendship that they extended to me while I was in Great Britain. Dr. Noble Frankland provided his time and his vast knowledge at the Imperial War Museum. I also must thank the staffs at the PRO, the Imperial War Museum, and the RAF Staff College.

In Germany, the staffs at the military archives in Freiburg and the *Militärgeschichtliches Forschungsamt* played an invaluable role in furthering my work. In particular, I must thank Dr. Manfred Messerschmidt, Dr. Jürgen Förster, Dr. Horst Boog, and especially Dr. Wilhelm Deist and Oberstleutnant Klaus Maier for their help and friendship. Major General Hans W. Asmus provided enormous patience, wisdom, as well as great courtesy and hospitality during my stay in Germany. I should also like to thank Oberst Werner Geissinger for his considerable help in proofreading the German as well as the English in the various drafts of this work. In the military archives in Freiburg, Frau Eleonore Müller was most helpful, always friendly, and invariably pleasant.

Finally, I must thank my wife Marjorie and my children, Alexandra and Spencer, for their support and love in all the separations that this project entailed.

Introduction

As with all military thought, a wide variety of political, historical, and economic factors guided the development of air doctrines in the period between the First and Second World Wars. Yet standing above all other influences was a revulsion against the mud and despair of the trenches. Thus, it is not surprising that an Italian senior officer, Giulio Douhet, would argue that airpower could prevent the repetition of a war that had cost Italy more than 400,000 dead. In terms of the first formulations of air doctrine, Douhet's thought did not prove particularly influential. In Britain, the development of doctrine, both within and outside of the Royal Air Force (RAF), already was well advanced by the end of the First World War.[1] Douhet may have exercised more influence on American doctrine, since various translated extracts of his work found their way into the library and schools of the American Air Service as early as 1922.[2] But the formulation of a precision bombing doctrine in the United States raises the question of how deeply his writings influenced early Army Air Corps pioneers.

Yet, Douhet's theories are symptomatic of intellectual attitudes current among military and civilian thinkers in the post-World War I era. They are, therefore, a useful point of departure. Douhet's central, single-minded argument was that the decisive mission for an air force was "strategic" bombing.[3] All other missions would only detract from this role and thus were considered counterproductive and a misuse of air resources. Douhet excluded the possibility of air defense, denied fighter aircraft a place in future air forces, and argued that close air support and interdiction were an irrelevant waste of aircraft. The *only* role for the air force of the future would be that of "strategic" bombing. Douhet further reasoned that the more heavily armed bomber would always prove superior to the fighter in air-to-air combat.[4] Underlying Douhet's arguments was a belief that bombardment of an enemy's population centers would shatter his morale and lead directly to the collapse of his war effort.[5] Such an attitude underlay most airpower theories between the wars and reflected a fundamental disbelief in the staying power of civilian societies.

Douhet's approach represented the hope that airpower and "strategic" bombing would enable international conflict to return to an era of short, decisive wars and thus would allow Europe to escape the mass slaughter of the last war. However, nowhere in Douhet's writings is there a sense of the technological and industrial underpinnings necessary for air war. This may subconsciously reflect the circumstance that Italy possessed none of the resources, expertise, or industrial requirements for such a war. It is worth noting, however, that most other theorists of the period were similarly reluctant to recognize the technological and industrial complexities of their subject. In retrospect, what makes the present-day conventional wisdom that Douhet was *the* prophet of airpower so surprising is the fact that his theory denigrated all the major missions of modern air forces except "strategic" bombing. Douhet dismissed air defense, tactical air, airlift, reconnaissance, and air superiority as immaterial. Not surprisingly, he also argued that airpower eliminated the requirement for armies and navies; consequently, there was no need for interservice cooperation.

The theories of Douhet and other early airpower advocates, with their stress on the notion that "strategic" bombing was the *exclusive* air mission, have exercised a great influence on the development of air forces since that time. Commentators on airpower have all too often tied their subject directly and exclusively to "strategic" bombing, while ignoring other possible applications. Air forces, however, have had to perform a wide variety of tasks other than "strategic" bombing. The real contribution of airpower to final victory in the Second World War lay in the very diversity of its capability. Ironically, the conduct of air operations in that war resembled, in many facets, the strategy of the previous conflict except that attrition came now in terms of aircraft and aircrews rather than mud-stained infantry. Month after month, year after year, crews climbed into their aircraft to fly over the European continent. Those in charge of the air battle came to measure success by drops in percentage points of bomber and fighter losses rather than in terms of yards gained. As one commentator has pointed out:

> Despite the visions of its protagonists of prewar days, the air war
> during the Second World War . . . was attrition war. It did not
> supplant the operations of conventional forces; it complemented
> them. Victory went to the air forces with the greatest depth, the
> greatest balance, the greatest flexibility in employment. The result
> was an air strategy completely unforeseen by air commanders . . .[6]

Thus, air war proved to have none of the decisive elements that prewar thinkers and advocates had so confidently predicted. Rather, air superiority and the utilization of airpower to break the opponent proved to be elusive and intractable problems. Enemy air forces could and did live to fight another day despite setbacks and defeat. Only the elimination of their supporting industries and resources, or the occupation of their bases by ground forces, guaranteed complete victory. The accomplishment of the former task proved extraordinarily difficult, while the latter indicated a degree of interdependence among air, ground, and naval forces that airpower advocates had so casually dismissed before the war. If the aircraft had added a new dimension to warfare, it had not changed the underlying principles.

While the concept of "strategic" bombing intrigued prewar air forces, practical factors—the "real world" of interservice relationships, defense priorities, political attitudes, and economic limitations—exercised an important influence over their establishment and development. Entirely different strategic factors determined control over the constitution and strategies of each different European air force, not to mention the Army Air Corps in the United States. To understand the course of those developments as well as the doctrine that guided the employment of airpower in the Second World War, one must grasp not only those factors influencing the air forces themselves but also the larger problems of national policy and strategy that influenced both politicians and the military.

The *Luftwaffe,* as with all military organizations, was a child of its time. The theories current throughout Europe in the 1920's and 1930's with respect to the future course of warfare in general and air war in particular also were present in Germany. Conversely, and not surprisingly, the peculiar forces that had guided and molded German history exercised their influence on the growth and development of the *Luftwaffe.* Like their counterparts in other nations, German airmen believed that their air force would be able to exercise an important, if not decisive, impact on a future war. To them, aircraft would be the definitive "strategic" weapon in the coming conflict.[7] Those currents within the German military, typified by Erich Ludendorff's conceptions of total war and the mobilization of the population, not only made the mass movement of the Nazi Party attractive to many officers but also led to a greater acceptance of airpower theories among the air force officer corps.[8] On the other hand, Germany's location and strategic situation presented the German military with a reality that they could not ignore; one major defeat on land might well seal the fate of the *Reich* before the *Luftwaffe* could have an impact. That represented a strategic situation quite different from that facing British and American airmen.

Besides reflecting its society, the *Luftwaffe* reflected the traditions and values of the Prussian officer corps. Like their brother officers in the army, *Luftwaffe* officers would prove imaginative, innovative, and highly competent in operational and tactical matters. They would, however, prove themselves lost in the higher realms of strategy and grand strategy, and it would be in those realms that the *Reich* would founder. After the war, the German generals and admirals would rush into print to prove that defeat had been largely the result of Hitler's leadership. In fact, their strategic concepts in the war proved to be as flawed as had the *Führer's.* The German generals and admirals aided and abetted Hitler's strategy in 1940; and when it succeeded beyond their wildest expectations with the fall of France, they reacted in awe, suspending reason for a blind faith in the invincibility of the *Reich* and its *Führer.* The strategic advice they tendered from that point forward ignored the industrial, economic, and political realities of war between industrialized nations that have existed since the American Civil War. The failure of German grand strategy and mobilization in 1940–41 insured not only the defeat of the German armed forces and the *Luftwaffe* in the coming years but a catastrophe for the German nation as well. Therefore, exploring the causes for the defeat of the *Luftwaffe,* the focus of this study, explains more than the downfall of an air force.

Notes

1. For a detailed discussion of this point, see the excellent work by Barry D. Powers, *Strategy Without Slide-Rule, British Air Strategy, 1914–1939* (London, 1976).

2. Robert F. Futrell, *Ideas, Concepts, Doctrine: A History of Basic Thinking in the United States Air Force, 1907–1964* (Montgomery, 1971), pp. 38–39.

3. For the purposes of this study, the use of the term "strategic" bombing will have the word strategic enclosed within quotation marks, as this author believes that the use of the word strategic by airpower enthusiasts to connote a particular form of bombing distorts the classical meaning of the word. The difficulty into which the misuse of this word has led historians might be best characterized by the following question: In May 1940, given Germany's military situation, what was the best strategic use to which the Luftwaffe could be put: supporting the army's drive to the channel and the crushing of French and British land power, or attacking French factories and cities? The answer is clear in a classical sense. Within the existing definitions of "strategic" and "tactical" bombing, it is not so clear.

4. General Giulio Douhet, *The Command of the Air* (London, 1943), pp. 16–17, 44, 55, 218, 239.

5. Edward Warner, "Douhet, Mitchell, Seversky: Theories of Air Warfare," *Makers of Modern Strategy,* ed. by Edward Mead Earle, 2nd edition (Princeton, 1971), p. 489.

6. William Emerson, "Operation Pointblank," Harmon Memorial Lecture, No. 4 (Colorado Springs, 1962), p. 41.

7. For the basic groundbreaking work on this point, I am indebted to a lecture given in September 1980 at the Air War College, Maxwell AFB, Alabama, by Oberstleutnant Klaus Maier of the Militärgeschichtliches Forschungsamt, Federal Republic of Germany. See the further discussion and amplification of this point in Chapter I and in my article, "The Luftwaffe Before the Second World War: A Mission, A Strategy?," *Journal of Strategic Studies* (September 1981).

8. See, in particular, the articles dealing with airpower that appeared in the *Militärwissenschaftliche Rundschau* from 1936 through 1939.

Origins and Preparation

Since World War II, American and British advocates of "strategic" bombing have criticized the *Luftwaffe* as being "in effect the handmaiden of the German army."[1] Such a view does not do justice to the complexity of the rearmament problem faced by the Third *Reich* in general and the *Luftwaffe* in particular. It also misses entirely the fact that a significant number of men within the *Luftwaffe*'s high command were converts to the doctrine of "strategic" bombing before the outbreak of World War II. That Germany was not able to wage a successful "strategic" bombing campaign in 1940 reflected merely the fact that German air strategists in the prewar period, like those in other nations, had considerably overestimated their ability to inflict punishing strategic damage with the weapons at hand. Before the war, the same trends that marked the air forces of Great Britain and the United States also were present in the officer corps of the *Luftwaffe*. But an important geographic consideration, the fact that Germany was a continental power, had an additional impact on German strategic thinking. In any conceivable conflict involving the military forces of the *Reich,* Germany faced the probability of land operations at the outset of hostilities. Thus, it would scarcely improve Germany's strategic position if — at the same time that the *Luftwaffe* launched aerial attacks on London, Paris, and Warsaw—Germany's enemies defeated the *Wehrmacht* on the border and overran Silesia, East Prussia, and the Rhineland.

THE STRATEGIC PROBLEM

Located in Central Europe with frontiers directly open to foreign military power, Germany, or the territory known before 1870 as "The Germanies," has faced strategic problems of a very different nature from those faced by Great Britain and the United States. Her vulnerability to invasion undoubtedly led German military leaders into the rather narrow concept that international conflict means war on land, and tended to force German military thinking into a concern for tactical and particularly operational matters. The experiences of the Seven Years War and the catastrophe of Jena/Auerstadt only served to reinforce such trends. Germany's strategic position, as well as the rather confined nature of the strategic arena in Western and Central Europe, also tended to make her military leaders pay scant attention to logistics. Put very simply, in the two World Wars British, and particularly American, generals had to think of logistics and supply before they considered operational matters. Their first

1

problem was how to get there. The Germans, on the other hand, were, in a sense, already there and had to solve the operational and tactical problems of war immediately. In the confined space of Central Europe their tendency to pay less attention to logistic matters was not necessarily disastrous. In the vast spaces of the Soviet Union, however, it was catastrophic in 1941.[2]

Adding to Germany's strategic vulnerability is the fact that industrial and economic power has increasingly dominated war since the mid point of the nineteenth century. Nations that do not have the ability to produce massive amounts of weapons, uniforms, ammunition, and supporting vehicles are not capable of conducting sustained war, and sustained war has been the mark of conflict between industrialized societies. The industrial revolution in the Ruhr in the nineteenth century gave Germany the industrial base from which to wage such a conflict. Ironically, the acquisition of that base opened Germany up to vulnerabilities in other areas. She possessed within her own territory virtually none of the raw materials necessary to the functioning of a wartime economy.[3] The only raw material she possessed in relative abundance was coal.[4] Moreover, the areas over which she was able to exercise considerable economic and diplomatic pressure (such as the Balkans) could provide only a relatively small percentage of the raw materials her wartime economy required. The great bulk of raw material imports vital to Germany's industrial base were open to interdiction by hostile powers, either by virtue of lying within enemy territory (as with the case of iron ore imports from the Briey Longwy basin in France) or by the fact that Germany's oceanic lines of communication over which they had to travel lay along the coasts of Great Britain.

World War I underlined Germany's economic vulnerability. By the end of the war, her population was on the brink of starvation, and her army was short of equipment and of such vital necessities as rubber and fuel. The inescapable reality that confronted Germany military planners, then, was that virtually all of the imports critical to the successful functioning of a war economy, oil, rubber, iron, aluminum ores, etc., would, from the outset of a major conflict on the European continent, be subject to blockade. Consequently, a basic principle in Hitler's long-range program was to gain control of the economic and raw materials of the European continent. The problem, obviously, was how to achieve that domination.

When Hitler came to power in January 1933, the tools available to extend Germany's strategic and economic reach seemed weak indeed. The serious limitations that the Versailles Treaty had placed on the size and nature of Germany's military forces had serious consequences on the defense industries of the nation. With no air force, a minuscule army, and an even smaller navy, Germany's military-industrial complex was almost nonexistent. Adding to the problem was the fact that the depression of the 1929-1933 period had severely damaged the economy's ability to support a massive armaments program. Politically, Hitler had to respond to that national crisis or risk the collapse of his revolution. Although from the minute he took power, Hitler drove the rearmament process as far and as fast as he could, rearmament, given the depth and strength of the armament industries, could not put enough of the unemployed back to work to overcome the economic difficulties.[5] Thus, Hitler's public works programs in effect represented an effort to build popular support for the regime by mitigating the depression until such time as the expansion of the industrial base allowed for an acceleration of armament production.

From the first, the Nazi regime was aware of the problem of raw materials. Yet efforts to alleviate shortages in particularly vulnerable sectors, such as the complete lack of natural petroleum sources, proved only partially successful. The oil problem is an excellent case in point. In order to maintain an increasingly motorized economy, meet the expanding demands of the rearming services, and cut down on dependence on foreign, insecure sources, the Germans devoted considerable resources to converting coal into petroleum products. In spite of substantial investments, however, synthetic production did not catch up with demand during the 1930's. While, in terms of consumption, the percentage of synthetic fuel steadily increased in this period, Germany imported more fuel in 1937 than she had at the beginning of the decade.[6] Demand had increased faster than production.[7] The fuel situation in the summer of 1938 reflects the magnitude of the problem. In June of that year, supplies in storage tanks covered only 25 percent of what mobilization requirements would be—or about four months of full wartime needs. Supplies of aviation lubricants were as low as 6 percent of mobilization requirements.[8] This was, of course, a reflection of Germany's inability to meet petroleum requirements from her own resources and her considerable problem in earning foreign exchange to buy strategic raw materials abroad.

In fact, a series of economic crises, caused by a lack of foreign exchange, marked the course of German rearmament throughout the 1930's.[9] Beginning in 1930, a worldwide depression caused a sharp dropoff in the value of German exports that continued through 1934. Thereafter, a marginal recovery took place. As a result, Germany's holdings of foreign exchange steadily dwindled, and this shortage of hard currency in the thirties set definite limits on the level of raw material imports available to support rearmament. As early as the fall of 1934, the Germans faced a running-down of stockpiles of raw materials and shortages of foreign exchange wherewith to buy replacements. Moreover, foreign suppliers were becoming doubtful as to the liquidity of the German economy and, as a result, would not deliver on credit. By the spring of 1935, stockpiles in nearly all areas had fallen dramatically; and for the remainder of the 1930's, the German economy lived a hand-to-mouth existence, desperately searching for sufficient foreign exchange to pay for imports.[10]

By 1937, the German economy was suffering serious shortages of steel because of a lack of ore imports, while the industry itself was operating at barely 83 percent of capacity.[11] These economic difficulties affected rearmament and most likely played a role in pushing Hitler into the confrontations of 1938. Here again, despite substantial financial gains made by the *Anschluss* with Austria, efforts to expand the rearmament program, to build up synthetic and munition industries, to begin the massive construction of the *Westwall* project, and to mobilize for the Czech crisis severely strained the German economy. In November 1938, Hermann Göring admitted that the German economic infrastructure had reached a point of maximum economic distress.[12] As a direct result, the *Oberkommando der Wehrmacht (OKW)*, the German armed forces high command, made major reductions in steel and raw material allocations to armament production.[13] Continuing difficulties led Hitler to announce to the *Reichstag* on January 30, 1939, that Germany must wage an "export battle" *(Exportschlacht)* to raise foreign exchange. Simultaneously, he announced further reduction in *Wehrmacht* allocations: steel, 30 percent; copper, 20 percent; aluminum, 47 percent; rubber, 14 percent.[14]

Problems stemming from insufficient foreign exchange and insufficient raw materials guided the course of German rearmament. Neither were available in sufficient quantity to build a massive "strategic" bombing force. Moreover, the army, given Germany's strategic position as a continental power, laid claims to resources that any rearmament program had to meet. Finally, the country's doubtful access to foreign supplies of petroleum products raised the question as to whether Germany could support an independent "strategic" bombing offensive. Thus, it is clear that economic constraints limited German air planners in the creation of the *Luftwaffe*, and the force they molded both before and during the war was influenced by strategic factors different from those guiding either the British or the Americans.

THE DEVELOPMENT OF THE *LUFTWAFFE*, 1933-39

With the onset of rearmament in 1933, the Germans faced considerable difficulties in the creation of an air capability. Given the facts that no German air force survived from the Great War, except as a camouflaged planning staff within the army, and that the capacity for civil aircraft production was inadequate for military purposes, the development of the *Luftwaffe* was an enormously complex task. Considering that within six and a half years this force would go to war and render vital support in the early campaigns, the Germans were successful in their efforts.

The first strategic problem on Hitler's ascension to power in January 1933 was the perception that a still-disarmed and vulnerable *Reich* faced the possibility of a preventive war, waged by Germany's neighbors to stop her resurrection as a military power. As Hitler told his generals shortly after he came to power, if France possessed any statesmen, she would wage war in the immediate future.[15] Thus, whatever theoretical advantages might accrue to Germany through the possession of a "strategic" bombing force in the late 1930's, the Third *Reich* faced the possibility of an imminent war. Future "strategic" bombing capabilities would do nothing for present military difficulties, while the tactical potential of a less sophisticated, more conventional air force would be more quickly realized for utilization in a contemporary military confrontation.

German interest in a "strategic" air weapon goes back to the early days of the First World War. Frustrated at the imposition of a distant blockade in 1914 by the Royal Navy, German naval strategists looked for a means to strike at the British Empire. As early as August 1914, Rear Admiral Paul Behncke, Deputy Chief of the Naval Staff, urged that the navy's Zeppelins attack London, the heart of the British Empire. Such attacks, he argued, "may be expected, whether they involve London or the neighborhood of London, to cause panic in the population which may possibly render it doubtful that the war can be continued."[16] Grand Admiral Alfred von Tirpitz noted in a letter of November 1914 that:

> The English are now in terror of the Zeppelin, perhaps not without reason. I contend here, ... I go for the standpoint of "war to the knife," but I am not in favor of "frightfulness" . . . . Also, single bombs from flying machines are wrong; they are odious when they hit and kill old women, and one gets used to them. If [however] one could set fire to London in thirty places, then what in a small way is odious would retire before something fine and powerful.[17]

When the Zeppelin campaign failed, the Germans attacked London with the heavier-than-air bomber. That campaign, even if it did not achieve great material damage, did lead to the creation of the Royal Air Force.[18]

The defeat of 1918 and the conditions of the Versailles Treaty eliminated aircraft from the German arsenal. Not only did the Treaty deny Germany access to new technology as represented by the submarine, the airplane, and the tank, but it severely limited the size and capability of Germany's military services. The victorious Allies, however, could not prevent the Germans from thinking about their experiences and the weapons of the last war.

Hans von Seeckt, father of the *Reichswehr,* insured that the minuscule army left to Germany included a small body of officers (180) who had had experience in the conduct of air battles in the Great War. As he did with the development of motorized/mechanized warfare, Seeckt showed considerable prescience with respect to airpower[19] and saw to it that its advocates possessed at least some voice within the army.[20] Limitations imposed by Versailles forced German aviation into a narrow framework. Nevertheless, extensive subsidies to civil aviation contributed to the survival of Germany's aviation industry, and preparations for air rearmament during the Weimar Republic played a significant role in the establishment of the *Luftwaffe* during the Nazi period.[21] Germany's lead in civil aviation was such that, by 1927, German airlines flew greater distances with more passengers than did their French, British, and Italian competitors together.[22] This experience in long-distance flying, navigation, and instrument flying obviously had a positive impact on developing the *Luftwaffe* in the interwar period.

Still, the problems facing the Nazis in January 1933 in the creation of an air force that could serve as an effective tool of diplomatic and military policy were enormous. Only a tiny cadre of experienced officers existed within the army and navy; *Lufthansa* experience was not directly convertible into a military force; and the German aircraft industry, weakened not only by the depression but also by internecine quarrels amongst its almost bankrupt firms, was not prepared for massive expansion.

The *Luftwaffe* was favored at its birth, however, by the fact that its patron and first leader, Hermann Göring, was Hitler's right-hand man. Göring's political pull insured that the *Luftwaffe* gained position as an independent service and that it enjoyed a privileged status in interservice arguments over allocation of funding and resources. While funding did not represent a problem in the early days of rearmament, by the late thirties serious economic difficulties impacted on all services—but on the *Luftwaffe* least of all because of Göring's position. Unfortunately, however, for the efficient functioning of the German command system, Göring, as Minister of Aviation, refused to subordinate himself to the Minister of War, Werner von Blomberg. Thus, Blomberg, who was responsible for coordinating and controlling the three services, faced an impossible task. His problems were further compounded by the fact that Göring, as Commander in Chief of the *Luftwaffe,* went around him at every opportunity.[23]

In the long run, Göring had a disastrous impact on the *Luftwaffe* but his position as number two in the political hierarchy prevented Hitler from removing him, even after his many failures demanded such action. Initially, Göring's political tasks as Hitler's chief aide during the consolidation of power (the establishment of the *Gestapo,* the savaging of the Communists, and the purge of Ernst Röhm and the S.A.) absorbed a substantial portion of *"der Dicke's"* time.[24] Thus, while Göring as *Reich* Air Minister and after March 1935 Commander in Chief played at the role, at least until 1936 others made the substantive decisions creating the new force. Göring's mental framework was that of a squadron-level fighter pilot which he had been in the First World War; and throughout his tenure as *Luftwaffe* commander, he remained largely ignorant of logistics, strategy, aircraft capabilities, technology, and engineering—in other words, just about everything having to do with airpower. Compounding his ignorance was the fact that he took a rather loose view of hard work, and his visits to the Air Ministry were sporadic at best. In July 1938, during an address to aircraft manufacturers, Göring even admitted that he saw Ernst Udet, at this time in charge of all the *Luftwaffe's* technical departments, only once a week.[25] The long-range implications of such leadership spelled disaster. Nevertheless, in the short term, his political pull was of great use in the establishment of an independent air arm.

Göring was particularly fortunate in his leading subordinate. Erhard Milch, Göring's and Hitler's selection for the position of State Secretary in the new Air Ministry, possessed tremendous drive, a thorough knowledge of the production capabilities of the German aircraft industry, a detailed understanding of its managers and designers, and, perhaps most importantly, excellent connections within the political leadership of the newly established Third *Reich*.[26] Milch's brashness and arrogance eventually led to conflict with more conventional *Luftwaffe* officers who had remained professional soldiers during the Weimar period. The latter never forgot that Milch had left the military after the war and eventually became the head of *Lufthansa*.

The other senior officers of the *Luftwaffe* came from the *Reichswehr*. Of particular note here is Blomberg's contribution to the establishment of the new service's officer corps. In 1933, on the occasion of the founding of the Air Ministry, Blomberg commented that the new *Luftwaffe* would require an elite officer corps with "a tempestuous spirit of attack."[27] More to the point, he insured that the army transferred first-class officers to the new service. Significantly, not only personnel with flying experience moved to the Air Ministry but also highly trained officers from the army's general staff transferred to the *Luftwaffe*. Blomberg offered Göring a choice between Walther Wever and the future Field Marshal Erich von Manstein for the position of Chief of Staff of the *Luftwaffe;* Göring chose the former. When Wever died in an aircraft crash in 1936, Blomberg initially considered offering Göring the future chief of the army's general staff, General Franz Halder, as a replacement.[28] Along with Wever, army luminaries such as Albert Kesselring and Hans Jeschonnek transferred to the *Luftwaffe*. Jeschonnek, among other accomplishments, had finished first in his class at the *Kriegsakademie,* usually a sure sign of promise for a quick rise to the top of the military profession.[29] By October 1933, 228 officers up to the rank of colonel had transferred from the older services. By January 1939, a further 70 had followed along with 1,600 noncommissioned officers (NCOs) and enlisted men. Blomberg demanded that individuals selected for transfer represent the "best of the best."[30]

The high quality of these officers should not obscure the fact that, in their short careers, the *Luftwaffe*'s officer corps and general staff never reached the level of homogeneity and competence that the army officer corps and general staff enjoyed. The simple mechanics of expansion alone ruled out such a possibility. From 1933 to 1935, the *Luftwaffe* developed a personnel strength of approximately 900 flying officers, 200 flak (antiaircraft) officers, and 17,000 men. In addition to those who transferred from the army, its officers came from a wide variety of sources; many pilots entered the *Luftwaffe* directly from civil aviation, while veterans of the First World War further fleshed out the officer corps. From this mixture, by the outbreak of the war the *Luftwaffe* had expanded to a strength of 15,000 officers and 370,000 men.[31] Within the officer corps alone, the sheer magnitude of the expansion resulted in an entirely understandable lack of coherence and a notable lack of strategic competence. Shortly after the surprise Japanese attack on Hawaii, Hitler asked his military staff where Pearl Harbor was, and none, including his *Luftwaffe* officers, could give him the answer.[32] Understandably, given the shortness of their service's lifespan, *Luftwaffe* officers had an immense task of catching up and maintaining currency in the technical aspects of their service. The result was that they became at best technocrats and operational experts with limited vision.[33] Thus, with perhaps the exception of Wever and to a lesser extent Milch, the officer corps showed a lack of understanding of the larger issues revolving around the interrelation between airpower and national strategy, defects which may, indeed, have been nothing less than fatal.

At the outset of rearmament in 1933, German planners had to decide what role the *Luftwaffe* would play within the framework of national strategy. In May 1933, Milch, the key figure in the *Luftwaffe*'s organization and development in the 1933-36 period, received a major study from one of his *Lufthansa* subordinates, Dr. Robert Knauss, on the strategic concept for the new air force.[34] Knauss' report contained major elements of Douhet's "strategic" bombing philosophy, Tirpitz's "risk theory," and what would today be regarded as "deterrence" doctrine. He believed that the purpose of the regime was the "restoration of Germany's great power position in Europe" and argued that since Poland and France, particularly the latter, would resist such a development, Germany faced the immediate possibility of a preventive war waged by these two powers. To overcome German military weakness through rearmament, thereby re-establishing Germany's status as a great power, Knauss suggested the rapid creation of a strong air force, whose decisive element would be the deterrent effect of a fleet of 400 four-engine bombers. He argued that destruction of the targets offered by modern industrialized society would halt the enemy's industrial production and that the bombing of population centers offered the possibility of breaking the enemy's morale. Thus, if Germany possessed a "strategic" bombing fleet, her putative enemies—Poland and France —would think seriously before incurring the risk of air attack on major population centers. Above all, Knauss argued that the creation of such a bombing fleet offered a greater possibility for affecting the European military balance than did the establishment of army divisions or the construction of naval surface units.

The creation of such a bomber force aborted for several reasons. First, the army was hardly enthusiastic about such a strategic conception. Colonel Konrad Gossler, head of the *Truppenamt*'s operation section, argued that there was no longer a clear separation between the homeland and the combat front. Thus, opposing air forces possessed the same opportunity to attack their enemy's homeland. Moreover, since the beginning of time, Gossler argued, each new weapon had led many to conclude that the old weapons of war were no longer needed. This had simply not happened. Finally, he objected that such a conception, if realized, "might destroy war by making it impossible for both sides." Such arguments would lead inevitably to pacifism.[35]

More decisive for the actual establishment of the *Luftwaffe* was the discovery that the German aircraft industry lacked the designers, industrial capacity, or experience to build such a "strategic" bombing fleet. During the summer of 1933, Milch and his planners found that their first production program could barely squeeze out of industry 1,000 aircraft, and most of them were training aircraft, to expand the flying base.[36] The "combat" aircraft hardly deserved that characterization. From a January 1933 industrial base of 4,000 workers, the aircraft industry expanded to 16,870 workers in 1934 and to 204,100 workers by the fall of 1938.[37] To a great extent, this represented Milch's great triumph as an organizer and bureaucrat.

While Milch played the decisive role in the administrative and industrial tasks of creating the *Luftwaffe,* Wever played a no-less-important role in formulating the new service's doctrine and strategy. He was not an unabashed advocate of "strategic" bombing but rather argued for a broadly based air strategy. Wever did not believe that the *Luftwaffe's* existence as a separate service gave it a mission entirely independent of the army and navy. Rather, he argued that its mission should complement those of the other services. Thus, the *Luftwaffe's* contribution to victory could involve attacks on an enemy's air forces, his army, his fleet, or even the destruction of his resources and armament industry. The conditions of the general situation and overall national strategy would determine in what form the air battle would be waged. While not denying the possible need for air defense or the importance of fighters, Wever felt that the "decisive weapon of air warfare is the bomber."[38]

Meanwhile, a careful analysis of Germany's strategic situation raised doubts as to whether "strategic" bombing should be the *Luftwaffe's* sole mission. A war game conducted during the winter of 1933-34 indicated that a bomber fleet alone could not immediately destroy the enemy's air fleet. The conclusion was that strong fighter forces, as well as antiaircraft guns, were necessary to protect the *Reich's* industrial and population centers.[39]

Wever's thinking on the subject of airpower was best summed up in the formulation of German air doctrine that first appeared in 1935: "Conduct of the Air War *(Die Luftkriegführung)."*[40] As with most German military doctrinal statements, this one was a clear, concise formulation. It was not meant to restrict or dogmatize but rather to give air force commanders the widest latitude and to encourage maximum flexibility. Among the chief points enunciated was the reiteration of Wever's point that the employment of the *Luftwaffe* should reflect the overall framework of national grand strategy. Within grand strategy, the critical tasks of the *Luftwaffe* would be the attainment and maintenance of air superiority, support of the army and the navy, attacks on enemy industry, and interdiction between front and homeland. "The nature of the enemy, the time of year, the structure of his land, the character of his people, as well as one's own military capabilities" would determine how airpower should be used.[41]

Wever's doctrinal statement stressed that air resources should not be used piecemeal nor should frequent changes be made in goals. In all likelihood, however, it would not be possible clearly to separate the struggle with an enemy air force from support provided to the army and navy. Unlike most airpower theorists, he showed a ready understanding for the fact that air superiority would be a most elusive goal. Changing technical capabilities, new production, and replacement of losses would all combine to allow the enemy to fight another day. While Wever felt that "strategic" bombing attacks on the enemy's industrial and economic sources of power could have an absolute impact, he warned that such an offensive might take too long to be decisive and thus be too late to help the army and the navy. He emphasized that only the strongest cooperation between the three services could achieve the overall objectives of national grand strategy. Air war against an enemy's industrial base should occur only when (1) there was an opportunity to affect quickly the war's course, (2) when land and naval preparations had prepared the way, (3) when there was a stalemate, or (4) when a decisive effect could be achieved only through the destruction of the enemy's economic sources of power.

Wever's death in the spring of 1936 was a major blow to the *Luftwaffe*. However, it did not result in cancellation of the four-engine "strategic" bomber project, as some have claimed.[42] In 1936, the Air Ministry cancelled the development of the four-engine Dornier Do 19 and Junkers Ju 89, because engines that could provide adequate power were not yet available from the German aircraft industry.* The failure to have a suitable engine available in 1936 and 1937 reflected the fact that German air rearmament did not begin until 1933. As a result, German engine research and development was in some important respects behind what was occurring in Great Britain and the United States. Moreover, the long lead-time required for engine development constrained German aircraft design throughout the 1930's. The Germans did embark on the He 177 project in 1937 in the belief that Heinkel could design and build a long-range "strategic" bomber by the early 1940's. The design of the He 177, in effect, represented an effort to shortcut the development of a high-powered engine for a heavy bomber by placing four engines within two nacelles. Heinkel designers expected that, by cutting down on the drag, they would have a bomber comparable to other four-engine aircraft with more powerful engines. Unfortunately for the *Luftwaffe,* they were never able to overcome the difficulties inherent in the design; hence the failure of the program reflected the failure of engineering and not a lack of interest in "strategic" bombing.[43]

Wever's broadly based approach to the question of airpower should not obscure the fact that his writings never denied the possibility that "strategic" bombing could play an important part in air warfare. Moreover, a significant portion of the *Luftwaffe*'s doctrinal thinking remained enamored with "strategic" bombing throughout the thirties. There was an obvious reason why this should be so: The concepts of total war and total mobilization had proved attractive to much of the German military throughout the interwar period. While Seeckt argued for establishment of an elite army, Ludendorff articulated the concept that modern war had become total. Unlike most interwar military thinkers who

---

*German aircraft designations do not contain a hyphen between manufacturer and model number. American designations do. The text will reflect national preferences.

sought to escape the horrors of World War I's mass warfare, Ludendorff embraced what had happened and argued that Germany must prepare in ruthless fashion during peace for the next war. Among other things, Ludendorff argued that war involved the entire population in the conflict, not just armies. In his view, economic production had become as important as battles on the frontline.[44] The 1918 collapse convinced him that Germany required a dictatorship for the next war and, even more importantly, that some method must be found to inspire the national unity that had come apart in the last months of the war.[45]

From the first, the Nazi Party appeared to be a particularly attractive means for insuring such unity of national will. Hitler's popularity with the masses offered the possibility of establishing a national cohesion that the conception of total war demanded.[46] Thus, what made the Nazi movement attractive to the military throughout the 1930's was the fact that it seemingly provided the psychological basis and preparation necessary for total war. *"Ein Volk, ein Reich, ein Führer"* was more than a slogan; in the mass rallies and propaganda displays, it guaranteed that the 1918 collapse would not recur. Thus, Ludendorff's conception of total war and the mass movement of the Nazi Party provided an affinity between the military and the National Socialist movement that helps explain the readiness of the officer corps to serve a party that hardly represented their upper-class attitudes.

Many within the *Luftwaffe* found in this political and psychological preparation for war a basis to argue that the next war would be a total war of the air and that, because of the national unity that the Nazis had created, Germany could better withstand such a struggle. In the May 1933 memorandum discussed above, Knauss argued that "the terrorizing of the enemy's chief cities and industrial regions through bombing would lead that much more quickly to a collapse of morale, the weaker the national character of his people is, and the more that social and political rifts cleave his society." Knauss assumed that a totalitarian society like Nazi Germany would prove more capable of enduring bombing attacks than would the fractured societies of Britain and France.[47] Such attitudes played an important role in *Luftwaffe* thinking throughout the remainder of the thirties.

Knauss himself went on from the Air Ministry to become the head of the new Air War College in Gatow. There, under his leadership, the emphasis remained solidly on "strategic" bombing until the outbreak of the war. Nearly all lectures concerned the "strategic" uses of airpower; virtually none discussed tactical cooperation with the army.[48] Similarly, in the military journals, emphasis centered on "strategic" bombing. The prestigious *Militärwissenschaftliche Rundschau,* the War Ministry's journal, which was founded in 1936, published a number of theoretical pieces on future developments in air warfare. Nearly all discussed the use of "strategic" airpower, some emphasizing that aspect of air warfare to the exclusion of others.[49] One author commented that European military powers were increasingly making the bomber force the heart of their airpower. The maneuverability and technical capability of the new generation of bombers were such that "already in today's circumstances the bomber offensive would be as unstoppable as the flight of a shell."[50] Major Herhudt von Rohden, eventually the head of the general staff's historical section, went so far as to argue that only the air force was in a position to attack the enemy in depth and to launch immediately "destructive attacks against the economic resources of the enemy from all directions." Moreover, von Rohden stressed, the *Luftwaffe* should not be an auxiliary to the other two services. Interservice cooperation did not mean dividing the *Luftwaffe* up and parceling out its personnel and materiel to support ground or naval tactical purposes. Rather, interservice cooperation meant using the *Luftwaffe* in "a unified and massed 'strategic' air war" that could provide for better long-range support.[51]

The failure of the *Luftwaffe* to progress further towards a "strategic" bombing capability is attributable to several factors. The first is that many within the *Luftwaffe* thought that their twin-engine aircraft gave them the ability to launch "strategic" attacks against Germany's most likely continental opponents—France, Czechoslovakia, and Poland. England presented greater problems, but even here General Felmy, Commander of *Luftflotte* 2 and charged with planning an air war against Britain in 1939, saw possibilities. Concluding the 1939 spring planning effort, Felmy admitted to his subordinates that the *Luftwaffe* did not yet possess any of the prerequisites for a successful "strategic" bombing offensive against Great Britain. He did suggest, however, that the panic that had broken out in London in September at the height of the Munich crisis indicated that a massive aerial onslaught directed against London might break Britain's powers of resistance.[52] A second factor lay on the technical side: The engineers never solved the He 177 design difficulties. Moreover, not only did Germany not possess the economic strength and resources to build a "strategic" bombing force on the scale of the British and American effort of 1943-44 but few airmen of any nation in the prewar period had foreseen the magnitude of the industrial and military effort that "strategic" bombing would require. Thus, it is not surprising that, in 1939, Germany was not much better prepared to launch a "strategic" bombing campaign than was Britain.

As previously mentioned, Wever's death in 1936 was disastrous for the future course of the *Luftwaffe* but in a sense other than that which most historians have suggested. First, he provided the glue that held the *Luftwaffe* together in the early rearmament years. He got on relatively well with other *Luftwaffe* leaders, including Milch, and all respected his qualities of intellect and leadership. Second, and equally important, Wever possessed both a practical military mind and a first-class strategic sense: he thought in terms of the long pull and not just immediate, operational problems. Given the financial and raw material constraints on rearmament, in the thirties Wever could not have created a "strategic" bombing force such as the United States Army Air Forces (USAAF) had in 1943 and 1944. Nevertheless, his presence would have mitigated the rather haphazard approach that characterized the *Luftwaffe* in the late thirties and early forties.

The caliber of Wever's successors underlines his importance to the *Luftwaffe*. Albert Kesselring, his immediate successor, was a troop leader *par excellence,* but overall he was not an effective Chief of Staff and did not get along well with Milch. The back-biting between the two led to Kesselring's replacement by Hans-Jürgen Stumpff within a year.[53] The latter proved little better than Kesselring; and, in February 1939, Göring named Hans Jeschonnek as Chief of the *Luftwaffe's* General Staff. Despite his brilliance at the *Kriegsakademie,* Jeschonnek proved no better than his predecessors. He was arrogant, shortsighted, and had had several bitter run-ins with Milch.[54] Moreover, Jeschonnek fell under Hitler's spell and swallowed the line that the *Führer* was the "greatest commander in history." As a result, he never possessed the independent judgment that his position required. Shortly after Munich, Hitler demanded a fivefold increase in the *Luftwaffe* by 1942, an impossible goal, given the economic constraints and the megalomaniacal proportions of the program. (Such a force would have required 85 percent of the world's aviation fuel and cost 60 million *RM,* a total equivalent to all German defense spending for the 1933-39 period.) Senior officers correctly concluded that there was no prospect of accomplishing such a plan. Jeschonnek, however, announced, "Gentlemen, in my view it is our duty to support the *Führer* and not work against him."[55] Such an attitude was not consistent with the traditions of the general staff, but fully conformed to Hitler's belief that his generals were there not to give advice but to carry out orders.[56]

The almost yearly changes in the position of Chief of Staff from 1936 to 1939 were not the only result of Göring's mishandling of the *Luftwaffe*. He now severely constrained Milch by balancing the State Secretary with others within the *Luftwaffe's* bureaucracy. Ernest Udet, a great fighter pilot in World War I and barnstormer of the 1920's, received an appointment as head of the *Luftwaffe's* technical departments as well as the Office of Air Armament where he controlled research and development for the *Luftwaffe*. Udet did not possess the technical or engineering skills to handle such responsibilities and was a dreadful administrator. He had no less than 26 separate departments reporting directly to him.[57]

In sum, Göring had neither the ability nor the background to run the enormously expanded *Luftwaffe*. Milch was increasingly isolated from the centers of power; and the other top leaders, such as Kesselring, Udet, and Jeschonnek, did not have Wever's strategic insight. Long-range planning and strategic thinking went by the boards, and the *Luftwaffe* increasingly became a force that reacted to day-to-day political and operational pressures.

The result of this increasingly chaotic organizational situation showed up most directly in the production programs of the late prewar period. Even considering their raw material shortages and their economic and foreign exchange difficulties, the Germans undercut the production capacity of their aircraft industry. Waste, obsolete production methods, and bad planning characterized the efforts of even the major manufacturers. Throughout the late 1930's, the

Germans produced numerous plans for aircraft production due to constantly changing goals and priorities. By 1939, aircraft production was only 70 percent of stated production goals (goals that were significantly lower than Hitler's demand for quintupling of the *Luftwaffe*).[58] The figures in Table I[59] reflect the shortfall between planned and actual production figures in the last years of peace.

TABLE I

Planned and Actual Aircraft Output, 1938 and 1939

1938 Plan Nos.	All Types	Combat	1939 Plan Nos.	All Types	Combat
6	5,800	4,129	8	9,957	7,095
7	6,021	3,971	10	8,299	6,051
7/8	6,154	3,710	10/11	8,619	6,357
Actual Production	5,235	3,350	Actual Production	8,295	4,733

The mobilization plans, drawn up by the general staff under Jeschonnek, and the production plans of Udet's technical experts continued to diverge—the former influenced by pressure from Göring and Hitler (and the real possibility of war), the latter under the impact of the distressing economic situation discussed at the beginning of this chapter. The repercussions of this situation were not immediately apparent since the *Luftwaffe*'s size and strength proved sufficient to meet initial wartime demands in Poland and France. But in long-range terms, this unbridgeable gulf between the general staff and the *Luftwaffe*'s technical departments made industrial planning almost irrelevant in the consideration of German strategy. There was no agency or person, except Göring, in overall charge of strategic planning, force structure, or industrial production. The results led directly to the situation of 1943-44.

Beginning in 1936, but with increasing force in 1937, the *Luftwaffe* transitioned into its second generation of aircraft. The emphasis from above on statistics complicated an inherently difficult process. As Göring stated, what mattered were numbers "to impress Hitler and to enable Hitler, in turn, to impress the world."[60] Milch at least mitigated some of the worst aspects of this numbers craze. In 1935, he recognized that most models in production were obsolescent and refused to increase their production levels. But to stop aircraft production just because nothing better was yet available would have been counterproductive, especially since a national goal was to expand aircraft production capacity. Fortunately for the *Luftwaffe*, the Ju 52, produced as a bomber during this period, proved an outstanding transport aircraft and formed the backbone of the *Luftwaffe*'s airlift force throughout the Second World

War.[61] Complicating the introduction of new aircraft were the difficulties experienced by German engine manufacturers in producing engines whose performance standards were comparable with those of American and British industry.[62] The fact that the Ju 52 was not an adequate bomber in any respect led to pressure from the bomber units for replacement. As a result, the Air Ministry rushed the Ju 86, He 111, and Do 17 into production before they had been thoroughly evaluated. None of the three was fully satisfactory; the Ju 86 was virtually useless, while the He 111 showed the most potential for improvement.[63]

The 1936 medium bomber program was meant to serve as an interim measure until a third generation of bombers arrived. Udet's growing love affair with the dive bomber had a disastrous effect on that program. In Spain, the *Luftwaffe* had experienced difficulty in hitting targets accurately from high altitude; the Ju 87 dive bomber was most accurate in putting bombs directly on target. From this experience, Udet concluded that every bomber should be a dive bomber. There were sound arguments for the need to achieve more accurate bombing, because the low production capacity of the German munitions industry in the late thirties did not allow for much wastage of bombs.[64] But the decision that the next generation of bombers should have the characteristics of dive bombers was manifestly impractical, if not impossible. The results were serious for both the Ju 88 and the He 177. In the case of the Ju 88 prototype, Udet's demand that it possess a dive-bombing capability, along with 50,000 other design changes, increased the aircraft weight from 7 to 12 tons with a concomitant loss in speed from 500 km/h to 300 km/h. Moreover, these changes delayed actual production by at least a year.[65] The additional requirement that the He 177 be able to dive bomb came in the middle of program development and virtually insured that, given an inherently complex engine design, the model would never evolve into an effective heavy bomber.[66]

Theoretically, the *Luftwaffe* based its approach to airpower on the belief that a flying unit was not combat-ready unless it possessed modern, reliable aircraft backed up by a first-class maintenance organization and supply system. Using this rationale, frontline units had to receive adequate numbers of replacement aircraft and reserves of spare parts. In an "after action" report on the Czech crisis, the chief of the *Luftwaffe's* supply services reported that these requirements had not yet been met.[67] Among other items, he underscored the fact that the number of aircraft engines in maintenance and supply depots represented only 4 to 5 percent of the total of engines in service. The basic cause of this situation was Göring's refusal to follow recommendations that the *Luftwaffe* devote 20 to 30 percent of production to provide adequate inventories of spare parts.[68] Instead, the Germans assigned production almost exclusively to firstline strength because of the political outlook of the top leaders and their fascination with numbers. This practice continued throughout the war. As a result, the *Luftwaffe* was chronically short of spare parts and had to cannibalize, a procedure that had a direct and negative impact on operational ready rates.

THE *LUFTWAFFE'S* IMPACT, 1933-39

The *Luftwaffe's* initial strategic purpose had been to deter Poland and France from launching a preventive war against the *Reich*. It was neither notably successful nor notably unsuccessful in this role. Hitler's diplomatic skills, particularly the 1934 Non Aggression Pact with Poland, were more important in altering the European diplomatic balance of power. The French, at least in the early period of German rearmament, were somewhat *blasé* about the implications of the *Luftwaffe*. As late as September 1937, one military leader told the British that with "a veritable forest of guns" over the Maginot Line, France could prevent the German air force from intervening in the land battle.[69] The following month, the French assured the visiting British Chief of the Imperial General Staff that they planned to strengthen the Maginot Line to counter German aircraft superiority and that they believed any "enemy would require an unrealizable supremacy of machines to get over the antiaircraft defenses. . . ."[70]

If at first the air threat did not impress the French, it certainly upset the British. Stanley Baldwin's remark that the bomber "would always get through" is ample testimony to British fears about the air threat. There is, of course, some irony here, because at least until 1937-38 Hitler did not seriously consider Great Britain as a possible opponent. Nevertheless, British alarms over the "growing air threat" and hopes of realizing an air limitation agreement between the European powers were a useful diplomatic tool that allowed Hitler to manipulate the island power.

If the threat of the *Luftwaffe,* along with the army's buildup in the mid-thirties, impressed many Europeans with the resurgence of German military power, the reality was a different matter. The conclusion drawn from an assessment of an April 1936 war game in the *Luftwaffe* staff warned that German air rearmament thus far was insufficient and inferior to that of the French air force.[71] Not until 1938 did the *Luftwaffe* begin to realize its potential. Before that point, events in southern Europe had already influenced the *Luftwaffe's* development.

While the Germans were completing the first stages of rearmament, the Spanish Civil War occurred. Hitler willingly provided substantial aid to the rebels, especially in the air, but regarded the war mostly as useful in distracting Europe's attention from the growing danger of Nazi Germany.[72] Spain was a helpful testing ground for the *Luftwaffe's* aircraft and tactics. The Ju 52 quickly showed its limitations as a bomber and was soon relegated to its World War II role as a transport; the He 51 biplanes proved inferior to Russian aircraft supplied to the Republic. By 1937, the Germans had introduced the Bf 109 fighter, the He 111 and Do 17 bombers, as well as a few Ju 87 dive bombers. All these aircraft soon indicated their relative worth. On the ground, the 88mm flak gun proved effective not only as an antiaircraft weapon but also against ground targets.[73] The fighter commander, Adolph Galland, however, felt that the combat experience gained in Spain led the *Luftwaffe* to overestimate the performance of antiaircraft weapons, thereby distorting future programs for the air defense of the *Reich*.[74]

Perhaps of greater importance, the Germans learned invaluable combat lessons in Spain which they quickly absorbed into their doctrine. The development of close air support and cooperation with the army came directly from the Spanish Civil War. Wolfram von Richthofen, Manfred's cousin, arrived in Spain out of favor with the Air Ministry in Berlin. Upon his arrival, his concept of air war was not substantially different from that of most other *Luftwaffe* officers at the time; in other words, close air support for the army ranked at the bottom of his priorities. However, once in his position as Chief of Staff to the Condor Legion, Richthofen recognized that his theories of airpower and Spanish political realities did not have much in common. The stalemate on the ground, the lack of suitable "strategic" targets, and the great Nationalist weakness in artillery led him to consider using his forces to support directly Franco's offensive against Bilbao.[75]

Against considerable opposition and without official sanction, Richthofen developed the technique and tactics of close air support for ground forces in offensive operations.[76] None of the elements required for such operations existed within the *Luftwaffe* before the offensive against the Basque Republic. To begin with, there was an overall lack of experience and technical expertise, because communication between ground and air units (particularly radio) did not yet exist. By the time Richthofen was through developing the concept and tactics, the Germans had recognized the necessity for closer cooperation and improved planning between ground and air units, had established close communication links and recognition devices, and had detailed *Luftwaffe* liaison officers to serve directly with frontline units. All of this was due to Richthofen's drive and imagination.[77]

The lessons of "strategic" bombing were more muted. On the one hand, one after-action report *(Erfahrungsbericht)* went so far as to emphasize the impact upon morale of bombing the Republic's work force, i.e., attacks resulting in supposedly bad discipline among the working class. Continuous attacks even by small bombing units against a single city, especially where antiaircraft defenses were insufficient, had "deeply impressed and depressed" the population.[78] Nevertheless, the *Luftwaffe*'s yearbook for 1938 suggested that "strategic" air warfare in Spain had not occurred for a variety of reasons. The Nationalists had been in a position to destroy utterly Madrid, Barcelona, and Valencia with incendiaries but had not done so because of the delicate political problems involved in a civil war. Franco had not attacked the major ports because these lay within the "international zone" and he had not authorized attacks on armament factories because Spain possessed so few.[79]

Conversely, Captain Heye of the *Seekriegsleitung* (naval high command) gained a different impression after talking with *Luftwaffe* officers during a 1938 visit to Spain. He reported on his return to Berlin:

> Disregarding the military success accompanying the *Luftwaffe's*
> use in immediate support of army operations, one gets the im-
> pression that our attacks on objects of little military importance,
> through which in most cases many women and children . . .
> were hit, are not a suitable means to break an opponent's re-
> sistance. They seem to strengthen his resistance. . . . The memory
> of the air attack on Guernica by the [Condor] Legion still today
> affects the population and permits no friendly feelings for Ger-
> many in the population of the Basques, who earlier were
> thoroughly friendly to Germany and in no manner Communistic.[80]

Significantly, whatever their attitudes towards the effects of bombing, the Spanish Civil War confirmed in some Germans' minds the belief that fighter aircraft and civil defense measures would be of importance in the coming war. In 1937, Udet increased the proportion of fighters to bombers from the existing 1-to-3 ratio to 1-to-2.[81] Moreover, unlike their counterparts in Britain, German airpower experts "believed that civil defense measures could appreciably reduce casualties in an air attack."[82]

Spain also indicated the difficulties of hitting targets by both day and night. The experience gleaned from night attacks proved generally beneficial, while the problem of hitting targets accurately in daylight missions helped push Udet towards his conception that every bomber should have a dive-bombing capability. At night, the Germans discovered the difficulties not only of finding targets but of hitting them.[83] This led to a recognition that navigational aids were critical for bad-weather and night operations. In March 1939, Kesselring admitted that even given a high level of technical competence, he doubted whether the average bomber crew could hit their target with any degree of accuracy at night or in bad weather.[84] To help overcome this difficulty, *Luftwaffe* scientists experimented with radio direction systems as an aid to navigation and as a technological answer to the problem of bombing targets in conditions of limited visibility. The *"Knickebein"* system, first used in the Battle of Britain, was a direct result.[85]

The introduction of a new generation of bombers and fighters after 1936 caused serious transition problems. High accident rates coupled with low in-commission rates continued to plague the transition program as late as the summer of 1938. At that time, *Luftwaffe* operational ready rates were surprisingly low. On August 1, 1938, the in-commission rate for bombers was 49 percent, for fighters 70 percent, and for the whole force 57 percent.[86] Only after drastically reducing flying and training time could the *Luftwaffe* bring its in-commission rate to a respectable level by the end of September 1938, shortly before the onset of the planned invasion of Czechoslovakia.[87] The level of air-crew training was equally deplorable. In August, the *Luftwaffe* possessed barely two-thirds of its authorized crew strength, and over 40 percent of the crews on duty were not fully operational. Table II[88] helps to point out the extent of the problem.

TABLE II
Aircrew Readiness, August 1938

Type of Aircraft	Authorized Number of Crews	Crew Training Status	
		Fully Operational	Partially Operational
Strat Recon	228	84	57
Tac Recon	297	183	128
Fighter	938	537	364
Bomber	1,409	378	411
Dive Bomber	300	80	123
Ground Attack	195	89	11
Transport	117	10	17
Coastal and Navy	230	71	34
TOTAL	3,714	1,432	1,145

Moreover, the chief of supply services pointed out that in an after-action report on the Czech crisis that:

> In the last months [before Munich], the following special measures were carried through concurrently: (1) equipping of many new units; (2) rearming of numerous units; (3) early partial overhaul for approximately 60 percent of frontline aircraft; (4) replacement of spare parts; (5) rebuilding of numerous aircraft in supply depots, units, and industry; (6) rearmament of many aircraft; (7) accelerated introduction of partially overhauled motors . . . ; (8) establishment of four new air groups and one new airfield . . . ; (10) preparation and resupply of mobilization supplies corresponding to the newly established units, rearmed units, and transferred units. . . . The compression of these tasks into a very short time span has once more and in clear fashion pointed out the known lack of readiness in the maintenance of flying equipment as well as among technical personnel. . . .
>
> The consequence of these circumstances was: (a) a constant and, for firstline aircraft, complete lack of reserves both as accident replacements and for mobilization; (b) a weakening of the aircraft inventory in the training schools in favor of regular units; (c) a lack of reserve engines and supplies for the timely equipment of airfields, supply services, and depots both for peacetime needs as well as mobilization.[89]

While the *Luftwaffe* was not prepared to face a military confrontation over Czechoslovakia,[90] it had a major impact on British and French diplomacy. Throughout the late 1930's, the British Chiefs of Staff had repeatedly warned their ministers about the German air danger. In late March 1938, they emphasized that in a military confrontation over Czechoslovakia, Germany would dominate the air and, moreover, that the entire *Luftwaffe* might concentrate on Britain as the most promising method of winning the war. In addition, they warned that while earlier studies had considered a possible air attack in 1939, an air offensive in 1938 would cause more damage because fewer defenses yet existed.[91] Upon his return from meeting Hitler at Godesberg, Chamberlain remarked to his Cabinet colleagues that he had just flown up the Thames and had imagined German bombers taking the same course.[92]

Nevertheless, in the final analysis, fears about the *Luftwaffe* probably were not decisive in molding the British response to German threats before Munich. In fact, by September 1938 many leading appeasers felt that the West could beat Germany in a war,[93] while the British military in late September came around to the view that "the latent resources of our Empire and the doubtful morale of our opponents under the stress of war give us confidence as to the ultimate outcome [of a war]."[94] But the terrible costs of World War I lingered in British minds and tempered the response. As the Foreign Minister, Lord Halifax, told the Cabinet he "could not feel we were justified in embarking on an action that would result in such untold suffering."[95]

The *Luftwaffe*'s effect on the French in 1938 can, at best, be described as causing both panic and a collapse in morale. After the French Chief of Air Staff had visited Germany in mid-August and had been shown a display of aerial might, he returned to Paris to advise his government that the French air force would last barely two weeks against the *Luftwaffe*.[96] The spectacle that the French Foreign Minister, Georges Bonnet, made in warning the German ambassador that an attack on Czechoslovakia would lead to war, while at the same time begging that Germany not put France in a position where she must honor her obligations, reflected desperate French fears concerning the German air threat.[97] At the end of September 1938, a senior general told the British military attaché that in a European war, "French cities would be laid in ruins [because] . . . they had no means of defense." He added that France was now paying the price for the years of neglect of her air force.[98] There was, of course, no more talk about a forest of guns over the Maginot Line.

What is surprising, given the predilection of some historians to argue that Munich saved Britain from the *Luftwaffe,* is the fact that the German air force had made almost no preparation to wage war against the British. In August 1938, a staff officer of *Luftflotte* 2, responsible for operations over the North Sea and against the British Isles, suggested that Germany's current capability to attack Britain would amount to pin pricks.[99] In late September, General Felmy, Commander of the Second Air Force, warned the high command that "given the means at his disposal, a war of destruction against England seemed to be excluded."[100] In May 1939, Felmy concluded an address by highlighting the lack of preparation for a "strategic" bombing offensive against Britain. He doubted whether the *Luftwaffe* could achieve more than a limited success in 1940 and admitted that it would not have one air division fully trained and prepared to attack Britain in the summer of 1939. Considering the Second Air Force's equipment, preparations for an air offensive on Britain were totally inadequate *(völlig ungenügend).*[101]

This state of affairs was a result of Germany's strategic situation. *Luftwaffe* planners had to face the fact that their first commitment would be to a major ground war. The conduct and the success of those operations would determine whether Germany would surmount her narrow economic and strategic base and thus be able to fight a protracted world war. If not, the war would end right there. In 1938, *"Fall Grün,"* the proposed attack on Czechoslovakia, would have involved the *Wehrmacht* in a major land campaign against the Czech Republic, leaving the army with only weak ground forces to protect the Polish and French frontiers. As was the case with *"Fall Weiss,"* the attack on Poland, the *Wehrmacht* would then have faced a major ground campaign in the west.[102]

The result of this strategic situation was that the *Luftwaffe* tied its plans for both 1938 and 1939 closely to the operations of the army. The tasks of the two air fleets assigned to support the invasion of Czechoslovakia were to destroy the Czech air force, to hinder the mobilization and movement of reserves, to support the army's advance, and only then to attack the enemy's population.[103] Similarly, the *Luftwaffe's* general staff underscored that the most important missions in the west would be to attack the French air force and prevent a breakthrough along the *Westwall* by Allied forces.[104] The same pattern repeated itself in 1939, except that this time Hitler refused to allow himself to be robbed of an opportunity to wage his "little war."

CONCLUSION

In conclusion, several features of prewar *Luftwaffe* doctrine deserve further elaboration. The first, and most obvious, is that the prevailing historical picture of a *Luftwaffe* tied closely to the army's coattails is no longer tenable. Most *Luftwaffe* leaders from Göring through the general staff believed, as did their counterparts in Britain and the United States, that "strategic" bombing was the chief mission of an air force and that, given such a role, the *Luftwaffe* would win the next war.[105] They probably did not consider the twin-engine aircraft at their disposal in 1937 and 1938 sufficient for a campaign against Britain, Russia, or the United States; but within the context of Central Europe, were not such aircraft adequate for attacking Warsaw, Prague, and Paris? Most Germans thought so, and certainly the leaders of the French and British air forces agreed with them. For the long run, the *Luftwaffe* had begun work on a four-engine bomber for more distant targets. Like most of their contemporaries in other air forces, *Luftwaffe* officers considerably overestimated the possibilities and potential of "strategic" air war, both in terms of industrial damage and of impact on morale. This was not surprising, since there was so little empirical evidence on which to base predictions. The prevalence of such attitudes within the *Luftwaffe's* officer corps helps explain the attack on Rotterdam as well as the seemingly casual shift from a strategy of air superiority to a direct attack on London during the Battle of Britain. Moreover, in their approach to "strategic" bombing, the Germans showed a greater awareness of the difficulties involved in finding and hitting targets at night or in bad weather than did other air forces. For instance, their preparations in developing blind-bombing devices like *"Knickebein"* were further advanced by a full two years than were those of the RAF.

When Adolf Hitler launched the *Wehrmacht* against Poland on September 1, 1939, to begin the Second World War, the *Luftwaffe* was in a considerably better position than it had been the previous fall. The staff and commanders had solved most of the teething problems that had marked the transition into a new generation of aircraft in 1937 and 1938. Air units possessed modern equipment, and antiaircraft and airborne forces gave the Germans capabilities that other European air forces could not match. In 1939, the *Luftwaffe* was close to realizing the potential of aircraft, while its doctrine of close air support and cooperation with the army placed it in the position to have a decisive impact on the coming battles beside the army's armored forces.

Nevertheless, there were problems. Above all, there were serious deficiencies in the character of the *Luftwaffe*'s leadership since most of those occupying top positions were incapable of thinking for the long pull. On the technical and production side, the Germans appeared well on their way to disaster. By the spring of 1939, British aircraft production was approaching German levels and in 1940 actually surpassed German output.[106] The fact that Göring had shunted Milch aside and turned the technical and production side over to Udet insured that this ominous trend would continue. Further exacerbating the *Luftwaffe*'s dangerous position were certain critical research and development decisions taken in the last month before the outbreak of war. In December 1938, Milch pushed through a major reorganization of the production system so that the aircraft industry could concentrate on developing a few superior aircraft.[107] In August 1939, shortly before the outbreak of war, Göring along with Udet, Milch, and Jeschonnek decided to constrict development and production. They placed strong development emphasis on the He 177, Ju 88, and Me 210.[108] While such emphasis was not meant to halt research and development on the next generation of aircraft, it did tend to slow down experimentation. When the Germans awoke to the danger in 1942, it was already too late; they had to fight the great air battles of 1943 and 1944 with basically the same equipment that they had used against Poland.[109]

As discussed above, there were factors pushing the Germans towards a broader conception of airpower than was the case in Britain and America. Economic reality placed severe limits on the nature and force structure of the *Luftwaffe* in the prewar period. Even more important than this limiting factor was Germany's general strategic placement in the heart of the European continent. Unlike British and American air strategists, German air strategists faced the prospect of a large-scale land battle from the moment that a war began and were never in a position to ignore entirely the demands of Germany's ground forces. Simultaneously, most German airmen believed that "strategic" bombing would be a decisive factor in the coming war. Thus, German air strategy was a combination of these two divergent elements. So, with the outbreak of hostilities, German airmen found themselves in strategic circumstances quite different from those they had originally envisioned. Unfortunately for the West, the broader based approach of Wever, along with a greater flexibility in *Luftwaffe* doctrine, corresponded more closely to the combat capabilities of aircraft in the late 1930's than did the almost exclusive "strategic" bombing doctrines of the RAF or the US Army Air Corps.[110] The real war of 1939 and 1940 was not the war for which most of the *Luftwaffe* had prepared, but it was a war in the initial stages to which it could and did adapt, and to which it applied airpower in cooperation with the army to gain an initial, devastating strategic victory that unfortunately, from the German perspective, could not be sustained.

Notes

1. For this view, see Dennis Richards, *The Royal Air Force, 1939–1945* (London, 1953), p. 29; Asher Lee, *The German Air Force* (New York, 1946), pp. 16–17; and even surprisingly Sir Charles Webster and Noble Frankland, *The Strategic Air Offensive Against Germany (SAOAG)*, Vol. I, *Preparation* (London, 1961), p. 125.

2. For the best discussions of the failures of German logistics in the Russian campaign see: Martin Van Creveld, *Supplying War* (New York, 1977); and Klaus Reinhardt, *Die Wende vor Moskau* (Stuttgart, 1972).

3. For a fuller discussion of the impact of the German economic situation on rearmament, see my dissertation: Williamson Murray, "The Change in the European Balance of Power, 1938-1939," Yale University dissertation, 1975, Chapter V.

4. For a discussion of the German coal situation, see: Institut für Weltwirtschaft an der Universität Kiel, "Die Kohlenversorgung Europas durch Grossdeutschland unter den gegenwärtigen kriegswirtschaftlichen Gesichtspunkten," Oct 1939, National Archives and Records Service (NARS) T–84/195/1560466.

5. For an outstanding discussion of this process see Gerhard L. Weinberg's brilliant study of Germany's foreign and strategic policies in the 1933-1936 period: *The Foreign Policy of Hitler's Germany, Vol. I, Diplomatic Revolution in Europe 1933-1936* (Chicago, 1970).

6. Abschrift einer Aufstellung der Überwachungsstelle für Mineralöl vom 3.5.38., "Deutschlands Mineralöl nach In- und Auslandsaufkommen in den Jahren 1928–1937 in 1000t," NARS T–77/282/1107267. There is an additional problem present here. The synthetic fuel process and its basic raw material, coal, were not conducive to the production of high-octane gasoline, and the Luftwaffe would have a major problem throughout the war in obtaining sufficient amounts of high-octane aviation fuel.

7. Speech by Korvettenkapitän Haensel, 4.3.39. während des Kriegsspieles des Marinekommandoamtes in Oberhof, p. 13, NARS T–1022/PG49089.

8. OKW Economic Staff, "Die Arbeiten des Wi Rü Amtes an der Mineralöl-Versorgung," p. 37, NARS T–77/282/1107267.

9. For a fuller discussion of these problems, see: Hans-Erich Volkmann, "Aussenhandel und Aufrüstung in Deutschland, 1933 bis 1939," *Wirtschaft und Rüstung am Vorabend des Zweiten Weltkrieges*, ed. by Friedrich Forstmeier and Hans-Erich Volkmann (Düsseldorf, 1975), p. 85.

10. Ibid., p. 89.

11. Dieter Petzina, *Autarkiepolitik im Dritten Reich* (Stuttgart, 1968), p. 103.

12. International Military Tribunal (IMT), *Trial of Major War Criminals (TMWC)*, XXXII, Doc. #3575PSS.

13. Ibid., Doc. #1301PS.

14. J. Düffer, *Weimar, Hitler und die Marine: Reichspolitik und Flottenbau, 1920-1939* (Düsseldorf, 1973), p. 504.

15. Edward W. Bennett, *German Rearmament and the West, 1932–1933* (Princeton, 1979), p.324.

16. Douglas H. Robinson, "The Zeppelin Bomber," *The Air Power Historian* (July 1961), p. 133.

17. Grand Admiral Alfred von Tirpitz, *My Memoirs*, Vol. II (New York, 1919), pp. 271–72.

18. For an excellent discussion of the German "strategic" bombing effort in World War I, see: Francis K. Mason, *Battle Over Britain* (New York, 1969), Chapter I.

19. For Seeckt's interest in the development of motorized forces and his recognition of their

importance for future defense policy, see: Reichswehrministerium, Chef der Heeresleitung, Betr: "Harzübung 8.1.22.," NARS T–79/65/000622.

20. For the best description of Seeckt's contribution to the carrying over of a portion of Germany's World War I air force into the body of the Reichswehr, see: Karl-Heinz Völker, "Die Entwicklung der militärischen Luftfahrt in Deutschland, 1920–1933," in *Beiträge zur Militär-und Kriegsgeschichte*, Vol. III, (Stuttgart, 1962), pp. 126–27.

21. For a discussion of the historiography surrounding the Weimar period's contribution to the Luftwaffe, see: Edward L. Homze's outstanding study *Arming the Luftwaffe, The Reich Air Ministry and the German Aircraft Industry, 1919–1939* (Lincoln, 1976), pp. 40–41. For the other outstanding study of the Luftwaffe after 1933, see: Karl-Heinz Völker, *Die deutsche Luftwaffe, 1933–1939: Aufbau, Führung und Rüstung der Luftwaffe sowie die Entwicklung der deutschen Luftkriegstheorie* (Stuttgart, 1967). From the small corps of flying officers within the Reichswehr, 97 army and 19 naval officers would reach general officer rank in the Luftwaffe. In addition, a number of army officers such as Kesselring and Wever would transfer to the Luftwaffe and then learn to fly after 1933. Völker, "Die Entwicklung der militärischen Luftfahrt in Deutschland, 1920–1933," pp. 284–88.

22. Ibid., p. 32.

23. It is worth noting that the army was no more willing to allow the establishment of a joint services high command.

24. For a discussion of Göring's role in the Nazi seizure of power, see Karl Dietrich Bracher, Wolfgang Sauer, and Gerhard Schulz, *Die Nationalsozialistische Machtergreifung* (Köln, 1960).

25. IMT, *TMWC*, XXXVIII, Doc. 140–R.

26. For an interesting study of Milch and his contribution to the Luftwaffe, see David Irving's *The Rise and Fall of the Luftwaffe, The Life of Field Marshal Erhard Milch* (Boston, 1973).

27. Wilhelm Deist, Manfred Messerschmidt, Hans-Erich Volkmann, Wolfram Wette, *Das deutsche Reich und der Zweite Weltkrieg*, Vol. I, *Ursachen und Voraussetzung der deutschen Kriegspolitik* (Stuttgart, 1979), p. 478.

28. Homze, *Arming the Luftwaffe*, pp. 60, 235.

29. Ibid., p. 236. It is worth noting that Jeschonnek had been a pilot in World War I and subsequently served mostly with the air planning staffs within the Reichswehr during the Weimar period.

30. Deist, *et al.*, *Das deutsche Reich und der Zweite Weltkrieg*, Vol. I., pp. 478–79.

31. Ibid., p. 479.

32. Horst Boog, "Higher Command and Leadership in the German Luftwaffe, 1935–1945," *Air Power and Warfare, Proceedings of the Eighth Military History Symposium, USAF Academy*, ed. by Colonel Alfred F. Hurley and Major Robert C. Ehrhart (Washington, 1979).

33. Dr. Boog's above cited article is particularly useful in his discussion of the intellectual limitations of the Luftwaffe's officer corps.

34. Bernard Heimann and Joachim Schunke, "Eine geheime Denkschrift zur Luftkriegskonzeption Hitler-Deutschlands vom Mai 1933," *Zeitschrift für Militärgeschichte*, Vol. III (1964), pp. 72–86.

35. Klaus A. Maier, Horst Rohde, Bernd Stegemann, and Hans Umbreit, *Das deutsche Reich und der Zweite Weltkrieg*, Vol. II, *Die Errichtung der Hegemonie auf dem europäischen Kontinent* (Stuttgart, 1979), p. 44.

36. For a full discussion of the different programs and the industrial and engineering problems that the Luftwaffe faced, see: Homze, *Arming the Luftwaffe*, Chapter IX.

37. Deist, *et al.*, *Das deutsche Reich und der Zweite Weltkrieg*, Vol. I, pp. 480–81; see Homze, *Arming the Luftwaffe*, p. 184, for a detailed breakdown of worker distribution within the aircraft industry.

38. See, in particular, Wever's lecture to the German Air War College, 1.11.35. "Vortrag des Generalmajors Wever bei Eröffnung der Luftkriegsakademie und Lufttechnischen Akademie in Berlin-Gatow am 1. November 1935," *Die Luftwaffe* (1936).

39. Karl-Heinz Völker, *Dokumente und Dokumentarfotos zur Geschichte der deutschen Luftwaffe* (Stuttgart, 1968), Doc. #184, p. 429.

40. "Die Luftkriegführung," Berlin 1935; copy made available to the author by Oberstleutnant Klaus Maier of the Militärgeschichtliches Forschungsamt, Freiburg, Federal Republic of Germany.

41. Ibid., paragraph 11.

42. See Herbert M. Mason, Jr., *The Rise of the Luftwaffe* (New York, 1973), pp. 213–15; Peter Calvocoressi and Guy Wint, *Total War* (London, 1972), p. 492; Dennis Richards, *Royal Air Force, 1939–1945*, Vol. I (London, 1953), p. 29; Basil Collier, *The Defense of the United Kingdom* (London, 1957), p. 121; Telford Taylor, *The Breaking Wave* (New York, 1967), p. 83; and Webster and Frankland, *SAOAG*, Vol. I, p. 125.

43. Völker, *Die deutsche Luftwaffe*, pp. 132–33; and H. Schliephake, *The Birth of the Luftwaffe* (Chicago, 1972), pp. 38–39. For further amplification on the failure to have a heavy bomber in the later 1930's, see Edward L. Homze's excellent piece, "The Luftwaffe's Failure to Develop a Heavy Bomber Before World War II," *Aerospace Historian* (March 1977). For a fascinating and groundbreaking work on the problems of engine development, see Edward W. Constant, III, *The Origins of the Turbo Jet Revolution* (Baltimore, 1980). See also C. Fayette Taylor, *Aircraft Propulsion, A Review of the Evolution of Aircraft Piston Engines* (Washington, 1971).

44. See the discussion by Hans Speier, "Ludendorff: The German Concept of Total War," *Makers of Modern Strategy*, ed. by Edward Mead Earle (Princeton, 1943). I would also like to thank Oberstleutnant Klaus Maier of the Militärgeschichtliches Forschungsamt for making available to me his lecture given at the Air War College in September 1980 in Montgomery, Alabama, that clarified the connection and importance of the concept of total war and its relationship to the development of Luftwaffe doctrine.

45. Erich Ludendorff, *Kriegsführung und Politik* (Berlin, 1922), pp. 328–33.

46. See the interesting discussion of this point in Deist, *et al.*, *Das deutsche Reich und der Zweite Weltkrieg*, Vol. I, pp. 124–25.

47. Heimann and Schunke, "Eine geheime Denkschrift zur Luftkriegskonzeption Hitler-Deutschlands vom Mai 1933," pp. 72–86.

48. See Air Ministry, *The Rise and Fall of the German Air Force (1933–1945)*, issued by the Air Ministry (ACAS) (London, 1948), p. 42.

49. See, in particular, Oberst (E) Frhr. v. Bulow, "Die Grundlagen neuzeitlicher Luftstreitkräfte," *Militärwissenschaftliche Rundschau* (1936); Major Bartz, "Kriegsflugzeuge, ihre Aufgaben und Leistung," (1936); and particularly Major Herhudt von Rohden, "Betrachtungen über den Luftkrieg," also *Militärwissenschaftliche Rundschau* 4 parts (1937).

50. Bartz, "Kriegsflugzeuge, ihre Aufgaben und Leistung," p. 210.

51. von Rohden, "Betrachtungen über den Luftkrieg," Part I, pp. 198–200.

52. BA/MA, RL7/42, Luftflottenkommando 2, Führungsabteilung Nr. 7093/39 g. Kdos, 13.5.39., Schlussbesprechung des Planspiels, 1939. Those who desire another example of how senior staff officers thought the Luftwaffe would wage an independent "strategic" air war should consult: Chef des Organisationsstabes im Generalstab der Luftwaffe Nr. 50/38 Chefsache, An den Chef des Generalstabes der Luftwaffe, "Organisationsstudie 1950," NARS T–971/36/0002.

53. Irving,*The Rise and Fall of the Luftwaffe*, p. 47.

54. Ibid., p. 69. Although many times, Milch's abrasive personality led him into major conflicts with his fellow Luftwaffe officers, the fault in this case seems to have lain with Jeschonnek.

55. Homze, *Arming the Luftwaffe*, pp. 223–24.

56. Deist, *et al.*, *Das deutsche Reich und der Zweite Weltkrieg*, Vol. I, p. 645.

57. Irving, *The Rise and Fall of the Luftwaffe*, p. 68.

58. R. J. Overy, "German Aircraft Production 1939–1942: A Study in the German War Economy," Cambridge University dissertation, 1977, p. 2; for a discussion of the prewar German production plans, see: R. J. Overy, "The German Pre-War Aircraft Production Plans: November 1936–April 1939," *English Historical Review* (1975).

59. Ibid., p. 11.

60. Homze, *Arming the Luftwaffe*, p. 106.

61. Deist, *et al.*, *Das deutsche Reich und der Zweite Weltkrieg*, Vol. I, pp. 484–85.

62. Homze, *Arming the Luftwaffe*, pp. 82–87 and 158–63.

63. Ibid., pp. 120–21.

64. For the surprisingly low capacity levels of the German munitions industry in the thirties, see: Bericht des Herrn Professor Dr. C. Krauch über die Lage auf dem Arbeitsgebiet der Chemie in der Sitzung des Generalrates am 24.6.41., NARS T–84/217/1586749.

65. Deist, *et al.*, *Das deutsche Reich und der Zweite Weltkrieg*, Vol. I, p. 490.

66. Homze, *Arming the Luftwaffe*, pp. 167–68.

67. Milch Collection, Imperial War Museum, Reel 55, Vol. 57, Der Chef des Nachschubamts, Nr. 3365/38, g. Kdos., Berlin, 3.11.38., Anlage L. E. 2. Nr. 15.222/38 g. Kdos, Berlin, Okt 1938, "Erfahrungsbericht über die Spannungszeit 1938," p. 3270.

68. Richard Suchenwirth, *The Development of the German Air Force, 1919–1939* (New York, 1970), p. 148.

69. PRO CAB 23/89, Cab 35(37), Meeting of the Cabinet, 29.9.37., p. 215.

70. PRO CAB 21/575, 15.10.37., "French and German Maneuvers," a note by Field Marshal Sir C. Deverell on his visit. The French, of course, might have been disguising their real fears from a thoroughly unreliable ally. Still, they spent little on their air force until the awakening of 1938.

71. Völker, *Dokumente und Dokumentarfotos zur Geschichte der deutschen Luftwaffe*, Doc. #196, p. 449.

72. Gerhard Weinberg, *The Foreign Policy of Hitler's Germany, 1933–1936* (Chicago, 1970), p. 298.

73. "Einsatz der deutschen Flakartillerie in Spanien," Aus Koehlers Flieger-Kalender 1940; "Flakeinsatz während des Feldzuges in Spanien," Auszug aus einer Ausarbeitung von Gen. Lt. Karl Veith vom Mai 1948, Karlsruhe Collection, Albert F. Simpson Historical Research Center (AFSHRC): K 113.302.

74. "Auswirkung der Erfahrungen in Spanien," Aus einer Ausarbeitung von Generallt. Galland über die Luftverteidigung des Reiches, 1946. Ibid.

75. Conversation with Generalmajor a.D. Hans W. Asmus, Baden-Baden, November 7 and 8, 1980, and letter from General Asmus, February 6, 1981.

76. Air Ministry, *The Rise and Fall of the German Air Force*, pp. 16–17.

77. "Lehren aus dem Feldzug in Spanien, Einsatz von Schlachtfliegern," aus einer Studie der 8. Abt. des Generalstabes aus dem Jahre 1944; Hans Hennig Freiherr von Beust, "Die deutsche Luftwaffe im spanischen Krieg," 2.10.56., p. 162, AFSHRC: K 113.302.

78. Maier, *et al.*, *Das deutsche Reich und der Zweite Weltkrieg*, Vol. II, p. 53.

79. Oberst Jaenecke, "Lehren des spanischen Bürgerkrieges," *Jahrbuch des deutschen Heeres, 1938* (Leipzig, 1939).

80. OKM, B. Nr., 1. Abt. Skl. la 961/38g.Kdos., Berlin, 14.7.38., Geheime Kommandosache, NARS T–1022/2957/PG48902.

81. Homze, *Arming the Luftwaffe*, p. 172.

82. PRO CAB 63/14, I. O. (S)1., 19.7.37., Air Raid Precautions Department, Intelligence Section, visit to Berlin of Major F. L. Fraser, "Interview with Ministeralrat Grosskreuz."

83. Von Beust, "Die deutsche Luftwaffe im spanischen Krieg," p. 140ff.

84. BA/MA RL 2 II/101, "Zusammenhänge zwischen Meteorologie und Taktik," Vortrag: General der Flieger Kesselring, Chef der Luftflotte 1., 1.3.39., p. 5.

85. See PRO AIR 20/1623, Air Scientific Intellience Report No. 6, "The Crooked Leg," 28.6.40., for a discussion of how British intelligence discovered the German system.

86. Air Historical Branch, Air Ministry, VII, Translations: Luftwaffe Strength and Serviceability Statistics, G 302694/AR/9/51/50.

87. BA/MA RL 7/164, Der Kommandierende General und Befehlshaber der Luftwaffengruppe 3., 1.12.38., "Erfahrungsbericht über die Spannungszeit 1938: Teil II."

88. Air Ministry, *The Rise and Fall of the German Air Force, 1933–1945* (London, 1948), pp. 19–20.

89. Milch Collection, Imperial War Museum, Reel 55, Vol. 57, Der Chef des Nachschubamts, Nr. 3365/38, g. Kdos., 3.11.38.; Anlage L.E. 2. Nr. 15.222/38, "Erfahrungsbericht über die Spannungszeit," p. 3270.

90. For a fuller discussion of this issue, see my article, "German Air Power and the Munich Crisis," *War and Society*, Vol. II, ed. by Brian Bond and Ian Roy (London, 1977).

91. Public Record Office (PRO) CAB 53/37, COS 698 (Revise), CID, COS Subcommittee, "Military Implications of German Aggression Against Czechoslovakia," 28.3.38., pp. 150–51.

92. PRO CAB 23/95, Cab 42(38), Meeting of the Cabinet, 24.9.3., p. 178.

93. Neville Henderson admitted that Germany might not last more than "a certain number of months." PRO FO 800/309, Part IV, letter from Henderson to Cadogan, 4.9.38. Halifax told the Cabinet in mid-September 1938 that "he had no doubt that if we were involved in war now, we should win it after a long time." PRO CAB 23/95, Cab 39(38), Meeting of the Cabinet, 17.9.38., pp. 98–99.

94. PRO CAB 53/41, COS 773, COS Subcommittee, "The Czechoslovak Crisis," 29.9.38.

95. PRO CAB 23/95, Cab 39(38), Meeting of the Cabinet, 17.9.38., pp. 98–99.

96. For General Vuillemin's visit to Germany, see: *Documents diplomatiques français (DDF)*, 2nd Series, Vol. X, Doc. #401, 18.8.38., Doc. #429, 21.8.38., and Doc. #444, 23.8.38. For what he told his government, also see: Paul Stehlin, *Temoignage. pour l'histoire* (Paris, 1964), pp. 86-91. For Vuilleman's advice at the end of the month, see: *DDF*, 2nd Series, Vol. XI, Doc. #377, 26.9.38.

97. *Akten zur deutschen auswärtigen Politik (ADAP)*, Series D, Vol. II, Doc. #422, 2.9.38.

98. PRO CAB 24/279, CP 206(38), Colonel Fraser to Phipps, 23.9.38., p. 52.

99. Vortragsnotiz über Besprechung mit Ia des Befehlshabers der Luftwaffengruppe Braunschweig, 25.8.38., NARS T–1022/2307/34562.

100. L. W. Gr. Kdo. 2, Führungsabteilung, Nr. 210/38, 22.9.38., "Planstudie 'Fall Blau'." Quoted by Richard Suchenwirth, *Hans Jeschonnek*, pp. 39-40.

101. BA/MA RL 7/42, RL 7/43, Luftflottenkommando 2., Führungsabteilung, Nr. 7093/39, 13.5.39., "Schlussbesprechung des Planspieles 1939."

102. For a fuller discussion of the overall strategic situation at the time of Munich in 1938, see my article: Williamson Murray, "Munich, 1938: The Military Confrontation," *Journal of Strategic Studies* (December 1979).

103. Concerning Luftwaffe planning for the invasion of Czechoslovakia, see in particular BA/MA RL 7/164, Der Kommandierende General und Befehlshaber der Luftwaffengruppe 3., 1.12.38., "Erfahrungsbericht über die Spannungszeit 1938."

104. IMT, *TMWC,* Vol. XXV, p. 381.

105. One of the surprising elements in the widespread willingness to accept the legend that the Luftwaffe was the "hand maiden" of the army is the fact that Göring never got along with the army, and it thus seems totally contradictory from what we know of his personality that he would accept a role that subordinated his air force to the army in overall German strategy.

106. Overy, "The German Pre-War Aircraft Production Plans: November 1936–April 1939," p. 796.

107. Milch Collection, Imperial War Museum, Reel 64, Vol. 65, p. 7400: 13.12.38., "Vortragsunterlagen für den Vortrag vor dem Herrn Generalfeldmarschall," p. 7419.

108. Homze, *Arming the Luftwaffe,* p. 229.

109. It should be noted that the Allies also fought these 1944 battles by and large with the aircraft in production or on the drawing boards.

110. See Appendix I for a description of the development of air doctrine in Britain and the United States.

II The Easy War

BACKGROUND TO THE INVASION OF POLAND

The German triumph over Czechoslovakia in September 1938 misled not only Hitler but his military as well and created the psychological conditions that contributed heavily to the decision to attack Poland the following year—a decision that precipitated the Second World War. Almost immediately after the signing of the Munich agreement, Hitler regretted that he had backed away from a limited war against Czechoslovakia. Further aggravating his displeasure was the fact that the Sudetenland's inclusion within Germany did nothing to relieve the *Reich*'s serious economic problems. Göring admitted in November 1938 that economic difficulties had reached the point where no more workers were available, factories were at full capacity, foreign exchange was completely exhausted, and the economy was in dire straits.[1] These economic troubles meant that, in early 1939, the regime had to reduce the *Wehrmacht*'s steel allocations by 30 percent, copper by 20 percent, aluminum by 47 percent, rubber by 30 percent, and cement from 25 percent to 45 percent.[2]

Under these conditions, the temptation to seize the remainder of Czechoslovakia and gain control of its industrial resources as well as its considerable holdings of foreign exchange was overwhelming. In March 1939, using Czech political troubles as an excuse, Hitler ordered the *Wehrmacht* to complete what the Munich agreements had begun. He threatened the Czech leader, Dr. Emil Hacha, by declaring that if Czechoslovakia refused to accede to German demands, "half of Prague would be in ruins from bombing within two hours, and that this would be only the beginning. Hundreds of bombers were waiting the order to takeoff, and they would receive that order at six in the morning, if the signatures were not forthcoming."[3]

But the seizure of Prague in March 1939 was one of the last of Hitler's peaceful conquests. (Several weeks later, the Nazis browbeat Lithuania into surrendering the port city of Memel.) The diplomatic explosion, resulting from the seizure of Prague, finally forced the British government to make a serious commitment to the continent and to alter the "business-as-usual" approach that they had taken towards rearmament. Yet, the new British course was due more to internal political pressure, precipitated by the British public's outrage, than to a basic change in the government's attitude. Great Britain now attempted diplomatically to bolster Europe against further Nazi aggression. However, British leaders did not yet regard war as inevitable and, as a result, did not seek to create military alliances against that eventuality. Their slow and hesitant approach towards Russia in the summer of 1939 hardly indicated serious preparation for war. Also during this period, the British offered the Germans a major economic loan if they behaved themselves—hardly the sort of policy to deter Adolf Hitler.[4]

The *Führer's* reaction to British criticism and diplomatic activity was at first outrage and then contempt. As he told his staff, he had seen his opponents at Munich and they were worms.[5] After hearing that the British had extended a guarantee to Poland at the end of March, he shouted: "I'll cook them [the British] a stew they'll choke on."[6] But as the summer progressed, Hitler seems to have convinced himself that Britain would not intervene in a military campaign against Poland. Both the aforementioned inadequacies of British diplomacy and the skill with which Hitler manipulated the European powers led him to conclude that he could get away with a small war on Poland. By signing the Nazi-Soviet Non Aggression Pact, thus removing the Soviet Union from the list of possible enemies, Hitler, in effect, isolated the Poles more thoroughly than he had the Czechs the previous year.

Further confirming Hitler in his small-war thesis was the consensus among the *Luftwaffe* that the threat of "strategic" bombing (or terror bombing) would serve to keep the Western Powers out of an eastern war.[7] Ironically, the unpreparedness of the *Luftwaffe* in the fall of 1938 played a role in Hitler's decision not to push the Czech crisis into a direct military confrontation but rather to negotiate at Munich. However, the spectacle that the British managed to make out of themselves that late September as they dug slit trenches and passed out gas masks played an important role in shaping Hitler's as well as the *Luftwaffe's* strategic thinking in 1939. As mentioned earlier, when speaking to his senior commanders, General Felmy, commander of *Luftflotte* 2, speculated in May 1939 on the moral pressure that a terror bombing campaign against London might offer. The events in Britain in the fall of 1938 suggested to Felmy that a high degree of war hysteria already existed there and that the Third *Reich* should take full advantage of such a state of affairs in contrast to the hesitant behavior of Germany's World War I government.[8]

That same month, the Fifth Section (intelligence) of the general staff echoed such sentiments. It reported that, compared to other European air forces, the *Luftwaffe* was the best prepared in every respect.

> Germany is, on the basis of all reports, the only state that in respect to equipment, organization, tactics, and leadership has advanced to a total conception of preparation and leadership of an offensive as well as defensive air war. This fact indicates a general advance in military preparedness and with it a strengthening of the whole military situation.

As proof of the value of air superiority, the intelligence experts pointed to the Italian success in Abyssinia and particularly to Germany's diplomatic triumph the previous autumn. They argued that panic in London and Paris over the threat of air attacks had contributed directly to the Munich surrender and suggested that the parliamentary systems of the Western Powers gave Britain and France considerably less flexibility in strategic policy than authoritarian Nazi Germany had. This line of reasoning led to the dangerous suggestion that it was "quite possible that in spite of [Western] pacts and promises to Eastern Europe, a conflict in that region would remain localized."[9]

In early July, both Hitler and Göring visited the *Luftwaffe*'s test station at Rechlin to examine the latest in research and development. The technical experts did a thorough job of implying that aircraft and equipment in the design and test stages were close to production. Although this was not the case, the demonstration provided one more confirmation to the *Führer* that the *Luftwaffe* not only possessed current superiority over its opponents but would maintain such superiority for the foreseeable future. In 1942, Göring recalled: "The *Führer* took the most serious decisions on the basis of that display. It was a miracle that things worked out as well as they did and that the consequences were not far worse."[10] While the Rechlin demonstration did not aim at supporting Hitler's inclination for a military solution to the Polish question but rather at convincing him that the *Luftwaffe* should receive more of the defense budget for the coming years, it undoubtedly helped to push Hitler towards the precipice.

On August 22, 1939, Hitler met with senior military officers to announce the reasons behind his inclination to settle accounts with Poland.[11] He gave pride of place to his historical uniqueness and the danger that he could "be eliminated at any time by a criminal or a lunatic." Second in importance was the fact that Germany's economic situation was precarious. "Because of the constraints on us, our economic situation is such that we can only hold out for a few more years." Four days later, Hitler summed up his general evaluation of the strategic situation in a letter to Mussolini:

> As neither France nor Britain can achieve any decisive successes in the west, and as Germany, as a result of the agreement with Russia, will have all her forces free in the east after the defeat of Poland, and as air superiority is undoubtedly on our side, I do not shrink from solving the eastern question even at the risk of complications with the West.[12]

What is interesting in the above calculation of risks is that the *Luftwaffe* played a role in two out of three factors the *Führer* cited. The belief in a short war against Poland, of course, rested on the army as well as the *Luftwaffe*, but clearly the German air force contributed to the belief that it would not take long to destroy Poland. The emphasis on air superiority undoubtedly represented a miscalculation that the *Luftwaffe* could deter the Western Powers by the mere threat of major air attacks against their population centers. As we now know Hitler was wrong, not so much in his estimate of Western leadership, for that remained cautious, overpessimistic, and unwilling to take risks, but rather in his failure to recognize that Western popular opinion was so incensed at German actions that Chamberlain and Daladier had no choice but to declare war in response to the German invasion of Poland.[13]

Hitler's remarks to his generals in August 1939, just prior to the invasion of Poland, raise an interesting historiographical question as to the nature of the war that the Germans expected to fight. Since the war, a number of Anglo-American historians have argued that before the war Hitler and the German high command developed a "*Blitzkrieg* strategy" which they then applied on the battlefields of Europe from 1939 to 1941.[14] The heart of this strategy supposedly was the close cooperation between tactical air and armored formations in making deep armored drives into enemy rear areas. By choosing such a strategy, the Germans, the argument runs, escaped the necessity of rearming in depth. On the armored side of the argument, such a theory presents several major difficulties. First, the German army's rearmament program did not emphasize the establishment of an armored force and there is no evidence that Hitler interfered in the formulation of army doctrine before the war.[15] As the previous chapter suggests, there were also problems relating to airpower. Close air support developed in Spain with little urging from the *Luftwaffe*'s high command in Berlin, while many German air force leaders and general staff officers remained enamored of the concept of "strategic" bombing. Hitler's emphasis on airpower in his August speech to the generals suggests that, at the beginning of the war, he placed higher reliance on the deterrent value and the actual capabilities of airpower in the coming war than most historians have allowed. The impact of the Polish campaign on German air strategy and the initial strategic response of Hitler to the war in the west provide further support for such a thesis.

THE POLISH CAMPAIGN AND THE "PHONY" WAR

In the early hours of September 1, 1939, German bombers and fighters delivered heavy attacks on targets throughout Poland. Unlike the previous year when the Czechs had fully mobilized by the end of September, the German attack caught the Poles in the process of mobilizing.[16] Interestingly, the *Luftwaffe* considered launching an all-out attack on military installations and armament factories in Warsaw to paralyze Polish resistance, but bad weather prevented the launching of such a "knockout" blow. By the time the weather had cleared, the interdiction and close air support aspects of operations were going so well that the general staff hesitated to shift the emphasis.[17] One must also note that at the conclusion of the Polish campaign, the *Luftwaffe* launched massive air assaults against military targets in Warsaw. In these raids, the Germans were not averse to any collateral damage inflicted on the civilian populace.

Complicating Poland's strategic difficulties at the beginning of the campaign was the fact that her high command had not separated operational from political requirements. To defend those areas regarded as politically essential, the Poles had distributed their forces in indefensible regions such as the Danzig Corridor and Silesia. As a result, their army was unable to defend itself and to carry out a prolonged resistance.[18]

Within the first days of the campaign, panzer units from General Walther von Reichenau's Tenth Army had broken out into the open, thereby achieving operational freedom. By September 6, tank units were halfway to Warsaw, the Corridor had been closed, and the Polish army was disintegrating. The Polish air force put up substantial resistance in the first days of the war; its pilots, as they did in the Battle of Britain, proved themselves not only tenacious and brave but highly skilled. Overwhelming German superiority, however, soon told.[19] For the first time in modern war, the combination of armored mobile formations supported by aircraft proved devastatingly effective.[20] Interdiction strikes made it impossible for the Poles to move large bodies of troops in the open, while efforts by Polish troops to fight their way out of encirclements, especially along the Bzura River, collapsed in the face of *Luftwaffe* bombing. These air attacks so demoralized the Poles that some troops threw away their weapons.[21]

After the fall of most of Poland, the Germans faced the problem of forcing the capital to surrender. Richthofen, in charge of the air assault on the city, requested permission to destroy Warsaw completely as "it would, in the future, be only a customs station." Operational orders from the *OKW* for the attack on the city were more restrained and required only that the bombardment aim at eliminating those installations judged essential for the maintenance of life in the city.[22]

By the end of September, not only had the Germans managed to destroy the Polish army and air force but Poland had ceased to exist as an independent nation. The *Wehrmacht* had won this victory at a surprisingly low cost. Polish losses were 70,000 dead, 133,000 wounded, and 700,000 prisoners, while German losses were only 11,000 dead, 30,000 wounded, and 3,400 missing.[23]

Despite the overwhelming victory, serious problems remained for the Germans to resolve in the areas of high strategy, the national economy, and the *Wehrmacht*'s actual versus anticipated military performance. In particular, the army high command *(Oberkommando des Heeres, OKH)* was most dissatisfied with the level of performance of even active-duty regular formations. Serious shortcomings had shown up throughout the regular army, while reserve and *Landwehr* units were well below the standards acceptable to senior army commanders.[24]

But the largest problem confronting Hitler was the fact that Germany faced a major European war. The *Luftwaffe* had not succeeded in deterring the West from honoring its obligations to Poland. Moreover, Hitler had calculated that the combination of the Nazi-Soviet Non Aggression Pact, supplies from the Balkans, and autarkic measures taken in the 1930's would mitigate the effects of an Allied blockade. He had assured his generals before the outbreak of war that Germany had little reason to fear a blockade, since it would "be ineffective due to our autarky and because we have economic resources in the East. We need have no worry. . . . The East will deliver us grain, cattle, coal, lead and zinc."[25] Reality, however, proved quite different. Import tonnage fell 57 percent. The value of imports had fallen from *RM* 472 million in January 1939 to *RM* 186 million in January 1940, while import tonnage declined from 4,445,000 tons the previous year to 1,122,000 tons.[26] With such problems, the long-term outlook appeared exceedingly dangerous. Moreover, petroleum reserves declined from 2,400,000 tons at the beginning of the war to 1,600,000 tons in May 1940,[27] while gasoline supplies fell from 300,000 tons in September 1939 to 110,000 tons in April 1940.[28]

This critical economic situation, caused by the outbreak of a wider European war than Hitler had expected, helps to explain an historical puzzle: Why throughout the fall and early winter of 1939 did Hitler push so strongly for an immediate offensive in the west?[29] Hitler felt that the *Wehrmacht* must move before the economy's difficulties affected German fighting strength. In early October, he warned that time favored Germany's enemies. "The danger, in case of a prolonged war, lies in the difficulty of securing from a limited food and raw material base [enough to sustain the] population, while at the same time securing the means for the prosecution of the war."[30] Hence, the pressure for an immediate offensive.

On the same day that Hitler was justifying the factors behind his strategy, he issued "Directive No. 6 for the Conduct of the War," in which he spelled out the territorial goals of the coming campaign as well as its strategic purposes:

> (a) An offensive will be planned on the northern flank of the western front through Luxembourg, Belgium, and Holland. This offensive must be launched at the earliest possible moment and in the greatest possible strength.
>
> (b) The purpose of this offensive will be to defeat as much . . . of the French army and . . . the forces of the allies fighting at their side, and at the same time to win as much territory as possible in Holland, Belgium, and northern France to serve as a base for the successful prosecution of the air and sea war against England and as a wide protective area for the economically vital Ruhr.[31]

Hitler's order that the armed forces launch a fall offensive in the west caused an enormous row with the generals. On the basis of "after action" reports from Poland and the western front, army leaders argued that their troops could not meet the demands that a western campaign would place on them.[32] In retrospect, the generals were correct: The fall and winter of 1939-40 provided the necessary time to bring regular, reserve, and *Landwehr* divisions up to the same high standard of performance.

Generally, the *Luftwaffe* seconded the army's efforts to postpone the western offensive.[33] Weather conditions in central Europe, however, probably played a big role in *Luftwaffe* calculations. The air staff was happier with the performance in Poland than was the army high command and, of course, the air force did not face the problem of training enormous numbers of reservists. Still, the pause between the end of the Polish campaign and the beginning of air operations against Norway allowed the Germans to augment considerably their air strength. On September 2, 1939, the *Luftwaffe* possessed 4,161 aircraft: 604 reconnaissance, 1,179 fighters, 1,180 bombers, 366 dive bombers, 40 ground attack, 240 coastal, and 552 transports. By the beginning of April 1940, the number had increased to 5,178 aircraft: 671 reconnaissance, 1,620 fighters, 1,726 bombers, 419 dive bombers, 46 ground attack, 230 coastal, and 466 transport.[34] In addition, the general quality of the bomber force rose somewhat with the widespread introduction of the Ju 88 into its squadrons.

Hitler's approach to Germany's strategic problems in the fall of 1939 further suggests a belief at the top level that the *Luftwaffe* could and would be the decisive weapon in the coming struggle. Historians have noted, as did the German generals of that time, that the fall offensive did not aim to achieve a decisive success against the French army. Rather, as Hitler's directive made clear, its fundamental aim was, while crippling as much of the Allied armies as possible, "to win as much territory as possible in Holland, Belgium, and northern France to serve as a base for the *successful prosecution of the air and sea war against England*" [my emphasis]. Such territorial gains would allow the German air force to strike at the heart of English power and also serve as a buffer against air attacks on "the economically vital Ruhr."[35]

The *Luftwaffe*'s chief of intelligence, "Beppo" Schmid, argued in late November 1939 for an exclusive air strategy. The *Wehrmacht*, he suggested, should not carry out any operations against the French, but rather the entire strength of the *Luftwaffe*, with whatever help the navy could provide, should concentrate against English imports. German air strategy would emphasize attacks on English ports and docks and, Schmid noted, "Should the enemy resort to terror measures—for example, to attack our towns in western Germany —here again [retaliatory] operations could be carried out with even greater effect due to the greater density of population of London and the big industrial centers."[36] While an *OKW* Directive of November 29 contained elements of Schmid's memorandum, Hitler was unwilling to go quite so far and risk all on an air-sea war against Britain before certain conditions had been met. The *OKW* stated that British imports could not be attacked until the army had either defeated the Allied armies in the field or until it had seized the coast opposite Britain.[37]

The great fall campaign never took place. Hitler himself does not seem to have abandoned the idea of such a campaign until January 1940, when an aircraft carrying the plan crash-landed in Belgium. Thereafter, Hitler, supported by Army Group A, forced the *OKH* to alter the plans for the western campaign to a massive armored thrust through the Ardennes. The new strategy aimed not at creating the strategic basis for an air and naval offensive against Britain but

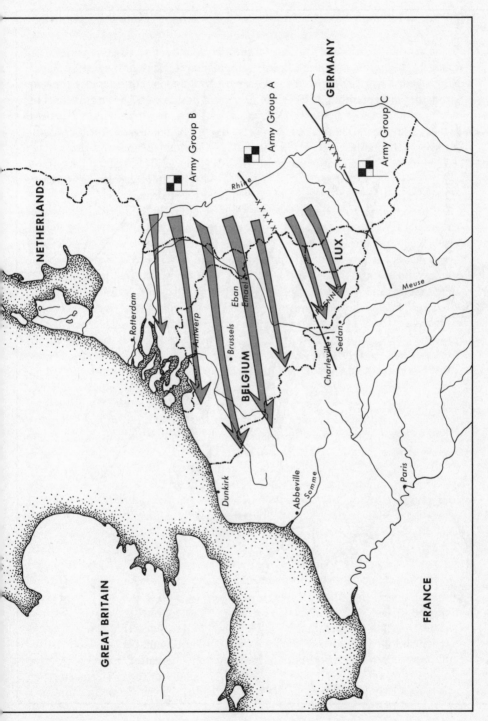

The Western Offensive: Initial Plan. Oct.-Nov. 1939

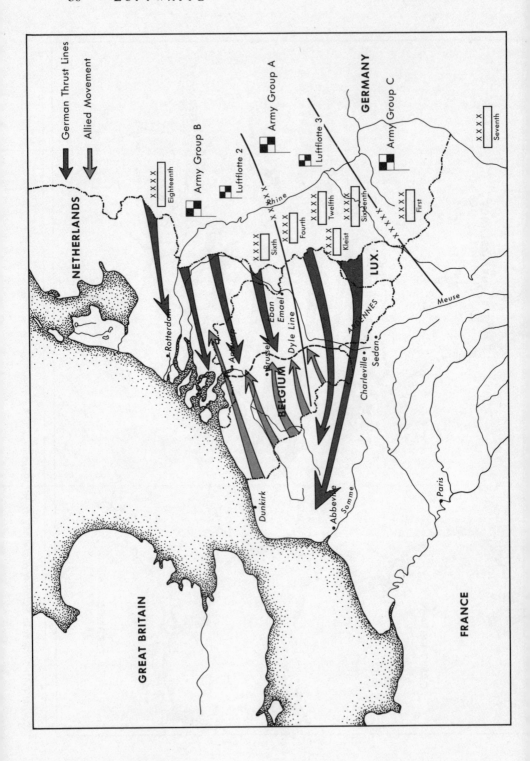

German Thrust Lines

Allied Movement

NETHERLANDS

GERMANY

Army Group C

Army Group A

Army Group B

Luftflotte 2

Luftflotte 3

XXXX Eighteenth

XXXX Seventh

XXXX First

XXXX Twelfth

XXXX Sixteenth

XXX Kleist

XXXX Sixth

XXXX Fourth

Rhine

Meuse

Rotterdam

Antwerp

Brussel

Eban Emael

Dyle Line

ARDENNES

BELGIUM

LUX.

Dunkirk

Charleville

Sedan

Abbeville

Somme

Paris

GREAT BRITAIN

FRANCE

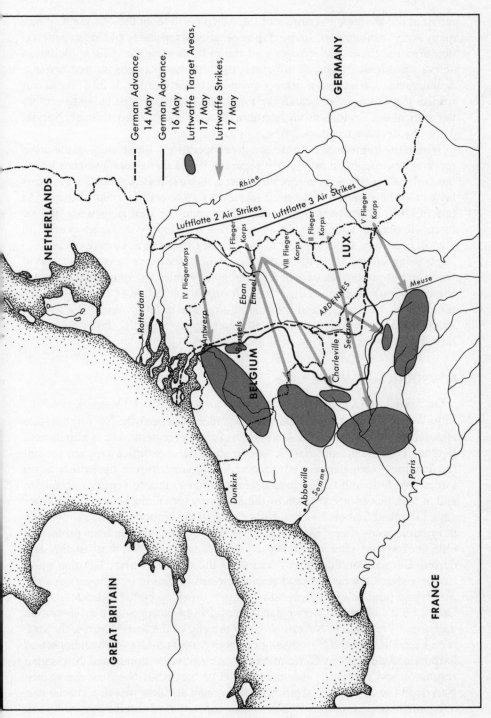

German Air Strikes in Support of the Western Offensive, 17 May 1940

rather at the strategic overthrow of the Allied position on the continent. While many army commanders doubted the operational feasibility of a deep-penetration armored drive, Hitler supported the radicals urging a rapid exploitation across the Meuse.[38] Almost concurrently, German planning turned towards Scandinavia. The *Altmark* affair convinced Hitler that the British would not respect the neutrality of Scandinavia and that Germany must move to protect her critical ore imports from northern Sweden that moved through Narvik. Thus, the decision to attack Norway in the spring.[39]

Within the framework of these two great operations, the strategy of the three services was integrated rather than separate. While there were instances where the *Luftwaffe* acted as an independent force, its basic mission in both campaigns lay within the carefully structured framework of overall German strategy. As one of Hitler's directives for the fall offensive in the west suggested, "the air force will prevent attacks by the Anglo-French air forces on our army and will give all necessary direct support to the advance."[40] It was not a case of the *Luftwaffe* being subordinated to the dictates of the army or the navy (in the case of Norway) but rather that overall air strategy fit within the conceptual design of the campaign's strategy. Thus, the *Luftwaffe*'s role followed closely Wever's thoughts on air strategy and the role of airpower in future wars. The general strategic conception and military purposes of the campaign had determined how the Germans would use their air resources.

SCANDINAVIA AND FRANCE

On April 7, 1940, German sea, land, and air forces struck Denmark and Norway. Within the first hours, Danish resistance collapsed. In Norway, despite almost complete surprise, the Germans were less successful. The occupation of Bergen, Trondheim, and Narvik went without serious difficulty, even though the landings were dangerously exposed to countermoves by British naval forces.[41] At Oslo and Christiansand, the Germans ran into serious opposition, and in both places intervention by the *Luftwaffe* turned the scales. In the latter case, German bombers silenced forts guarding the harbor entrance so that the navy could land troops. Despite their ancient equipment, the forts protecting Oslo shelled and sank the heavy cruiser *Blücher* and, for most of the day, denied German landing forces access to the city. However, German paratroopers seized the airport, and reinforcements rushed in by air overawed the Norwegian population. The breathing space provided by the defenders of the Oslo fjord did allow the Norwegian government to escape and to set in motion measures of resistance. Nevertheless, by the end of the first 24 hours, the strategic situation from the Norwegian perspective was hopeless. With all important harbors and airfields in German hands, the *Luftwaffe* dominated Norwegian resistance and prevented the intervention of the Royal Navy except against Narvik. In the course of operations, the German air force played a crucial role in maintaining air superiority, in providing support to advancing ground forces, and in supplying widely scattered forces.[42]

No matter what the tactical successes of the Norwegian campaign might have been, the impact of the campaign on Germany's strategic situation was negative for the short as well as the long haul. In the latter, Norway proved a strategic drain throughout the Second World War. Moreover, the conquest of the Lorraine ore fields in the campaign against France mitigated the need for Swedish iron ore. Those imports, while useful, were never decisive.[43] The short-range strategic impact was even more dubious. By the time naval operations in Norwegian waters were over, the German navy had ceased to exist as an effective surface force. By mid-June, Admiral Erich Raeder, Commander in Chief of the navy, was down to one heavy cruiser, two light cruisers, and four destroyers; the remainder of the fleet was either at the bottom of the ocean or in drydock undergoing repair.[44] The naval staff compounded the inevitable naval losses that went with such a campaign by what can only be categorized as strategic incompetence. In late May and early June, afraid that the war would end before its two battle cruisers had significantly engaged enemy forces, the naval high command risked the *Gneisenau* and *Scharnhorst* in strategically pointless operations in northern waters. As a result, both were seriously damaged and did not return to service until December 1940.[45] Considering that, as early as May 20, Raeder broached with the *Führer* the possibility of an invasion of Britain, such a frittering-away of naval strength in the north is quite surprising.[46]

With the initiation of operations against Scandinavia, the Germans completed preparations for a move against the West. On May 10, 1940, the *Wehrmacht* began an offensive aimed at the strategic overthrow of its opponents. Operations against Holland and northern Belgium by Army Group B confirmed the expectations of the Allies as to German strategy and fixed their attention away from the decisive threat. Meanwhile, German armor moved through the Ardennes until it reached the Meuse. By the evening of the 13th, Panzer Group Kleist had three bridgeheads across the river. Within less than two days, the Germans had achieved operational freedom and were rolling towards the English Channel. At that time, Germany's opponents believed that the *Wehrmacht* enjoyed overwhelming superiority. As we now know, except in the air (and even here German superiority was not overwhelming), the Germans did not enjoy a significant, quantifiable advantage.[47] Their victory resulted from an operational plan whose serious risks were more than offset by corresponding advantages that would not have been present in a more conventional operation. Second, German training and doctrine were more realistic and demanding than those of their opponents. Third, the army and the *Luftwaffe* had closely integrated their plans to meet the overall demands of German strategy.

German air attacks that accompanied the start of the offensive aimed at achieving air superiority over the Low Countries and northern France. In the first hours, a significant portion of the *Luftwaffe*'s effort struck at Allied air forces and their ground organizations. Neither the Dutch nor the Belgians were capable of putting up serious resistance, because most of their equipment was obsolete. The British had stationed a significant force of bombers and fighters

("Hurricanes") in northern France to support the British Expeditionary Force.[48] The French air force, unfortunately, was in great disarray as it was transitioning to a newer generation of aircraft (as had the *Luftwaffe* in 1937-38 and the RAF in 1938-39 with similar results). The French were, in fact, having considerable difficulty in equipping squadrons with new aircraft as well as maintaining operational ready rates. In early 1940, some French squadrons ran in-commission rates of barely 40 percent, and the pressure of operations only compounded their difficulties.[49] The Allies' defeat in the campaign should not obscure the fact that the French air force fought well, and its experienced pilots, often in inferior equipment, fought tenaciously.[50]

The first German air strikes against the Belgians and Dutch virtually eliminated their air forces as possible factors in the campaign; the British and French also suffered heavy aircraft losses on the ground and in the air. But the first day's operations did not come lightly. On May 10, the Germans lost 83 aircraft (not including Ju 52's), including 47 bombers and 25 fighters, equalling the worst losses for a day in the Battle of Britain. On the following day, the Germans lost a further 42 aircraft, including 22 bombers, 8 dive bombers, and 10 fighters.[51]

In the north, Dutch resistance collapsed in the face of the German assault. By the third day, the 9th Panzer Division had reached the outskirts of Rotterdam. On May 14, the 54th Bomber Wing shattered the center of that city and killed over 800 and rendered 80,000 homeless despite the fact that negotiations were already in motion to surrender the town. After the war, quite naturally, there was a paucity of individuals willing to accept responsibility. Whether or not the bombing was a deliberate act of terror, as Telford Taylor suggests, it "was part of the German pattern of conquest—a pattern woven by Hitler and the *Wehrmacht.*"[52] The next day, to avoid the possibility that the *Luftwaffe* would destroy another city, the Dutch Commander in Chief surrendered all his forces in Holland. At that time, the Germans were not hesitant to note the connection.[53]

Significantly, the *Luftwaffe* launched few attacks on Allied forces advancing into Belgium to meet Army Group B's drive. Rather, it shielded General Gerd von Rundstedt's forces, which were moving through the Ardennes, from the prying eyes of Allied reconnaissance aircraft. By the 12th, *Luftflotte* 3 reported general superiority over its opponents, and German aircraft then turned increasingly to attacks on the Allied transportation network and to supporting the advance of ground forces. Reinforcing the impression made by air attacks in the early days of the campaign, there was the psychological impact of German paratrooper operations. *Luftwaffe* airborne forces seized strategic bridges throughout Belgium and Holland, while German glider forces captured the supposedly impregnable fortress of Eban Emael. Such successes had an impact out of all proportion to German paratrooper strength.[54] By materially aiding Army Group B's advance, they furthered the impression of Allied commanders that the *Wehrmacht*'s offensive weight lay in the north.

Like the German army, the *Luftwaffe* had prepared for the coming campaign with ruthless efficiency. Richthofen had honed his "Stukas" to a fine edge.[55] Now on the banks of the Meuse, the work paid off. On the 13th, German infantry (an integral part of the panzer divisions) began to cross the river. Guderian had carefully worked out plans with his air counterpart, General Bruno Loerzer, Commander of *Fliegerkorps* II. The two had decided that the *Luftwaffe* would provide continuous support rather than a massive, one-shot attack. It would thus force French artillerymen and infantry to keep their heads down while German infantry made the crossing. Despite interference at higher levels, the plan went like clockwork.[56] Continuous "Stuka" attacks on French reservists holding the line had a devastating effect.[57] By nightfall, the Germans had established a secure bridgehead; by the next day, tanks were across; and by the 15th, the panzers were in the open and had a clear run to Abbeville. The use of dive bombers to support the Meuse crossings played a major role in one of the most decisive strategic victories in the military history of the 20th century.

The value of the general air superiority that the *Luftwaffe* was able to achieve over the Ardennes showed clearly in the efforts of Allied air forces to destroy the bridges German engineers had thrown across the Meuse. Despite extraordinary bravery that bordered on the suicidal and losses that reached the level of 56 percent of the RAF bombers dispatched, the Allies were able only to hinder, not to halt, the movement across the Meuse.[58] Allied air attacks on May 15 gave the Germans on the ground severe knocks (Guderian's XIX Panzer Corps had a particularly hard time) but no air force could sustain losses on the level suffered that day. On the 16th the Germans, as they began their roll towards the English Channel, noticed a considerable let-up in Allied air pressure.

Exploitation by German armored formations proceeded with the utmost dispatch. What is remarkable is the speed with which short-range fighters and dive bombers moved forward to support ground forces that were rapidly drawing out of range. By the 17th, within 24 hours of the French evacuation, German fighters were establishing their operational base at Charleville, west of the Meuse. For several days, fuel, ammunition, parts, and ground personnel flew in by Ju 52's because the army's movement into the ever-deepening pocket had choked the Meuse bridges. The forward operating base was so short of fuel that ground personnel siphoned all but the minimum amount of gasoline from every noncombat aircraft landing at Charleville. This rapid deployment forward was due entirely to an air transport system of Ju 52's.[59] The system supported the army as well as the air force in its drive to the Channel; and shortly after the fighters had moved to Charleville, the *Luftwaffe* flew in 2,000 army technicians to establish a tank-repair facility at the same location.[60]

The next stage of the campaign led to one of the more controversial episodes in the war, the famous "stop order" that resulted in the eventual escape of most of the British Expeditionary Force and large numbers of Frenchmen through Dunkirk. Available evidence contradicts the well-publicized post-war testimony of German generals that Hitler was responsible for halting the movement of

German tank forces short of Dunkirk. The most careful reconstruction suggests that Generaloberst Gerd von Rundstedt and Hitler, supported by a number of other senior officers, stopped the armor before it could cut Allied forces off from Dunkirk.[61] Given the extent of German success and their understandable nervousness, as well as a desire to protect their armored forces for the anticipated conquest of France, the stop order made sense at the time. Interwoven with this German caution was a considerable underestimation of how swiftly the British could organize and conduct a withdrawal operation. On May 25 Göring compounded what was in retrospect a serious strategic mistake by suggesting to Hitler that the *Luftwaffe* could by itself destroy what was left of Allied armies in the Low Countries.[62] Hitler found Göring's proposal sufficient to delay further the ground offensive against the Dunkirk perimeter. By the time the army moved forward, the opportunity had been lost; the enemy had entrenched and begun a full-scale evacuation.

Over Dunkirk, the *Luftwaffe* suffered its first serious rebuff of the war. As Galland has noted, the nature and style of the air battles over the beaches should have provided a warning as to the inherent weaknesses of the *Luftwaffe*'s force structure.[63] Admittedly, the Germans fought at a disadvantage. Although positioned forward at captured airfields, the Bf 109 was at the outer limits of its range and possessed less flying time over Dunkirk than did the "Hurricanes" and "Spitfires" operating from southern England. German bombers were still located in western Germany and had even farther to fly. Thus, the *Luftwaffe* could not bring its full weight to bear, with the result that when its bombers hammered those on the beaches or embarking, the RAF intervened in a significant fashion. British fighter attacks often prevented German bombers from performing with full effectiveness. Both sides suffered heavy losses. During the nine days from May 26 through June 3, the RAF lost 177 aircraft destroyed or damaged; the Germans lost 240.[64] For much of the *Luftwaffe,* Dunkirk came as a nasty shock. *Fliegerkorps* II reported in its war diary that it lost more aircraft on the 27th attacking the evacuation than it had lost in the previous ten days of the campaign.[65]

The destruction or forced evacuation of the entire Allied left wing in the Low Countries (consisting of the most mobile and best trained divisions) made the defense of France hopeless. Nevertheless, the remaining French forces put up a creditable defense in early June, suggesting what they might have accomplished if they had had better leadership in May. Their hopeless military position made defeat quick and brutal. To a certain extent, the strategic collapse of the entire western position has obscured the significant attrition of German armored and air forces that took place during the fighting. At the beginning of the western offensive, the army had 2,574 tanks.[66] By the armistice, the Germans had lost 753 tanks or nearly 30 percent of their armored forces.[67] *Luftwaffe* losses of aircraft were on a similar scale (see Tables III,[68] and IV[69]). While Bf 109 losses remained somewhat lower than other categories of combat aircraft, pilot losses in the single-engine fighter force (see Table V[70]) suggest a high correlation between aircraft and crew losses.

Tables III through V underscore the extent of German losses in the Battle of France. They suggest that the tendency to view the Battle of Britain as a separate episode from the defeat of France does not do justice to the resistance of Allied air forces in the spring of 1940 and distorts the fact that for five months, from May through September, the *Luftwaffe,* with only a short pause, was continually in action. Thus, the break in morale that bomber pilots over London were reported to have suffered in mid-September 1940 was the result not only of the strain of fighting over Britain but of operations that had been continuous since the previous May.

THE BATTLE OF BRITAIN

Serious aircraft losses during the spring campaign greatly weakened the *Luftwaffe* before the Battle of Britain. Had that been the only disadvantage under which the *Luftwaffe* operated, German strategic problems would have been daunting enough, given the difficulties of mounting a major combined arms operation. Unfortunately for the Germans, the strain that recent battles had imposed on their military structure represented only a small portion of the problem; a whole host of strategic, economic, tactical, and technological problems had to be faced and surmounted before the *Reich* could solve the "British question."

What made an inherently complex task impossible was the overconfidence that marked the German leadership in the summer of 1940. Hitler, basking in a mood of preening self-adulation, went on vacation. During a visit to Paris after the signing of the armistice, tours of World War I battlefields, and picnics along the Rhine, the last thing on Hitler's mind was grand strategy.[71] The high command structure, however, was such that without Hitler there was no one with either the drive or strategic vision to pick up the reins—a state of affairs precisely in accord with the *Führer*'s wishes.

Until mid-July 1940, Hitler believed that England would sue for a peace that he would have happily extended to her. As early as May 20, Hitler had remarked that England could have peace for the asking.[72] Nothing in British behavior in the late 1930's suggested that Hitler's expectation was unrealistic. In fact, there were still some within the British government who regarded Churchill's intransigence with distaste. In late May, Lord Halifax, the Foreign Secretary, expressed his alarm at the relish with which Churchill approached his task, while "Rab" Butler, Under Secretary of State for Foreign Affairs, told the Swedish minister in London that "no opportunity would be neglected for concluding a compromise peace if the chance [were] offered on reasonable conditions."[73]

Churchill, furious at Butler's indiscretion, passed along a biting note to Halifax. Butler's whining reply that he had been misunderstood and had meant no offense indicates how much things had changed since Churchill had assumed power.[74] But one must stress that Churchill's toughness as the nation's leader reflected a new mood in Britain. In late June 1940, Admiral Dudley Pound told the French liaison officer at the Admiralty that "the one object we had in view

TABLE III

German Aircraft Losses (Damaged and Destroyed)—May-June 1940

Destroyed on Operations

Type Aircraft	Strength 4.5.40.	Due to Enemy Action	Not Due to Enemy Action	Total	Destroyed Not on Operations	Total Destroyed	Losses as Percent of Initial Strength
Close Recce	345	67	5	72	6	78	23%
Long-Range Recce	321	68	18	86	2	88	27%
Single-Engine Fighters	1,369	169	66	235	22	257	19%
Twin-Engine Fighters	367	90	16	106	4	110	30%
Bombers	1,758	438	53	491	30	521	30%
Dive Bombers	417	89	24	113	9	122	30%
Transport	531	188	18	206	7	213	40%
Coastal	241	20	16	36	3	39	16%
TOTAL	5,349	1,129	216	1,345	83	1,428	28%

Damaged on Operations

Type Aircraft	Due to Enemy Action	Not Due to Enemy Action	Total	Damaged Not on Operations	Total Damaged	Total Damaged and Destroyed	Total Damaged and Destroyed as Percent of Initial Strength
Close Recce	13	4	17	1	18	96	28%
Long-Range Recce	12	8	20	1	21	109	34%
Single-Engine Fighters	33	92	125	25	150	407	30%
Twin-Engine Fighters	20	6	26	3	29	139	38%
Bombers	116	47	163	40	203	724	41%
Dive Bombers	20	7	27	1	28	150	36%
Transport	8	14	22	5	27	240	45%
Coastal	3	5	88	4	12	51	21%
TOTAL	225	183	488	80	488	1,916	36%

TABLE IV German Aircraft Losses, 1940

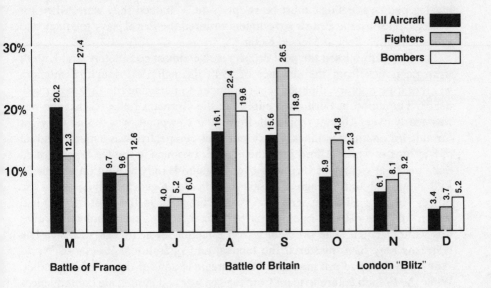

Legend: All Aircraft (black), Fighters (grey), Bombers (white)

	M	J	J	A	S	O	N	D
All Aircraft	20.2	9.7	4.0	16.1	15.6	8.9	6.1	3.4
Fighters	12.3	9.6	5.2	22.4	26.5	14.8	8.1	3.7
Bombers	27.4	12.6	6.0	19.6	18.9	12.3	9.2	5.2

Battle of France   Battle of Britain   London "Blitz"

Table V   BF 109 Fighter Pilot Losses 1940

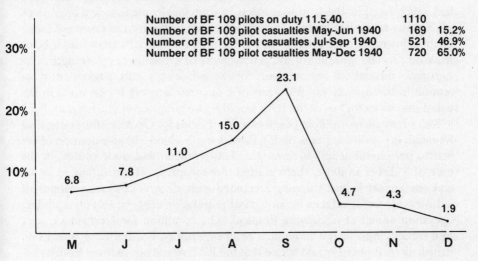

Number of BF 109 pilots on duty 11.5.40.	1110	
Number of BF 109 pilot casualties May-Jun 1940	169	15.2%
Number of BF 109 pilot casualties Jul-Sep 1940	521	46.9%
Number of BF 109 pilot casualties May-Dec 1940	720	65.0%

M	J	J	A	S	O	N	D
6.8	7.8	11.0	15.0	23.1	4.7	4.3	1.9

was winning the war and that it was as essential for them [the French] as for us that we should do so. . . . All trivialities, such as questions of friendship and hurting people's feelings, must be swept aside."[75] Indeed they were, when for strategic reasons, the British government ordered the Royal Navy to attack and sink the French fleet at Mers-el-Kebir.[76]

The Germans missed the new British resolve almost completely, and Hitler's strategic policy from the summer of 1940 through 1941 sought a method, whether it be military, diplomatic, or political, to persuade the British to make peace. The mood in Berlin was euphoric; the Germans believed that the war was nearly over. All that remained, from their viewpoint, was to find the right formula for ending hostilities. Confirming this perspective was a memorandum of late June in which Alfred Jodl, the number two man in the *OKW,* suggested that "the final victory of Germany over England is only a question of time."[77] Jodl's approach to the English "problem" reflected a general failing within the officer corps of all three services. As the campaign in the west in 1940 had shown, the tactical and operational performance of German military forces was without equal. The problem lay on a higher level: that of strategy. The Germans may have mastered the tactical and operational lessons of World War I, but they had not mastered the strategic lessons of that terrible conflict. While the French failure to learn from the last war had immediate consequences in May 1940, German unwillingness to face that war's strategic lessons had an even more catastrophic impact on the history of Germany.

German strategic planning and discussions throughout the summer of 1940 reflect, in glaring fashion, a failure to grasp the essentials of strategy. The navy had squandered its battle cruiser assets in strategically meaningless operations off Norway in the late spring. The army drew up a plan for the proposed cross-channel invasion, code named "Sea Lion," that one can charitably describe as irrelevant to and ignorant of the general state of available naval strength. The *Luftwaffe* throughout the summer, following Göring's lead, paid minimal attention to the operational problems of a channel crossing by the army in the belief that its victory over the RAF would make an invasion unnecessary.[78]

Jodl's June memorandum posed two possibilities for German strategy against England: (a) "a direct attack on the English motherland; (b) an extension of the war to peripheral areas" such as the Mediterranean and trade routes. In the case of a direct strategy, there existed three avenues: (1) an offensive by air and sea against British shipping combined with air attacks against centers of industry; (2) terror attacks by air against population centers; and (3) a landing operation aimed at occupying England. The condition for German success, Jodl argued, must be the attainment of air superiority. Furthermore, attacks on British aircraft plants would insure that the RAF would not recover from its defeat. Interestingly, Jodl suggested that air superiority would lead to a diminishing capacity for the RAF bomber force to attack Germany. It is in this context that German attacks in the coming struggle on Bomber Command's bases must be seen. By extending the air offensive to the interdiction of imports and to the use of terror attacks against the British population (justified as reprisal attacks), Jodl believed that the *Luftwaffe* would break British willpower. He commented that German strategy would require a landing on the British coast only as the final blow *("Todesstoss")* to finish off an England that the *Luftwaffe* and navy had already defeated.[79]

On June 30, 1940, Göring signed an operational directive for the air war against England. After redeployment of its units, the *Luftwaffe* would first attack the RAF, its ground support echelons, and its aircraft industry. Success of these attacks would create the conditions necessary for an assault on British imports and supplies, while at the same time protecting German industry. "As long as the enemy air force is not destroyed, it is the basic principle of the conduct of air war to attack the enemy air units at every possible favorable opportunity—by day and night, in the air, and on the ground—without regard for other missions." What is apparent in early *Luftwaffe* studies is the fact that the German air force regarded the whole RAF as the opponent rather than just Fighter Command. Thus, the attacks on Bomber Command bases and other RAF installations were the result of an effort to destroy the entire British air force rather than of bad intelligence. Parenthetically, the losses in France directly influenced Göring's thinking. He demanded that the *Luftwaffe* maintain its fighting strength as much as possible and not allow its personnel and materiel to be diminished because of overcommitments.[80]

In retrospect, the task facing the Germans in the summer of 1940 was beyond their capabilities. Even disregarding the gaps in interservice cooperation —a must in any combined operations—the force structure, training, and doctrine of the three services were not capable of solving the problem of invading the British Isles. The Norwegian campaign had virtually eliminated the *Kriegsmarine* as a viable force. Thus, there were neither heavy units nor light craft available to protect amphibious forces crossing the Channel. The lack of escorting forces would have made "Sea Lion" particularly hazardous because it meant that the Germans possessed no support against British destroyer attacks coming up or down the Channel. The Admiralty had stationed 4 destroyer flotillas (approximately 36 destroyers) in the immediate vicinity of the threatened invasion area, and additional forces of cruisers, destroyers, and battleships were available from the Home Fleet.[81] Even with air superiority, it is doubtful whether the *Luftwaffe* could have prevented some British destroyers from getting in among the amphibious forces; the *Kriegsmarine* certainly could not have done so. The landing craft that circumstances forced the Germans to choose, Rhine River barges, indicates the haphazard nature of the undertaking, as does the tenuous links to supplies and reinforcements that the Germans would have had across the Channel. Just a few British destroyers among the slow-moving transport vessels would have caused havoc.

Air superiority itself represented a most difficult task, given *Luftwaffe* strength and aircraft capabilities. Somewhat ironically, the strategic problem confronting the Germans in the summer of 1940 represented in microcosm that facing

Allied air forces in 1943. Because of the Bf 109's limited range, German bombers could strike only southern England where fighter protection could hold the loss rate down to acceptable levels. This state of affairs allowed the RAF a substantial portion of the country as a sanctuary where it could establish and control an air reserve and where British industrial power, particularly in the Birmingham-Liverpool area, could maintain production largely undisturbed. Moreover, the limited range of German fighter cover allowed the British one option that they never had to exercise: Should the pressure on Fighter Command become too great, they could withdraw their fighters north of London to refit and reorganize; then when the Germans launched "Sea Lion," they could resume the struggle. Thus in the final analysis, the *Luftwaffe* could do no more than impose on Fighter Command a rate of attrition that its commanders would accept. The Germans were never in a position to attack the RAF over the full length and breadth of its domain. Similarly in 1943, Allied fighters could grapple with the Germans only up to a line approximately along the Rhine. On the other side of the line, the *Luftwaffe* could impose an unacceptable loss rate on Allied bombers. Not until Allied fighters could range over the entire length and breadth of Nazi Germany could Allied air forces win air superiority over the continent.

The rather long preparatory period between the end of the French campaign and the launching of the great air offensive against the British Isles was due to more than just German confidence that the war was over and that Britain would accept peace. The losses suffered by the *Luftwaffe* in the spring and the extensive commitments of its aircraft and aircrews in the May-June battles demanded considerable time for rest and recuperation as well as for the integration of fresh crews into bomber and fighter units. Moreover, the speed of the German advance had caused several major redeployments of air units to keep up with ground operations. The attack on Britain now required another major redeployment and the preparation of permanent airfields and facilities for an extended campaign. The logistical difficulties involved in establishing a new base structure far from Germany were considerable.

Further complicating the *Luftwaffe*'s tasks was an inadequate intelligence system. While the gap between British and German capabilities was not yet wide, the British were on the way towards gaining a decisive edge in intelligence collection.[82] Already the British had enjoyed their first successes in breaking into the German "enigma" coding system, and poor signal discipline by the *Luftwaffe* throughout the war provided the British with easy access to German air force communications traffic. How much impact "Ultra" (the comprehensive generic term for intelligence based on intercepted and decoded German messages) had on the Battle of Britain is not entirely clear. The official historian of British intelligence in the war claims that it had no direct impact on the battle, while another historian argues that "Ultra" indicated German targets for the August 15 attacks early enough for Air Marshal Sir Hugh Dowding, Commander in Chief of Fighter Command, to use the decrypts in his conduct of that day's air battles.[83] What is clear is that "Ultra," in combination with 'Y' Service intercepts of German radio traffic, gave the British an increasingly accurate picture of the German order of battle as air operations continued into September.[84] Finally, the Battle of Britain witnessed the integration of British scientists directly into the intelligence network. The combination of scientists with signals and other intelligence gave the Allies a detailed picture of German scientific advances as well as of the enemy's tactics and operations. Conversely, the German picture of Allied developments remained almost opaque.[85] The first clear break in scientific intelligence came when the British—on the basis of a few scraps of information drawn from crashed aircraft, the interrogation of captured aircrews, and several "Ultra" messages—deduced the nature of the German blind bombing system, the so-called *"Knickebein"* method.[86] This was the first of many triumphs.

The undervaluing of intelligence and a concomitant underestimation of enemy capabilities marked *Luftwaffe* operations throughout the war.[87] These defects showed up in appreciations written by the *Luftwaffe*'s intelligence section for the air offensive on Britain. However, given the successes of May and June and the overestimation of airpower then current in the air forces of the world, it is perhaps understandable that the Germans misjudged their opponents. In a study dated July 16, 1940, *Luftwaffe* intelligence estimated the "Hurricane" and "Spitfire" well below their actual performance capabilities, made no mention of Britain's radar-controlled air defense system, and ended on the optimistic note that "the *Luftwaffe,* unlike the RAF, will be in a position in every respect to achieve a decisive effect this year."[88]

The initial *Luftwaffe* estimate on the duration of the coming campaign was four days for the defeat of Fighter Command in southern England, followed by four weeks during which German bombers and long-range fighters would mop up the remainder of the RAF and destroy the British aircraft industry.[89] On July 21, Göring intimated to his commanders that beside the RAF, the British aircraft industry represented a critical target for winning air superiority. Above all, the initial strategic goal must be the weakening of the morale and actual strength of British fighter units. Interestingly, Göring suggested that his fighter forces exercise maximum operational latitude, and to this end commanders should not tie them too closely to the bombers. Such a strategy would allow the fighters to use their speed and maneuverability.[90] Three days later, *Fliegerkorps* I delineated four direct missions for the *Luftwaffe* in the coming battle. The first and most important was to win air superiority by attacks on the RAF and its industrial support, particularly the engine industry; second, to support the Channel crossing by attacks against the enemy fleet and bombers, and eventually through direct aid for the army; third, to attack British ports, supplies, and imports; and finally, independent of the first three tasks, launch ruthless retaliatory terror attacks on major British cities.[91]

The first phase of the battle, lasting from the beginning of July until early August, involved exploratory operations over the Channel, as the Germans sought to draw Fighter Command out and to close this important waterway to British shipping. On July 1, Dowding had at his disposal 462 "Hurricanes" (347 in commission, 75%) and 279 "Spitfires" (191 in commission, 68%).[92] Opposing him the *Luftwaffe's* Second and Third Air Forces by July 20 controlled nearly 2,600 aircraft, including 1,131 medium bombers (769 in commission, 68%), 316 dive bombers, (248, 79%), and 809 single-engine fighters (656, 81%).[93] Before the initiation of a full-scale air campaign, German efforts over the Channel aimed at wearing down Fighter Command and putting a stop to British shipping. In retrospect, it can be seen that the German strategy represented a serious error. It allowed Fighter Command and its controllers considerable experience with German procedures and tactics. It also enabled the British to work some of the bugs out of their radar systems as well as to build up the confidence of radar operators in the system. Early mistakes, such as that of July 11 when British controllers scrambled 6 "Hurricanes" to meet one lone raider and the fighters ran into a raid consisting of at least 40 aircraft, were repeated with decreasing frequency.[94] By the beginning of July, both Fighter Command and its support structure were adapting to the German pressure.

The opening air battle was fought at considerable cost to both sides. By the second week of August, the British had lost 148 aircraft while the *Luftwaffe* had lost 286, including 105 Bf 109s.[95] But British fighter-pilot losses during the first month were serious: 84 pilots, or 10% of the basic force.[96] Nevertheless, Dowding and his command had more fighter aircraft and pilots at the end of the month than they did at the beginning. Given what the RAF had learned thus far in the combat, it is surprising how little the Germans were able to divine about the strengths of Fighter Command. A *Luftwaffe* intelligence report at the beginning of August stated:

> As the British fighters are controlled from the ground by R/T their forces are tied to their respective ground stations and are thereby restricted in mobility, even taking into consideration the probability that the ground stations are partly mobile. Consequently, the assembly of strong fighter forces at determined points and at short notice is not to be expected. A massed German attack on a target area can therefore count on the same conditions of light fighter opposition as in attacks on widely scattered targets. It can, indeed, be assumed that considerable confusion in the defensive networks will be unavoidable during mass attacks, and that the effectiveness of the defenses may thereby be reduced.[97]

While "Eagle Day" (the day the Germans were to launch their main aerial assault) did not officially take place until August 13, on the 11th Fighter Command noted a significant upswing in operations. On that day, a major raid on Britain's southern ports resulted in swirling dogfights that cost the British dearly. No. 11 Group lost 27 fighter pilots, killed, wounded, or missing, no less than 7% of its available pilots. German losses were also heavy; 39 aircraft were destroyed (although only 12 Bf 109 pilots were lost).[98] For the succeeding

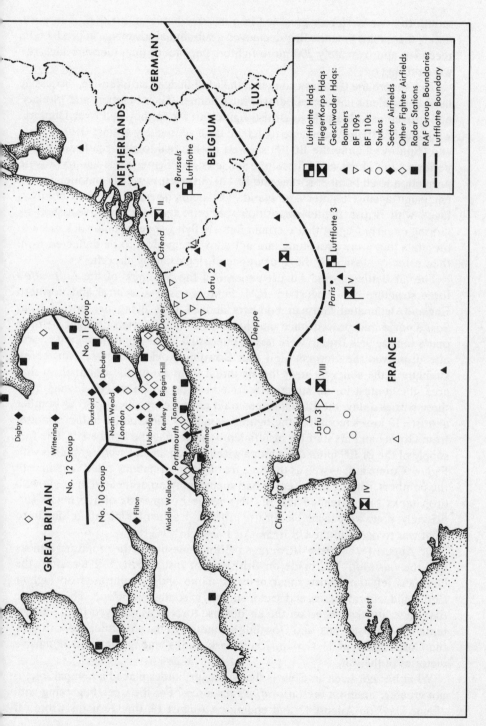

Battle of Britain: The Opposing Forces

month the two air forces grappled in a massive battle of attrition. It is worth noting that at this time the British enjoyed a substantial advantage in production, receiving approximately 200 more fighters per month than German factories were turning out.[99]

Even before the Germans launched their full-fledged air offensive, distressing tactical problems had appeared over the Channel. Their bombers and "Stukas" had proven as vulnerable to British fighter attack as they had over Dunkirk, while the Bf 110 proved unable to defend itself adequately against "Hurricanes" and "Spitfires." Only the Bf 109 showed itself equal to the "Spitfire" and superior to the "Hurricane." Thus, the single-engine fighter force had to provide protection to all bomber sorties and Bf 110 missions, as well as conduct its own campaign against Fighter Command. The helplessness of German bombers faced with British fighter opposition was reflected in a directive issued by Göring in early August that German fighters flying cover should stick close to the units they were protecting and not allow themselves to be deflected from their primary mission by the appearance of single enemy aircraft.[100]

The air battles in mid-August underlined the weakness of the *Luftwaffe's* force structure. On August 15, RAF fighters based in central and northern England decimated German bombers and Bf 110's flying unescorted from Scandinavia and proved once and for all that unsupported daylight bomber operations against Britain were nearly impossible. RAF opposition in the north also disproved the German view that Dowding would concentrate his entire strength in the south to meet the air threat from across the Channel. In that area, the contest for air superiority lasted a little over a month. Flying up to three sorties a day, the Bf 109 force could not be everywhere; and as bomber and Bf 110 losses mounted, the fighter squadrons came under unfair criticism from Göring and his staff for insufficiently protecting the bombers.[101] The fuel supply of the Bf 109 limited the arena within which the *Luftwaffe* grappled with Fighter Command, as well as the time that fighter formations could remain with the bombers. The Condor Legion had successfully experimented in Spain with drop tanks that extended the Bf 109's range by upwards of 125 miles; surprisingly, none were available for use in 1940—a state of affairs quite similar to what was to occur in the US Army Air Forces in 1943.[102]

On August 15, an easily discouraged Göring questioned the promising attacks that the *Luftwaffe* had made on British radar installations.[103] Thereafter, the Germans left the British radar network alone and concentrated on Fighter Command, aircraft bases, and sector stations in southern England. The pressure that these attacks placed on the air defense forces has received justifiable attention from historians, and Dowding's conduct of the air battle, supported by the Commander of 11 Group, Keith Park, ranks among the great defensive victories of the war.

What has not been so clear is that these air battles placed a comparable, if not greater, strain on the *Luftwafffe's* resources. For the week beginning with "Eagle Day" on August 13 and ending on August 19, the Germans wrote off approximately 284 aircraft, or 7 percent of their total force structure, or approximately 10 percent of all aircraft deployed in the three air fleets facing Britain as of July 20.[104] For August, aircraft losses were 774 from all causes, or 18.5 percent of all combat aircraft available at the beginning of the month.[105] Pilot losses had even more serious implications. Table VI[106] suggests that both the British and the German forces were using up their fighter pilots at an extraordinarily fast rate. It is doubtful whether the crew losses in the *Luftwaffe's* bomber force were any less, and it is definite that crew losses in the "Stuka" and the Bf 110 forces were even higher.

TABLE VI
Fighter Pilot Losses
RAF Fighter Command (Hurricanes and Spitfires), *Luftwaffe* (BF 109 force)

	RAF		LUFTWAFFE	
	Total losses All causes	Percentage loss of fighter pilots*	Total losses All causes	Percentage loss of fighter pilots*
July	84	10%	124**	11%
August	237	26%	168	15%
September	264	28%	229	23.1%

*Based on number of pilots available at the beginning of the month.
**May include some late returns from the Battle of France.

A sustained battle of attrition now took place: it began in the middle of August and lasted into the first week of September. During that period the *Luftwaffe* put extraordinary pressure on Fighter Command and its support structure. During the last ten days of August, Dowding's forces lost no less than 126 "Spitfire" and "Hurricane" pilots (14%)[107] and Park had to alter No. 11 Group's tactics considerably. Fighter pilots were no longer allowed to pursue German aircraft out over the Channel and all British fighter interceptions would attempt to attack German bombers rather than fighters.[108] Sixty percent of the British pilots lost were experienced aircrews, while replacements were coming directly from Operational Training Units (O.T.U.).[109] Losses in Fighter Command reached the point that the Air Staff was forced to transfer pilots directly from Bomber Command and to cut the O.T.U. course in half to get pilots out to the fighter squadrons.[110] But if the British were having a tough time the Germans were having an even nastier experience. Fighter Command's tenacious resistance led Göring to put the Bf 109 force on a tighter and tighter leash in terms of protecting the bombers. Moreover, the single-engine fighter force now had to protect the Bf 110s.[111] But as Table VII[112] indicates, the Germans were going through the same decline of skill levels among aircrews as new and untrained pilots and crews were rushed out of Operational Training Units to rebuild the front-line strength of squadrons that were being savaged by the fighting over Britain. The steady drain of fighter pilots on both sides is

TABLE VII

Pilot Availability and Losses 1940
BF 109 Squadrons

	Fighter Pilots available at beginning of month	Operationally ready fighter pilots at beginning of month	%	Fighter pilot losses during month	%
May	1110	1010	91%	76	6.8%
June	1199	839	70%	93	7.8%
July	1126	906	80.5%	124	11%
August	1118	869	77.7%	168	15%
September	990	735	74.2%	229	23.1%

clearly suggested by the figures in Table VIII.[113] Table IX[114] suggests the level of aircraft losses that accompanied the aircrew losses; while Table X[115] indicates the cumulative total of aircraft losses from May through September.

The impact of losses over southern England combined with inclinations already present in *Luftwaffe* doctrine to induce a change in German air strategy early in September. Attacks on Britain's air defense system through September 6 had given no indication that Fighter Command was weakening. As a result, Göring—at Kesselring's urging and with Hitler's support—turned to a massive assault on the British capital. This all-out effort, directed at London's East End and docks, accorded well with Douhet's theories and the Germans' own belief that ruthlessness could pay extra dividends.

Hitler's conversion to the assault on London reflected a predilection that haunted the *Luftwaffe* in the coming years: his insatiable fascination with a retaliatory air strategy in reply to enemy bombings. On September 4, the *Führer* declared in Berlin: "When they declare they will attack our cities in great measure, we will eradicate their cities. . . . The hour will come when one of us will break, and it will not be National Socialist Germany!"[116]

The results of the great September 7 raid on the London docks were indeed spectacular. During the night of September 7-8, London firemen fought nine fires that rated more than 100 pumps, and one fire on the Surrey Docks that rated more than 300 pumps.[117] The attack of September 7 did not entirely step over the line into a clear terror bombing because the primary target was the London docks, but there clearly was an assumed hope of terrorizing the London population. The relief to Fighter Command provided by this change in German strategy benefited not so much the exhausted fighter crews who still faced considerable fighting but rather the ground infrastructure of the British air defense system (the maintenance personnel, airfields, and sector stations needed to keep the aircraft flying).

The night bombing and daylight probes of the next week put heavy pressure on both London's inhabitants and German bomber crews. However, not until

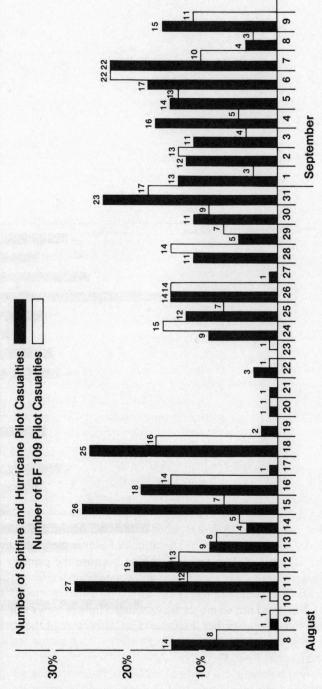

Table VIII Fighter Pilot Losses (All Causes) (RAF and Luftwaffe)

■ Number of Spitfire and Hurricane Pilot Casualties

□ Number of BF 109 Pilot Casualties

Table VIII continued

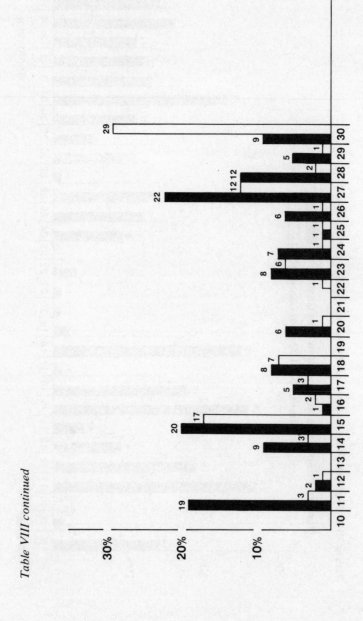

TABLE IX

Aircraft Losses, July-September 1940

Destroyed on Operations

Type Aircraft	Strength 29.6.40.	Due to Enemy Action	Not Due to Enemy Action	Total	Destroyed Not on Operations	Total Destroyed	Total Destroyed as Percent of Initial Strength
Close Recce	312	1	2	3	5	8	3%
Long-Range Recce	257	47	14	61	9	70	27%
Single-Engine Fighters	1,107	398	79	477	41	518	47%
Twin-Engine Fighters	357	214	9	223	12	235	66%
Bombers	1,380	424	127	551	70	621	45%
Dive Bombers	428	59	10	69	19	88	21%
Transport	408	3	1	4	11	15	4%
Coastal	233	38	29	67	14	81	35%
TOTAL	4,482	1,184	271	1,455	181	1,636	37%

Damaged on Operations

Type Aircraft	Due to Enemy Action	Not Due to Enemy Action	Total	Not on Operations	Total Damaged	Total Damaged and Destroyed	Total Damaged and Destroyed as Percent of Initial Strength
Close Recce	0	3	3	9	12	20	6%
Long-Range Recce	6	8	14	5	19	89	35%
Single-Engine Fighters	47	83	130	55	185	703	64%
Twin-Engine Fighters	49	11	60	5	65	300	84%
Bombers	118	118	236	98	334	955	69%
Dive Bombers	22	6	28	21	49	137	32%
Transport	1	1	2	9	11	26	6%
Coastal	4	6	10	12	22	109	47%
TOTAL	247	236	483	214	697	2,339	52%

TABLE X

Aircraft Losses, May-September 1940

Destroyed on Operations

Type Aircraft	Strength 4.5.40.	Due to Enemy Action	Not Due to Enemy Action	Total	Destroyed Not on Operations	Total Destroyed	Aircraft Destroyed in May-Sep Period as of Initial Strength
Close Recce	345	68	7	75	11	86	25%
Long-Range Recce	321	115	32	147	11	158	49%
Single-Engine Fighters	1,369	567	145	712	63	775	57%
Twin-Engine Fighters	367	304	25	329	16	345	94%
Bombers	1,758	862	180	1,042	100	1,142	65%
Dive Bombers	417	148	34	182	28	210	50%
Transport	531	191	19	210	18	228	43%
Coastal	241	58	45	103	17	120	50%
TOTAL	5,349	2,313	487	2,800	264	3,064	57%

September 15 did the *Luftwaffe* launch another massive daylight attack on London. This strike represented the climactic moment of the battle. On earlier occasions the Germans had lost more aircraft, but the stunning impact of a Fighter Command that was rested and prepared by a week of less critical operations broke the back of the attack. Unlike the previous week when the *Luftwaffe* had devastated the London docks, the bombers now scattered over London and ran for the coast. As a consequence, there was no concentrated pattern to the bombing.[118]

The failure of the daylight offensive in September led to the cancellation of "Sea Lion" and to a rethinking of German air strategy against Britain as part of an overall reassessment. The Germans now turned to a night bombing offensive. The strategic problem that faced the *Luftwaffe* was how exactly it could conduct this campaign. As with the air superiority battle of August and early September, this problem was, in many ways, similar to that facing those directing the Allied "strategic" bombing campaign of 1943 and 1944. German planners had to decide whether the *Luftwaffe* should deliver the weight of its attack against a specific segment of British industry such as aircraft factories, or against a system of interrelated industries such as Britain's import and distribution network, or even whether it should strike a blow aimed at breaking the

morale of the British population. The bombing offensive against London, referred to as the *Blitz,* attempted to achieve simultaneously all three strategies,
none of which proved decisive.[119] As with the daylight attacks, the *Luftwaffe*
did not possess the strength or the capabilities to achieve these objectives, and
the direct attacks on British military industrial targets and population centers
only spurred British desires to repay the Germans in kind.[120]

One aspect of the German night bomber offensive deserves closer scrutiny.
The switch to night bombing resulted from a realistic appreciation that there
were not enough German fighters to protect the bombers from devastating
British fighter attacks. The night effort led to a drastic falloff in bomber losses
as a result of combat; and through the winter of 1941, British night fighter and
antiaircraft defenses were generally ineffective against German intruders. While
combat-related losses were low, the accident rate remained high. *Luftwaffe*
crews flew these combat missions at night and in bad weather, or trained in
less-than-perfect conditions to achieve the flying proficiency required. Thus, to
list only combat losses considerably understates the attrition that took place.
From October to December 1940, bomber losses from noncombat causes ran
well over 50 percent of all losses each month; while for the whole period,
63.5 percent of bomber losses resulted from noncombat causes (see Table XI[121]).

CONCLUSION

As is the case in most wars, those who participated in or observed the Battle
of Britain and the *Blitz* drew conclusions compatible with their own views on
force structure and doctrine. Nevertheless, in every sense, those directing the
Luftwaffe came off least well in the "lessons learned" analysis. Although the
Germans had suffered the hardest psychological knocks, since it was their air
offensive that had failed, their reaction seems best represented by Jeschonnek's
remark shortly before the invasion of Russia: "At last, a proper war!"[122] Before
going on to examine the full implications of such a statement, one should note
that Jeschonnek and the general staff paid minimal attention to the attrition
that had taken place not only in the Battle of Britain but in the land campaign
that had preceded it. Thus, willfully and confidently, they embarked on a
campaign to conquer the largest nation in the world with an air force that,
quantitatively, was virtually the same size as it had been the previous year and
was arguably weaker in terms of crew experience and training. Moreover, industrial production of aircraft had stagnated for the third consecutive year.

For the British, the Battle of Britain confirmed what operations over the
Heligoland Bight had indicated the previous December—daylight bomber
operations in the face of enemy fighters were not possible. Surprisingly, German
night operations, which often did not achieve either concentration or accuracy
in bombing, did not raise the question of the accuracy of the RAF's bombing
over German territory. Not until the summer of 1941, on the basis of Bomber
Command's own operations, did the British recognize that only one-third of

TABLE XI

German Bomber Losses, October-December 1940

	Total No. of Bombers at Beginning of Month	Bombers Destroyed Due to Enemy Action	Bombers Destroyed on Operations But Not Due to Enemy Action	Bombers Destroyed Not on Operations	Total Destroyed
October 1940	(28.9.40.) 1,420	64	78	29	171
November 1940	(2.11.40.) 1,423	14	57	13	84
December 1940	(30.11.40.) 1,393	62	58	9	129
TOTAL	Average 1,412	140	193	51	384

their bombs were falling within 5 miles of the target (a target circle equal to 78.54 square miles).[123] Nor did the fact that massive German bombing of London had strengthened, rather than diminished, British morale make much impression. On this very point, Air Marshal Sir Charles Portal, Commander in Chief of the RAF, remarked at the time that the Germans surely could not take the same level of pounding as had the British people.[124]

The American assessment of the tactical lessons was equally short-sighted. Army Air Forces' observers attributed the high loss rate of German bombers at the hands of British fighters to inadequate defensive armament and airframe size, to flying missions at too low a level, and to poor formation discipline under attack.[125] The Army Air Forces' plan of employment, drawn up in August 1941 for America's possible entrance into a European war, argued that "by employing large numbers of aircraft with high speed, good defensive power, and high altitude," its bombers would be able to penetrate deep into the heart of Germany in daylight without unbearable losses.[126] The impediment that the Bf 109's lack of range placed on German bomber operations did not receive proper recognition until the American disaster over Schweinfurt in October of 1943 had again underscored the need for long-range fighter support. According to American official historians, such an oversight "is difficult to account for."[127]

In one critical respect, however, the British and American air forces drew the correct lesson from the Battle of Britain. Both air forces concluded that the German force structure was inadequate to meet the demands of the battle. Encouraged by an overestimation of actual German air strength, both air forces set targets for their industrial production and force structure that demanded enormous increases in air strength. Thus, at the same time that the Germans continued a minimum program of air armament, Britain and the

United States set in motion preparations that gave them a decisive quantitative edge in the later years of the war. The air struggle of those years rested, as it did in the 1940 battles, ón numbers of aircraft, industrial capacity and production, and availability of trained aircrews. Thus, the basis of Allied superiority rested on the production programs drawn up in 1940 and 1941 by both sides.

Notes

1. IMT, *TMWC*, Vol. XXXII, Doc. #3575, p. 413.

2. Jost Dülffer, *Weimar, Hitler und die Marine, Reichspolitik und Flottenbau 1920–1939* (Düsseldorf, 1973), p. 504.

3. William L. Shirer, *The Rise and Fall of the Third Reich* (New York, 1960), pp. 446–47.

4. For a fuller discussion of this criticism of British policy, see my study *The Change in the European Balance of Power, 1938-1939* (Princeton, 1984), Chapters X and XI. This is a fundamentally different view than that expressed by Gerhard Weinberg in *The Foreign Policy of Nazi Germany*, Vol. II (Chicago, 1981). Readers interested in the subject are invited to compare the differing interpretations.

5. IMT, *TMWC*, Vol. XXVI, Doc. #798PS, p. 338.

6. Shirer, *The Rise and Fall of the Third Reich*, p. 467.

7. I am indebted to Oberstleutnant Dr. Klaus Maier of the Militärgeschichtliches Forschungsamt for this line of argument.

8. BA/MA RL 7/42, RL 7/43, Luftflottenkommando 2., Führungsabteilung, Nr. 7093/39, 13.5.39., "Schlussbesprechung des Planspieles 1939."

9. Maier, *et al., Das deutsche Reich und der Zweite Weltkrieg*, Vol. II, pp. 63–64.

10. Quoted in David Irving, *The War Path, Hitler's Germany, 1933–1939* (New York, 1978), p. 225; for further discussion of this visit, see Irving, *The Rise and Fall of the Luftwaffe*, pp. 73–74.

11. *Documents on German Foreign Policy (DGFP)*, Series D, Vol. VII. Doc. #192, 22.8.39.

12. Ibid., Vol. VII, Doc. #307, 26.8.39.

13. See the outstanding article on the real attitudes within the Chamberlain Cabinet by Peter Ludlow, "The Unwinding of Appeasement" in *Das "Andere Deutschland" im Zweiten Weltkrieg*, ed. by L. Kettenacker (Stuttgart, 1977).

14. For the economic side of such a strategy, see Burton Klein, *Germany's Economic Preparations for War* (Cambridge, 1959), and Alan Milward, *The German Economy at War* (London, 1965). On the military side of the argument, see Larry Addington, *The Blitzkrieg Era and the German General Staff, 1865–1941* (New Brunswick, 1971). For a recent restatement of the theory, see F. H. Hinsley, E. E. Thomas, C. F. G. Ransom, R. C. Knight, *British Intelligence in the Second World War*, Vol. I (London, 1979), Chapter 1.

15. For a fuller discussion of these issues, see Murray, *The Change in the European Balance of Power, 1938-1939*, Chapter I.

16. Maier, *et al., Das deutsche Reich und der Zweite Weltkrieg*, Vol. II, p. 117.

17. "The Luftwaffe in Poland," a study produced by the German Historical Branch (8th Abteilung), 11.7.44., AHB, Translation No. VII/33.

18. For a fuller discussion of the planning and conduct of operations in the Polish campaign, see: Robert M. Kennedy, *The German Campaign in Poland 1939* (Washington, 1956); and Maier, *et al., Das deutsche Reich und der Zweite Weltkrieg*, Vol. II, Part IV.

19. For an interesting discussion of the Polish campaign in the air, see J. S. Orworski, "Polish Air Force Versus Luftwaffe," *Air Pictorial*, Vol. 21, Nos. 10 and 11, October and November 1959.

20. In fact, it can be argued that it was only in Poland that the Germans integrated armored formations and close air support into a coherent operational concept. It was only in Poland that a significant body within the German army's high command became convinced that an armored exploitation strategy was in the offing.

21. Maier, *et al., Das deutsche Reich und der Zweite Weltkrieg*, Vol. II, p. 124; for a detailed account of the battle along the Bzura, see Rolf Elbe, *Die Schlacht an der Bzura im September 1939 aus deutscher und polnischer Sicht* (Freiburg, 1975).

22. "German Bombing of Warsaw and Rotterdam," Air Historical Branch, Translation VII/132.

23. Maier, *et al.*, *Das deutsche Reich und der Zweite Weltkrieg*, Vol. II, p. 133.

24. For a fuller discussion of the state of the German army after the Polish campaign and its efforts to correct its deficiencies, see my article in *Armed Forces and Society* (Winter 1981), "The German Response to Victory in Poland: A Case Study in Professionalism."

25. IMT, *TMWC*, Vol. XXVI, Doc. #798 PS, pp. 342–43.

26. Schlesisches Institut für Wirtschafts- und Konjunkturforschung, "Zahlen des deutschen Aussenhandels seit Kriegsbeginn," August 1940, pp. 2–7, NARS T–84/195/1560551.

27. Bericht des Herrn Professor Dr. C. Krauch über die Lage auf dem Arbeitsgebiet der Chemie in der Sitzung des Generalrates am 24.6.41., "Treibstoff-Vorräte," NARS T–84/217/1586749.

28. In particular, see Harold C. Deutsch, *The Conspiracy Against Hitler in the Twilight War* (Minneapolis, 1968), who regards Hitler's desire for a western offensive in the fall as completely irrational.

29. Maier, *et al.*, *Das deutsche Reich und der Zweite Weltkrieg*, Vol. II, p. 267.

30. OKW files: "Denkschrift und Richtlinien über die Führung des Krieges im Westen," Berlin, 9.10.39., NARS T–77/775.

31. H. R. Trevor-Roper, ed., *Blitzkrieg to Defeat, Hitler's War Directives* (New York, 1965), Directive #6 for the Conduct of the War, 9.10.39., p. 13.

32. For a fuller discussion of these "after action" reports and their impact on army thinking, see my article "The German Response to Victory in Poland: A Case Study in Professionalism."

33. Maier, *et al.*, *Das deutsche Reich und der Zweite Weltkrieg*, Vol. II, p. 242.

34. Air Historical Branch, Translation No. VII/107, "Luftwaffe Strength and Serviceability Tables, August 1938–April 1945 (compiled from the records of VI Abteilung Quartermaster General's Department of the German Air Ministry). Dates for the figures are September 2, 1939, and April 6, 1940.

35. Trevor-Roper, *Blitzkrieg to Defeat*, Directive #6 for the Conduct of the War, 9.10.30., p. 13.

36. "Proposal for the Conduct of Air War Against Britain," made by General Schmid of the German Air Force Operations Staff (intelligence), 22.11.39., AHB, Translation No. VII/30.

37. Trevor-Roper, *Blitzkrieg to Defeat*, Directive #9, "Instructions for Warfare Against the Economy of the Enemy," 29.11.39., p. 18.

38. See, in particular, Guderian's description of the major argument in the March conference between himself and Generals Halder and Busch. Heinz Guderian, *Panzer Leader* (London, 1952), pp. 90–92. For fuller accounts of arguments within the German high command over the proper strategy for the coming campaign, see: Telford Taylor, *The March of Conquest* (New York, 1958); Alistair Horne, *To Lose a Battle, France 1940* (London, 1969); Hans-Adolf Jacobsen, *Fall Gelb. Der Kampf um den deutschen Operations plan zur Westoffensive 1940* (Wiesbaden, 1957); Hans-Adolf Jacobsen, *Dokumente zur Vorgeschichte des Westfeldzuges 1939–1940* (Göttingen, 1956).

39. Taylor, *The March of Conquest*, p. 90.

40. Trevor-Roper, *Blitzkrieg to Defeat*, Directive #6 for the Conduct of the War, 9.10.39., p. 14. These instructions for the immediate operational employment of the Luftwaffe do not contradict the thesis that the purpose of the campaign was to create the conditions for a strategic offensive (air and naval) against Britain. For a fuller description of Luftwaffe tasks, see: ObdL, Führungsstab Ia Nr. 5330/39, 7.12.39. Weisung Nr. 5, Luftkrieg im Westen. AFSHRC: K 113.306.2.

41. The misreading of these German naval operations by the Admiralty and by Churchill in particular must be counted as one of the great British failures of the Second World War.

42. The clearest account of the campaign in English is contained in Taylor, *The March of Conquest;* see also T. K. Derry, *The Campaign in Norway* (London, 1952); S. W. Roskill, *The War at Sea, 1939–45* (London, 1954); and Maier, *et al.*, *Das deutsche Reich und der Zweite Weltkrieg*, Vol. II.

43. For the best discussion on the importance of Swedish iron ore imports to the Reich, see: Rolf Karlborn, "Sweden's Iron Ore Exports to Germany 1933–1944," *Scandinavian Economic History Review*, No. 1 (1965).

44. Maier, *et al.*, *Das deutsche Reich und der Zweite Weltkrieg*, Vol. II, p. 224.

45. Ibid., 221–24. It should be stressed that the navy risked these ships partially to gain an advantageous position for the post-war budget debates.

46. Raeder claims in his memoir that he only raised the issue of a possible invasion to pre-empt the topic. His strategy thereafter indicates that from the start, he never considered an invasion a serious possibility. See Erich Raeder, *Struggle for the Sea* (London, 1952), p. 331.

47. For a numerical comparison of the forces employed in this campaign, see in particular R. H. S. Stolfi, "Equipment for Victory in France in 1940," *History* (February 1970). There is, of course,

another aspect and that is the qualitative difference. See also my article in *Armed Forces and Society*, "The German Response to Victory in Poland: A Case Study in Professionalism."

48. For the disposition of RAF forces in France at the start of the 1940 campaign, see Major L. F. Ellis, *The War in France and Flanders, 1939–1940* (London, 1953), map between pages 34 and 35.

49. See, in particular, Patrice Buffetot and Jacquer Ogier, "L'armée de l'air française dans la campagne de France (10 mai-25 juin 1940)," *Revue historique des Armées*, Vol. II, No. 3, pp. 88-117.

50. For an interesting discussion of the relative experience level of pilots in the French and German air forces, see: J. Curry, "Hawk 75 in French Service," *American Aviation Historical Society Journal*, Vol. II, No. 1 (Spring 1966), pp. 13–30.

51. "Der Einsatz der deutschen Luftwaffe während der ersten 11 Tage des Frankreichfeldzuges," Auszüge aus den täglichen Lagemeldungen des Oberbefehlshabers der Luftwaffe, Abt. Ic., AFSHRC: K 113.306–3, v. 2.

52. Taylor, *March of Conquest*, p. 203.

53. See the diary entry for General von Waldau's diary: Auszugweise Wiedergabe aus dem persönlichen Tagebuch des Generals von Waldau vom März 1939–10.4.42 Chef des Luftwaffenführungstabes. AFSHRC: K 113.306–3, v. 2.

54. Seventy German paratroopers ended up on top of Eben-Emael and were sufficient to force the surrender of the fort with its 1,200 defenders. "Der Handstreich auf die Werk-Gruppe Eben-Emael am 10. Mai 1940," NARS T–971/35/1019.

55. KTB VIII Fl. Korps, BA/MA RL8/45.

56. For Guderian's account, see *Panzer Leader*, pp. 79–82. See also "Der Bericht der Luftwaffe über die Durchführung," Auszug aus den täglichen Luftlagemeldungen des Oberbefehlshabers der Luftwaffe-Lagebericht Nr. 251, 14.5.40, AFSHRC: K 113.306–3, v. 2; and KTB VIII Fl. Korps, BA/MA RL 8/45.

57. For the collapse of the French infantry under "Stuka" attack, see Horne, *To Lose a Battle, France, 1940*, pp. 290–92.

58. Major L.F. Ellis, *The War in France and Flanders, 1939-1940* (London, 1953), pp. 55-56.

59. "Das Jagdgeschwader 27 des VIII. Flieger-Korps im Frankreichfeldzug, 1940," Generalmajor a. D. Max Ibel, 25.6.53., BA/MA, RL 10/591.

60. Generaloberst Halder, *Kriegstagebuch*, Vol. I, ed. by Hans-Adolf Jacobsen (Stuttgart, 1964), diary entry for 16.5.40.

61. See the carefully worked out argument in Taylor, *The March of Conquest*, pp. 255–63.

62. Testimony by former Chief of Intelligence Schmid on 18.6.54., AFSHRC: K 113.306–3, v. 3.

63. Adolf Galland, *The First and the Last* (New York, 1954), p. 6.

64. Ellis, *The War in France and Flanders*, p. 246. The German losses, it should be noted, were for the entire western theater of operations, but most of the Luftwaffe's effort was concentrated in this time period over Dunkirk.

65. "Einsatz des II. Fliegerkorps bei Dünkirchen am 27.5.40.: Schwerer Tag des II. Fliegerkorps," AFSHRC: K 113.306–3, v. 3.

66. Guderian, *Panzer Leader*, p. 75.

67. Maier, *et al.*, *Das deutsche Reich und der Zweite Weltkrieg*, Vol. II, p. 294.

68. These two tables are drawn from two major compilations of the Air Historical Branch. They are AHB, Translation VII/107, "Luftwaffe Strength and Serviceability Tables, August 1938–April 1945"; and Translation VII/83, "German Aircraft Losses, September 1939–December 1940." These tables, in turn, were compiled from the German Quartermaster records then in the hands of the AHB.

69. BA/MA RL 2 III/1025, gen. Qu. 6 Abt. (III A), "Front-Flugzeug Verluste," 1940.

70. Based on the figures in BA/MZ, RL 2 III/707, Gen. Qu.6.Abt. (I), Übersicht über Soll, Ist-bestand, Einsatzbereitschaft, Verluste und Reserven der fliegenden Verbände. These tables were usually about 5 days behind actual losses. Therefore there is some distortion and in fact the Germans clearly lost more pilots in May than in June (but many of the losses in May were not reported until June). What matters are the trends and the overall implications of those trends.

71. For Hitler's mood after the defeat of France, see Telford Taylor, *The Breaking Wave* (New York, 1967), pp. 53–54.

72. IMT, *TMWC*, Vol. XXVIII, Jodl diary entry for 20.5.40.

73. The Earl of Birkenhead, *Halifax* (Boston, 1966), p. 458; and Llewellyn Woodward, *British Foreign Policy in the Second World War* (London, 1962), p. 53.

74. For the British files on this incident, see PRO FO 371/24859 and FO 800/322.

75. PRO ADM 205/4 undated and unsigned memorandum.

76. For a full discussion of the British attack on the French fleet at Mers-el-Kebir, see the thoughtful study by Arthur Marder in *From the Dardanelles to Oran* (London, 1974), Chapter V.

77. Chef WFA, 30.6.40., "Die Weiterführung des Krieges gegen England," IMT, *TMWC*, Vol. XXVIII, pp. 301–03.

78. Maier, *et al.*, *Das deutsche Reich und der Zweite Weltkrieg*, Vol. II, pp. 378–79.

79. Chef WFA, 30.6.40., "Die Weiterführung des Krieges gegen England," IMT, *TMWC*, Vol. XXVIII, pp. 301–03.

80. BA/MA RL 2II/27, "Allgemeine Weisung für den Kampf der Luftwaffe gegen England," ObdL, Führungsstab Ia Nr. 5835/40, 30.6.40.

81. Roskill, *The War at Sea*, Vol. I, pp. 248–49.

82. For the intelligence advantage that the British enjoyed, see: R. V. Jones, *The Wizard War* (New York, 1978); Hinsley, *et al.*, *British Intelligence in the Second World War*, Vol. I; Ronald Lewin, *Ultra Goes to War* (New York, 1978); and Brian Johnson, *The Secret War* (London, 1978).

83. Hinsley, *et al.*, *British Intelligence in the Second World War*, Vol. I, pp. 176–77; and Harold Deutsch, "Ultra and the Air War in Europe and Africa," *Air Power and Warfare*, pp. 165–66. For the German view on Ultra's impact, see Maier, *et al.*, *Das deutsche Reich und der Zweite Weltkrieg*, p. 384.

84. For the contribution of "Y" Service, see Aileen Clayton, *The Enemy is Listening* (London, 1980).

85. See, in particular, Jones, *Wizard War* and Solly Zuckerman, *From Apes to Warlords* (London, 1978).

86. In particular, see PRO AIR 20/1623 Air Scientific Intelligence Report No. 6, "The Crooked Leg," 28.6.40., for R. V. Jones' initial report and estimation of the "Knickebein" system.

87. See particularly, Boog, "Higher Command and Leadership in the German Luftwaffe, 1935–1945," *Air Power and Warfare*, p. 145.

88. Mason, *Battle Over Britain*, Appendix K, OKL, 16,7.40., Operations Staff Ic.

89. Basil Collier, *The Defense of the United Kingdom* (London, 1957), p. 160.

90. BA/MA RL 2 II/30, "Besprechung Reichsmarschall am 21.7.40."

91. BA/MA RL 8/1 Generalkommando I. Fliegerkorps Abt. I a Nr. 10260/40, 24.7.40., "Gedanken über die Führung des Luftkrieges gegen England."

92. Mason, *Battle over Britain*, p. 130.

93. Based on figures in Air Ministry, *The Rise and Fall of the German Air Force*, p. 76; Mason, *Battle over Britain*, p. 186; and "Luftwaffe Strength and Serviceability Tables, August 1938-April 1945," Air Historical Branch, Translation No. VII/107.

94. Collier, *The Defense of the United Kingdom*, pp. 166-171.

95. Ibid., p. 171.

96. Based on the daily loss tables for July available in Mason, *Battle over Britain*.

97. Quoted in Air Ministry, *The Rise and Fall of the German Air Force*, p. 80.

98. Percentages based on number of pilots available on August 1. See Mason, *Battle over Britain*, p. 203.

99. Based on figures given in Mason, *Battle over Britain*, p. 121, and The United States Strategic Bombing Survey, *The Effects of Strategic Bombing on the German War Economy* (Washington, D.C., 1945), p. 277.

100. BA/MA RL 2 II/30, H. Qu., 2 August 1940, Aktenvermerk.

101. See Galland, *The First and the Last*, pp. 24–29.

102. Ibid., p. 24.

103. BA/MA RL 2 II/30, Besprechung am 15.8.40.

104. The figures of Luftwaffe aircraft written off (60 percent or greater damage) comes from the loss tables in Mason, *Battle Over Britain*, pp. 241-43, 247, 263-64, 272-73, 274, 281-84, 286-87; the 7 percent figure represents total Luftwaffe aircraft types involved in the Battle of Britain as of August 10 based on AHB, Translation No. VII/107, "Luftwaffe Strength and Serviceability Tables, August 1938–April 1945"; while the 10 percent figure represents aircraft deployed in the three air fleets as of July 20, Mason, *Battle Over Britain*, p. 128.

105. Figures based on: AHB, Translation No. VII/107, "Luftwaffe Strength and Serviceability Tables, August 1938-April 1945"; and AHB, Translation VII/83, "German Aircraft Losses, September 1939-December 1940."

106. Based on the tables in Mason, *Battle over Britain*, and on BA/MA, RL 2 III/707, Gen. Qu.6.Abt. (I), Übersicht über Soll, Istbestand, Einsatzbereitschaft, Verluste und Reserven der fliegenden Verbände.

107. Based on the tables in Mason, *Battle over Britain*.

108. Ibid., p. 285.

109. Ibid., p. 274.

110. Collier, *Defense of the United Kingdom*, p. 200.

111. Mason, *Battle over Britain*, pp. 284-285, 289.

112. Based on the figures in BA/MA, RL 2 III/708,709, Gen. Qu.6.Abt. (I), Übersicht über Soll, Istbestand, Einsatzbereitschaft, Verluste und Reserven der fliegenden Verbände.

113. Based on the tables in Mason, *Battle over Britain* for August and September.

114. AHB, Translation VII/83, "German Aircraft Losses, September 1939–December 1940."

115. Ibid.

116. Quoted in Maier, *et al., Das deutsche Reich und der Zweite Weltkrieg*, Vol. II, p. 386.

117. Mason, *Battle Over Britain*, p. 363.

118. Ibid., pp. 387–91.

119. For an excellent discussion of various arguments over target selection and strategy in the post-September 15 period, see: Maier, *et al., Das deutsche Reich und der Zweite Weltkrieg*, pp. 388–96.

120. Air Marshal 'Bert' Harris recalls taking Sir Charles Portal up to the roof of the Air Ministry to watch the spectacular results of one of the December raids on London. Harris interview, RAF Staff College, Bracknell, England.

121. Table drawn from AHB, Translation No. VII/83, "German Aircraft Losses, September 1939–December 1940"; and AHB, Translation No. VII/107, "Luftwaffe Strength and Serviceability Tables, August 1938–April 1945."

122. Irving, *The Rise and Fall of the Luftwaffe*, p. 123.

123. Webster and Frankland, *SAOAG*, Vol. IV, Annexes and Appendices, p. 205.

124. Dennis Richards, *Portal* (London, 1979), p. 146. The similarity between Portal's comment and Knauss' argumentation is indeed striking. See Chapter I of this book, p. 10.

125. Haywood S. Hansell, Jr., *The Air Plan that Defeated Hitler* (Atlanta, 1972), pp. 53–54.

126. Craven and Cate, *The Army Air Forces in World War II*, Vol. I, p. 149.

127. Ibid., p. 604.

III ▌▌▌ The Turn to Russia

THE STRATEGIC PROBLEM

If early summer 1940 brought Hitler an unimagined, easy triumph over France, it also brought unanticipated strategic problems. Hitler had expected the British to recognize their hopeless situation and sue for peace. He seems, however, to have given almost no thought to what options Germany possessed should Britain reject his offer[1]. The unrealistic optimism that characterized the air offensive against the British Isles marked the German approach towards their strategic problems throughout the 1940–41 period. As Italian Foreign Minister Galeazzo Ciano noted after a visit to Munich in June 1940, Hitler resembled a successful gambler who "has made a big scoop and would like to get up from the table, risking nothing more."[2] Ciano's description was most apt, for Hitler did, indeed, wish to escape a war against Britain. He calculated, quite correctly, that those who stood most to gain from a British defeat were the Japanese and the Americans and not the Germans.[3] Thus, the road that policymaking within Germany travelled up to the beginning of "Barbarossa" led (1) from a direct air offensive on Britain to persuade the British of their hopeless position and to allow an unhindered move against Russia; (2) to a search for an indirect strategy to defeat the British; (3) to increasing interest in attacking the Soviet Union to remove a major buttress in Churchill's strategic policy; and, finally, (4) to the decision to invade Russia as the basis for realizing Hitler's long-term ideological goals.[4]

What the Germans misread, however, was the real significance of the victory over France in 1940. Their success did not mean that Germany had won the war, as Jodl's memorandum of June 30, 1940, suggested.[5] Rather, it meant that Germany had acquired the economic and raw material resources to fight a long war. The nature and direction that a protracted war might take would depend on the strategic choices that the Germans were now to make; nevertheless, no matter what strategy Hitler and his advisers chose, the *Reich* was in for an extended and difficult struggle. The refusal of Germany's political and military leaders to recognize that fact destroyed whatever small chance Germany had to realize her inordinate goals and contributed directly to the catastrophe of 1945. Above all, this failure in grand strategy reflected the unwillingness of the German military to comprehend the nature of warfare between the great powers in the modern age. This led to the unrealistic belief that victory over France represented a return to the era of the short war.

With Britain's rejection of peace, Hitler sensed the strategic basis for Churchill's decision. As he suggested to Halder, the British hoped that both the Soviet Union and the United States would intervene in the war against Germany.[6] In this Hitler was correct, for Churchill had indeed based his hard line on the belief that Russia and America could not, in their own self-interest, allow Germany to dominate Europe.[7] With that strange mixture of intuition and ignorance that characterized Hitler's makeup, the *Führer* urged on his military advisers the possibility of a quick, late summer campaign against the Soviet Union to remove that prop from British policy. His military advisers eventually were able to persuade him that such a campaign, late in the year, made no sense.[8]

Yet, Hitler's interest in a possible strike against Russia in the summer of 1940 does not indicate that he had firmly set Germany's course for the following summer.[9] Rather as it became clear by mid-September that the RAF would hold its own and that "Sea Lion" was no longer a viable option, Hitler turned to the peripheral strategy which Jodl had urged in June. In the early fall of 1940, Hitler approached Spain and Vichy France about helping Fascist Italy attack British interests in the Mediterranean, North Africa, and the Middle East. Such an approach might have worked in the early summer of 1940 when the *Wehrmacht*'s reputation was at its highest. But having suffered defeat in the skies over Britain, it was not so easy to forge an alliance among powers whose interests and appetites were mutually exclusive. Hitler fully recognized the diplomatic difficulties when he commented before meeting with Franco and Pétain that the need of the hour was a gigantic fraud.[10]

Conversations with the French and particularly the Spanish led nowhere, and upon return to Berlin Hitler remarked that he would sooner have "three or four" teeth pulled than face another conversation with Franco. Hitler had missed the bus.[11] In the early summer in the full flush of victory, he might well have persuaded Spain to participate. After Mers-el-Kebir, had he granted substantial concessions to France in terms of the eventual peace treaty, he might also have enlisted Vichy support. However, with the *Wehrmacht*'s overwhelming success, he felt no need to cut Spain in on the loot or to mitigate the onerous terms he wished to impose on France. Now in the fall of 1940, it was too late; the Spanish and the French recognized that the war was not over. The former made impossibly high demands concerning the price for Spain's entrance into the war; the latter decided to wait on further events despite bitterness against the British for Mers-el-Kebir.

There remained only the Russians as a means of pressuring the British. Since Hitler had hoped to end the war in the west so that he could solve the eastern question, one can wonder how seriously the *Führer* ever considered the possibility of a closer alliance with Russia. Nevertheless, in November 1940, the Soviet Foreign Minister, Vyacheslav Molotov, arrived in Berlin to explore further cooperation between the dictatorships. The Russians overplayed their hand. Stalin seems to have believed his diplomatic position was stronger than, in fact, it was. Thus, Molotov was at his most truculent, brushing aside German suggestions that the Soviets interest themselves in the Persian Gulf, Iran, and India. While such goals were not entirely out of the range of Soviet expectations, Molotov emphasized more concrete and immediate aims in Europe. Among other items, he suggested that Finland, the Balkans, and the Dardanellés all lay within the Soviet sphere of interest. What undoubtedly made the Germans choke was Molotov's proposal that a two-nation commission control the Skagerrak, entrance and exit to the Baltic—the proposed nations being the Soviet Union and Denmark. Adding further to the German discomfort were Molotov's tactless contradictions of the *Führer* and his justly famous rejoinder to Joachim von Ribbentrop's (the German Foreign Minister) comment that Britain was finished; why then, he asked, were they in an air raid shelter?[12]

Molotov's behavior, typical of Soviet diplomatic practices that have subsequently worked so well in dealings with the West, made a disastrous impression on his hosts and undoubtedly contributed to the German decision to settle matters with the Soviets that coming summer. There had been, moreover, a general deterioration in relations between the two powers since the summer of 1940.[13] Stalin had taken advantage of German preoccupation in the west to incorporate Lithuania, Latvia, and Estonia into the Soviet Union. More threatening to German interests was the Russian move against Rumania in July 1940, when the Soviets forced their neighbor to surrender not only the province of Bessarabia (covered by the Nazi-Soviet Non Aggression Pact) but the province of Bukovina as well (not covered by the agreement).

Hitler's reply to what he regarded as a threat to German interests in the Balkans, particularly Rumanian oil, was direct and forceful. Complicating the diplomatic situation was the fact that Hungary and Rumania were on the brink of war over the province of Transylvania.[14] To the Germans, such a disruption of Balkan relations was unacceptable. Under pressure from both Ribbentrop and Ciano, the Rumanians surrendered substantial territory to Hungary.[15] With that difficulty cleared up, the Germans turned to bolster a Rumanian regime badly shaken by a serious diplomatic defeat. The Germans moved with their usual speed. In early September, they supported the establishment of a pro-German military regime under General Ion Antonescu. At the end of the month, they sent a military "mission" consisting of a motorized infantry division, supported by flak and air units, to protect the oil region and to demonstrate German support for the new regime. One of the "mission's" major tasks was: "In case a war with Soviet Russia is forced upon us, to prepare for the commitment of German and Rumanian forces from the direction of Rumania."[16]

These German moves, all without consultation, elicited a vigorous response from the Russians. They protested strongly against the Vienna Accords that had settled the difficulty between Rumania and Hungary, and the movement of German motorized troops into Rumania could not have contributed to a Soviet sense of well-being.[17] Equally disturbing, in view of Soviet interests in the Baltic, was a Finnish-German agreement that allowed the Germans to transport substantial forces through Finland to northern Norway. Of the 4,800 troops involved in the move, 1,800 remained in Finland for a considerable period. Under these circumstances, the Russians had every right to be suspicious.[18] Given these frictions, the rapacious nature of the two dictators' appetites, as well as Hitler's belief that only in the east could Germany achieve the living space she needed, the conflict between Russia and Germany was indeed inevitable. Had Molotov been more tactful and tractable, it is still unlikely that the Russians could have delayed the coming confrontation for long.

Nevertheless, Molotov's visit did precipitate a quick decision by Hitler. Within a little over a month, Hitler issued Directive No. 21, "Operation Barbarossa," to the armed forces. It stated: "The German *Wehrmacht* must be prepared *to crush Soviet Russia in a quick campaign* even before the conclusion of the war against England."[19] The directive itself reflected a culmination of the planning process that had begun during the preceding summer.[20] Before examining the outlines of German military and strategic planning, one need only note that Hitler had set the final direction to German grand strategy. From this point forward, the Germans began serious preparations to destroy the Soviet Union in a swift, fast-moving campaign in which the *Wehrmacht* would drive into the heart of the Eurasian continent.

DISTRACTIONS

Unfortunately for the Germans, difficulties now arose in the south. In June 1940, believing that the war was over and the time propitious to loot the British and French empires, the Italians joined the war. Most Italians, particularly those in the upper classes—the military and Royalist circles, as well as the Fascists—wildly applauded Mussolini's war declaration, a declaration that Franklin Roosevelt so aptly described: "On this tenth day of June 1940, the hand that held the dagger has stuck it into the back of its neighbor."[21] The Italian armed forces, however, were woefully unprepared for any military commitments. The army possessed obsolete equipment, a faulty doctrine, and a thoroughly inadequate table of organization. The navy was acquiring an up-to-date battle fleet but had no desire to use its ships in combat. The Italian air force, supposedly heirs of Douhet, could not provide an accurate count of the aircraft at its disposal.[22] These deficiencies, which became so glaringly obvious in coming months, had nothing to do with the bravery of the Italian people; rather, they had to do with military organizations that did not exist to fight. As General Ubaldo Soddu described his military career: ". . . when you have a fine plate of *pasta* guaranteed for life, and a little music, you don't need anything more."[23]

The Germans soon paid for their belief that Mussolini had reformed the capabilities of the Italian military. The *Reich* assigned the Italians the task of pinning down British forces in the Mediterranean. Hence, the Italian characterization of their Mediterranean effort as a "parallel war." That was an apt description for, in fact, there was little military cooperation between the Axis powers until the following winter when the Germans had to take over because of Italian military ineptitude.

Disaster came soon enough. Despite an explicit German warning in late September not to stir up trouble in the Balkans, the Italians blithely went their own way.[24] In October 1940, in an effort to parallel the German move into Rumania, they attacked Greece. With little preparation, no strategic planning, and at the onset of bad weather, Mussolini launched his forces into the highlands of northern Greece. The result was a military defeat with serious strategic implications. Italian incompetence had upset the Balkans and had provided an entree into the region for the British.

Worse news soon followed. In November, "Swordfish" torpedo bombers, flying off the carrier *Illustrious,* attacked the Italian fleet in the harbor of Taranto. By the time two strike forces of 12 and 9 aircraft had completed their mission, they had sunk 2 new and 2 older Italian battleships and had altered permanently the Mediterranean naval balance in the Royal Navy's favor.[25]

The collapse of Italian ground forces in North Africa in December 1940 completed the catalogue of disasters. Beginning on December 9, British mechanized units within the space of two months destroyed an Italian army that had invaded Egypt and moved forward into Libya to capture Bardia, Tobruk, and Benghazi, and by the beginning of February the British threatened to drive the Italians entirely from North Africa. With the fall of Tobruk on January 12, 1941, the British had captured well over 100,000 Italian troops and destroyed nearly the entire Italian army in North Africa.[26] The Italians, with their "parallel war," had wrecked the Axis' strategic position not only in the Balkans but also in the Mediterranean.

The Germans now had no choice but to restore stability to the southern flank before "Barbarossa." As early as August 1940, they had considered sending a panzer corps to Libya to aid in the drive to Suez, but the Italians had rebuffed the offer.[27] The destruction of much of the Italian battle fleet at Taranto and the military disaster in Greece forced Hitler to stronger action. On November 20, after pointed recriminations at the lack of diplomatic discipline and military incompetency of Italy, the *Führer* proposed that Germany send strong air units to Sicily to make long-range attacks on the British fleet in the eastern Mediterranean.[28] The Italians, in no position to refuse any offer of help, speedily acquiesced. By the beginning of January 1941, *Fliegerkorps* X, mostly drawn from units operating in Norway, had arrived at bases in Sicily. By mid-January, nearly 200 German bombers and long-range fighters were operating against the Royal Navy and its lines of communications in the central and eastern basins of the Mediterranean. The impact of the *Luftwaffe* on naval and air operations in the Mediterranean theater was immediate and direct.[29]

The disasters that overtook Italian ground forces in Libya forced Hitler to increase the level of aid. By the end of December, the military situation looked so bleak that the German Embassy in Rome suggested that only a joint Mediterranean command, dominated by German officers, could save the situation.[30] For political reasons, Hitler rejected the proposal to take over directly the Italian war effort. Nevertheless, he could not escape the need to bolster Italy in North Africa with significant ground forces. On January 11, he ordered the army to prepare a blocking force for service in Libya. At the same time, he allowed *Fliegerkorps* X to move to North Africa to support Axis ground forces.[31] By mid-February, Hitler had added a panzer division to an initial commitment of one light division. Commander of the new German forces in Africa was a recently promoted lieutenant general, Erwin Rommel.

The emphasis on the North African campaign by many Anglo-American historians should not obscure the fact that the Mediterranean remained a strategic backwater for Hitler—an area in which the Germans consistently minimized the forces committed.[32] Rommel's task was to prevent an Italian collapse and to pin down as many Commonwealth forces as possible; he was notably successful in this endeavor. Moreover, criticism of his capabilities as a strategist missed the point that Rommel never received the resources necessary for a wide ranging strategic campaign. Although Rommel's surge into Egypt in the spring of 1942 was not, as it turns out, capable of overturning Britain's Middle Eastern position, it did manage to unbalance the British so thoroughly that not until the following October were they able to utilize their overwhelming superiority in the theater. For the *Luftwaffe,* the Mediterranean represented a peripheral theater from January 1941 through the fall of 1942. The *Luftwaffe*'s mission in the Mediterranean largely involved attacks on the island of Malta, support for the Africa Corps, attacks on the British fleet, an increasing commitment to protect the tenuous supply lines between Africa and Europe, and support for the ineffective Italians. As German liaison officers noted early in the war, the Italians had neither the personnel nor the production rate to support a sustained air war.[33]

Because the Germans were using a defensive strategy in the Mediterranean, they had to restore order to the Balkans before "Barbarossa" could begin. British aid to Greece, in the form of RAF squadrons, alarmed Hitler who particularly feared air attacks on the oil fields and refineries of Rumania.[34] Further *Wehrmacht* deployments into Rumania in the late fall initiated preparations both for "Barbarossa" and the elimination of Greece as an opponent. However, both geographic and diplomatic difficulties hindered the buildup; bad weather in December 1940 and January 1941, combined with Rumania's primitive transportation system, caused serious delays. Moreover, Bulgaria, worried about Turkey, hesitated to allow German troops access to its territory. Not until the end of February did the Germans assuage Bulgarian fears, and only on March 1 did their troops cross the Danube to begin deployment against Greece.[35]

As the German army prepared to invade Greece, Hitler pressured Yugoslavia to join the Axis and to provide additional routes for the offensive. Here the truculence that has marked much of Serbian history stymied Hitler's objectives. Shortly after the Regent acceded to German demands, Serbian officers overthrew his regime. Unfortunately, the plotters proved surprisingly hesitant to accept British support; they failed to recognize that their actions had so antagonized Hitler that war was inevitable.[36] Furious, Hitler was not the sort to hesitate. Afraid that the Yugoslavs represented a threat to the southern flank of German armies invading Russian, not to mention the attack on Greece, Hitler determined to remove Yugoslavia from the list of independent Balkan nations.

The spring 1941 campaign heralded the return of major air operations for the *Luftwaffe* after the period of relative calm lasting from December 1940 through March 1941. However, the onset of this new campaign differed from that of the year before. This time, the *Luftwaffe* would face increasing commitments with no recuperative periods until its final defeat in 1945. Hitler's anger at what he regarded as a Yugoslav betrayal insured that the *Luftwaffe* received a mission well beyond a role of strict military utility. On March 27 in War Directive #25, he emphasized that "Yugoslavia, even if it makes initial professions of loyalty, must be regarded as an enemy and beaten down as quickly as possible." The *Luftwaffe*'s first objective would be: "As soon as sufficient forces are available and the weather allows, the ground installations of the Yugoslav air force and *the city of Belgrade* will be destroyed from the air by continual day and night attacks [my emphasis]."[37]

German military planning exhibited its usual adaptability to changing circumstances. As Halder admitted later, the *OKH* had already prepared the theoretical groundwork for an attack on Yugoslavia; all that remained was to solve the practical difficulties of moving troops and supplies for the expanded campaign.[38] In little more than a week after the *coup,* the Germans had altered Twelfth Army's dispositions in Bulgaria to include Yugoslavia in its mission and had established the Second Army in southern Austria and Hungary along the Yugoslav frontier. Armored forces from the two armies, one advancing from the north and the other from the south, would strike deep into Yugoslavia at Belgrade. Meanwhile, Twelfth Army would bypass Greek defenses by swinging through Yugoslavia to take the Greeks in the flanks and rear.[39] Along with these new deployments went an extensive redeployment of the *Luftwaffe*. Nearly 600 aircraft moved from various bases within the *Reich* to support the extension of the campaign to Yugoslavia; some units were deployed from bases as far away as southern France. *Luftwaffe* strength for the coming offensive now exceeded 1,000 aircraft.[40] The reasons behind such a drastic increase in aircraft strength become readily apparent in reviewing the orders directing the air attacks on Yugoslavia. The campaign's strategic plan specifically excluded bombing either industrial plants or the transportation network, since the Germans hoped to utilize the Yugoslav economy as soon as possible for their own needs. However, *the* major task, concurrent with achieving air superiority, was "the destruction of Belgrade through a great air attack." That attack would begin in the morning with a direct bombing of the city's center with 75 percent high explosives and 25 percent incendiaries; after a quick turnaround, the bombers would return that same afternoon with 40 percent high explosives and 60 percent incendiaries. The change in bomb load reflected a desire to cause as many fires as possible "to ease the problem of marking the city for the night attack." Night bombers would drop 50 percent high explosives and 50 percent incendiaries. Further bombings of Belgrade would occur on D+1. The code word for the operation was "Punishment,"[41] an accurate description of Hitler's feelings. By the time the Germans had completed their attacks on a city that the Yugoslavs had declared open, 17,000 people had died.[42] Hitler had exacted his measure of revenge.

The campaign was a stunning repetition of the success the previous spring. Within less than a week, German mechanized forces had captured the ruins of Belgrade. German spearheads supported by the *Luftwaffe* sliced through the land.[43] By April 17, organized resistance had ended with the surrender of the remnants of the Yugoslav army.[44] The drive to the south against the Greeks and British did not last much longer. The sweep through Yugoslavia not only outflanked Allied forces facing Bulgaria but also cut off the Greek's First Army fighting the Italians in Albania. By April 22, German armored and air units had broken through the pass at Thermopylae, and the remainder of the campaign was a race to see whether the Royal Navy could evacuate British troops before German armor could cut off their escape.[45] There was one climactic clash to the campaign. On May 20, German airborne forces dropped on Crete. However, they met an unexpectedly warm reception. In fact, on the basis of the first day's operation, it looked as if the Germans might fail entirely. Not only did the paratroopers not capture a landing strip but the survivors were isolated and under great pressure. Only faulty leadership and coordination around the Maleme airfield allowed the Germans to seize that airbase and to fly in reinforcements. Air superiority gave the paratroopers critical support and prevented the Royal Navy from bringing to bear its full weight.[46] Despite the successful outcome, the Germans indeed had received a bloody nose in Crete. Altogether, their losses totalled nearly 4,000 men or one-quarter of the attacking force. Out of the 500 transport aircraft, the *Luftwaffe* had to write off 146 as total losses, while a further 150 were damaged.[47] Because of the operation's high cost, Hitler considered the day of large paratrooper operations as finished.

In retrospect, the Balkan campaign was only a footnote in the war. It did not significantly postpone the invasion of Russia. The delay in the Russian campaign resulted more from supply and organizational difficulties and poor ground and weather conditions associated with the late spring than from the attack on Greece and Yugoslavia.[48] At the most, Balkan operations affected the freshness and staying power of units transferred from operations in the south to the Russian campaign. Ironically, the campaign in the Balkans succeeded too well. The advance of armored spearheads had been so quick and the collapse so sudden that the Germans were not able to round up thousands of Greek and Yugoslav soldiers left in the backwater areas of those countries. Rapid redeployment of German units to "Barbarossa" assignments allowed those soldiers to roam the countryside; they soon formed the basis for the considerable guerilla movements throughout the area. By 1942, these guerrillas were tying down large numbers of Germans and were preventing the *Reich* from fully utilizing the resources of the southern Balkans.

For the *Luftwaffe,* the spring of 1941 offered the last easy campaign. Nevertheless, even before "Barbarossa," aircraft losses were rising ominously. Operations in the Balkans, as well as an increased effort against British cities to disguise the redeployment to the east, pushed the loss rate (all aircraft) from 2.6 percent (written off) in January 1941 to 7.2 percent in April, and to 7.5 percent in May.[49] The loss rate for bombers (written off) climbed in the same period from 4.8 percent in January, to 5.5 percent in February, to 8.6 percent in March, to 10.6

percent in April, and to 12 percent in May. Thus, the strain on resources was already mounting before operations in the east began. Furthermore, official German reaction among the ruling hierarchy to the loss rate suggests a general indifference to the potential impact that such losses might have in sustained combat operations in Russia.

BARBAROSSA: BACKGROUND

The decisive campaign of the Second World War was the German invasion of Russia in 1941. The defeat of that effort reflected the failure of German leaders to prepare the economic and productive capacity of the *Reich* and western Europe for war on a continental rather than a western European scale. Thus, in a certain sense, the production and industrial decisions made by the German leadership in the summer of 1940 represented a decisive turning point in World War II. In effect, Germany's leadership had sealed her fate before the campaign opened.

Hitler had turned to Russia in the summer of 1940 as a possible solution to the British dilemma. While the idea of a fall 1940 campaign had to be shelved temporarily, contingency planning for an invasion of Russia began almost at once. By the end of July 1940, serious planning was underway in the *OKH*. On August 5, General Erich Marcks presented a strategic study that sketched in outline a framework for the proposed campaign. Marcks posited as the main strategic aim the destruction of Soviet armed forces. The *Wehrmacht* would advance at least as far as the line Archangel-Gorki-Rostov to prevent the possibility of bomber attacks against Germany. The main thrust would occur north of the Pripyat marshes and attempt the capture of Moscow. Subsidiary drives in the north and south would protect the flanks of the advance on the capital and prevent a Soviet spoiling attack on Rumanian oil resources. Marcks suggested that the decisive battles would occur in the first few weeks with the armored drive playing the critical role; these penetrations would hopefully destroy the main body of the Red Army in the border areas. The study estimated a slight numerical advantage in favor of the *Wehrmacht* and certainly a decisive qualitative superiority. Once German troops had pierced the Red Army's forward lines and had begun the exploitation phase, Marcks believed that the Soviet command and control system would collapse, allowing the Germans to destroy Soviet armies piecemeal. The study suggested that a period of between nine and seventeen weeks would be necessary to achieve the campaign's objectives.[50]

Further studies in the fall of 1940 followed the direction that Marcks had suggested. While certain problems emerged in the war gaming of operations, such as the distances involved in Russia, most officers concurred with the proposed strategy with its emphasis on gaining a swift military victory by advancing on Moscow. However, Hitler did not agree fully, and the *Führer* emphasized that after the capture of the border areas, the advance on Moscow would not proceed until German forces had captured Leningrad.[51] The emphasis in Hitler's strategy was on gaining Soviet economic resources as quickly as possible. Thus, right from the beginning, there was a dichotomy in German strategy between Hitler's emphasis on capturing economic spoils and the army's preoccupation with strictly military factors. This was the first direct interference by the *Führer* in "Barbarossa's" planning process; as in France, he would involve himself deeply in operational matters.

There are several elements in the planning process that require amplification. The first is that, while Hitler and the *OKH* held somewhat different views as to the proper strategy for the campaign's later stages, all substantially underestimated the Red Army's numerical strength, Soviet industrial resources, and the inherent logistical difficulties involved in waging a campaign on a continental scale.[52] There were, of course, reasons for such underestimations of the Red Army; the pernicious effect of the purges as well as the depressingly poor showing of Soviet military forces in Poland and Finland were all too obvious. Moreover, the Germans found it difficult to build an accurate picture of Soviet industrial potential. In Stalin's police state, intelligence agents did not last long. For security reasons, Hitler forbade deep reconnaissance flights into the Soviet Union until shortly before the invasion, and the *Luftwaffe* did not possess reconnaissance aircraft with the range to reach the Urals.[53] Nevertheless, there were glimpses behind the curtain of Soviet security. Shortly before "Barbarossa," the Russians allowed several German engineers to see the new aircraft factories in the Urals and the extensive production that was already underway; their reports went unheeded.[54]

This underestimation of Russian capabilities lay not only in misreadings of Soviet resources but in the nature of the war that Hitler was launching. This war was more than a political or strategic struggle. It was an ideological war, a crusade, waged to encompass not simply the defeat of an enemy nation but the utter destruction and subjugation of a whole people. The purposes for this campaign in Hitler's eyes were to (1) capture the *Lebensraum* (living spaces) for the Germanic peoples, (2) destroy the Jewish-Bolshevist regime, (3) root out and destroy the Jewish population (along with several other unfortunate nationalities), (4) reduce the Russian people to a servile mass, and (5) capture the resources to conduct a war against the Anglo-Saxon powers. It is now clear that the German military, with few exceptions, concurred with the ideological framework within which Hitler determined to wage "Barbarossa."[55] From the first, the *Führer* made clear to his commanders that the coming campaign

> was a battle of extermination. . . . Annihilation of Bolshevik commissars and communist intellectuals. . . . The struggle must be conducted against this poison. There is no question of the laws of war. . . commissars and members of the secret police are criminals and must be treated as such [i.e., shot].[56]

Shortly before the beginning of "Barbarossa," the head of the *Luftwaffe*'s air mission in Rumania returned from meeting Göring to report to his leading subordinates that "the *Reichsmarschall* has clearly ordered that among Russian prisoners each Bolshevik functionary is to be immediately shot without any judicial proceedings. That right [to shoot communists] every officer possesses."[57] If there were some opposition to the "commissar order," it was not widespread. As the head of the army's Rumanian mission suggested, war had returned to the religious and ideological basis of the Thirty Years' War: Germany's opponents were the financiers, Freemasonry, and the financial and political power of the World Jewry.[58] Far too many officers acquiesced in outrages, such as the murder of hundreds of thousands of Jews by SS commando teams (Einsatzgruppen), while the starvation of literally hundreds of thousands (if not millions) of prisoners was directly attributable to Wehrmacht authorities.[59]

The widespread acceptance of Hitler's goals and attitudes throughout the officer corps made possible the terrible atrocities that occurred. It was not merely a matter of Hitler and the SS. On the political side of the invasion, the scale of criminality quickly disabused disaffected Russians and Ukrainians of the notion that the Germans might be their liberators. German atrocities rallied the population to the defense of a thoroughly unpopular and vicious regime. On the military side, a sense of a racial and cultural superiority, shared by most German officers, contributed to an underestimation of Russia's powers of resistance. As sophisticated a general officer as Günther Blumentritt could claim in 1941 that "Russian military history shows that the Russian as a combat soldier, illiterate and half-Asiatic, thinks and feels differently."[60] Given such attitudes, it is not surprising that many German soldiers, as well as their leader, expected that once they kicked in the door, the structure —ruled by Jewish subhumans—would collapse.[61]

One of the more glaring defects in mapping out the preinvasion strategy was the scant attention the Germans paid to the logistical difficulties of supporting troops deep inside Russia. The general assumption seems to have been that the first great rush of mechanized forces would carry to Smolensk and destroy the Red Army in the border areas. Thereafter, depending on railroads, German troops would exploit the initial success to finish the campaign. Surprisingly, the units scheduled to repair railroads leading to Smolensk lay at the bottom of army priorities—a reflection of an unduly optimistic approach to logistics.[62] Compounding this casual attitude towards logistics was the failure to appreciate the distances involved in traversing Russia. The push to Smolensk and from there to Moscow represented a logistical problem on a vastly different scale from the campaign in the west against France.

For the Luftwaffe, the awesome geographic size of Russia presented comparable logistical difficulties. What is more, the major commitments occupying the air force from June 1940 on had allowed almost none of the periods of rest the army had enjoyed to conserve and rebuild strength. Göring claimed after the war that he had opposed the invasion; but his remarks to General Georg Thomas, head of the OKW's economic section, that such a war was simply a "problem of the necessary supply organization" suggests that he was as overconfident as the rest.[63] Hitler's Directive #21 stressed that the Luftwaffe's first task was to eliminate the Russian air force and to prevent it from interfering with the advance on the ground; after gaining air superiority, the Luftwaffe was to support the army. Interestingly, the directive explicitly ruled out attacks on the enemy's armament industry "during the main operations. Only after the completion of the mobile operations may such attacks be considered—primarily against the Ural region.''[64] The assumption was that ground operations would proceed so rapidly that the *Wehrmacht* would soon occupy Soviet industrial centers; thus, it made no sense to destroy what would soon be in German hands. No one considered or even thought it possible that the Soviets would transfer much of their military industrial complex behind the Urals.

The extension of the war to Russia meant that the *Luftwaffe* now faced the prospect of war on two fronts (three fronts if one considers the Mediterranean a separate theater).[65] What should have alarmed senior German military and civilian officials was that, despite a drastic increase in commitments, there had been virtually no change in the number of aircraft in the force structure from the previous year. (See Table XII.[66])

TABLE XII
German Aircraft Strength

	May 11, 1940	June 21, 1941
Close Recce	335	440
Long-Range Recce	322	393
Single-Engine Fighters	1,356	1,440
Night Fighters		263
Twin-Engine Fighters	354	188
Bombers	1,711	1,511
Dive Bombers	414	424
Ground Attack	50	
Coastal	240	223
TOTAL	4,782	4,882

A revealing statistic in Table XII is the fact that the *Luftwaffe* began the invasion of Russia with 200 fewer bombers than it had possessed at the start of operations against the West; German bomber production had not kept pace with losses over the course of the year.

The *OKL (Oberkommando der Luftwaffe,* German air force high command) detailed three air fleets to cooperate directly with the three army groups in the subjugation of the Soviet Union. Two thousand seven hundred seventy aircraft, or 65 percent of the frontline strength of the *Luftwaffe,* moved east against the Russians; through the spring of 1943, the bulk of the *Luftwaffe* would remain tied to the eastern front.[67] Facing the Germans was a Soviet air force estimated at 8,000 aircraft, with somewhere around 6,000 deployed in European Russia.[68] Like the army, the *Luftwaffe* believed that after the first day's operations had broken the back of the Soviet air forces, the Russians would not recover. Moreover, Russia seemingly offered an opportunity to replicate the victorious effort against France with none of the frustrations of the aerial assault on the British Isles. Thus, Jeschonnek's remark ''at last a proper war'' represented more than just the relief of an air staff that had suffered the only German defeat thus far in the war. Flight crews also were glad to terminate increasingly dangerous and ineffective night missions over Great Britain.[69] By February 1941, RAF countermeasures had so neutralized

German blind bombing devices that scarcely 20 percent of bombs dropped were falling near their targets. The rest were landing in the countryside.[70]

In retrospect, considering the opposing force structures, the difficulties and extent of the theater and the overconfidence within the high command, the Germans did better than they should have. Their enormous tactical successes through the fall of 1941 were as much the result of Stalin's incompetence as of German military brilliance. In his search for internal security, the soviet dictator had quite literally destroyed his army's officer corps in a purge that lasted from 1937 through 1939.[71] Unfortunately, the purge had hit hardest at those in the high command who possessed the most realistic sense of operational and tactical matters, including the strategic difficulties that Russia would face in a major European war.[72]

Stalin compounded the problems facing his armies in his reaction to the German victory over France. The Russians overplayed their diplomatic hand in the fall of 1940; then when ominous signals accumulated as German troops deployed to the east, Stalin lost control of the situation. He disbelieved the evidence that pointed to a German invasion. Admittedly, the Germans threw considerable misinformation at the Soviets, and the cover plan for "Barbarossa" was a carefully worked out attempt to throw the Russians off the scent.[73] The last minute deployment of air units to operating bases in East Prussia and along the frontier also helped deceive the Soviets. Not until June 19 did *Fliegerkorps* VIII move to East Prussia from deep inside Germany where it had replenished supplies and drawn new aircraft and crews.[74]

Finally on the evening of June 21, Stalin allowed his high command to issue a strategic warning to troops on the frontier. The warning from Moscow came so late that it reached few frontline units.[75] Surprise was almost complete, and the dispairing signal of a border patrol—"We are being fired on, what shall we do?"—indicates the level of unpreparedness. The reply from higher headquarters—"You must be insane, and why is your signal not in code?"—points out the disadvantages under which the Soviets began the campaign.[76]

BARBAROSSA: THE INVASION

In the early morning hours of June 22 from the Baltic to the Black Sea, the *Wehrmacht* stormed across the frontier. German aircraft, crossing the frontier at high altitudes in order not to alert Soviet defenses, dropped to attack altitude and pulverized Russian airfields. Still unalerted, Soviet air units had their aircraft lined up in neat rows facilitating the *Luftwaffe*'s task. Those few aircraft that managed to scramble soon fell to the guns of German fighters. The extent of the surprise is shown by *Fliegerkorps* IV, which on the first day reported destroying 142 enemy aircraft on the ground and only 16 in the air.[77] By noon of the 22nd, the Russians had lost 528 aircraft on the ground and 210 in the air in the western district. For the entire front, Russian losses totalled no less than 1,200 planes in the first eight and one-half hours.[78]

The situation on the ground forced the Soviets to commit their remaining air resources in a desperate effort to stabilize the collapse. Ill-trained, ill-equipped, and ill-prepared, Soviet aircrews floundered in impossible formations and in obsolete aircraft;[79] the slaughter of Soviet aircraft resembled the destruction of the Japanese fleet air arm in the "Marianas' turkey shoot" of 1943. The attacks on Soviet airbases and ground support organizations led to a general collapse of the Russian air force's ability to control its units. Desperate appeals, radioed in clear text from air units to higher headquarters, gave the impression of a thoroughly chaotic situation.[80] Milch recorded in his diary the destruction of 1,800 Soviet aircraft on the first day, followed by 800 on June 23, 557 on the 24th, 351 on the 25th, and 300 on the 26th.[81] Whether, in fact, the *Luftwaffe* had managed to destroy that many aircraft is beside the point; a defeat of immense proportion had overtaken the Red Air Force—a catastrophe overshadowed only by events on the ground.

On the main battlefronts, aided by *Luftwaffe* close air support and interdiction missions, German armies surged forward against a collapsing opponent. Within four days, Manstein's panzer corps had advanced nearly 200 miles to the Dvina River; and by the end of the month, the entire Russian position in the Baltic region was in shreds. The greatest disaster occurred, however, on the central front in an enormous double envelopment around the cities of Bialystok and Minsk. When the armored pincers of Panzer Groups 2 and 3 met behind Minsk, they enclosed elements from four Soviet armies. By the time that mopping-up operations had finished on July 9, the Germans had claimed 287,704 prisoners and destruction of 2,585 tanks.[82] Probably another quarter of a million Soviet soldiers had died or been wounded in operations leading up to this final collapse. The German drive, however, did not remain stationary. As the infantry hurried forward to encompass and destroy the pocket, mechanized forces from Panzer Groups 2 and 3 swung out again to meet on July 19 at Smolensk to complete another envelopment of Soviet forces. By the time that they had reduced the Smolensk pocket, the Germans had captured a further 100,000 prisoners, 2,000 tanks, and 1,900 guns.[83] Only in the south did the Germans fail to gain a significant success. Nevertheless, even there Army Group South closed up on Kiev and was breaking into the big bend of the Dneper River. On July 3, Halder noted optimistically:

> On the whole, one can already say that the task of destroying the mass of the Russian army in front of the Dvina and Dneper has been fulfilled. I believe the assertion of a captured Russian general to be correct that we can calculate on meeting east of the Dvina and Dneper only disjointed forces which alone do not possess the strength to hinder German operations substantially. It is, therefore, truly not claiming too much when I assert that the campaign against Russia has been won in fourteen days. Naturally, it is not yet ended. The extent of the theater and the tenacity of resistance that will be conducted with every means will still claim many weeks.[84]

Yet, the advance to Smolensk stretched supply lines to the breaking point. As the Smolensk cauldron died down at the end of July, the Germans found it almost impossible to supply their forward spearheads. The distance to the railheads, the movement of infantry to support the mechanized forces, and the exhaustion of the motorized supply system created a logistical nightmare. Further complicating the serious supply situation were Soviet attacks launched from within and without the Smolensk pocket to break through the German encirclement. The intensive fighting made heavy demands on ammunition stocks of divisions in the forward lines so that the transportation system had to bring up ammunition, and thus there was no opportunity to stockpile fuel for the next advance.[85] By July 23, Halder admitted that the existing situation where frontline units were living a "hand-to-mouth" existence in terms of their supplies was making it impossible to build up stockpiles for the next push.[86] Thus, the infamous August pause during which the German army remained virtually stationary at Smolensk and in the north resulted not only from disagreements within the high command as to the next objective and the need to refresh exhausted mechanized units but also from a logistical system that could barely supply frontline forces, much less build up reserves.[87]

The demands placed on the frontline units reflected the grievous underestimation that the Germans had made of Russian strength. Often badly led and consisting of ill-equipped and ill-trained troops, Russian counterattacks strained the entire German structure. Halder admitted on August 11 that:

> [The] whole situation shows more and more clearly that we have underestimated the colossus of Russia—a Russia that had consciously prepared for the coming war with the whole unrestrained power of which a totalitarian state is capable. This conclusion is shown both on the organization as well as the economic levels, in the transportation, and above all, clearly in infantry divisions. We have already identified 360. These divisions are admittedly not armed and equipped in our sense, and tactically they are badly led. But they are there; and when we destroy a dozen, the Russians simply establish another dozen.[88]

These Soviet attacks on Army Group Center failed to gain any appreciable tactical success and clearly expended an immense number of Russian lives. Yet, in the long run, they had an important strategic impact. The wear-and-tear on German units, attacked in the Yel'nya and Smolensk battles, was perhaps of greater importance than any tactical victory Soviet forces might have gained. The battle of attrition had begun with a terrible vengeance. Having advanced as far as they had in the entire French campaign, the Germans discovered the geographical difference between continental distances and those in Central Europe. The Russians possessed strategic depth; and even if they had not fully utilized it in the first months, it was an inevitable strategic advantage.

For the *Luftwaffe*, these same factors were operative. The deeper that flying units moved into Russia, the more precarious became their supply situation. By mid-July, air units were crying for fuel and ammunition; and within the jumble moving forward to support the spearheads, the *Luftwaffe*'s logistical system functioned no more efficiently than that of the army. *Fliegerkorps* VIII reported as early as July 5 that fuel was lacking even though the corps had already limited its missions.

Laconically, Richthofen noted: "Supply is for us the greatest difficulty in this war."[89] The funnel-shaped nature of the theater also operated against the *Luftwaffe*. As the *Wehrmacht* moved deeper into Russia, the front widened. As a result, the *Luftwaffe* had to cover greater distances with forces that weakened as losses mounted. Moreover, as the army spread out, the tendency became more pronounced to use air units as fire brigades to patch up frontline difficulties. Air force commanders were not necessarily happy with such a state of affairs but often had no choice other than to use their air resources to support the army.[90] This should not suggest that the *Luftwaffe* involved itself solely in aiding ground forces. In late July with the seizure of bases near Smolensk, it launched major raids against the Russian capital.[91] Richthofen, Commander of *Fliegerkorps* VIII, expected great results from these attacks and noted hopefully on July 13 that the first massed attack *(erster grosser Angriff)* on Moscow "could cause a catastrophe. All the experts calculate that a famine exists in the 4 million population of the capital."[92] When transferred to the north in August, Richthofen ordered a firebomb attack on Leningrad; the next day, he noted that two small and one large conflagrations, 1.5 kilometers wide, burned in the city's center with smoke clouds reaching great height.[93] Nevertheless, for the most part, the demands and tempo of ground operations kept the *Luftwaffe* sufficiently occupied to preclude significant aerial attempts at city busting.

The air losses suffered by *Fliegerkorps* VIII in twelve days (August 10 to 21) while supporting I Army Corps in its effort to cut the main Moscow-Leningrad railroad dramatizes the impact of attrition on *Luftwaffe* strength. In this period supporting the advance of one army corps, *Fliegerkorps* VIII lost 10.3 percent of its aircraft (destroyed or written off as the result of operations), with 54.5 percent of its aircraft damaged but reparable. During this action, the air corps had 3.9 percent of its flying personnel killed, 5.7 percent wounded, and 2.9 percent listed as missing for a 12.5 percent total casualty rate.[94]

Aiding the *Luftwaffe* in its support of the army's advance was the flexible supply and maintenance system already discussed in relation to the French campaign. Units moved forward rapidly behind advancing spearheads; and as the campaign's emphasis shifted from one front to another, bomber and fighter units moved swiftly to new bases and areas of operation. Such flexibility allowed the *Luftwaffe* to give maximum support to the armored drives and helped the army push ever deeper into Russian territory.[95] Nevertheless, the continual movement of units across the Russian landscape was not without cost. These shifts strained the maintenance and supply system to the breaking point so that by late fall 1941, operational aircraft ready rates were way down, thereby having a negative impact on the whole force structure.

After considerable argument between Hitler and his generals and after a modicum of resupply had occurred, forward movement began again at the end of August. In the north, Field Marshal Ritter von Leeb's forces, supported by mechanized units detached from the central front, drove to the suburbs of Leningrad and isolated that city except for a tenuous link across Lake Ladoga. Hitler forbade Leeb from taking

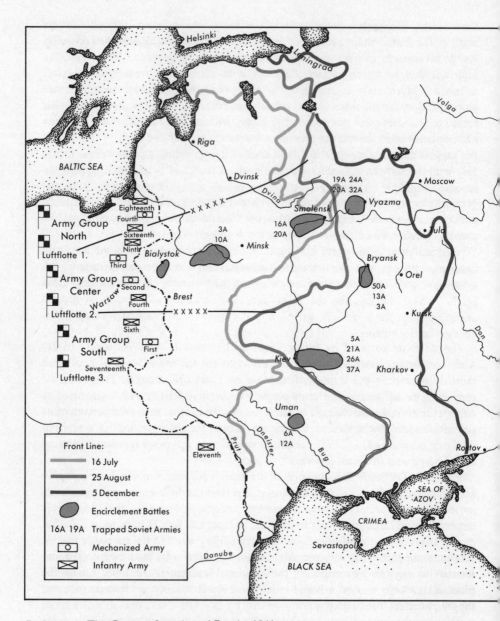

Helsinki

Leningrad

Volga

Riga

BALTIC SEA

Dvinsk

Dvina

XXXXX

Smolensk

19A 24A
20A 32A

Vyazma

Moscow

Eighteenth
Fourth

Army Group
North

Luftflotte 1.

Sixteenth

Ninth

Third

Bialystok

3A
10A

Minsk

16A
20A

Tula

Bryansk

Orel

Army Group
Center

Second

Warsaw

Fourth

Brest

XXXXX

50A
13A
3A

Kursk

Luftflotte 2.

Sixth

Army Group
South

First

Seventeenth

Luftflotte 3.

Kiev

5A
21A
26A
37A

Kharkov

Don

Front Line:

16 July

25 August

5 December

Encirclement Battles

16A 19A   Trapped Soviet Armies

Mechanized Army

Infantry Army

Eleventh

Uman

6A
12A

Dneister

Prut

Bug

Rostov

SEA OF
AZOV

CRIMEA

Sevastopol

Danube

BLACK SEA

Barbarossa: The German Invasion of Russia, 1941

the city and ordered him to starve it into submission. By the end of the winter, 1 million civilians within Leningrad had died of famine.[96] In the south, a more immediate disaster threatened the Russians. Thanks largely to Stalin's military ineptitude, Guderian's Panzer Group 2 broke loose from the central front and drove almost straight south to link up with General Ewald von Kleist's Panzer Group 1.[97] Behind the encompassing arms of the panzer armies lay a vast pocket of Soviet troops around Kiev. By the time that cleanup operations had ended, the Germans claimed to have taken 655,000 prisoners. The Soviets asserted after the war that only 677,000 Russian soldiers had been in the region at the end of August and that 150,000 managed to escape before resistance collapsed.[98] The figures are meaningless; they can only symbolize a human tragedy of unimaginable extent. What is clear is that the Germans had torn to ribbons the entire southern theater of operations; German troops could now move forward as fast as their vehicles, supplies, and weather conditions would permit.

The catalogue of Russian disasters was not yet complete. Satisfied that his decision to divert strength from Army Group Center to the army groups on the wings had paid dividends, Hitler returned to the strategy his generals had urged in August: a great offensive aimed at destroying Russian armies lying in the center and at capturing Moscow. The operation's code name was "Typhoon." Setting the tone for the coming weeks, Hitler issued a proclamation demanding that attacking troops complete the work of the campaign and end twenty-five years of Bolshevism in Russia—a system of rule equalled only by capitalistic plutocracy. ("The support of these systems is also the same in both cases: the Jew and only the Jew.")[99] German armored strength concentrated again on the central front, and again the Soviets allowed wishes to delude their view of reality. The German halt in the center after July, the diversion of armored forces to the north and south, as well as the lateness of the season persuaded the Russians that they need not worry about an offensive against Moscow. However, Guderian's Panzer Group 2 hustled up from the Ukraine. On September 30, two days before the other armies, Guderian began his drive towards Orel. On October 2, the other German armies attacked, supported by 1,387 aircraft.[100] The offensive caught the Red Army unaware; two panzer armies blasted through the forward positions and moved swiftly to exploit the breakthrough. On October 3, German tanks, surprising Russian defenses and passing trams that were still operating, drove into Orel. So fast had the Germans moved that the Russians could not even begin evacuation of that town's industrial plant. By October 6, Bryansk had fallen, and Russian command and control over the entire central front collapsed.[101]

The advance came so swiftly and the collapse so suddenly that Moscow received its first indications of disaster through Hitler's speech on October 5 that spoke of a "final decisive offensive." The Russians had no specific knowledge of what Hitler was speaking except for the fact that communications no longer existed with the Western Army Group.[102] On October 5, Russian reconnaissance pilots reported a German armored column some 25 kilometers long advancing on the great highway from Smolensk to Moscow. Despite efforts by the NKVD (Soviet Secret Police) to arrest the pilots as "panic mongers," their reports gave Moscow its first indication of the extent of the collapse.[103] The Germans had ripped open Soviet frontlines from Bryansk to Vyazma and were encircling two vast groupings of Russian armies: the first of three armies around Bryansk and the second of five armies around Vyazma. Officially, the Germans claimed 658,000 prisoners in the double encirclements.[104] Again, the totals are meaningless. One can only note that for the second time within a little over a month, an immense disaster had overtaken the Red Army. So great was the booty in prisoners and materiel that the *Reich*'s press chief, at the instigation of Hitler and Goebbels, announced that the Soviet Union was finished and the war virtually over.[105]

Despite these catastrophes, the situation was by no means hopeless. The Germans had begun "Typhoon" with a minimum of supplies.[106] Even more telling was the onset of poor weather in the fall; the German advance slowed to a crawl in the last half of October, while *Luftwaffe* support almost ceased. Flying off primitive dirt strips located at the end of long supply lines, air units found it as difficult to provide the army with close air support as the army found it to advance. From a level of over 1,000 sorties per day before the onset of bad weather, the sortie rate fell to 559 on October 8 and to 269 on the 9th.[107]

The threat to Moscow persuaded Stalin to bring Marshal Georgi Zhukov from Leningrad to defend the capital. With a firm hand in control, the Soviets reknit their defenses with surprising swiftness as the enemy advance bogged down in autumn mud. Nevertheless, the onset of bad weather should not obscure the fact that there was nothing unusual about such weather; if anything, the period of mud lasted for a shorter period than usual.[108] In retrospect, the Germans should have shut down the campaign after the victory of Bryansk/Vyazma. The supply situation had become so difficult that barely enough resupply got through to keep the advance moving. Consequently, there was no leeway to build up reserves or to send forward the critical winter clothing and equipment that the troops would desperately need when winter struck.[109] The offensive continued. The German high command, in the face of steadily worsening weather, turned reality upside down. It would push the last battalion of reserves into the front. Unlike the Marne campaign of World War I, German generals assured themselves, this time they would not withdraw.[110] While those at Army Group Center and in the field were too close to conditions to underestimate the difficulties of future operations, Hitler and the *OKH* planned wide ranging operations deep behind Moscow for which neither troops nor supplies existed. This undoubtedly resulted from a poor appreciation for condition in the field that, in turn, led to a general overconfidence as to the capabilities of German forces and a complete underestimation of Russian forces.[111] For the frontline troops advancing under dreadful conditions, Hitler's overconfidence showed itself not only in impossible demands but with the mid-November withdrawal of much of *Luftflotte* 2 for service in the Mediterranean. Thus, support for the drive on Moscow almost entirely devolved on the shoulders of Richthofen's *Fliegerkorps* VIII.[112]

At the beginning of November, the arrival of cold weather brought an end to the mud, and the advance began again. By now, however, under Zhukov's inspiring (and ferocious) leadership, the Russians had recovered. Militia units, divisions pulled from quiet segments of the front, and Siberian reinforcements trundled through Moscow in a desperate effort to keep the Germans at bay outside the capital. The clawing resistance bought precious time until full winter conditions set in, thus weakening German strength further. By the beginning of December, the Germans had reached Moscow's suburbs; that was as far as they got. On December 5, Zhukov counterattacked, and in appalling winter weather the entire German front threatened to come apart.

The *Luftwaffe* played a decreasingly important role as the Battle of Moscow approached. Conversely, the Red Air Force, once thought destroyed, mounted increasingly effective attacks supporting the Moscow defenders. A primary reason was that the fighting on the eastern front had brought the *Luftwaffe* to desperate straits. Operational ready rates for combat aircraft throughout the force structure sank towards dangerous levels; and in conditions of mud, bad weather, and increasing cold (not to mention the difficulties in supply), maintenance personnel found it almost impossible to maintain aircraft. By the beginning of October, the in-commission rate for the *Luftwaffe*'s bomber force had sunk below 40 percent, while only 58 percent of single-engine fighters were in commission. The rate for all aircraft hovered near 53 percent.[113] Further complicating the *Luftwaffe*'s problem of flying missions at the end of tenuous supply lines was the fact that its aircraft were flying off primitive dirt strips, while the Red Air Force was using more permanent facilities in the vicinity of Moscow.

Hitler's gamble to conquer Russia in one summer had failed. Germany now faced immense commitments in the east with an army and air force that through attrition during the summer and fall had lost their cutting edge. In fact, it was only at this point that the Germans, faced with the possibility of massive defeat in Russia, began to mobilize their economy and the national economies of their already subjugated foes for the long pull.

To add to his difficulties in the east, Hitler gratuitously declared war on the United States after the Japanese had destroyed the American battle fleet at Pearl Harbor. In doing this, he made it virtually certain that American resources and military power would appear in Europe at the earliest possible hour and would add to *Wehrmacht* requirements in Russia, in the Mediterranean, and in the west. Why Hitler extended German strategic responsibilities at the desperate hour when his forces in front of Moscow were collapsing is hard to fathom. It seems most likely, as is so often the case in human affairs, that Hitler's decision was an instinctive, illogical reaction to a desperate situation.[114] With events in Russia slipping beyond his control, America offered Hitler a psychological object at which to strike. Undoubtedly contributing to Hitler's mood was a sense of frustration that he had felt over the summer and fall of 1941 as the US Navy increasingly intervened in the Battle of the Atlantic. Now in December 1941, the United States, humiliated at Pearl Harbor, presented an inviting and vulnerable target for his navy's submarine force. The declaration of war on December 10, however, allowed the Roosevelt administration to present America's entry into the war in a wider context than merely the surprise attack on Pearl Harbor, somewhat diverting the public's clamor for revenge against Japan. Thus, it was Hitler's actions that provided the political basis for Roosevelt's decision to support a "Germany first" strategy.

PRODUCTION AND STRATEGY, 1940–41

Between July 1940 and December 1941, the Germans lost the air war over Europe for 1943 and 1944. Ignoring the severe attrition that had occurred even in the Battle of France, they paid little attention to the fact that their aircraft industry had changed neither its approach nor its production rate substantially from what it had been during the opening months of the war. The negative impact of this situation needs no great elaboration considering the fact that aircraft loss and replacement rates for 1941 were approximately equal. The impact of aircraft and crew losses on the *Luftwaffe*'s force structure, the strain of sustained operations on the maintenance and supply systems, and the difficulties encountered in attempting to escalate the *Luftwaffe*'s involvement had a synergistic effect that placed the *Luftwaffe* in a precarious situation by the winter of 1941–42. Moreover, these interrelated factors largely determined the *Luftwaffe*'s fate in the upcoming air battles of 1943 and 1944.

The greatest strain on the *Luftwaffe* in 1941 resulted from operations conducted in the east beginning on June 22. Unlike the Battle of France or the Battle of Britain, attrition in Russia involved low loss rates combined with sustained operations over an extended period. The cumulative effect of these small "acceptable" losses was no less decisive in its impact than was the Battle of Britain. Table XIII[115] gives a detailed picture of the cumulative impact of those losses through the fall of 1941 on the eastern front.

TABLE XIII

Crew and Aircraft Losses on the Eastern Front—June 22–November 1, 1941

	Average Monthly Strength	Average Monthly Losses: Damaged and Destroyed	Percent	Average Crew Strength	Average Monthly Crew Losses	Percent	Percent Loss: Four-Month Period
Close Recce	323	92	28.5	539	51	9.5	38
Long-Range Recce	238	54	22.7	270	31	11.5	46
Single-Engine Fighters	661	240	36.3	800	73	9.1	36.4
Twin-Engine Fighters	77	22	28.6	84	11	13.1	52.4
Bombers	836	268	32.1	901	126	14	56
Stukas	293	60	20.5	345	24	7	28
Coastal	34	5	14.7	24	2	8.3	33.2
TOTAL IN EAST	2,462	741	30.1	2,963	318	10.7	42.8

Yet, the losses in Russia through November 1941 only reflect a part of the severe burden that the *Luftwaffe* experienced in 1941 (see Tables XIV,[116] XV,[117] XVI,[118] and XVII[119]). Due to the "Blitz" against the British Isles in the winter of 1941, the Balkan campaign, and air commitments in the Mediterranean as well as "Barbarossa," the *Luftwaffe* had gone through its entire inventory of aircraft in just twelve months. (See Table XVII.)

By the end of 1941, German aircraft production and crew training programs could no longer keep up with losses; and by January 1942, conditions forced frontline units to rob transition schools of crews a month before their scheduled course completion. By February, the quartermaster general no longer knew how many aircraft he would receive due to chaotic conditions in the aircraft industry.[120] Thus, by late winter, the general staff could not accurately forecast either how many aircraft or crews the *Luftwaffe* would receive in the next month, not to mention succeeding months.[121] From this point forward, the staff would squeeze out of industry and out of transition schools as much as possible each month and shove new crews with decreasing skill levels and new aircraft into the frontline units.

Compounding the difficulties was a supply and maintenance system that revealed little capacity for functioning over the long distances that the *Luftwaffe* now covered. What had sufficed within the limited frontiers of prewar Germany could not meet the needs of an air force committed from the Bay of Biscay to the gates of Moscow and from the North Cape to North Africa. The supply system, particularly in Russia, no longer functioned effectively. Milch in a visit to the eastern front discovered that hundreds of inoperable aircraft were lying about on forward airfields. They had either broken down or been damaged in combat, and spare parts were not flowing forward to repair these aircraft.[122] Because supply and

Table XIV   German Aircraft Losses 1941 (All Types)

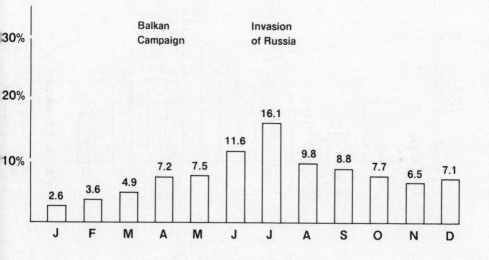

Table XV   German Bomber Losses 1941

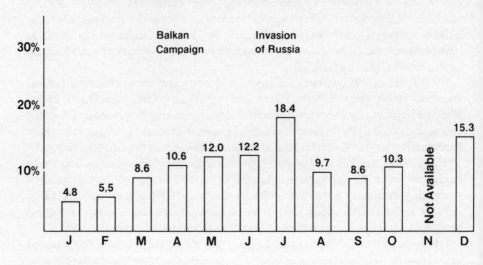

Table XVI   German Fighter Losses 1941

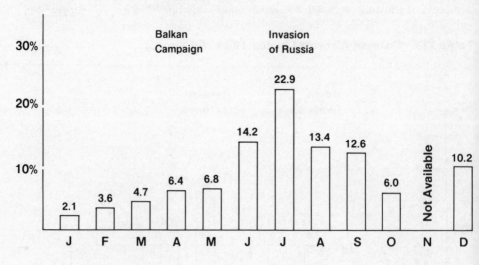

TABLE XVII

German Losses, All Causes—1941 (Not Including November)

| | Aircraft Written Off | | | | | |
	Aircraft Authorized, Jan 1941	Actual Strength 4.1.41.	Due to Enemy Action	Not Due to Enemy Action	Total	Percent of January Strength
Close Recce	372	384	165	98	263	68.5
Long-Range Recce	276	356	195	95	290	81.5
Single-Engine Fighters	1,202	841	622	705	1,327	157.8
Twin-Engine Fighters	435	384	246	217	463	120.6
Bombers	1,715	1,339	1,154	644	1,798	134.3
Stukas	467	456	225	141	366	80.3
Transport	444	415	159	155	314	75.7
Liaison	200	*	40	56	96	*
Coastal	162	122	43	42	85	69.7
TOTAL	5,273	4,297	2,849	2,153	5,002	115%

*Data not available.

Aircraft Damaged, 1941 (Not Including November)

| | Not Reparable at Unit Level | | | Reparable at Unit Level | | | |
	Due to Enemy Action	Not Due to Enemy Action	Total	Due to Enemy Action	Not Due to Enemy Action	Total	Total Aircraft Damaged
Close Recce	21	26	47	76	108	184	231
Long-Range Recce	16	28	44	20	94	114	158
Single-Engine Fighters	166	463	629	80	350	430	1,059
Twin-Engine Fighters	38	77	105	23	119	142	257
Bombers	187	439	626	130	538	668	1,294
Stukas	29	56	85	27	74	101	186
Transport	9	54	63	38	112	150	213
Liaison	7	48	55	5	87	92	147
Coastal	2	2	4	3	10	13	17
TOTAL	475	1,193	1,658	402	1,492	1,894	3,562

maintenance were separate from operational units, a wide gulf had grown up between frontline units and their logistical support establishment in the *Reich*. Furthermore, the *Luftwaffe*'s organizational structure divorced supply and maintenance from operations, thereby hindering vital communications between these two divisions. More often than not, the special needs of one were not meaningfully addressed by the other.[123]

The pressure of continuous air operations on the *Luftwaffe*'s maintenance infrastructure also had its effect. Over the winter of 1940–41, the Germans experienced a considerable period without combat in which to reconstitute and to rebuild flying units strained by the fighting in 1940. The bombers, however, with their heavy commitments in the night offensive against British cities, did not enjoy such recuperation. But beginning in April 1941, with the campaign in the Balkans, the demands of far-flung campaigns burdened the entire structure. The result was a slow but steady decline in the *Luftwaffe*'s "in-commission" rates to a nadir in the winter of 1941–42 (see Table XVIII[124]).

Besides maintaining aircraft "in commission," the *Luftwaffe* had the concomitant problem of filling cockpits. The loss rate, as already suggested, had reached the point where the *Luftwaffe* pushed pilots out of training schools as rapidly as possible to bring aircrew strength to acceptable levels. What now happened was that operational units completed what the schools could no longer finish. The process in many units involved working new pilots into squadron operations on a gradual basis while hopefully minimizing their exposure to hazardous missions. Then as experience increased, squadrons assigned the pilots to more dangerous tasks until they were fully combat-ready.[125] Such a system was undoubtedly the only one that frontline units could follow given the state of pilot training. It had, however, two pernicious side effects. The first was that it maximized the exposure to danger of experienced aircrews, thus increasing their losses. This, in turn, led to higher percentages of untrained or partially trained personnel in the combat units. The second, and equally disastrous, effect was that untrained pilots in the dangerous and primitive conditions of frontline airfields had a higher accident rate than normal. The normal rate was high enough given a lax attitude towards flying safety throughout the war.[126] But the combination of a weak flying safety program along with untrained and unskilled pilots flying off primitive airstrips was deadly. As Table XVII indicates, the *Luftwaffe* was destroying three of its own aircraft for every four destroyed by the enemy, and the number of damaged aircraft from noncombat accidents was an intolerable burden on an already overstrained maintenance system.

The attrition over the summer and fall of 1941 led to a steady deterioration in the experience level of aircrews. From the summer of 1941, the *Luftwaffe* entered a period in which losses proceeded at such a pace that a recovery in terms of crew flying experience could only come with a long halt to operations. However, failure in Russia in 1941 virtually insured that the *Luftwaffe* would never receive a respite. In fact, the increase of Allied air efforts in the Mediterranean and west meant that the demands on the German air force would continually increase, thus exacerbating

Table XVIII   Luftwaffe "In-Commission" Rates 1941

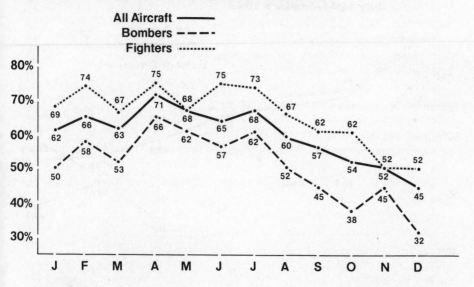

an already serious situation. This deterioration of aircrew skill level shows up most clearly in Table XIX[127] in the two column summarizing losses not due to enemy action.

The most dangerous trend in 1941 was a production program that one can perhaps best describe as inadequate. The Germans had entered the war with a surprisingly low production rate. However, given the resource limitations under which they worked, production levels reflected economic reality. The victories of 1940, however, fundamentally altered Germany's strategic and economic situation. Not only had the Germans captured large stockpiles of raw materials in France and the Low Countries but the modern industrial plant of those nations was now under their control. Moreover, the success in the west made Eastern Europe, including the Soviet Union, more amenable to cooperation with the *Reich;* finally the occupation of France gave the Germans direct access to Spanish and Moroccan raw material resources (particularly tungsten and iron ores).

With these resources at their disposal, the Germans were in a position to organize the new conquests in tandem with their own war economy in order to increase drastically their armament production. They did no such thing.[128] There were several basic reasons for this failure. This omission did not, one must stress, result from a belief in a so-called *"Blitzkrieg"* strategy. Rather, the Germans now allowed themselves to be deluded by the speed of the first victories over Poland and France into believing that they could continue armament production at the prevailing low level. The overconfidence marking the approach to "Seal Lion" and "Barbarossa" were symptomatic of a wider malaise: Nothing was impossibe for the rulers of the Third *Reich*! The issue here is not that the Germans built tanks or

**Table XIX   Percent of Fully Operational Crews
July 1941-January 1942**

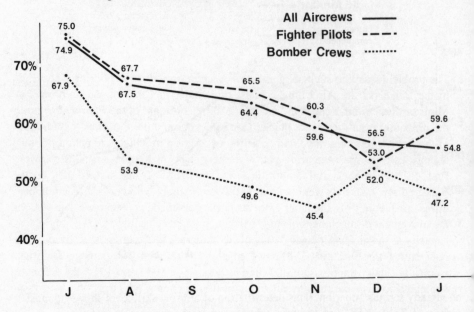

artillery pieces at the expense of aircraft, but rather they made minimal alterations in the production of all major weapon systems after the fall of France in spite of a radically different raw material and industrial situation. Symptomatic of this situation in the summer of 1940 was the Army ordnance office's rejection of Hitler's proposal that tank production be increased from 100 to 800 per month because such a level would be too expensive and require too many skilled workers.[129] But as late as February 1941, a major economic journal noted that "Germany is entering the final struggle with so overwhelming a superiority of armament capacity that the result can no longer be in doubt."[130]

Certainly, the losses in tanks and aircraft in the French campaign should have raised serious doubts as to existing rates of production; the same could be said for the Battle of Britain. However, no one in the *Luftwaffe*, with the possible exception of Milch, became particularly worried over the continuing lag in production. Only the failure of the Russian campaign spurred Hitler to reorganize the economy prompting a dramatic expansion of production. Nevertheless, the *Führer* himself was not completely at fault, since few senior officials had pushed for major increases in production.

Further complicating a rational utilization of Europe's economic resources were the ideological perceptions of the German leadership. Göring indicated the ideological basis coloring the Nazi approach to economic problems when he stated in 1942:

> Basically, I consider all of occupied France as a conquered country.
> It seems to me that in earlier times the thing was simpler. In earlier
> times, you pillaged. He who had conquered a country disposed of
> the riches of that country. At present, things are done in a more
> humane way. As for myself, I still think of pillage
> comprehensively.[131]

The problem was that such an approach was counterproductive. Göring's positions in the *Reich* (as the Air Minister and Commander in Chief of the *Luftwaffe*, as Minister of the Four-Year Plan, and as a leading confidant of the *Führer*) increased the probability that his views guided German economic policy. Thus, exploitation of the French economy involved a looting expedition in which competing military authorities (in France the army got the largest share of the loot as its troops were first on the scene), civil authorities, and industrial firms divided the booty. Captured raw materials went straight to the *Reich* along with considerable numbers of machine tools.[132] In the latter case, such transfers made no economic sense,[133] for the movement of machine tools to Germany could not possibly increase productive capacity as the aircraft industry was already underutilized with most factories on 8-hour shifts, once a day. The looted machine tools went into storage facilities. Ironically, under the pressure of Allied air attacks in 1943 and 1944, the Germans attempted to disperse the aircraft industry into occupied countries; the looting of 1940 and 1941, however, proved a severe hindrance as many tools were no longer available.[134] Moreover, the failure to use factories in occupied countries in 1941 and 1942 meant that when the Germans reopened plants, they discovered machinery and facilities in poor condition.

The badly thought-out looting of occupied countries stands in contrast to the occupation of Czechoslovakia in 1939. When the Germans seized Prague in March 1939, economic authorities refused to allow the transfer of raw material stockpiles to the *Reich,* since this would allow Germany to maintain Czech production and to utilize Czechoslovakia's industrial potential to the fullest. They were correct in that assumption, for not only did Czech industry substantially aid German armament but it also earned substantial foreign exchange up to the outbreak of war.[135] Similarly, the *Luftwaffe* found Czechoslovakia extremely useful in supporting its own production plans. By the end of 1939, Udet had placed orders for 1,797 Czech aircraft. Indeed, the Czech aircraft industry proved useful in serving its new masters.[136]

In the case of France, however, things worked out quite differently. In all of 1941, the French aircraft industry produced only 62 aircraft for the *Luftwaffe* (Holland only 16), while Czech plants produced 819.[137] The reason is quite apparent. In the case of Czechoslovakia, the Germans were still in a difficult strategic and economic situation, and they, therefore, eagerly incorporated Czech potential into their economic system. The euphoria after victory over France, however, led most of the *Luftwaffe*'s leadership to disregard the low production figures for German industry and to ignore the possible integration of western European economies, including France, into the German war effort.

Exacerbating all of the production problems was a major labor shortage. With so many German men mobilized for service with the army, a large deficit existed in manpower available for industry. In Britain, women filled many of the shortages caused by the rapid expansion of the armed forces.[138] However, Germany's ideology interfered directly with economic good sense—Hitler refused to allow the widespread use of women in the factories as had occurred in World War I. The result was that in the summer and fall of 1941, an acute shortage of workers existed throughout the armament industry. There were not enough German men to go around. While the Germans had millions of prisoners of war captured in the Polish and western campaigns, most of those worked in the countryside to keep German agricultural production at acceptable levels.

But there was a manpower pool of enormous potential in the summer of 1941: the hundreds of thousands of prisoners that were falling into German hands as the *Wehrmacht* surged into Russia. However, ideology intervened with a vengeance. Hitler refused to allow the transfer of any of these prisoners to the *Reich* for work either on farms or in factories.[139] Thus, while German industry was desperately short of workers, hundreds of thousands of Russian soldiers were starving to death in inadequate *Wehrmacht* prisoner of war camps. By February 1942, of the 3,900,000 Russian soldiers that the Germans claimed to have captured, only 1,100,000 remained alive; of these, only 400,000 were capable of being moved to the *Reich* to work in industry.[140] Ciano recorded in his diary in late November 1941 Göring's macabre sense of humor about this terrible situation:

> Göring told me that hunger among the Russian prisoners had reached such an extreme that in order to start them toward the interior it is no longer necessary to send them under armed guard; it is enough to put at the head of the column of prisoners a camp kitchen, which emits the fragrant odor of food; thousands and thousands of prisoners trail along like a herd of famished animals.[141]

As Germany's chief economic czar, the *Reichsmarschall* was cognizant of the shortages in the work force. His remarks underline the callous attitudes toward the *"Untermensch"* and a frivolous approach to Germany's dangerous economic situation.

The basic cause of the *Luftwaffe*'s production problems in 1941 lay not only in the dilettantism of the higher Nazi leadership but also with a military leadership that did not understand the difficulties involved in producing modern weapons in large numbers and who evinced little worry about enemy production capabilities. As mentioned in Chapter I, Göring in 1937 and 1938 had largely removed Milch from control over the production and technical aspects of the *Luftwaffe*. Udet, Milch's replacement, possessed neither the temperament nor the technical background to handle his new responsibilities. Jeschonnek, on the general staff side, showed little interest in the dull nonoperational requirements of planning and carrying through a production program. Thus, even before the war the plans of the general staff and of Udet's production planners had diverged. Now in a war in which *Luftwaffe* commitments were widening, production figures remained virtually stationary. Table XX[142] indicates the extent of Germany's aircraft production.

TABLE XX
Production of German Aircraft—1939–1941

	Fighters	Bombers	Transports	Trainers	Others	Total
1939	1,856	2,877	1,037	1,112	1,413	8,295
1940	3,106	3,997	763	1,328	1,632	10,826
1941	3,732	4,350	969	889	1,836	11,776

The impact of these levels of aircraft production on frontline units became obvious as the war continued. German industry was not producing aircraft at a rate sufficient to replace losses at the front and in accidents. As a result, the difference between the number of aircraft authorized and actually present increased as operations attrited frontline strength. In September 1939, combat units had possessed virtually a full complement of aircraft. As production failed to keep up with loss rates, it became ever more difficult to sustain authorized levels, and even the most favored organizations had to operate well below authorized strength (see Table XXI[143]).

TABLE XXI
Authorized Actual Strength, Combat Aircraft—
September 1939–March 1942

	Authorized	Actual	Percent of Authorized Aircraft
September 1939	2,950	2,916	98.9
December 1939	3,313	3,258	98.3
March 1940	4,034	3,692	91.5
June 1940	3,714	3,327	89.6
September 1940	3,547	3,015	85.0
December 1940	3,792	3,050	80.4
March 1941	4,100	3,853	94.0
June 1941	4,228	3,451	81.6
September 1941	4,318	3,561	82.5
December 1941	4,344	2,749	63.3
March 1942	4,623	2,876	62.2

When combined with the operational ready rates for late 1941, the figures in Table XXI present a thoroughly depressing picture of the *Luftwaffe*'s combat strength. One aircraft type in particular, the bomber, had reached the point where the *Luftwaffe* had hardly any capability left. In December 1941, the bomber force possessed only 47.1 percent of its authorized strength; only 51 percent of that force was in commission. Thus, from an authorized strength of 1,950 bombers, the

Luftwaffe had only 468 in commission on December 6, 1941, or 24 percent of authorized aircraft.[144]

The cause of this shortfall lay directly at the door of Udet's poor administration, with a sizeable portion of the blame also to be shared among Göring, Jeschonnek, and the aircraft industry. Udet had possessed neither the capability nor background to assume responsibility for technical development and production. At one point, he admitted that he understood nothing of industrial processes and even less about the engineering of large aircraft.[145] The result of such a situation was that for a three-year period, the Air Ministry provided little leadership or guidance to manufacturers. Udet's offices became involved in producing a series of production plans that bore no relationship to what was occurring in industry. After each demand for an increase in production, his staff invariably revised downwards plans to reflect the results.[146] Moreover, introduction of new aircraft types or new models of existing aircraft "meant that the large planned increases were subject to sudden and sharp revision downwards, even when strategy demanded otherwise."[147]

Yet, the top leadership also bears responsibility for the production crisis of 1941. Hitler, despite occasional interest in technical matters, intervened hardly at all in *Luftwaffe* production during the early war years. Contrary to his relations with the army, Hitler delegated much authority over air force matters to Göring; and while he did set industrial priorities, he was poorly informed about what was going on with *Luftwaffe* production. While it suited Göring to keep the *Führer* uninformed, he himself also possessed little knowledge through the spring of 1941 of what was happening. Udet did provide a scapegoat for subsequent production failures,[148] but Göring and his staff deserve a full measure of blame for their concurrence with production levels during this period.

The crisis came to a head in the summer of 1941. Udet's office could no longer hide the growing disparity between planned and actual production totals when *Luftwaffe* strength in the field reached scandalously low levels. To help overcome this industrial shortfall, Göring reinserted Milch into the production process. Shortly before the beginning of "Barbarossa," Göring granted the State Secretary wide powers over the aircraft industry that included the right to close or to requisition factories, to confiscate raw materials, to transfer or dismiss designers, and in general to reorganize industrial production. As with previous orders from the *Reichsmarschall*, Milch was to quadruple production.[149] This time, however, Göring had given the brief to a man who did understand modern production methods and industrial practices.[150]

Over the summer of 1941, Milch supplanted Udet and assumed control of the technical offices that Udet had controlled.[151] The gradual exclusion of Udet from the centers of power within the Air Ministry as well as Milch's less-than-tactful behavior contributed to the former's suicide in the fall of 1941. Undoubtedly, the nightmarish situation that Milch discovered in industry and within these offices contributed to Udet's death. But before his death, Udet, with Milch's backing, produced a plan in July 1941 calling for a radical restructuring of German industry to accelerate production.[152] A more detailed, longer-range plan came out in

September under Milch's guidance. Based on a change in priorities after the completion of "Barbarossa,"[153] Milch's production projection demanded nearly 50,000 aircraft from industry by March 1944. For 1942, the so-called "Göring plan" asked for approximately 33 percent more aircraft than had been produced in 1941. For fighter aircraft, the Göring plan asked for a 61.1 percent increase in monthly fighter production in 1942 and a 20.5 percent increase in bomber production. By the end of 1943, Milch foresaw a rise in the monthly production rate for fighters to 625 (a 101 percent rise over the 1941 average) and for bombers to 656 (an increase of 81.2 percent over 1941 production).[154]

Unlike Udet who had gloomily assumed in June 1941 that given the resources, the work force, and the industrial capacity then available, the aircraft industry could not substantially increase production.[155] Milch took a different line. In a speech to the aircraft industry's chief industrialists, Milch outlined the production increases enumerated in the new plan. He demanded that the industrialists judge what was possible and what was not. Further, he refused to allow industry to proceed with serial production of new aircraft, because he demanded the mass production of existing types.[156] Delays imposed by the search for quality were a major factor in minimizing aircraft production. Indeed, the quality versus quantity dilemma was a factor Milch never succeeded in reconciling with the German industrial system. Right through 1944, German aircraft possessed the finest upholstered crew seats; thousands of man-hours were wasted in machining bulkheads and minor fittings, while parts taking no strain or requiring no precision were finished to close tolerances. The completed aircraft represented a finely finished product compared to their American and British counterparts; but where there were hundreds of the latter, one found only tens of the former.[157]

One of the major excuses that aircraft manufacturers had presented for the low rate of aircraft production in the first war years was a lack of raw materials, especially in the light metals sector so essential to an increase in production. Sending out inspectors to check on industrial procedures, Milch discovered widespread waste of raw materials throughout the aircraft industry: The production of one type aircraft engine was wasting approximately 1,500 pounds of aluminum. Moreover, industry had built up large stockpiles, and Messerschmitt factories were even using aluminum to build tropical shelters and ladders for use in vineyards.[158] Milch was able to put a stop to many of these practices, and it was soon apparent to those in charge of the aircraft industry that a firm hand had now grasped control.

The change of responsibility within the Air Ministry had, fortunately for Germany's opponents, come too late. For 1941, the Western Powers had outproduced Germany's aircraft industry by a wide margin (see Tables XXII,[159] XXIII,[160] and XXIV[161]).

In fighters alone, Anglo-American production totals for the last quarter of 1941 were nearly 400 percent greater than Germany's; in twin-engine aircraft, the lead was 169 percent; and in four-engine aircraft, a whopping 4,033 percent.[162] The levels for 1941, however, only reflected a small portion of Germany's problem. The British and Americans had been planning major increases in production since the summer of 1940. Considering the potential of American industry, those preparations had been on a far grander scale than Germany could ever consider. Now in the summer of 1941, the Germans began to change their approach, but it was only after Udet's suicide in November 1941 that Milch gained general authority.

Most of the leadership remained blissfully ignorant of the terrible danger facing the *Reich*. With great glee, Goebbels recorded every Anglo-American disaster in early 1942, while dismissing as idle Yankee boasting the American production figures.[163] Göring casually replied to warnings of the industrial potential of the United States that Americans "could only produce cars and refrigerators."[164] The German Embassy in Washington sent a number of warnings during 1940 that while America's national defense was still woefully lacking in nearly every respect, production would represent a serious threat by 1941 and increasingly each year thereafter. The cautionary forebodings made little impression.[165] Milch was not so sanguine having seen American industry at work,[166] but only in late 1941 had he gained full control of aircraft production.

CONCLUSION

For the second year in a row, the *Luftwaffe* had lost nearly its entire complement of aircraft. The German air force could not look forward, as it had in 1940 after the

Table XXII   Average Monthly Production by Half Years: Fighters

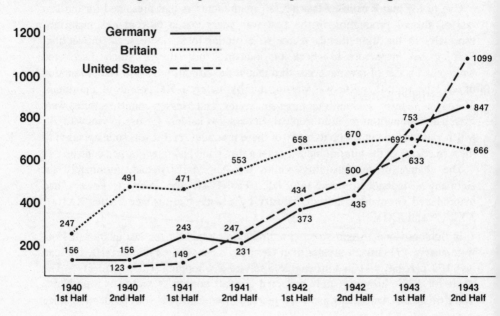

**Table XXIII   Average Monthly Production by Half Years:
Twin-Engine Aircraft**

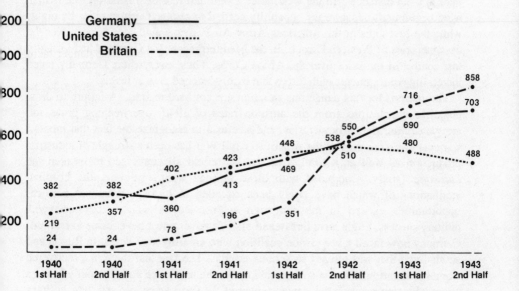

**Table XXIV   Average Monthly Production by Half Years:
Four-Engine Aircraft**

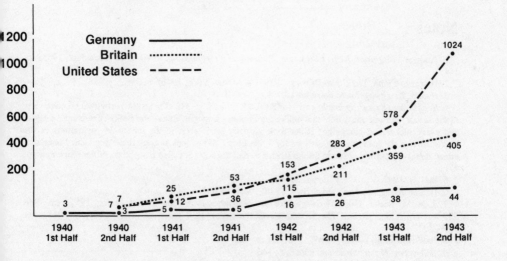

Battle of Britain, to a period of recuperation. The failure in front of Moscow meant that the war in the east would continue with its ever-vaster commitments and its interminable distances. In the west, after a year and half of frustration, the British were beginning to acquire the capability needed to savage German cities by night, while the first units of the American Army Air Forces would soon appear over the daytime skies of Western Europe. In the Mediterranean, the Germans had virtually lost control of the skies over the Africa Corps. Thus, everywhere Germany faced increasing commitments with forces that barely reached prewar levels.

The reasons for this dangerous situation are not hard to find. A failure to draw objective conclusions from the attrition rates of 1940, overweening pride and arrogance after the early victories, and a refusal to recognize the fact that modern war ever since the time of the American Civil War has been a struggle of industrial production as well as a conflict on the battlefield all converged to weaken the *Luftwaffe* fatally. Combined with these failings went a regime, the criminal inclinations of which have rarely been equalled in history. Whatever political opportunities existed in the campaign against Russia which, combined with military success, might have threatened Stalin's government never came to fruition. Germany now faced a worldwide coalition with an army near defeat in Russia and an air force that was already in serious trouble. The fact that the *Reich* recovered from this situation and managed to hold on for the next three and one-half years is a remarkable comment on the staying power of the German people and their military institutions, if not their good sense. Nevertheless, the defeat in front of Moscow represented the decisive military turning point of World War II. From this point on, Germany had no chance to win the war; and with her inadequate production, she faced enemies who would soon enjoy overwhelming numerical superiority in the air and on the ground.

Notes

1. Andreas Hillgruber, *Hitlers Strategie. Politik und Kriegführung, 1940–1941* (Frankfurt, 1965), p. 144.

2. Galeazzo Ciano, *The Ciano Diaries, 1939–1943* (New York, 1946), p. 266.

3. Halder, *Kriegstagebuch*, entry for 13.7.40., Vol. II, p. 21.

4. See Halder, *Kriegstagebuch*, entry for 30.6.40., Vol. I, p. 375. This is the partially subjective view of the author, but one must note that unlike the French campaign, unlike the Balkan campaign of 1941, and every succeeding campaign, Hitler took virtually no interest in the day-to-day operations of the Luftwaffe and the planning preparations for ''Sea Lion.'' This does suggest that ''Sea Lion'' operation aimed largely at putting pressure on the British to end the war. See also Hillgruber, *Hitlers Strategie*, p. 171.

5. IMT, *TMWC*, Vol. XXVIII, pp. 301–03.

6. Halder, *Kriegstagebuch*, entry for 13.7.40., Vol. II, p. 21.

7. J. R. M. Butler, *Grand Strategy*, Vol. II, *September 1939–June 1941* (London, 1957), pp. 209, 239–41; Winston Churchill, *The Second World War*, Vol. II, *Their Finest Hour* (Boston, 1948), pp. 119–72.

8. Jodl's testimony, IMT, *TMWC*, Vol. XV, p. 428.

9. Hillgruber, *Hitlers Strategie*, note 6, p. 146.

10. Halder, *Kriegstagebuch*, entry for 3.10.40., Vol. II, p. 124.

11. Galeazzo Ciano, *Ciano's Diplomatic Papers* (London, 1948), p. 402.

12. For details of the meeting between Molotov and Ribbentrop, see *DGFP*, Series D, Vol. XI, Docs. #325, 13.11.40.; #326, 16.11.40.; #328, 15.11.40.; #329, 18.11.40.

13. For a full discussion of Soviet foreign policy and motives during this period, see Adam Ulam's brilliant work *Expansion and Coexistence* (New York, 1974); see also Gerhard Weinberg, *Germany and the Soviet Union, 1939–1941* (Leiden, 1954).

14. *DGFP*, Series D, Vol. X, Docs. #384, #393.

15. Ibid., Doc. #413.

16. DGFP, Series D, Vol. XI, Doc. #84, 21.9.40.

17. Ibid., Docs. #1, 1.9.40.; #7, 3.9.40.

18. Ibid., Docs. #91, 23.9.40.; #142, 2.10.40.; #148, 4.10.40.; #178, 14.10.40.; #197, 19,10.40. The Germans did claim that the 1,800 troops remaining in Finland would be reduced to 100 men as soon as the move had finished.

19. Ibid., Doc. #532, 18.12.40.

20. See the discussion in Klaus Reinhardt, *Die Wende vor Moskau, Das Scheitern der Strategie Hitlers im Winter 1941/42* (Stuttgart, 1972), pp. 16–17.

21. Franklin D. Roosevelt, *The Public Papers and Addresses of Franklin D. Roosevelt* (London, 1941), p. 263. For the best discussion of those military and political factors involved in wartime Italy, a country that rivaled the Third Reich and Stalin's Russia in mendacity if not in competence, see Bernard M. Knox's brilliant dissertation, "1940. Italy's 'Parallel War', " Yale University dissertation (1976).

22. This generalization on the state of Italian preparation is drawn from Knox, "1940. Italy's 'Parallel War', " pp. 21–77, and my dissertation, "The Change in the European Balance of Power," Chapter 7. For the inability of the Italian air force to report its numbers accurately, see Knox, p. 57. The air force Chief of Staff reported to Mussolini in April 1939 that the air force possessed 3,000 aircraft; the navy's intelligence service, spying on the air force, could only locate 982.

23. Bernard M. Knox, "Fascist Italy Assesses Its Enemies, 1935–1940," a paper delivered at Harvard University, John F. Kennedy School of Government, July 1980.

24. *DGFP*, Series D, Vol. XI, Doc. #73, 20.9.40.

25. Captain S. W. Roskill, *The War at Sea*, Vol. I (London, 1976), pp. 300–01.

26. Major General I. S. O. Playfair, *The Mediterranean and the Middle East*, Vol. I, *The Early Successes Against Italy* (London, 1974), pp. 272–93.

27. *Kriegstagebuch des Oberkommandos der Wehrmacht, (KTB OKW)*, Vol. I, ed. by Hans-Adolf Jacobsen (Frankfurt am Main, 1965), entry for 9.8.40., p. 17. See also Walter Warlimont, *Inside Hitler's Headquarters* (New York, 1964), p. 110. For the Italian rebuff of German offers of help, see *DGFP*, Series D, Vol. XI, Doc. #149, 4.10.40.; and note p. 462.

28. *DGFP*, Series D, Vol. XI, Doc. #369, 20.11.40.

29. Playfair, *The Mediterranean and the Middle East*, pp. 315–21.

30. *DGFP*, Series D, Vol. IX, Doc. #583, 30.12.40.; see also #597, 2.1.41.

31. Trevor-Roper, *Blitzkrieg to Defeat*, Directive #22, pp. 53–54.

32. See, in particular, B. H. Liddell Hart, *History of the Second World War* (New York, 1971), who devotes 103 pages to the North African campaign in 1941–42 and only 53 pages to the German campaign in Russia in 1941–42.

33. BA/MA, RL 2 II/38, Verbindungsstab zur italienischen Luftwaffe, Nr 2212/41, 11.2.41., "Kriegsgliederung der italienischen Fliegertruppe. Stand 11.7.41."

34. *DGFP*, Series D, Vol. XI, Doc. #368, 20.11.40.

35. Martin L. van Creveld, *Hitler's Strategy 1940–1941, The Balkan Clue* (Cambridge, 1973), pp. 114–30.

36. J. R. M. Butler, *Grand Strategy*, Vol. II, *September 1939–June 1941* (London, 1957), p. 449.

37. Trevor-Roper, *Blitzkrieg to Defeat*, Directive #25, p. 61.

38. van Creveld, *Hitler's Strategy 1940–1941*, p. 145.

39. For the best concise history of the war in the Balkans, see George Blau, *The German Campaigns in the Balkans (Spring 1941)* (Washington, 1953).

40. Air Ministry, *The Rise and Fall of the German Air Force*, p. 123.

41. BA/MA, RL 7/657, Luftflottenkommando 4, Führungsabteilung Ia op Nr 1000/41, Wein, 31.3.41., "Befehl für die Luftkriegführung Jugoslawien."

42. Irving, *The Rise and Fall of the Luftwaffe*, p. 118.

43. For the effect of air operations on the Yugoslav army, see BA/MA, RL 7/656, Auszug aus dem Tagebuch der jugosl. Obersten Heeresleitung.

44. *KTB OKW*, Vol. I, entry for 18.4.41., p. 382.

45. See Blau, *The German Campaign in the Balkans*.

46. See Hans-Otto Mühleisen, Kreta 1941, Das Unternehmen 'Merkur' (Freiburg, 1968).

47. Ibid., p. 102.

48. For an interesting discussion of this point, see van Creveld, *Hitler's Strategy 1940–1942*, pp. 172–78.

49. BA/MA, RL 2 II/1025, Genst. 6.Abt. (III A), Front-Flugzeug-Verluste. May's loss rate was distorted and considerably higher than shown because the transport losses in the Crete operation had not yet been reported.

50. George E. Blau, *The German Campaign in Russia—Planning and Operations (1940–1942)* (Washington, 1955), pp. 6–12.

51. *DGFP*, Series D, Vol. XI, Doc. #532, 18.12.40.

52. Hillgruber, *Hitlers Strategie*, pp. 210–11.

53. Reinhardt, *Die Wende vor Moskau*, p. 19.

54. Blau, *The German Campaign in Russia*, p. 42. See also Guderian, *Panzer Leader*, p. 143, for his remark that a tour of German tank production facilities during which the Russians had claimed that the Germans were hiding both their latest tank designs and other factories had alarmed him.

55. I am indebted to Jürgen Förster of the Militärgeschichtliches Forschungsamt for discussing his work with me in this field. His work will appear in the fourth volume of the Forschungsamt's history of World War II. For a summary of this work, the reader should consult "Hitler's War Aims Against the Soviet Union and the German Military Leaders," *Militärhistorisk Tidskrift* (Stockholm, 1979).

56. Halder, *Kriegstagebuch*, entry for 30.3.41., Vol. II, p. 337.

57. BA/MA, RL 9/85, Kommandeurbesprechung vom 18.6.41., Deutsche Luftwaffenmission in Rumänien.

58. BA/MA, R 31–1/24. Der Befehlshaber der deutschen Heeres-Mission in Rumänien, Stabsbesprechung, 9.10.40.

59. See, in particular, Förster's "Hitler's War Aims Against the Soviet Union and the German Military Leaders." For the treatment of Soviet prisoners of war, see: Christian Streit, *Keine Kameraden, Die Wehrmacht und die sowjetischen Kriegsgefangenen 1941–1945* (Stuttgart, 1978).

60. Quoted in: Reinhardt, *Die Wende vor Moskau*, p. 21.

61. Ibid., p. 27. What is so surprising about all of this is that in the First World War, it had taken the German army three years of hard fighting to beat the Russians; they had, thus, been there before, and post-war protestations about having been surprised by conditions in Russia are not credible considering the German experience in World War I.

62. For an interesting discussion of the problems of logistics and supply in the Russian campaign, see Martin van Creveld, *Supplying War* (Cambridge, 1977), Chapter V.

63. Reinhardt, *Die Wende vor Moskau*, p. 25.

64. DGFP, Series D, Vol. XI, Doc. #532, 18.12.40.

65. Göring admitted as much. See the speech of the head of the Air Mission in Rumania briefing senior officers in that country on the contents of a meeting of senior German air force generals at Karinhall. BA/MA, RL 9/85, Kommandeurbesprechung vom 18.6.41. Deutsche Luftwaffenmission in Rumänien.

66. "Luftwaffe Strength and Serviceability Tables, August 1938–April 1945," AHB, Translation No. VII/107.

67. Air Ministry, *The Rise and Fall of the German Air Force*, p. 165; see also for similar figures: Olaf Groehler, "Stärke, Verteilung und Verluste der deutschen Luftwaffe im zweiten Weltkrieg," *Militärgeschichte*, 1978, pp. 322–23.

68. Blau, *The German Campaign in Russia*, p. 42.

69. By fall 1941, losses in night operations by He 111's had reached the point where He 111's were pulled off of operations even at night in the west. BA/MA, RL 3/50, Kommando der Erprobungsstellen der Luftwaffe, Nr 15520/42 g. Kdos "Gedanken über das mittlere Kampfflugzeug."

70. See the discussion in Hinsley, *British Intelligence in the Second World War*, Vol. I, pp. 326–28.

71. For a fuller description of the course of the purges, see Robert Conquest, *The Great Terror, Stalin's Purge of the Thirties* (London, 1968), Chapter VII.

72. See John Erickson, *The Road to Stalingrad* (New York, 1975), Chapter I.

73. For an interesting and informed discussion of the intelligence background to "Barbarossa," see Barton Whale, *Codeword Barbarossa* (Cambridge, 1973).

74. BA/MA, RL 8/49 Russland-Feldzug 1941: VIII Fliegerkorps. See also Air Ministry, *The Rise and Fall of the German Air Force*, pp. 162–65, for the movement of German air units to the east.

75. Erickson, *The Road to Stalingrad*, pp. 101–35.

76. Seymour Freiden and William Richardson, eds, *The Fatal Decisions* (New York, 1956), p. 56.

77. BA/MA, RL 8/31 Generalkommando des IV. Fliegerkorps Abt. Ic, "Lagebericht v. 22.6.41."

78. Erickson, *The Road to Stalingrad*, p. 118–19.

79. Albert Kesselring, *A Soldier's Record* (New York, 1953), p. 90.

80. BA/MA, RL 8/31 Generalkommando des IV. Fliegerkorps Abt. Ic, "Lagebericht v. 22.6.41."

81. Irving, *The Rise and Fall of the Luftwaffe*, p. 123.

82. Erickson, *The Road to Stalingrad*, pp. 150–59. Reinhardt, *Die Wende vor Moskau*, p. 28, gives the following figures: 330,000 prisoners, 3,000 artillery pieces, and 3,332 tanks. Halder, *Kriegstagebuch*, Vol. III, p. 56, gives 289,874 prisoners, 2,585 captured and destroyed tanks, 1,449 artillery pieces, and 246 aircraft.

83. Blau, *The German Campaign in Russia*, p. 49.

84. Halder, *Kriegstagebuch*, Vol. III, p. 38.

85. van Creveld, *Supplying War*, pp. 168–69.

86. Halder, *Kriegstagebuch*, Vol. III, p. 106.

87. See, in particular, van Creveld, *Supplying War*, pp. 167–80.

88. Halder, *Kriegstagebuch*, Vol. III, p. 170.

89. BA/MA, RL 8/49 Russland-Feldzug 1941: VIII Fliegerkorps.

90. Ibid.

91. BA/MA, RL 10/17 Auszug aus dem Frontflugbuch des ehem. StffFw. Fritz Hoyer, Stabsstaffel Kampfgeschwader 2 vom 24. Juni bis 29.10.41.

92. BA/MA, RL 8/49 Russland-Feldzug 1941: VIII Fliegerkorps.

93. v. Richthofen Tagebuch, entries for 8.9.–9.9.41.

94. BA/MA, RL 8/47 Generalkommando I. A. K., Abt, Ia 545/41, 16.9.41., "Einsatz des Fliegerkorps VIII vom 10.–21.8.41.," Appendix I, Tätigkeit des VIII. Fliegerkorps bei der Unterstützung des Durchbruchs des I. A. K. bis zur Eisenbahnlinie Leningrad-Moskau vom 10.8.41.–21.8.41.

95. For the movement of Luftwaffe units on the eastern front, see particularly Air Ministry, *The Rise and Fall of the Luftwaffe*, pp. 167–70. See also BA/MA, RH 19II/661D, "Der Feldzug gegen die Sowjet Union: Kriegsjahr 1941: Bearbeitet in der Führungsabteilung des Oberkommandos der Heeresgruppe Nord"; and also Auszug aus dem Frontflugbuch des ehem. StffFw. Fritz Hoyer, Stabsstaffel Kampfgeschwader 2.

96. Harrison Salisbury, *The 900 Days, The Siege of Leningrad* (New York, 1969), p. 582.

97. Erickson, *The Road to Stalingrad*, pp. 198–210.

98. Ibid., p. 210.

99. BA/MA, RH 19 III/6561 D, "Der Feldzug gegen die Sowjet Union: Kriegsjahr 1941: Bearbeitet in der Führungsabteilung des Oberkommandos der Heeresgruppe Nord."

100. Reinhardt, *Die Wende vor Moskau*, p. 67.

101. For a more complete discussion of the Kryansk/Vyazma disaster, see Reinhardt, *Die Wende vor Moskau*, pp. 67–74; and Erickson, *The Road to Stalingrad*, pp. 214–19.

102. Lieutenant General K. F. Telegin, "German Breakthrough," quoted in *Stalin and His Generals*, ed by Seweryn Bialer (New York, 1969), p. 273.

103. Reinhardt, *Die Wende vor Moskau*, pp. 68–69; and Erickson, *The Road to Stalingrad*, pp. 216–17.

104. Blau, *The German Campaign in Russia*, p. 79.

105. Reinhardt, *Die Wende vor Moskau*, pp. 74–75.

106. Ibid., pp. 56–57.

107. Ibid., p. 73.

108. Ibid., pp. 78–79.

109. van Creveld, *Supplying War*, p. 174.

110. Kurt Assmann, *Deutsche Schicksalsjahre* (Wiesbaden, 1951), p. 275.

111. Reinhardt, *Die Wende vor Moskau*, pp. 84–86, 93.

112. Air Ministry, *The Rise and Fall of the German Air Force*, pp. 172–73. See also Kesselring, *A Soldier's Record*, pp. 107, 115–17. Fliegerkorps VIII was scheduled to follow Luftflotte 2 to the Mediterranean.

113. Air Historical Branch, "Luftwaffe Strength and Serviceability Tables, August 1938–April 1945," Translation No. VII/107.

114. For another view of Hitler's decision, see Hillgruber, *Hitlers Strategie*, pp. 553–54.

115. BA/MA, RL 2III/715, Gen. Qu. 6.Abt. (I), "Übersicht über Soll, Istbestand, Verluste und Reserven der fliegenden Verbände," 1.11.41.

116. BA/MA, RL 2III/1025, Genst. 6.Abt. (III A), Front-Flugzeug-Verluste, 1941.

117. Ibid.

118. Ibid.

119. Ibid.

120. BA/MA, RL 2 III/717, Gen. Qu. 6. Abt. (I), "Übersicht über Soll, Istbestand, Verluste und Reserven der fliegenden Verbände."

121. BA/MA, RL 2 III/718, Gen. Qu. 6. Abt. (I), "Übersicht über Soll, Istbestand, Verluste und Reserven der fliegenden Verbände."

122. Irving, *The Rise and Fall of the Luftwaffe*, p. 131.

123. Air Division, Control Commission for Germany, British Element, "A Study of the Supply Organization of the German Air Force, 1935–1945," (June 1946).

124. Air Historical Branch, "Luftwaffe Strength and Serviceability Tables, August 1938–April 1945," Translation No. VII/107.

125. Conversation with Lieutenant General Hannes Trautloft, a.D., Baden Baden, Federal Republic of Germany, November 7, 1980.

126. Letter from Major General Hans W. Asmus, February 6, 1981.

127. The following percentages are drawn from RL 2 III/715, 716, 717: Gen Qu. 6. Abt. (I), "Übersicht über Soll, Istbestand, Verluste und Reserven der fliegenden Verbände."

128. For a fuller discussion of the economic inadequacies of German production in the 1940–1941 period, see the discussion in Reinhardt, *Die Wende vor Moskau*, Chapter I. Reinhardt accepts the "Blitzkrieg" theory, but his analysis of the actual production situation is excellent.

129. Guderian, *Panzer Leader*, p. 114.

130. The United States Strategic Bombing Survey (USSBS), *The Effects of Strategic Bombing on the German War Economy* (Washington, 1945), p. 151.

131. A. S. Milward, *The New Order and the French Economy* (Oxford, 1970), p. 77.

132. For the most detailed examination of the Luftwaffe's failure to utilize properly the economic resources of Europe, see Richard Overy's outstanding article, "The Luftwaffe and the German Economy 1939–1945," *Militärgeschichtliche Mitteilungen* 2/79.

133. One must note that in terms of Nazi ideology, such actions made excellent sense given the purposes for which Hitler had waged this war.

134. For a fuller discussion of these points, seè Overy, "The Luftwaffe and the German Economy," pp. 66–67.

135. Deist, *et al.*, *Das deutsche Reich und der Zweite Weltkrieg*, Vol. I, pp. 333–34.

136. Overy, "The Luftwaffe and the German Economy," p. 55.

137. Ibid., p. 59.

138. Although there were limits to what one could do with this expedient, by 1943 the British had virtually exhausted all their sources for workers. See John Ehrman, *Grand Strategy*, Vol. V, *August 1943–September 1944* (London, 1956), p. 41.

139. Reinhardt, *Die Wende vor Moskau*, p. 104.

140. Ibid., p. 188.

141. Ciano, *The Ciano Diaries*, p. 411.

142. USSBS, *The Effects of Strategic Bombing on the German War Economy*, Appendix Table 102, p. 277.

143. These figures are drawn from Webster and Frankland, *SAOAG*, Vol. IV, Appendix xxviii, pp. 501–04.

144. The above calculations are based on figures drawn from Webster and Frankland, *SAOAG*, Vol. IV, Appendix xxviii, p. 502; and AHB, "Luftwaffe Strength and Serviceability Tables, August 1938–April 1945," Translation VII/107.

145. E. Heinkel, *He 1000* (London, 1965), p. 180.

146. Irving, *The Rise and Fall of the Luftwaffe*, p. 120.

147. Overy, "German Aircraft Production, 1939–1942," p. 34. Overy's Cambridge University dissertation is the most careful examination of the failures involved in the production of aircraft in the early war years. All of the points discussed in the above analysis are examined in greater detail in this admirable work.

148. Göring conference, 9.10.43., Milch Documents, Imperial War Museum, Vol. LXIII, p. 6309.

149. Göring to Milch, June 1941, Milch Documents, Imperial War Museum, Vol. LVII, p. 3213. See also Richard Suchenwirth, "Command and Leadership in the German Air Force" (Air University, 1969), pp. 99–101.

150. Conversation with Generalleutnant Hannes Trautloft, a.D., Baden Baden, November 7 and 8, 1980. Trautloft, who was on the fighter staff with Milch in 1944, described Milch as "the only general director we had—the only senior officer who understood the problems of modern industry."

151. Irving, *The Rise and Fall of the Luftwaffe*, Chapter VIII.

152. Overy, "German Aircraft Production, 1939–1942," pp. 43–44.

153. Trevor-Roper, *Blitzkrieg to Defeat*, Directive #32a, 14.7.41.

154. Figures based on *USSBS, ESBGWE*, Appendix Table 102, "Number of German aircraft produced by types, annually 1939–1944 and monthly 1941–1944," and BA/MA, RL 3/999 C Amts-Programm, "Lieferplan," 15.9.41.

155. Irving, *The Rise and Fall of the Luftwaffe*, p. 124.

156. Overy, "German Aircraft Production, 1939–1942," pp. 45–46.

157. Conversation with Oberstleutnant i.G. Werner Geissinger, GAF, Air War College, Maxwell AFB, March 10, 1981.

158. Irving, *The Rise and Fall of the Luftwaffe*, p. 126.

159. The above figures are based on Appendix xxxiv, Webster and Frankland, *SAOAG*, Vol. IV, p. 497.

160. Ibid.

161. Ibid.

162. Ibid.

163. Goebbels, *The Goebbels Diaries, 1942–1943*, ed. by L. Lochner (New York, 1948), pp. 41, 65, 104, 169, 251.

164. Asher Lee, *Goering, Air Leader* (New York, 1972), p. 58.

165. See among others *DGFP*, Series D, Vol. XI, Doc. #60, 14.9.40.

166. Irving, *The Rise and Fall of the Luftwaffe*, p. 127.

IV On the Brink: January–October 1942

THE EAST

As with 1941, the eastern theater of operations remained the focus of *Luftwaffe* operations throughout 1942.[1] (See Table XXV.[2]) Although the German air force faced critical deployments and tasks elsewhere, the bulk of German aircraft remained in the east until events in the fall required shifts in air resources. The war in the east in the summer of 1942 superficially resembled the swift advance of 1941 with a rapid surge towards the Caucasus and Stalingrad, but inherent supply and maintenance difficulties intensified as the *Luftwaffe* operated from bases deep inside Russia and far from its sources of supply. Moreover, the attrition that had occurred during 1941 forced the *Luftwaffe* to operate with considerably less effectiveness because of less well-trained crews than it had in 1941. Finally, one must note that geographic and climatic problems, complicated by difficulties facing ground forces that were outnumbered and losing their qualitative superiority, precluded the *Luftwaffe* from developing any new role in the east other than helping extricate the army out of increasingly dangerous situations. Perhaps, considering the balance of forces in the east, ground and air, there was no other choice. Overall, *Luftwaffe* attrition rates for the year showed an alarming rise over those of 1941 (see Tables XXVI,[3] XXVII,[4] and XXVIII[5]).

As indicated in Chapter III, the German failure in front of Moscow in December 1941 and Russian counterattacks provoked a crisis in the German high command and threatened the collapse of the eastern front. The Russian counteroffensive caught the Germans on the point of final exhaustion, short of supplies, and with few preparations to meet the winter weather. Hitler excused his and the high command's culpability by claiming that severe winter weather had come surprisingly early,[6] but such claims did little to help troops that were fighting in temperatures 20° below zero. As the collapse threatened to become general, the *Führer* sacked Brauchitsch and other senior commanders and assumed the position of Commander in Chief of the army himself.[7]

Weather conditions accelerated the attrition of men through frostbite and of equipment through cold. By December 16, Panzer Group 2 was down to 40 tanks in operable condition. Sixth Panzer Division possessed only 350 riflemen and no tanks by the 13th, while 7th Panzer Division had a combat strength of barely 200 men.[8] In such conditions, Russian attacks threatened to destroy the army in the east. This eventuality did not occur for two reasons. The first was that the vast blood letting of the summer and fall had left the Russian army with limited resources to achieve its objectives. The second factor dovetailed with the first. After the first flush of

able XXV   German Losses June-December 1942 by Theater

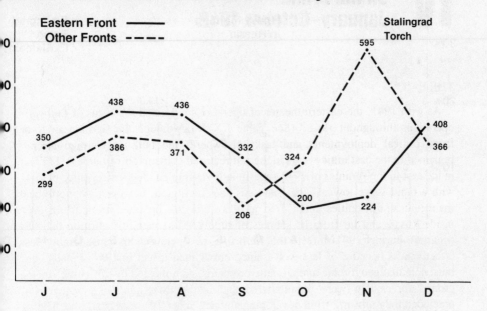

Table XXVI   German Aircraft Losses 1942 (All Types)

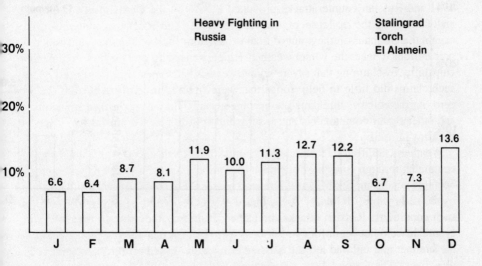

Table XXVII German Bomber Losses 1942

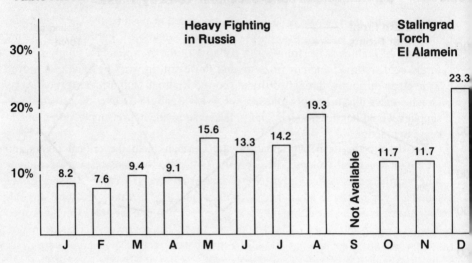

Table XXVIII German Fighter Losses 1942

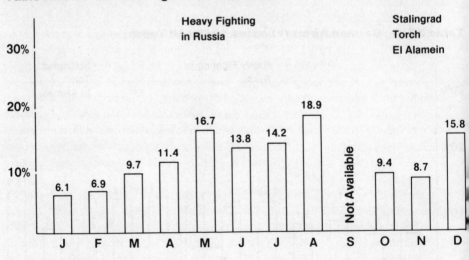

victories in December, Stalin became overconfident; overruling Zhukov, he set wide-ranging strategic goals that were beyond the capabilities of his forces.[9] The result was that everywhere Soviet forces succeeded in pushing the Germans back; nowhere did they succeed in fully exploiting the situation.[10] Further complicating German difficulties at the front was a collapse of the *Wehrmacht*'s supply system. In the cold, railroad engines froze up and those still in working condition moved with great difficulty through drifting snows. Railroad authorities warned Army Group Center that in temperatures below −15° Centigrade, over 50 percent of its supplies would not get through, and in heavy snow the entire supply system might cease to function.[11]

Yet despite the desperate situation, the Germans held the critical points and prevented a general collapse. In February 1942, the Russians opened a hundred-mile gap between Army Group North and Army Group Center. Russian forces failed to exploit their advantage, however, and the Germans escaped the full consequences of the breakthrough. Nevertheless, this time the Red Army managed to isolate two pockets of German troops: the first of approximately brigade strength around Kholm, the second containing the better part of two army corps (six divisions with 100,000 men) near Demyansk.[12] Hitler ordered the forces trapped to hold in what was optimistically termed the Demyansk "fortress."[13] The responsibility for resupplying the beseiged forces fell on the *Luftwaffe*'s already overburdened shoulders.

By the time that the spring thaw arrived in late March, the immediate crisis was over. Both sides wearily faced each other with armies that had fought themselves to exhaustion. Attrition of the German army, however, insured that it would never again reach the level of efficiency that it had displayed at the beginning of "Barbarossa." On March 25, 1942, Halder recorded German losses in the east as 32,485 officers and 1,040,581 NCOs, and men from forces that had numbered 3.2 million at the start of the invasion (33.52 percent).[14] This total did not include those reporting sick. Considering that these totals included support troops, attrition of combat units had undoubtedly exceeded 50 percent. Equipment losses were on a similar scale. By March 1942, tank losses had reached 3,486 from a tank force numbering 3,350 in June 1941, and which had received only 873 replacement tanks.[15] Not surprisingly, the number of tanks ready for action on the eastern front on March 30, 1942, was 140.[16] Losses in artillery, trucks, and support vehicles were comparable.

The winter crisis only intensified *Luftwaffe* problem areas (inadequate production and maintenance, and declining crew capabilities). The failure to defeat Russia, unlike the situation the previous year, meant that the *Luftwaffe* faced inescapable commitments with no possibility of a lull in operations during which it could rehabilitate exhausted flying units. Generally, however, the *Luftwaffe* was better prepared for cold weather than the army. The air transport system enabled it to evade supply bottlenecks and to move winter clothing forward to its units in Russia. Nevertheless, the weather was no kinder to the *Luftwaffe*'s ground transportation system; by January 1942, only 15 percent of the 100,000 air force vehicles in the east remained in working condition.[17] Vehicle shortages forced some units to use shovels and peasant sleds to clear snow from airfields. The cold itself presented numerous problems from starting aircraft to performing simple maintenance. Mechanics had to preheat tools before beginning work and repeat the heating operation several times thereafter while working in the open.[18] Special weather conditions in Russia demanded special procedures and the development of specific equipment items, most of which could not be available until the following winter.

Moreover, the army's plight forced air force commanders to commit their resources to aid frontline crises, while heavy losses of artillery increased demands for close air support. The fact that the *Luftwaffe* possessed few ground support aircraft led to the use of bombers in this role, thus increasing their loss rate. This tactical misuse of bombers continued unabated throughout the war, but the imperatives of the ground situation often offered no other choice. Not only was this an inefficient use of aircraft but each bomber loss involved the wastage of more crew, more instruments, more engines, and more raw materials than in the case of a single-engine ground attack aircraft.[19]

In the desperate battles on the eastern front, *Luftwaffe* antiaircraft units, especially those equipped with 88mm antiaircraft guns, played a valuable part in fighting Russian tanks. Because partisan activity made rear areas insecure and Russian breakthroughs threatened forward operating fields, the *Luftwaffe* used support and staff personnel in January 1942 to defend airfields. But what was defensible as necessity soon became indefensible as common practice. Deciding that the *Luftwaffe* was overmanned with maintenance and support personnel, Göring ordered establishment of *Luftwaffe* field divisions for frontline service. Led by untrained officers and NCOs, such units suffered disproportionately heavy casualties. Moreover, such shortsightedness, which characterized so much of the *Luftwaffe*'s approach, resulted in the enlistment of maintenance and service troops for duty as frontline riflemen.[20] Thus, at the same time that Milch and his staff prepared for a rapid expansion in aircraft strength, Göring was squandering the expertise of trained technicians who already were having difficulty in keeping sufficient numbers of *Luftwaffe* aircraft flying.

The aerial resupply of beleaguered ground forces in the Kholm and Demyansk pockets added to commitments, while the success of aerial resupply set a dangerous precedent for the following fall. In this case, aerial supply worked because a variety of factors were different from those involved in the Stalingrad relief operation. First, the front stabilized near the pocket, and forward operating airfields were thus only a short distance from the troops they supplied. Moreover, these forward operating bases were accessible to airfields in the former Baltic countries and were tied directly to the *Luftwaffe*'s infrastructure in Germany. Consequently, it was relatively easy to move aircraft and supplies forward.

Unfortunately for the *Luftwaffe*, it had never possessed the resources to build a sizeable independent transport force; rather a significant percentage of transport aircraft served to transition future bomber pilots from single to multiengine aircraft.

Thus, the only way to build up airlift capability for emergency situations like Demyansk and Stalingrad was to strip training establishments of instructors, pupils, and aircraft; in other words, to shut schools down. But the losses in training resources, particularly in instructor pilots, were not only irreplaceable but were enormous in their cumulative impact. Nevertheless, in the short term, both the Kholm and Demyansk airlifts succeeded in their narrow tactical goals. The pockets held until relieving forces broke through in May. The airlift in support of the Demyansk pocket flew 14,455 missions, moved 24,303 tons of weapons and supplies and 15,445 soldiers into the pocket, and 22,093 wounded out: a performance that averaged between 100 and 150 missions and 265 tons per day.[21] But the cost was inordinately high. By the time the army relieved the pocket in May 1942, the *Luftwaffe* had lost 265 transport aircraft, or 30 percent of its transport force at the end of February.[22] The negative impact on training was, of course, substantial.

Having weathered the last crises in late winter, the Germans now faced the problem of what their strategy should be for the coming year. Halder, who had remained as Chief of Staff, argued for a defensive strategy in the east in which the army would launch no major offensives but rather husband and rebuild its strength.[23] Hitler, convinced that he alone had prevented a disaster during the winter, disagreed. Ever the gambler, he determined to knock the Soviets out of the war. But this decision would prove difficult to execute given the extent of losses since "Barbarossa" had begun. In fact, only by tasking their allies—the Hungarians, the Italians, and the Rumanians—to defend large segments of the front were the Germans able to build up their forces for the summer offensive.

The condition of the German army gave little cause for optimism. At the end of March 1942, *OKH* reported that out of 162 divisions in the east, 8 were suitable for offensive operations, 3 could be brought up to full offensive capability after a short rest, and 47 could perform limited offensive tasks. The rest were only suitable for defensive warfare.[24] In an effort to upgrade the combat capability of deficient divisions, the army reorganized itself. The results, however, were less than satisfactory. Army Groups North and Center lost virtually all motor vehicles so that their divisions were no longer capable of even limited mobile operations.[25] Of 65 divisions detailed for the coming offensive, only 21 either had trained as new units or had received rehabilitation in rear areas. The remaining 44 divisions had reinforced and rehabilitated while serving in the frontline. Shortages of vehicles and horses severely limited the mobility of infantry divisions, while the spearhead divisions of panzer and motorized infantry possessed only 80 percent of their authorized motor vehicles.[26]

On April 5, 1942, Hitler issued Directive #41 for the summer offensive. Army Group Center would remain on the defensive, and Army Group North would undertake a limited offensive against Leningrad to link up with Finland. The main effort lay in the south, "with the aim of destroying the enemy before the Don [River], in order to secure the Caucasian oil fields and the passes through the

Caucasus mountains themselves.''[27] The primary strategic aim of the campaign was oil. Considering Germany's serious oil shortage, the emphasis on oil made sense.[28] What did not make sense was the belief that German forces possessed the strength and logistical capacity to reach the main oil fields, to seize them undamaged, and to hold them long enough to allow exploitation of their production.

The *Luftwaffe's* task .was to bolster the army's advance. It would provide air cover for ground redeployments in support of operation *"Blau"*; should the enemy seek to strengthen defending forces, German bombers were to attack his transportation system. When the offensive began, the *Luftwaffe* would seek to maintain air superiority while attacking enemy ground forces. Early in Directive #41, Hitler suggested that the purpose of the offensive was "to wipe out the entire defensive potential remaining to the Soviets and to cut them off, as far as possible, from their most important centers of war industry."[29] However, Hitler cast his strategy so as to achieve the capture of the Soviet Union's oil production region, a goal which—as already suggested—was virtually unattainable given the forces available. Thus, there was no possibility of cutting the Soviets off "from their most important centers of war industry" except to deprive Russia of a limited percentage of her oil production. Nowhere in his directive did the *Führer* suggest using the *Luftwaffe* to strike Soviet industry or petroleum production; given the megalomaniacal extent of Hitler's summer aims and the weaknesses of the ground forces, the *Luftwaffe* would be completely employed in supporting the army's drive.

Before the main summer offensive began, Hitler decided to eliminate Soviet forces on the Crimea Peninsula. On May 8, Eleventh Army, supported by *Fliegerkorps* IV and VIII, attacked the Russians on the Kersch Peninsula. Aided by a continuous flow of close air support, Manstein's ground forces broke through Russian positions and routed substantial Soviet forces. On May 19, Halder recorded the successful completion of operations and the capture of 150,000 prisoners with considerable equipment.[30] While the Germans mopped up Kersch, the Russians launched a spoiling offensive on the southern front. They hoped to dislocate German preparations by capturing the critical transportation center of Kharkov. After initial success, the Russians ran into strong resistance. Soviet infantry pressed Sixth Army back on Kharkov, but the Russians hesitated to unleash their armor. Having hesitated, they lost the opportunity. The Germans had reserves in the area; Kleist's First Panzer Army, supported by Richthofen's "Stukas," sliced northwards and in one great sweeping thrust isolated the Izyum salient and attacking Russian forces. Once again, Stalin turned a serious military situation into catastrophe. He refused to allow a withdrawal until too late. By the end of May, the Germans had destroyed two Russian armies and badly mauled three others. Two hundred thousand prisoners marched westward to work in German slave labor camps; probably as many lay dead in the wreckage of defeat. Not only had the Germans eliminated Russian reserves on the southern front but the Russians had lost the better part of their armored forces.[31]

One final preparatory operation came before the summer offensive began. Mainstein regrouped his forces, while Richthofen's "Stukas" returned from

Kharkov: their target, the fortress city of Sevastapol. On June 2, the German air and artillery bombardment began and continued without interruption for the next five days. *Fliegerkorps* VIII flew up to 1,000 sorties per day, while Manstein's troops fought their way through the Russian forts and defensive system.[32] On the 19th, Richthofen noted with satisfaction that the city's center was a sea of flames from air attacks with smoke clouds reaching 1,500 meters and stretching from Sevastapol to the Sea of Azov and the Kersch Peninsula.[33] By the beginning of July, resistance had collapsed; Richthofen's *Fliegerkorps* VIII moved north to support the main summer offensive.

Many historians have argued that the summer and fall of 1942 represented the decisive turning point in the history of World War II. The evidence does not support such a contention. The surge forward of German armies in Russia and in the Mediterranean region represented the last spasmodic advances of Nazi military power; there was no prospect of achieving a decisive strategic victory. By the spring of 1942, attrition had reduced both sides in Russia to desperate straits. While the Germans enjoyed a small qualitative edge, the explanation for their successes in the summer lay in the Soviet blunders in the Crimea and at Kharkov in the spring. However, the numerical scales were rapidly turning against the *Wehrmacht,* as Soviet production hit full stride and as Western aid reached Russia in increasing quantities. In the Mediterranean, the scales had already tilted against the Germans; the British collapse in North Africa in May is explicable only in terms of gross military incompetence.

We have already delineated the weaknesses of ground forces available for the summer; the *Luftwaffe* presented a similar depressing picture. The *Luftwaffe* deployed approximately 2,750 aircraft in the east, the bulk being assigned to Army Group South for the summer offensive. But major commitments in the Arctic as well as the need to aid the hard-pressed and equipment-starved northern and center army groups required significant numbers of aircraft. As a result, only 1,500 aircraft were available to support the main drive.[34]

On June 28, the summer offensive began as Fourth Panzer and Second Army jumped off. Three armored, three motorized infantry, and nine infantry divisions led the opening phase that hit the Bryansk Front. Led by "Stukas" and other bombers from *Fliegerkorps* VIII, German armor broke through and raced for Voronezh.[35] By July 2, the Germans had advanced 80 kilometers; and as the official Russian history suggests, the situation was near disaster.[36] Meanwhile on June 30, Sixth Army attacked from north of Kharkov to complete a pincer movement south of Voronezh. This time, however, the pincer arms closed around few Russians. The Soviet high command had finally absorbed the lessons of the past year; when threatened with encirclement, it pulled troops back without hesitation. This response to German breakthroughs characterized Soviet strategy throughout the summer, and prompt withdrawals denied the Germans the successes they had enjoyed the previous summer.[37]

Now in early July, Hitler divided Army Group South into two separate commands, Army Group B in the northern sector and Army Group A in the southern

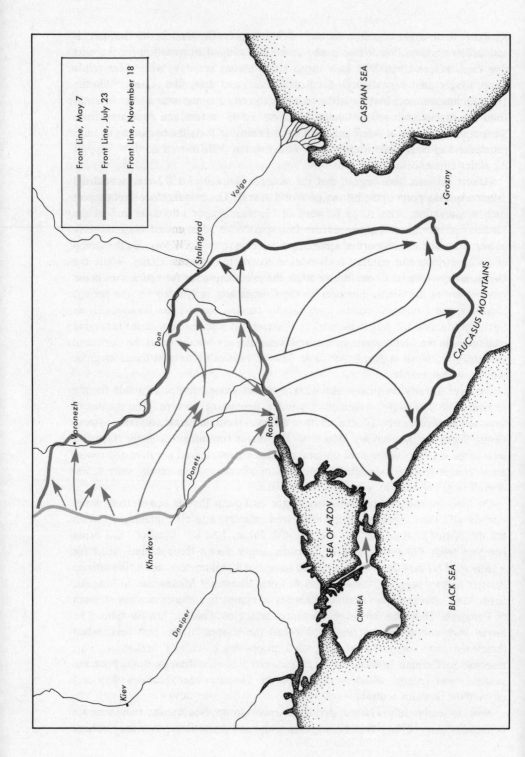

Front Line, May 7

Front Line, July 23

Front Line, November 18

CASPIAN SEA

Volga

Grozny

Stalingrad

CAUCASUS MOUNTAINS

Don

Voronezh

Rostov

Donets

Kharkov

SEA OF AZOV

BLACK SEA

CRIMEA

Dneiper

Kiev

sector. He also made major changes in the command structure to facilitate his control over operations. While Army Group B moved south from Voronezh to clear out the Don River bend, Army Group A, spearheaded by First Panzer Army, drove east to Voroshilovgrad and then southeast to seize the Don bridges at Konstantinovskaya.[38] As the advance gathered momentum, some of the signs of a collapse in the command and control system that had existed the previous summer reappeared on the Russian side.[39] Nevertheless, although losing much of its equipment in the process, most of the Red Army managed to escape.

Hitler's baleful influence was soon apparent. In mid July, he fired Bock, while relations between the *Führer* and the army's Chief of Staff were increasingly strained. Halder, recognizing the limited nature of German fighting strength, was not fooled by the initial success. Hitler, however, was now thinking in grandiose terms. Further encouraging his dreams was his own serious underestimation of the Soviet's ability to resist further German advances. As the *OKW* War Diary noted on June 25, Hitler believed that Russian resistance would be considerably less than in 1941, and that Army Group South could execute the phases for operation *"Blau"* with less difficulty and more quickly than originally planned.[40] In late July, he demanded that Army Group A "occupy the entire eastern coastline of the Black Sea, force a passage of the Kuban," drive towards Grozny, and thrust through to the Caspian Sea in the Baku area. Simultaneously, Army Group B was to "thrust forward to Stalingrad, smash the enemy forces concentrated there, . . . , and . . . block . . . land communications between the Don and the Volga [Rivers], as well as the Don itself."[41] Thus, not only did Hitler direct the advance along widely diverging axes but the objectives of Army Group A were so diverse that the attempt to gain all insured that German forces would gain none. Hitler also made clear his growing interest in Stalin's city, for one of the *Luftwaffe*'s major tasks was to insure "the early destruction of the city of Stalingrad."

The *Luftwaffe*'s mission in this last great, wide-ranging German offensive of the war represented a replay of the previous year. By and large, its units maintained air superiority over the entire front and severely hampered Soviet reconnaissance and bombing efforts.[42] German aircraft played an important role in breaking up Soviet counterattacks in the first days of *"Blau."* The *Luftwaffe*'s interdiction of Soviet forces disrupted supplies and, in one case, caught two reserve divisions in the open—150 kilometers east of Stalingrad—and butchered them. Richthofen trumpeted in his diary about a "beautiful bloodbath *(Tolles Blutbad!)*"[43] During this period, most assigned aircraft supported the army's advance. For July and August, *Luftwaffe* reports to *OKW* headquarters contained the constant refrain that battle emphasis in the east lay "in supporting the army's advance *(Schwerpunkt Kampfeinsatz zur Unterstützung der Angriffsarmeen)*."[44]

As in 1941, the Germans inflicted heavy aerial losses on their Russian opponents, while losing relatively few aircraft themselves. But a constant attrition of air units took place, and the cumulative effect of such losses was devastating. From May through September 1942, *Luftwaffe* bomber units in the east lost approximately 120 bombers per month, while fighter losses were almost exactly the same. Aircraft losses on the eastern front were approximately 60 percent of all *Luftwaffe* losses for all theaters (see Table XXV[45]). For bomber squadrons, monthly losses represented approximately 15 percent of total actual strength for all theaters. Fighter losses averaged nearly 20 percent per month.[46] In spite of this steady attrition lasting over five months, the Germans maintained unit aircraft strength on the eastern front at a uniform level. In August and September, the general staff withdrew a number of long-range bomber wings that had suffered particularly heavy losses, but prompt replacement by rehabilitated and refreshed units from the zone of the interior kept frontline strength at the same level.[47] But improved supply and replacement procedures designed for maintaining strength should not disguise the overall state of the *Luftwaffe* in the east—a state which as early as June 26, the *OKW* War Diary described as "strained."[48]

Adding to *Luftwaffe* difficulties was the fact that as the army hurtled forward, the distances over which supplies moved rapidly increased. Army Group South was already the farthest removed of the army groups from the supply system. As Sixth Army, with its supporting flak and air force units, approached Stalingrad in August, the nearest supply system railhead was 350 kilometers behind in Stalino. With severe shortages of motorized transport, the *Wehrmacht* faced an increasing logistical problem as the advance continued.[49] At the end of July, the drive into the Caucasus ran out of fuel; and while *Luftwaffe* transport units helped to alleviate some shortages, the bulk nature of fuel made it impossible to alter fundamental supply realities.[50] Consequently, the utilization rate began to fall as units deployed forward to new airfields to support advancing ground forces. Poor communications and the slow arrival of supplies, as well as the primitive conditions found on forward operating bases, added to the *Luftwaffe's* problems.[51]

As German forces surged into the Caucasus, Hitler undercut their efforts. He was now entranced with Stalingrad and on August 1 ordered the transfer of Fourth Panzer Army (two German and Rumanian Corps, the equivalent of eight divisions) from Army Group A to Army Group B. By mid-August, the Germans had cleared out the Don bend and were preparing to cross the Don and to seize Stalingrad. On the 23rd, General von Wietersheim's panzer corps crossed that river in a surprise attack and within one day had advanced to the Volga north of Stalingrad, a distance of 60 kilometers. Aerial support provided by *Fliegerkorps* VIII, 1,600 sorties, 1,000 tons of bombs, with the loss of only 3 aircraft (and a claim of 91 Russian aircraft shot down) facilitated the rush forward. That afternoon, Richthofen, now Commander of *Luftflotte* 4, launched massive aerial attacks on the city itself.[52] For the next week, Stalingrad felt the fury of German air attacks as the *Luftwaffe* supported the army by trying to break the will of Stalingrad's defenders and population.

From this point forward, the Nazi effort centered on the struggle for Stalingrad—a struggle minimizing the flexibility and adaptability of German units while maximizing the dogged determination of their Russian opponents. The house-to-house struggle sucked more and more troops into the dying city. What German strategy had once viewed as a blocking position for the advance into the

Reichsmarschall Hermann Göring and *Generaloberst* Hans Jeschonnek (*AFSHRC*)

Ernst Udet and Willi Messerschmitt (*AFSHRC*)

General Walther Wever, First Chief of Staff (*AFSHRC*)

Feldmarschall Erhard Milch visiting the front (*AFSHRC*)

Feldmarschall Albert Kesselring with Werner Mölders (*AFSHRC*)

Air Defence of the *Reich*: Trautloft and Galland at war games with First Fighter Wing, Nov–Dec 1943 (*AFSHRC*)

Adolf Galland: fighter ace
extraordinaire (*General Galland*)

Hannes Trautloft in his Bf 109S
(*General Trautloft*)

The interim bomber: the He 111 (*official USAF photo*)

The cancelled 'strategic' bomber: the Do 19 (*AFSHRC*)

The flawed 'strategic' bomber: the He 177 (*AFSHRC*)

B-17 formation attacking Brunswick (*official USAF photo*)

B-17s under attack by Fw 190 over Bremen, 29th November 1943 (*official USAF photo*)

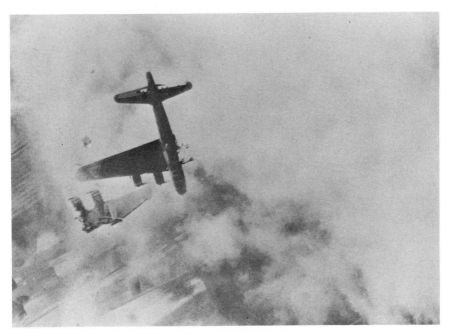

The cost (*official USAF photo*)

The cost: B-17 falling out of formation (*official USAF photo*)

The defenders: the Fw 190 (*official USAF photo*)

Mainstay of the night fighter force—the Bf 110G (*official USAF photo*)

Mainstay of the fighter force: the Bf 109G (*official USAF photo*)

The flawed long-range fighter: the Bf 110 (*DAVA*)

The 'fast' bomber: the Ju 88 (*official USAF photo*)

Bf 109E (*DAVA*)

Do 17 (*DAVA*)

The 'fast' bomber: the Ju 88 (*AFSHRC*)

Attrition: Bf 109 pilot bales out (*official USAF photo*)

The *Luftwaffe*, 1945

Caucasus now became the focal point for Hitler. By the end of October, the Germans had captured most of the city, but Russian resistance clung tenaciously to the banks of the Volga. In the south, Army Group A remained halted at the end of its long supply lines. Everywhere on the eastern front, the Germans now lay in overextended positions. Meanwhile, their Russian opposition, unlike the previous year, had conserved and built up its strength. Beginning in mid-October, increasing numbers of Soviet aircraft challenged the *Luftwaffe*. By early November, Russian aerial interdiction efforts were seriously interfering with Sixth Army's supplies.[53]

Even rising aircraft production in Germany had little impact on the force structure, because commitments and opposition that the *Luftwaffe* faced were extracting an even higher price. The attrition on the eastern front from May through October 1942 represented a major portion of the *Luftwaffe*'s overall strength. In this time frame, bomber losses (aircraft written off) in Russia equalled 51 percent of all bombers at the end of April, while the corresponding figure for single-engine fighters was 48.6 percent.[54] Thus, Hitler's decision to defeat the Soviet Union in 1942 insured that neither the *Luftwaffe* nor the army would receive a respite to recuperate from the winter defeats of 1942. Perched precariously at the end of long lines of communications and with its strength severely attrited, the *Wehrmacht* awaited the crushing Russian counterblow.

THE MEDITERRANEAN

As in 1941, the Mediterranean had remained a side show for the Germans through most of 1942. Air and ground forces deployed in North Africa represented the minimum required to fend off the British. The fact that Rommel with these forces had won great tactical victories is a tribute to his genius. Nevertheless, his success inevitably led to a rise in the forces deployed against him on the ground as well as in the air.

The British, saddled with a series of incompetent commanders on the ground, were well served in the air. From May 1941, Arthur Tedder, one of the outstanding airmen of the war, commanded the RAF in the Middle East, while his deputy, Sir A. "Mary" Coningham, led the air forces assigned to support Eighth Army. Tedder and Coningham built up a force in the 1941–42 period that showed extreme versatility in its employment in close air support, air superiority, and short- and long-range interdiction missions. While the RAF in the Mediterranean gained numerical and qualitative superiority over the *Luftwaffe*, difficulties complicated the execution of a successful British air strategy. Perhaps the most daunting were the enormous distances that British forces had to traverse within this theater. The distance between Tripoli and El Alamein was 1,500 kilometers, equal to that from East Prussia to Moscow. Moreover, supply lines reached from Britain around the African continent, while the aircraft ferrying system, although involving less distance, crossed Central Africa and thus presented considerable logistical difficulties.

Moreover, the British suffered from interservice coordination problems. Early in his command, Tedder recognized the interrelationship between the efforts of the three services and that, without a strategic conception, British armed forces could not achieve decisive results. As he noted in his memoirs:

> The campaign in North Africa provide a prime example of the complementary roles played in the Second World War by all three services. The brunt of the desert battles fell upon the Army and the Royal Air Force; the eventual intention was to turn out of North Africa, bag and baggage, the Italian and German forces. By seeming paradox, this object could not be achieved without success at sea. . . . By a further paradox, such superiority at sea could after 1941 be secured only by the exercise of airpower and could certainly not be secured by surface forces alone.[55]

Tedder found it difficult to cooperate with the army which could not understand the particular advantages as well as limitations of the air weapon.[56] On one occasion in 1942, he wrote home that the army's performance resulted from "an excess of bravery and a shortage of brains."[57] The result of such failings in army training, doctrine, and leadership largely nullified British air superiority over the desert battlefield.[58] It was one matter to control the airspace over the battlefield; it was another to translate that superiority into direct success when cooperation with the army broke down or if ground commanders consistently lost to inferior forces.

British air and naval forces operating from Malta were a thorn for the Italian logistics to North Africa from the onset of the Mediterranean war. By late 1941, what had began as a nuisance had now become a strategic threat. In September 1941, the British sank 38.5 percent of the tonnage sent from Italy to Libya. In October, the figure reached 63 percent and in November an astonishing level of 77 percent.[59] British forces undoubtedly received considerable help from "Ultra" decrypts of Axis cypher traffic, making convoy operations relatively easy to pinpoint and attack. This intolerable pressure on Rommel's logistical system helps explain the sudden transfer of *Luftflotte* 2 into the theater in November. The fact that these forces represented a substantial portion of the aircraft supporting the advance on Moscow does, however, raise an interesting question about the *OKW*'s strategic priorities.

Indeed the arrival of new air units in Sicily in December 1941 allowed the Germans to clear the waters around Malta and protect Axis convoys from British interference. Shipping losses fell to a more acceptable level of 20–30 percent. However, until logistical preparations had been accomplished, Kesselring could not launch an aerial offensive aimed at destroying Malta.[60] Beginning in early April 1942, the air offensive on Malta began. By May 10, Second Air Fleet had flown 11,000 sorties against the island fortress and placed the garrison and local population in desperate straits.[61] The question now facing the Germans was whether to proceed with an airborne and naval invasion. After considerable debate within the Axis' high commands, Hitler vetoed the operation. In retrospect, given the enormous logistical difficulties in the theater, Malta's capture would only have made a marginal difference to the North African situation.[62] Nevertheless, the failure to seek a decision forced the *Luftwaffe* to leave strong forces in Sicily to harass Malta—a further dispersal of limited air resources.[63]

In the summer of 1942, despite Rommel's brilliant successes in the spring, the Mediterranean balance was shifting against the Axis. On the ground, the British were accumulating a numerical superiority that outweighed whatever qualitative superiority the Germans still enjoyed. Even more important was the fact that in July, Eighth Army acquired a commander who refused to tolerate the "nice chap" syndrome that had so hampered the British army.[64] By October, the British possessed an impressive numerical superiority. Although the Mediterranean campaign operated on a smaller scale, the similarities between the strategic situation in the Mediterranean and those existing in Russia are striking. German air and ground units at the end of long lines of communications faced massive enemy buildups with little prospect of reinforcement. The situation represented a recipe for strategic disaster.

THE WEST: BRITISH EFFORTS[65]

With the outbreak of war in September 1939, the British government placed severe limitations on Bomber Command's freedom of action; it forbade RAF bombers from attacking any target that might involve civilian casualties.[66] Nevertheless, the British learned much·from the "Phony War." The first lesson, one that burned itself into British sensibilities for the remainder of the war, was the massacre of "Wellington" bombers by German fighters in December 1939. After this disaster, most RAF senior commanders were dubious about the potential of daylight bomber operations over well-defended airspaces.[67] The second lesson involved problems associated with bad weather and long-range flying by British bombers over hostile territory in night leaflet raids—raids that "Bomber" Harris claimed provided the Germans with their toilet paper needs for much of the war.[68]

The German invasion of France and the Low Countries in May 1940 removed most restrictions on bomber activity.[69] For the next ten months, Bomber Command launched its aircraft against specific targets in Germany, especially oil plants and transportation systems. The initial hope was that "the accuracy of night bombing [would] differ little from daylight bombing."[70] By the spring of 1941, the nature of the problem had emerged. In August of that year, an analysis of mission photographs indicated that only one in three British aircraft was hitting within 75 square miles of its target.[71] In fact, given the lack of navigational aids, Bomber Command had a difficult time in hitting cities. On October 1, 1941, with Karlsruhe and Stuttgart as targets, British bombers "were reported over Aachen, Eupen, Malmedy, Coblenz, Neuwied, Kreuznach, Frankfurt am Main, Wiesbaden, Limburg, Darmstadt, Mainz, Worms, Trier, Offenburg, Saarfels, Nuremberg, Erlangen, Bamberg, Bayreuth, Coburg, Pegnitz, Aschaffenburg, Schweinfurt, Würzburg, Regensburg, Weiden, and Chemnitz."[72]

The weight of such evidence pushed Bomber Command and the Air Staff towards "area" bombing, a euphemism for what was to be a "city busting" campaign. But if the considerable difficulties in hitting targets at night pointed in this direction, the doctrinal frame of reference established before the war made "area" bombing an attractive strategy. As early as September 11, 1940, Sir Charles Portal—still Commander of Bomber Command—urged his government to announce the names of 20 German cities targeted for reprisal raids "for each night of indiscriminate bombing by the enemy."[73] In May 1941, Churchill circulated to the Cabinet a paper by Trenchard. The former Chief of Air Staff (CAS) argued that Germany's population was "particularly susceptible to air bombing." Admitting that only 1 percent of the bombs dropped hit their target, he concluded that:

> This means that if you are bombing a target at sea, then 99 percent of your bombs are wasted, but not only 99 percent of the bombs are wasted but 99 percent, too, of the pilots and of the training which went to produce them. . . . If, however, our bombs are dropped in Germany, then 99 percent which miss the military target all help to kill, damage, frighten, or interfere with Germans in Germany, and the whole 100 percent of the bomber organization is doing useful work and not merely 1 percent of it.

Such a policy, Trenchard admitted, might involve heavy casualties in aircraft and crews, "but the counting of our losses has nothing to do with the soundness of the plan once you accept the view that the nation can stand their casualties. The pilots in the last war stood it, and the pilots of this war are even better, and, I feel, would welcome a policy of this description."[74]

This movement towards the use of "area" bombing received its final impetus in March 1942 when Churchill's scientific advisor, Lord Cherwell, presented the Prime Minister with a carefully structured argument in favor of a systematic attempt to destroy German cities. The heart of Cherwell's argument lay in his belief that the destruction of housing was the best method to break German resistance.

> Investigation seems to show that having one's house demolished is most damaging to morale. People seem to mind it more than having their friends or even relatives killed. At Hull, signs of strain were evident though only one-tenth of the houses were demolished. On the above figures, we should be able to do ten times as much harm to each of the 58 principal German towns. There seems little doubt that this would break the spirit of the people.[75]

The basic problem for Cherwell's argumentation was that Bomber Command was already suffering serious losses at night, while other theaters were making demands on bomber production. The raid of November 7, 1941, underscored the damage that the *Reich*'s night defenses could inflict on British bombers. From a force of 400 aircraft, Bomber Command lost 37, or 9.25 percent. Aircraft attacking specific targets suffered even higher losses: bombers attacking Berlin lost 12.5 percent of their number, at Mannheim 13 percent, and in the Ruhr Valley 21 percent. Night no longer provided an impenetrable veil for bomber operations; as it turned out, this would not be the last time that circumstances would force Bomber Command to rethink its basic strategy and tactics.[76]

In January 1942, disenchantment with the results of the bombing offensive thus far led to the appointment of Sir Arthur Harris as leader of Bomber Command. Harris possessed an unshakeable belief that, with the necessary resources, his command could win the war by itself. Fortified by a strong personality and intolerant of differing views, Harris was an ideal leader to shake the lethargy from the command. Interestingly, it was not until late 1942 that Harris became a complete convert to an "area" bombing strategy.[77] Nevertheless, as suggested above, the realities were already pushing him in that direction.

Harris established excellent relations with the Prime Minister, and over the course of the spring and summer of 1942, he bombarded Churchill with memoranda.[78] In these he argued forcefully that only a resolute and sustained bombing offensive could defeat Germany and that diversion of aircraft to protect British shipping, to support the army, or to attack Axis forces in the Mediterranean was a gross misuse of airpower.[79] Harris became especially vociferous over the diversion of aircraft to support the war on submarines.

> The strength of Coastal Command, which is composed largely of suitable bomber types, is today almost the equal of Bomber Command. It achieves nothing essential, either to our survival or to the defeat of the enemy. It abates little, not even the possessiveness of the Admiralty. It aids by preventing a few shipping losses—a very few. These few losses we can bear awhile if we do not further embarrass our shipping position by adding to our difficulties the transportation and support of vast armies overseas. . . . Coastal Command is therefore merely an obstacle to victory. By redirecting Coastal Command to the offensive, it could, in conjunction with Bomber Command, do . . . more harm to the enemy naval situation and the enemy war situation as a whole than it can do or has in years of waste and misemployment in its present wrong and mainly futile occupations.[80]

As a new commander, Harris understood that his command desperately needed operational successes for its morale as well as for the survival of its primary mission as a city buster in view of the pressures to divert four-engine aircraft to other tasks. The appearance of the first significant navigational aid, *Gee,* aided the accomplishment of this task. The first demonstration of *Gee*'s effectiveness came in early March 1942, when British bombers devastated the Renault armament factory near Paris.[81] The second demonstration came later in the month with a low level attack on Lubeck, described by Harris as "built more like a firelighter than a human habitation." Post-raid photo reconnaissance indicated that the bombing had destroyed 40 to 50 percent of the city. At the end of April, the command blasted Rostock and a nearby Heinkel factory.[82]

But Harris' greatest triumph of the year came in May. By scratching together every aircraft in the command and in its operational training units, he put 1,000 aircraft over Cologne and swamped the night defenses to achieve an unheard of bombing concentration. The raid was a success. With a relatively low loss rate (40 bombers or 3.8 percent of the attacking forces), Bomber Command destroyed much of the city. Later photo reconnaissance indicated that the attack had destroyed 600 acres of Cologne of which 300 lay in the center. The greatest success of the raid may, however, have rested in the political capital it provided Harris. The next 1,000 bomber raid, following soon after Cologne, again underlined the limitations under which the command operated. In early June, Harris sent his bombers against Essen; and with less favorable conditions, the bombers achieved no concentration. In fact, the German high command only reported "widespread raids over West Germany."[83]

While one more 1,000 bomber raid occurred in 1942, Harris, having made his point, now began the long process of building up his command. The introduction of the "Lancaster" bomber, further aids for blind bombing, and creation of a pathfinder force (the latter with considerable opposition from Harris) resulted in a gradual rise in the command's destructive potential. But as the British advanced, so too did the Germans. By August, the Germans were jamming Gee, and the new pathfinder force faced the same navigational and target-finding problems that had for so long plagued the command. Not only that, but there were no target-marking bombs available.[84] If the results from 1942 failed to achieve another striking success, the command at least built up its strength and gathered invaluable experience for 1943.

The British did not confine their efforts solely to night bombing. The RAF expended considerable effort throughout 1941 and 1942 in daylight operations, although there was some doubt concerning the bomber's ability to survive without fighter protection. Nevertheless, after the start of "Barbarossa," some senior British officers hoped that the RAF could launch day bombing sorties, protected by fighters, against targets on the continent such as airfields and important factories. In this way, the RAF would force the Germans to fight. Code name for these operations was "Circus." Unfortunately, the results did not meet expectations. The Germans withdrew fighter units from the coast to airfields deep in France and Belgium. There, they could choose whether to fight or not, and British fighter forces, operating at extreme ranges, faced the problem that Bf 109's had confronted in 1940. Moreover, there were relatively few targets of importance to the Nazi war effort; therefore, the Germans fought only when circumstances favored them.[85]

There was, of course, a solution: either extend the range of existing fighters or design a long-range fighter specifically to protect deep penetration raids. But the RAF showed little interest in drop tanks, and the Air Staff dismissed the notion that British industry could develop a long-range fighter of sufficient capability to take on German fighters. In March 1940, prodded by Dowding who argued that the RAF needed a long-range fighter to protect international trade, Air Vice Marshal W. S. Douglas, Assistant Chief of Air Staff, suggested:

> It must, generally speaking, be regarded as axiomatic that the long-range fighter must be inferior in performance to the short-range fighter. . . . The question had been considered many times, and the

> discussion had always tended to go in circles. . . . The conclusion
> had been reached that the escort fighter was really a myth. A fighter
> performing escort functions would, in reality, have to be a high
> performance and heavily armed bomber.[86]

Unfortunately, Douglas' view reflected most views in the Air Ministry. Portal informed Churchill in June 1941 that a long-range fighter could never hold its own against short-range fighters; thus, the former could never fly where they could expect opposition from the latter. Churchill's response to this gloomy conclusion was that such a view closed "many doors."[87]

Confirming the Prime Minister's assessment were disastrous losses suffered in 1942 by RAF bombers during unaccompanied daylight operations into Germany. In April 1942, 12 "Lancasters" made a low level, deep penetration attack on the M.A.N. Works in Augsburg. The RAF initiated heavy fighter sweeps and bombings of coastal targets to distract German fighters. Nevertheless, over northern France, 20 to 30 Bf 109's jumped the "Lancasters" and shot down 4. The bombers encountered no further fighters but lost three more aircraft to flak in the target area, while the remaining five aircraft received damage. In December 1942, a major attack on the Phillips Radio Works in Eindhoven lost 16 percent of the attacking force of 93 bombers, while a further 57 percent were damaged.[88]

Thus far, we have highlighted the attrition of German air units in World War II. One must emphasize, however, that such losses were endemic to all air forces. From May to September 1942, Bomber Command lost 970 aircraft. In May, the command's average strength had been 417 aircraft. Thus, the loss rate works out to approximately 233 percent in a five-month period.[89]

In August 1942, another air force entered the lists against the *Luftwaffe*. Flying at 23,000 feet, 12 B–17's attacked the marshalling yards at Rouen, while 6 others flew against a diversionary target. Four "Spitfire" squadrons provided protection on the run-in, while five "Spitfire" squadrons covered the withdrawal.[90] No losses occurred; and by October 1942, General Ira Eaker informed General Carl "Tooey" Spaatz that this experience indicated that the B–17 could "cope with the German day fighter." In November, Eaker, on the basis of the first 1,100 missions, claimed that German fighters were no match for close formations of American bombers; losses on those first 1,100 missions had totalled only 1.6 percent. Unfortunately, what Eaker left unsaid was the fact that most missions had enjoyed intensive fighter support. Those attacks, however, that had flown to the fringes or beyond of fighter range had suffered a loss rate of 6.4 percent, and no missions had yet reached the *Reich*.[91] Thus, daylight and unaccompanied bomber attacks on Germany remained very much in question.

THE GERMAN RESPONSE: AIR WAR IN THE WEST

Germany had entered the war with large fighter and flak forces. However, the air defense system, although not intended to protect the civilian population, was behind the British. This reflected the fact that German strategy was by definition aggressive and offensively oriented. The *Luftwaffe* trained its fighter forces for offensive operations in enemy airspace. Consequently, the burden of defending the *Reich* fell on the flak units. However, the relative freedom with which RAF bombers crossed the night skies over Germany during the summer of 1940 raised serious questions. As a result, at almost the same time as the British, the Germans began work on the problem of night controlled, aerial interception.

From the beginning, the Germans had emphasized the role of flak in the defense of the *Reich*. This partially resulted from a misreading of the lessons of Spain where antiaircraft had proven effective against low flying aircraft, the profile of most missions in that war.[92] But despite the relative ineffectiveness of flak against high altitude targets, the Germans continued to place strong emphasis on flak throughout the war for use against enemy aircraft. Two factors played a role in this crucial decision. Hitler found antiaircraft guns more congenial than aircraft and more within his frame of reference. Also important was the fact that antiaircraft guns, blasting into the night, provided the population with a psychological crutch no matter how ineffective the weapons might be. Goebbels, with support from the *Gauleiters* (Nazi district leaders), berated Milch as late as 1943 because there were insufficient antiaircraft guns for defense of the cities.[93] The use of antiaircraft guns, however, did involve diversion of scarce aluminum resources that would have been better spent on aircraft.[94]

In July 1940, the *Luftwaffe* established the 1st Night Fighter Division in Brussels under General Joseph Kammhuber.[95] The general staff combined various units, including a few flights of Bf 109's, a flight of Do 17's, and one combined flak-searchlight regiment. Initially, defense of the *Reich* involved a combination of intruder attacks on British bases with a searchlight zone over the *Reich* for fighter aircraft to attack illuminated bombers. The first tactic showed promise, but Hitler halted intruder operations in the summer of 1941 in view of mounting bomber losses against Russia. Thereafter, he rarely allowed German night fighters or bombers to attack RAF bombers in their lair. Thus, from 1941, Germany's air defense emphasized passive operations with few offensive thrusts.

To help defend the fatherland, Kammhuber's defensive measures involved the extensive use of searchlight belts in western Germany working in tandem with Bf 109's. At the beginning, these efforts depended on acoustical devices to locate approaching bombers. Not surprisingly, the fighters achieved few successes since *Luftwaffe* fighters could hardly locate the bombers, a situation quite analogous to the RAF's inability to find German cities. Beginning in October 1940, the Germans introduced Würzburg radar units into the struggle with the first set in Holland. By late 1941, Kammhuber had established a belt of radar stations reaching from Denmark to Holland and then south through Belgium and northern France. The system provided early warning as well as ground control intercept (GCI) stations to support a growing force of night fighters with their own radar sets. Kammhuber established a tight system in which each GCI station controlled one fighter operating in a designated area that was a portion of the larger belt. Helped substantially by the experimentation of Major W. Falk, Kammhuber's air defense forces represented a formidable threat to Bomber Command's operations by the start of 1942. What had been a thin line in front of the Ruhr in early 1941 had become a defensive system of considerable depth and extent by the following year.[96] The system did have one obvious weakness. With only one German GCI station and fighter over a given area, Bomber Command was in a position to swamp the defenses if it could feed its aircraft through the German defensive system in a concentrated stream.

Unfortunately for Germany's cities, these efforts raised only occasional interest in the high command or in the *Luftwaffe*'s general staff. Throughout 1941 and 1942, most eyes remained centered on Russia. There were admittedly some nasty shocks in the spring of 1942. Heavy air raids on Lubeck and Rostock disturbed some in the high command, and Goebbels found time to rage in his diary about the destruction of art by British barbarians.[97] Lubeck, however, was hardly of decisive importance for Germany; and while the *OKW* noted the attacks on Rostock, it gave the raids no particular significance.[98]

The attack on Cologne was another matter. The *Luftwaffe*'s underestimation of the attacking force and a miscalculation of Hitler's mood exacerbated the impression created by the destruction.[99] Calculating that air defense forces had accounted for 37 British bombers (in fact the British lost 40[100]), the *Luftwaffe* urged that in view of what it termed a 50-percent success, the *Reich*'s propaganda services issue a victory bulletin. Not only did Hitler refuse the request in sharp terms but he pointedly remarked that the bomber force contained a higher number of aircraft than estimated. Disregarding enemy propaganda claims, Hitler argued, the damage on the ground indicated that something extraordinary had occurred.

On June 3, Hitler received Jeschonnek and gave the Chief of Staff a severe dressing down. He ridiculed *Luftwaffe* estimates on the bomber force attacking Cologne and its efforts to "gloss over or to describe what was a catastrophe as a defensive victory." In the conversation, Hitler made two further comments fraught with significance for Germany's future. First, he suggested that the only reply to such "terror" raids was retaliation in kind. Also, Hitler pointed out quite correctly that these raids signaled an attempt to establish an aerial second front. He concluded his discussions with Jeschonnek by remarking that: "I never hide from the truth, but I must see clearly in order to be able to draw correct conclusions."[101]

Fortunately for Bomber Command, despite efforts to launch further 1,000 plane raids, it did not again in 1942 achieve the success of the Cologne attack. Thus, Hitler did not draw the correct conclusions. As the *OKW* War Diary reported British failures in descriptions of widely dispersed efforts, the threat slipped from German consciousness.[102] Consequently, Kammhuber's night defense forces received only minimal reinforcements. From 116 aircraft assigned to night air defense in September 1940, the force grew to 250 aircraft in September 1941 and to 345 aircraft in September 1942.[103] However, had further Colognes occurred in 1942, Kammhuber might have received the resources in late 1942 and early 1943 that the night defenses received in response to the Hamburg catastrophe of July

1943, which ultimately enabled them to decimate Bomber Command in early 1944.

In reaction to the spring raids of 1942, the Germans launched a series of night retaliatory raids against British cities. Shortly after the Rostock raid, a member of the German foreign office announced that the *Luftwaffe*, using the Baedekker tourist guide, would strike the name of each British city destroyed off the list.[104] The British in response termed these summer 1942 night raids, "Baedecker" raids. In reality, the raids achieved little significant damage; bomber losses were high, particularly in training units which lost heavily among instructional crews.[105] Not only had further attrition taken place in the hard-pressed bomber forces but once again the Germans had sacrificed long-range interests, the training of future combat aircrews, for short-term expedience.

In March 1941, Göring held a major conference for units in the west. After describing in detail the coming air offensive against Britain, he secretly admitted to Adolf Galland and Werner Mölders that "there's not a word of truth in it." Forces would transfer from France to the Russian theater leaving only a few fighters in the west.[106] Although only approximately two fighter wings remained in the west for the next year and a half, many of the best fighter crews remained in that theater. Similarly, the best equipment went to the west; industry supplied the Fw 190's to the western theater first, and only the latest model Bf 109's fought over France and Belgium.[107] Small in numbers (no more than 180 aircraft), the western fighter forces were among the best in the *Luftwaffe*.

The daylight aerial defense of the west soon pulled back to bases deep in France and Belgium from which German fighters met the "Circus" operations on more or less equal terms. At the farthest extension of "Spitfire" range, the Germans could choose whether to fight or not. Although numerically superior in operations over western Europe, the British at no time dominated the *Luftwaffe*. When they wished to do so, the Germans could challenge the RAF in most effective fashion. Two examples—the breakout of the *Scharnhorst* and *Gneisenau*, and the Dieppe raid of August 1942—underline the conditions of the 1942 western air battle.

In the first case, the two battle cruisers had lain in French ports for nearly a year under attack from British bombers. Worried by the possible loss of one or both of these ships to air attack and afraid that the Allies might invade Scandinavia, Hitler ordered the ships to break through the Channel to Germany from whence they could eventually move to northern waters. In charge of the air cover, Galland drew on two fighter wings in France as well as one from Germany; he began the operation with approximately 250 fighters. In a well-coordinated effort, the Germans brought the ships home. Despite the fact that mines damaged both battle cruisers, German fighter aircraft kept the RAF from intervening in a decisive fashion.[108]

The Dieppe tragedy does not need a full recapitulation here, but the air action that day is worthy of note. In August 1942, Allied forces raided the port of Dieppe; the purpose of the attack was to seize the port and test planning theories for an eventual invasion of the continent. The raid itself was a dismal tactical failure. Canadian troops never got past the sea wall; most were butchered on the beaches. As naval units struggled to get the survivors off, the *Luftwaffe* intervened in rising numbers and a major air battle took place. By the end of the operation, the *Luftwaffe* had written off 21 fighters (4 Bf 109's and 17 Fw 190's) and 27 bombers (7 Ju 88's, 1 He 111, and 19 Do 217's).[109] The British, however, in addition to considerable ground losses, lost 1 destroyer to air attack and 106 aircraft.[110] While the direct impact of Dieppe was of little importance, the raid's strategic lessons had a critical effect on the war's future. The Germans drew the wrong conclusions and believed that Dieppe indicated that at its start the coming Allied invasion would attempt to seize a major port.[111] Such a conclusion greatly aided deception plans surrounding "Overlord." On the Allied side, British and American commanders concluded that seizure of a builtup area, such as a port city, represented too hazardous an operation. Thus, they determined to take the port with them (the "Mulberry" harbors). The second vital lesson drawn was that local air superiority over western France and the Low Countries was insufficient for the success of such a complex operation. Rather, the Allies needed complete air superiority over western Europe, a circumstance that only the defeat of the *Luftwaffe* could achieve.

There is one parenthetical aspect of the air war that touches tangentially on this study and that is the role of aircraft in the war on trade. Fortunately for Britain, the war at sea raised minimal interest in Göring. Thus, despite a great opportunity, the *Reichsmarschall*'s willingness to cooperate with the navy was almost nonexistent.[112] The general staff did select two bomber wings in the summer of 1939 to operate against British trade, while the seizure of Narvik in April 1940 revealed the long-range potential of the Fw 200, the "Condor." Nevertheless, despite the time required to train bomber crews in navigation over water, Göring used these specialized crews in the bombing offensive against Britain in the summer and fall of 1940. By March 1941, *Fliegerführer Atlantik* (air commander, Atlantic) possessed a total of 83 aircraft (21 "Condors," 26 He 111's, 24 He 115 torpedo bombers, and 12 Ju 88/Me 110 reconnaissance aircraft). By July, the number had increased to 155 aircraft, a force hardly capable of inflicting decisive damage on British convoys. Despite the scarcity of aircraft, long-range "Condors" had a serious impact on the naval war. In January, German aircraft sank 20 ships for a total of 78,517 tons, while U-boats sent to the bottom 21 vessels (126,782 tons). The following month, "Condors" sank 27 ships (89,305 tons); thereafter, British countermeasures restricted the threat.[113] Nevertheless, these successes by a small number of aircraft indicate what the Germans might have achieved with more resources.

In 1942, the efforts of the *Luftwaffe*'s antishipping forces centered on northern waters. Failure in the east led the Germans to make a major effort to shut off western aid reaching Russia through Murmansk. In 1941, the Germans had constructed a series of airfields in northern Norway to support ground forces operating in the Arctic. These fields proved useful when the *Luftwaffe* turned to attacking North Cape convoys. The first aerial attacks, launched against convoy PQ 16, managed to sink 7 out of 34 ships. The next operation, against PQ 17, was more successful and resulted in destruction of 23 out of 34 ships. For the *Luftwaffe*, this attack represented its last major success against Allied shipping. The next

Murmansk convoy in the fall possessed aircraft carrier protection, and British fighters extracted heavy losses from attacking aircraft. Soon thereafter, however, the *Luftwaffe* shut down operations in Arctic waters because the invasion of North Africa resulted in the transfer of antishipping units from the North Cape to the Mediterranean.[114] In the final analysis, German efforts to attack British shipping by air achieved disproportionate successes for the level of effort expended. Nevertheless, while suggesting what the *Luftwaffe* might have accomplished with more resources, the war against Allied commerce never aroused Göring's interest, and the opportunity vanished.

GERMAN PRODUCTION, 1942: PERFORMANCE AND IMPLICATIONS

Milch's 1942 production program, the so-called "Göring program," had largely been predicated on the winning of the Russian campaign.[115] The army's failure in front of Moscow raised serious difficulties for the possibility of increasing aircraft production. Heavy equipment losses in Russia, combined with ongoing military operations in the east, gave Hitler no choice but to switch industrial priorities back to army production.[116] Three weeks after Hitler's decision, Milch noted to Jeschonnek what the impact would be:

> (a) Instead of a transfer of workers from the army to *Luftwaffe* tasks, a heavy withdrawal of air force workers [in favor of the army].
>
> (b) Industrial capacity already surrendered by the army to the air force to be returned.
>
> (c) Unexpectedly strong limitations on raw material allocations—for example, only one-half of expected copper.
>
> (d) Extraordinary reductions in construction projects in support of weapons and industry.
>
> (e) Similar difficulties and no adjustments with the machine tool industry.[117]

Thomas estimated that production priorities would mean that the aircraft industry could complete only 60 percent of the "Göring program."[118]

In fact, no such reduction occurred. Despite the fact that the aircraft industry possessed the same work force and aluminum allocation that it had had in 1941, aircraft production began a dramatic acceleration that would continue into 1943 and 1944. From an average monthly production of 981 aircraft in 1941 (311 fighters and 363 bombers), German production rose to 1,296 per month in 1942, a 32 percent increase (434 fighters, 39.5 percent; and 545 bombers, 50 percent). In December 1942, production reached 1,548 aircraft, a 58 percent increase over December 1941, including 554 fighters (110 percent) and 674 bombers (69 percent).[119] As suggested earlier, this dramatic increase was largely due to one man, Erhard Milch.

To begin with, Milch established a close working relationship with the new armaments czar, Albert Speer, who had succeeded Dr. Fritz Todt after the latter's death in an aircraft crash. In addition to Todt's powers, Speer received far wider latitude than Todt had ever possessed. Only the *Luftwaffe* remained independent of Speer's direct control, although cooperation between Speer and Milch removed much of the friction characterizing previous relationships.[120] Nevertheless, the army's desperate condition in the east and high ammunition expenditures in the great land battles on the eastern front forced Milch to make-do with what the *Luftwaffe* had received in previous years.

While the Germans possessed significant resources of aluminum, aircraft production faced serious competition from other users. In 1941, 5,116 tons of aluminum per month (16 percent of all allocations) went to ammunition production for the three services (for fuses, incendiaries, tracers, etc.). Milch noted to Göring that this equalled the aluminum necessary to produce 1,000 Do 217's or 4,000 Bf 109's.[121] Altogether, aircraft construction received 74 percent of aluminum production.[122] From the last quarter of 1941, allocations to aircraft production began to run seriously in arrears and that situation remained constant throughout 1942.[123] While Milch waged a running battle to increase aluminum allocations for the aircraft industry, he undertook substantive measures to improve manufacturing efficiency. First, he cracked down on wasteful practices that had characterized German industry; aluminum allocations to manufacturers now depended on actual use in the production of each aircraft rather than an absurdly high industry-wide average set by the Air Ministry. By 1943, recycling of scrap aluminum as well as crashed aircraft had increased available aluminum by 57 percent. Also, important was the fact that substitute materials, such as steel alloys and wood, stretched aluminum allocations.[124] Success was dramatic. In 1942, with 15,000 fewer tons of aluminum, German industry produced 3,780 more aircraft weighing a total of 28,628 more tons.[125]

On the labor side of aircraft production, Milch and industry leaders achieved similar results. Through 1941, the aircraft industry had received a disproportionate share of labor resources, undoubtedly because of Göring's position as leader of the Four Year Plan. In late 1941, however, Hitler ended the *Luftwaffe*'s favored position; and over the course of 1942 despite a massive influx of foreign laborers into Germany, the aircraft industry received few new workers.[126] Beginning in the summer of 1941, Milch had demanded that the aircraft industry rationalize production methods and use raw material allocations as well as its work force better. The result of such pressure was a steady increase in productivity from 1941 through 1943 (although not nearly as marked as in the United States) as German industry introduced mass production methods.[127] But no matter how revolutionary the new methods were in terms of German industrial practices, aircraft manufacturers never came close to equalling what occurred in the United States where, as one historian of the strategic bombing offensive has noted, American industry was turning out aircraft like "cans of beans."[128]

Despite Milch's drive to increase production, there remained considerable skepticism in the general staff as to the size of the proposed program. As late as

March 1942, Jeschonnek objected to Milch's urgings for a rapid increase in fighter production. He remarked, "I do not know what I should do with more than 360 fighters!"[129] By June, the Chief of Staff had modified his opinion and written Milch that the general staff foresaw a need for a monthly production of at least 900 fighters by the winter of 1943–44.[130] Nevertheless, in view of the attrition rates of 1940 and 1941, Jeschonnek's March comment can only be described as remarkable.

The impact of Milch's success was favorable for the short run. Given the difficulties that the *Luftwaffe* had experienced at the end of 1941, this was not surprising. With heavy commitments in Russia, indicators such as unit strength as a percentage of authorized strength underwent gradual improvement over the spring and summer of 1942.[131] Encouraging also for frontline commanders was the fact that operational ready rates also began a slow climb from the depths of winter 1941–42. From a low of 39 percent for all combat aircraft (44 percent for fighters and 31 percent for bombers) in late January 1942, the in-commission rate had risen to 69 percent for combat aircraft by late June (75 percent for fighters and 66 percent for bombers). Thereafter, however, heavy operations in the east and commitments over great distances resulted in a fall in overall operational ready rates to as low as 59 percent and no higher than 65 percent for the remainder of the year.[132] If the *Luftwaffe* had recovered some strength, the patient was still in serious condition.

The most discouraging of the 1942 indicators confronting the *Luftwaffe* was the fact that increased aircraft losses accompanied rising production. In fact, by June 1942 the *Luftwaffe* possessed only 60 more combat aircraft than one year earlier (June 21, 1941: 4,882 aircraft; June 20, 1942: 4,942 aircraft). For the remainder of 1942 as commitments multiplied, aircraft strength fell until by the end of the year the Germans had less than 4,400 combat aircraft.[133] Thus, not only were the Germans losing more aircraft in numerical terms but attrition in absolute terms now took place at a faster rate than in 1941. The attrition taking place through October 1942 (see Table XXIX[134]) underscores the demands on the *Luftwaffe* as the *Wehrmacht* made its last lunge forward. By the end of October, in terms of its operational ready rate, its force structure, and its attrition thus far in the year, the *Luftwaffe* was dangerously overextended.

CONCLUSION

The *Luftwaffe*'s problems in 1942 directly reflected the catastrophic failure of German grand strategy in Russia. In a larger sense, however, the root of those problems lay in the unjustified overconfidence that had marked German strategic and industrial planning after the stunning victory over France. Because the Germans had done so little to expand production despite control over most of Europe, the *Reich*'s ground and air forces faced enemies who possessed a growing material superiority. Hitler's gamble in the summer of 1942 in the east further exacerbated German numerical inferiority. For the *Luftwaffe*, the imbalance was becoming unmanageable. Disregarding the difficulties in Russia, the *Luftwaffe* confronted in

TABLE XXIX

German Losses, All Causes—January-October 1942

Aircraft Written Off

	Average Strength, Jan 1942	Due to Enemy Action	Not Due to Enemy Action	Total	Percent of January Strength
Close Recce	280	70	73	143	51%
Long-Range Recce	400	236	136	372	93%
Single-Engine Fighters	1,500	868	866	1,734	115.6%
Twin-Engine Fighters	490	331	244	575	117.3%
Bombers	1,750	1,101	648	1,749	99.9%
Stukas	440	315	162	477	108.4%
Transport	970	250	256	506	52.2%
Liaison	270	73	91	164	60.7%
Coastal	230	33	40	73	31.7%
TOTAL	6,330	3,277	2,516	5,793	91.5%

Aircraft Damaged: January-October 1942

	Not Reparable at Unit Level			Reparable at Unit Level			Total Aircraft Damaged
	Due to Enemy Action	Not Due to Enemy Action	Total	Due to Enemy Action	Not Due to Enemy Action	Total	
Close Recce	43	34	77	37	49	86	163
Long-Range Recce	47	116	163	20	38	58	221
Single-Engine Fighters	202	681	883	133	470	603	1,486
Twin-Engine Fighters	88	181	269	39	118	157	426
Bombers	329	566	895	90	294	384	1,279
Stukas	46	83	129	28	50	78	207
Transport	21	90	111	23	143	166	277
Liaison	10	91	101	14	65	79	180
Coastal	0	3	3	2	4	6	9
TOTAL	786	1,845	2,631	386	1,231	1,617	4,248

the west an Anglo-American industrial capacity that in the last quarter of 1942 outproduced Germany by 250 percent in single-engine fighters, by 196 percent in twin-engine aircraft, and by 20,077.7 percent in four-engine bombers. While some of the West's production went to the Pacific and to Russia, the rising wave of Allied production was becoming clear.[135] It would soon swamp Germany's aerial defenders.

Notes

1. *KTB OKW*, Vol II, ed. by Andreas Hillgruber, p. 166.
2. BA/MA, RL 2 III/1181–1185, Flugzeugunfälle und Verluste bei den fliegenden Verbänden.
3. BA/MA, RL 2 III/1025, 6.Abt. (III A), Front-Flugzeug-Verluste, 1942.
4. Ibid.
5. Ibid.
6. Trevor-Roper, *Blitzkrieg to Defeat*, Directive #39, 8.12.41., p. 107.
7. Albert Seaton, *The Russo-German War, 1941–45* (New York, 1971), p. 212.
8. Reinhardt, *Die Wende vor Moskau*, pp. 206, 210.
9. Erickson, *The Road to Stalingrad*, pp. 297–98; see also Kurt von Tippelskirch, *Geschichte des Zweiten Weltkrieges* (Bonn, 1951), p. 237.
10. See Halder, *Kriegstagebuch*, Vol. III, entries for 29.12.41., 30.12.41., 31.12.41., 2.1.42., which begin with the following comments: 29.12.: "Ein sehr schwerer Tag!"; 30.12.: "Wieder ein schwerer Tag!"; 31.12.: "Wieder ein schwerer Tag!"; and 2.1.: "Ein Tag wilder Kämpfe."
11. Reinhardt, *Die Wende vor Moskau*, p. 216.
12. Hermann Plocher, *The German Air Force Versus Russia, 1942*, USAF Historical Study No. 154 (Air University, 1967), pp. 69–70.
13. Halder, *Kriegstagebuch*, Vol. III, entry for 22.2.42., p. 405.
14. Ibid., entry for 25.3.42., p. 418.
15. Burkhart Müller-Hillebrand, *Das Heer 1933–1945*, Vol. III, *Der Zweifrontenkrieg* (Frankfurt am Main, 1969), Table 2 "Verluste, Panzerkampfwagen," Blau, *The German Campaign in Russia*, p. 41; and Reinhardt, *Die Wende vor Moskau*, p. 258.
16. Reinhardt, *Die Wende vor Moskau*, p. 258.
17. Irving, *The Rise and Fall of the Luftwaffe*, p. 144.
18. Plocher, *The German Air Force Versus Russia, 1942*, pp. 105, 107.
19. Ibid., p. 13.
20. Ibid., pp. 68, 139–40. See also von Richthofen's order for the combing out of 30 percent of rear service personnel, BA/MA, RL8/49, Korpsbefehl des komm. General des VIII. Fl. K., 25.2.42.; and Richthofen's disapproval in October 1942 of Göring's intention to establish 20 Luftwaffe field divisions: "Luftflotte 4 vor Stalingrad: unter Gen. Oberst Frhr. v. Richthofen," AFSHRC: K 113.309–3, v. 9, diary entry for 15.10.42.
21. "Versorgung Demjansk und Cholm," Morzik Nr 227, 2.2.56., AFSHRS: K 113.3018–4.
22. "Luftwaffe Strength and Serviceability Tables, August 1938–April 1945," AHB, Translation No. VII/107.
23. Seaton, *The Russo German War*, p. 258.
24. Hans-Adolf Jacobsen, *Der Zweite Weltkrieg in Chronik und Dokumenten* (Darmstadt, 1962), p. 690.
25. Reinhardt, *Die Wende vor Moskau*, p. 259.
26. Blau, *The German Campaign in Russia*, p. 138.
27. Trevor-Roper, *Hitler Directs the War*, Directive #41, 5.4.42., p. 116. There was, of course, a corollary objective in gaining control of the oil. Seizure of the oil in the Caucasus would deny that oil to the Russians.
28. Shortages in diesel fuel for the navy had become so acute by the end of 1941 that one author has described the 1942 period as one of "crisis" in which the navy, including the U-boat forces, lived "hand to mouth." See Wilhelm Meier-Dornberg, *Die Ölversorgung der Kriegsmarine 1935 bis 1945* (Freiburg, 1973), pp. 68–71.
29. Trevor-Roper, *Hitler Directs the War*, Directive #41, 5.4.42., p. 116.

30. Halder, *Kriegstagebuch*, Vol. III, entry for 19.5.42., p. 444.

31. Erickson, *The Road to Stalingrad*, pp. 345–47.

32. *The Great Patriotic War of the Soviet Union 1941–1945, A General Outline* (Moscow, 1974), pp. 119–20.

33. Richthofen, "Kriegstagebuch," 12.7.42.

34. Air Ministry, *The Rise and Fall of the German Air Force*, pp. 178–79.

35. Blau, *The German Campaign in Russia*, p. 143.

36. *The Great Patriotic War of the Soviet Union*, p. 125.

37. Tippelskirch, *Geschichte des Zweiten Weltkrieges*, p. 283.

38. Blau, *The German Campaign in Russia*, pp. 146–48.

39. *The Great Patriotic War of the Soviet Union*, p. 126.

40. *KTB OKW*, Vol. II, entry for 25.6.42., p. 448.

41. Trevor-Roper, *Blitzkrieg to Defeat*, Directive #45, 23.7.42., p. 129.

42. Erickson, *The Road to Stalingrad*, p. 356.

43. Richthofen, "Tagebuch," entry for 21.8.42.; "Luftflotte 4 vor Stalingrad: unter Gen. Oberst Frhr. v. Richthofen," AFSHRC: K 113.309–3, v. 9.

44. *KTB OKW*, Vol. II, entries for 2.7.42., 6.7., 9.7., 10.7., 13.7., 14.7., 16.7., 17.7., 18.7., 19.7., 20.7., 24.7., 26.7., 27.7., 28.7.

45. These tabulations are based on the author's calculation of losses reported to the Luftwaffe quartermaster general in BA/MA, RL 2 III/1181, 1182, 1183. These reports indicate the day on which aircraft were lost, although the monthly loss reports the quartermaster general submitted to the general staff reflected the day on which the loss report arrived in Berlin. There was generally a four-day to one-month slippage between the actual loss and its report to Berlin. Thus, the author's retabulation for the 1942–43 period represents the most accurate picture that one can get of actual losses when they occurred. One must add that, as in all administrative organizations, not every loss was reported, although the incentive to do so was strong since it was on the basis of these loss reports that the supply service issued replacement aircraft. Unfortunately, direct loss tables for 1944 seem to have been lost; consequently, some figures for 1944 are more difficult to specifically tabulate. Nevertheless, drawing on the information contained in other tables, one can establish a clear trend to Luftwaffe losses. We shall, of course, do so in succeeding chapters.

46. Percentages based on average number of squadrons serving on the eastern front, August 1942: *KTB OKW*, Vol. II, entries for 13.8.42., 17.8.42., 22.8.42.

47. Air Ministry, *The Rise and Fall of the German Air Force*, pp. 178–79.

48. *KTB OKW*, Vol. II, entry for 26.6.42., p. 452.

49. See, in particular, v. Richthofen's discussion with those in charge of the supply system in "Luftflotte 4 vor Stalingrad unter Gen. Oberst Frhr. v. Richthofen," entry for 15.8.42., AFSHRC: K 113.309–3, v. 9.

50. Tippelskirch, *Geschichte des Zweiten Weltkrieges*, p. 285; and Blau, *The German Campaign in Russia*, pp. 155–56.

51. Plocher, *The German Air Force Versus Russia*, pp. 217, 229.

52. "Luftflotte 4 vor Stalingrad unter Gen. Oberst Frhr. v. Richthofen," entry for 23.8.42., AFSHRC: K 113.309–3, v. 9.

53. Manfred Kehrig, *Stalingrad, Analyse und Dokumentation einer Schlacht* (Stuttgart, 1974), p. 120.

54. German bomber losses for this period were: 676 aircraft written off, including 633 fighters. German strength on April 30 was: 1,319 bombers and 1,302 fighters. These figures are based on the author's calculations of Luftwaffe loss tables in BA/MA, RL 2 III/1181, 1182, 1183, and Air Historical Branch, "Luftwaffe Strength and Serviceability Tables, August 1938–April 1945," Translation No. VII/107.

55. Marshal of the Royal Air Force Lord Tedder, *With Prejudice* (London, 1966), p. 244.

56. Ibid., pp. 106–07, 116, 163, 194.

57. Ibid., p. 217.

58. Why the British army should have had exceeding difficulty is examined in Brian Bond's scrupulously accurate account of the interwar period: *British Military Policy Between the Two World Wars* (Oxford, 1980). For another participant's evaluation of the British army in 1941–42, see Erwin Rommel, *The Rommel Papers*, ed. by B. H. Liddell Hart (London, 1953), pp. 132, 185, 211, 222, 262, 298, 308, 332, 341, 366, 519–20, 523.

59. Richard Suchenwirth, *Historical Turning Points in the German Air Force War Effort*, USAF Historical Studies No. 89 (Maxwell AFB, 1959), p. 90.

60. Kesselring, *A Soldier's Record*, pp. 123–24.

61. *KTB OKW*, Vol. II, entry for 10.5.42., p. 348.

62. This is especially true considering the fact that Rommel's supply lines ran from Greece to Bengasi in the summer of 1942. For German logistical difficulties in the theater, see van Creveld, *Supplying War*, Chapter VI.

63. *KTB OKW*, Vol. II, p. 348.

64. See, in particular, Tedder's comments in *With Prejudice*, p. 313.

65. The following summary of events is based on the account in Webster and Frankland, *SAOAG*, Vol. I, and Anthony Verrier, *The Bomber Offensive* (London, 1968). For a discussion of the development of British and American air doctrines, see Appendix I.

66. Sir Arthur Harris, *Bomber Offensive* (New York, 1947), p. 36.

67. Webster and Frankland, *SAOAG*, Vol. I, p. 195.

68. Harris, *Bomber Offensive*, p. 36.

69. The change in Prime Minister from Neville Chamberlain to Winston Churchill undoubtedly contributed to the decision for a more ruthless bombing policy.

70. Webster and Frankland, *SAOAG*, Vol. I, p. 216.

71. For the full Butt report, see Webster and Frankland, *SAOAG*, Vol. IV, Appendix 13, report by Mr. Butt to Bomber Command on his examination of night photographs, 18.8.41.

72. Webster and Frankland, *SAOAG*, Vol. I, p. 185.

73. PRO AIR 14/1925, letter from Portal to the Under Secretary of State, Air Ministry, 11.9.40.

74. PRO PREM 3/31, COS (41) 86 (0), 28.5.41., "The Present War Situation Mainly Insofar as it Relates to Air."

75. PRO AIR 8/440, Lord Cherwell to the Prime Minister, 30.3.42. See Verrier, *The Bomber Offensive*, pp. 97–98, for the failure of the British Cabinet to consider seriously Lord Tizard's objections to Cherwell's calculations.

76. Frankland and Webster, *SAOAG*, Vol. I, pp. 185–86.

77. Ibid., p. 346.

78. See particularly the Harris memoranda of 17.6.42., 28.6.42., and 3.9.42., as well as Leo Amery's sharp analysis of the weaknesses in Harris' arguments (letter to Churchill, 1.9.42.) in PRO PREM 3/19.

79. For Harris' outrage at the diversion of bomber aircraft to the Mediterranean as well as Tedder's reply, see Tedder, *With Prejudice*, pp. 253–54.

80. PRO PREM 3/19, Harris memorandum 17.6.42. This is indeed a remarkable miscalculation of the role of Coast Command in winning the Battle of the Atlantic. For that task, see Slessor, *The Central Blue*, Chapter XVII.

81. Webster and Frankland, *SAOAG*, Vol. I, pp. 387–88.

82. Ibid., p. 391–94.

83. Ibid., pp. 406–11.

84. Ibid., p. 432.

85. Ibid., pp. 235–36.

86. PRO AIR 16/1024, Minutes of the 20th Meeting of the Air Fighting Committee, held at Air Ministry, White Hall, 12.3.40.

87. Webster and Frankland, *SAOAG*, Vol. I, p. 177.

88. Ibid., pp. 439–43.

89. This calculation is based on the figures available in Table A of Max Hasting's *Bomber Command* (New York, 1979), and Appendix 39 of Webster and Frankland, *SAOAG*, Vol. IV, p. 428.

90. Wesley F. Craven and James L. Cate, *The Army Air Forces in World War II*, Vol. I (Chicago, 1948), pp. 663–64.

91. Thomas A. Fabyanic, "A Critique of Air War Planning, 1941–44," (Saint Louis University dissertation, 1973), pp. 125–27.

92. "Auswirkung der Erfahrungen in Spanien," Aus einer Ausarbeitung von Generallt. Galland über die Luftverteidigung des Reiches, 1946, AFSHRC: K 113.302, v. I.

93. Goebbels, *The Goebbels Diaries*, entry for 10.4.43., p. 322. For Hitler's demand that heavy emphasis remain on the flak program, see BA/MA, RL 3/60 Besprechungsnotiz nr 46/42, 6.3.42. Karinhall, Göring, Milch, Jeschonnek, v. Brauchitsch (Haupt).

94. For a further discussion of this point, see the following section.

95. The following discussion of German night fighter tactics is drawn from the extensive review of night air defense written for the RAF by General Josef Kammhuber at the end of the war, hereafter referred to as "Development of Night Fighting."

96. See the maps delineating the expansion of the system in Verrier, *The Bomber Offensive*, p. 175. For a study discussing the expansion of the night defense system as well as requirements for equipment, see: BA/MA, RL 7/579, "Denkschrift über die Luftverteidigung Herbst und Winter 1941/42 im Bereich Luftwaffenbefehlshaber Mitte," Luftwaffenbefehlshaber Mitte, Führungsabteilung I, 116 Nr. 2500/41, 1.8.41. See also Air Ministry, *The Rise and Fall of the German Air Force*, pp. 185–92

97. Goebbels, *The Goebbels Diary*, pp. 154, 155, 158, 160, 186, 193.

98. *KTB OKW*, Vol. II, entries for 25.4., 26.4., and 27.4.42., pp. 328–29.

99. The following account is based on *KTB OKW*, Vol. II, entries for 31.5., 2.6., and 3.6.42., pp. 394, 398–400.

100. Webster and Frankland, *SAOAG*, Vol. I, p. 407.

101. *KTB OKW*, Vol. II, entry for 3.6.42., p. 400. See also Nicolaus von Below, *Als Hitlers Adjutant 1937–1945* (Mainz, 1980), pp. 311–12.

102. Beginning in July 1942, Luftwaffe reports were recorded in the OKW War Diary. For the general aimlessness of the British attacks, see *KTB OKW*, Vol. II, entries beginning with 1.7.42., pp. 467ff.

103. AHB, "Luftwaffe Strength and Serviceability Tables," Translation No. VII/107.

104. Goebbels, *The Goebbels Diaries*, pp. 200–01.

105. Air Ministry, *The Rise and Fall of the German Air Force*, p. 196.

106. Galland, *The First and the Last*, pp. 54–55.

107. Webster and Frankland, *SAOAG*, Vol. I, p. 490.

108. BA/MA, RL 8/252, "Erfahrungsbericht über Vorbereitung und Durchführung des Unternehmens Donnerkeil," Generalmajor Max Ibel, a.D.; see also Galland, *The First and the Last*, pp. 96–108.

109. Based on the figures in BA/MA, RL 2 III/1182 Genst. Gen. Qu. (6. Abt.), Flugzeugunfälle und Verluste bei den fliegenden Verbänden, August 1941.

110. Roskill, *The War at Sea*, Vol. II, p. 250–52.

111. Friedrich Ruge, *Der Seekrieg, 1939–1945* (Stuttgart, 1954), pp. 36–38.

112. The following discussion on the air war against British trade is drawn from the Air Ministry's *The Rise and Fall of the German Air Force*, pp. 110–19.

113. Roskill, *The War at Sea*, Vol. I, pp. 362–63.

114. Air Ministry, *The Rise and Fall of the German Air Force*, pp. 114–15. To be accurate, one must note that German submarines and the threat of surface units were also involved in the attacks on the Murmansk convoys.

115. See Der Staatssekretär der Luftfahrt und Generalinspekteur der Luftwaffe, Betr.: Steigerung der Rüstung, gst. Nr. 675/41, An den Herrn Generalquartiermeister, 15.10.42., AFSHRC: K 113.82, v. 2.

116. Georg Thomas, *Geschichte der deutschen Wehr- und Rüstungswirtschaft 1918–1943/5* (Boppard am Rhein, 1966), Thomas to Keitel, Betr.: Forderungen an die Rüstung, 23.12.41., p. 470, and Hitler: Denkschrift, 3.1.42., p. 478. See also BA/MA, RL/315, Oberkommando der Wehrmacht, Wi Rü Amt/Ru (IIa), Nr 130/42 Betr.: Rüstung 1942, 14.1.42.

117. BA/MA, RL 3/864, Der Staatssekretär der Luftfahrt und Generalinspekteur der Luftwaffe, 144/42, geh, Kdos., 23.1.42., An den Herrn Chef des Generalstabes.

118. Thomas, *Geschichte der deutschen Wehr-und Rüstungswirtschaft*, Thomas to Keitel, Betr.: Forderungen an die Rüstung, 23.12.41.

119. Figures for German aircraft production drawn from USSBS, *The Effects of Strategic Bombing on the German War Economy*, Appendix Table 102.

120. Albert Speer, *Inside the Third Reich* (New York, 1970), pp. 203, 244, 265, 275, 276, 336, 339.

121. See BA/MA, RL 3/50, Der Staatssekretär der Luftfahrt und Generalinspekteur der Luftwaffe, Nr 118/41 g. Kdos., Dem Herrn Reichsmarschall, 24.10.41.

122. BA/MA, RL 3/64, Industrierat des Reichsmarschalls für die Fertigung von Luftwaffengeräten, Umstellausschuss, Stand der Umstellarbeiten Mitte November 1942, 21.11.41., Anlage 1.

123. See the excellent discussion in Overy, "German Aircraft Production," pp. 197–99.

124. Ibid., pp. 201–02.

125. USSBS, *The Effects of Strategic Bombing on the German War Industry*, Appendices Tables 101, 102.

126. Overy, "German Aircraft Production," pp. 206–10.

127. Richard J. Overy, *The Air War 1939–1945* (London, 1980), pp. 168–70.

128. Verrier, *The Bomber Offensive*, p. 326.

129. Irving, *The Rise and Fall of the Luftwaffe*, p. 148; Irving cites much supporting evidence for Milch's frustration at the low level of fighter production that Jeschonnek was suggesting. There were some in German industry who recognized the danger that America's industrial potential represented for

the Reich and urged major increases in German aircraft production. See BA/MA, RL 3/54, Fr., W. Siebel, Wehrwirtschaftsführer, An Generaloberst Udet, 7.10.40.; and Der Leiter der Wirtschaftsgruppe Luftfahrt-Industrie, Pr. 312/41 La/Wp, 24.12.41., von Rohden Collection, NARS T–971/68.

130. BA/MA, RL 3/865, Generalstab, Generalquartiermeister, 6. Abt. Nr. 3474/42, 23.6.42., Betr.: Flugzeug-Forderungen, An den Staatssekretär und Generalinspekteur der Luftwaffe.

131. See the figures in Webster and Frankland, *SAOAG,* Vol. IV, pp. 501–04.

132. Figures based on totals for 24.1.42. in AHB, "Luftwaffe Strength and Serviceability Tables, August 1938–April 1945," Translation No. VII/107.

133. Ibid.

134. Based on figures in the quartermaster loss returns for aircraft losses: BA/MA, RL 2 III/1025, 6.Abt. (III A) Front-Flugzeug-Verluste, 1942.

135. Based on the table in Webster and Frankland, *SAOAG,* Vol. IV, Appendix XXIV, p. 497.

V Attrition on the Periphery: November 1942–August 1943

The German successes in the spring and summer of 1942 deceived the participants at that time as thoroughly as they have historians since. For the British, Rommel's advance to El Alamein represented a part of German strategy in which a second great pincer arm advancing from the Caucasus would link up with the Africa Corps in the Middle East.[1] Such megalomania was, of course, part and parcel of Hitler's approach to grand strategy, but the means simply did not exist for such wide-ranging aims.[2] Arguments between Hitler and his generals in the summer reflected a divergence between the latter's more realistic assessments and the *Führer*'s intuitive dreams. There was, however, no showdown; Hitler removed those who raised uncomfortable issues. Thus, German strategy in 1942 was entirely of his own making (unlike the previous year); and in November, Hitler's miscalculation of the balance in the Mediterranean and in the east led him to make major strategic mistakes. These decisions forced the *Wehrmacht* to fight on the periphery against enemies who enjoyed a rising numerical superiority. For the *Luftwaffe*, Hitler's resolve was a catastrophe, for he committed his air force to an avoidable battle of attrition under great disadvantages. The impact of the resulting attrition was immediate and direct. Not only did these air battles savage frontline squadrons but aerial transport operations to supply Stalingrad and Tunisia mortgaged the entire training program. For losses suffered in various theaters in 1943, see Tables XXX[3] and XXXI[4].

THE WAR IN THE EAST: NOVEMBER 1942–AUGUST 1943

While the advance into the Caucasus slowed because of logistical difficullties and while Sixth Army exhausted itself at Stalingrad, the Soviets built up their reserves and prepared for a great counteroffensive. Unlike the previous winter during which the Red Army had sought after far-reaching goals and as a result had achieved none of them, the Russians now planned a limited offensive: its target, the German Sixth Army. Despite the desperate situation of Stalingrad's defenders, the Soviets fed in minimal replacements, enough to keep the defenders going but no more.[5]

Soviet intentions and capabilities remained veiled to the Germans. Hitler was confident that his summer offensive had broken the Red Army and that the *Wehrmacht* could go over to the defensive without fear. On October 14, he signed "Operational Order Nr. 1" in which he argued that the Soviets could no longer rebuild their shattered forces and that the German army must hold the line over the

Table XXX   German Losses by Theater January-November 1943

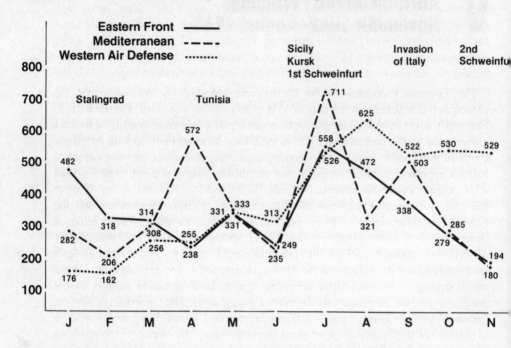

Table XXXI   German Fighter Losses 1943 (Number of Aircraft)

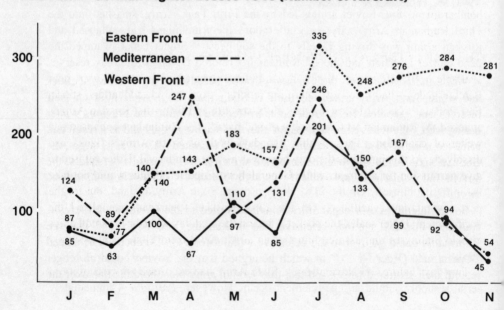

winter "to create the conditions necessary for the final destruction of our most dangerous opponent."[6] But Hitler was hopelessly optimistic. Sixth Army was enmeshed in Stalingrad and was seriously short of ammunition, fuel, and reserves.[7] These shortages severely limited that army's strategic and tactical mobility. Even more threatening was the fact that both flanks were up in the air. To the south lay the Fourth Rumanian Army with few reserves and little German support. To the north, on the great flank sweeping from the Russian city of Voronezh along the Don, lay three allied armies, the Second Hungarian, Eighth Italian, and Third Rumanian, with the barest corseting of German troops. Nowhere on the southern front did the Germans possess a strategic reserve, while tactical reserves along the entire front were few.

In explaining Stalingrad and the refusal to allow a breakout, one must understand the relationship among theaters. At the beginning of November 1942, Hitler's attention centered on the Mediterranean. The front at El Alamein had collapsed; and on November 2, Rommel informed *OKW* that he could no longer hold. A failure to inform Hitler immediately caused a blowup,[8] but Hitler's tantrum could not restore the situation. Meanwhile, intelligence reported a massive movement of Allied shipping into the Mediterranean. No one in *OKW* was sure of Allied intentions, but Hitler and Göring ruled out the possibility of a strike against French Northwest Africa.[9] In the following week, disaster piled upon disaster: Rommel's retreat continued, Anglo-American forces landed in Algeria and Morocco, French resistance collapsed, and events forced the Germans to occupy Vichy France. In this desperate situation, Hitler's attention remained glued on the Mediterranean as German forces seized Tunisia to counter Allied occupation of Algeria and Morocco.

For our purposes here, one need only note these distractions on Hitler when the storm in the east broke—and break it did! On November 19 after a hurricane bombardment, four Soviet armies led by the Fifth Tank Army, smashed into the Third Rumanian Army. By early afternoon, the Rumanians had collapsed and Russian armor was driving rapidly to the southeast.[10] Soviet tanks swamped the 22nd Panzer Division and the 1st Rumanian Armored Division (the only reserves available). By afternoon, *OKW* headquarters—located with the *Führer* near Berchtesgaden—had received "alarming reports" from army headquarters, still in East Prussia.[11] On the following day, Fifty-seventh and Fifty-first Russian Armies attacked the Rumanian VI Corps south of Stalingrad. The Rumanians collapsed in a welter of confusion. Thus, within two days both of Sixth Army's flanks had dissolved. At this juncture, the only hope was a swift withdrawal. Hitler refused to give permission for a retreat, while Generaloberst Friedrich Paulus would not take the initiative himself. On the 21st, Hitler ordered Sixth Army to stand, but for the next several days vacillated. On the 23rd, Russian spearheads completed the encirclement; Hitler sealed the pocket's fate on the next day when he ordered Paulus to hold Stalingrad and assured him that an airlift could meet Sixth Army's supply needs.

Two days before, on November 21, Sixth Army had examined the possibility of aerial resupply should an encirclement occur. However, *Luftflotte* 4 immediately warned Paulus and his staff that the *Luftwaffe* did not possess the transport capacity for such an effort. On the 21st, Richthofen cautioned both Sixth Army and the general staff that such an effort was not in the offing. On the next day, *Luftwaffe* commanders on the southern front again warned Sixth Army that they could not support an encircled army by air. However, Paulus' Chief of Staff commented that there was no other choice other than aerial resupply.[12] While the warning signals at the front were unambiguous, the situation was far from clear in the high command. Despite notice from Richthofen to the *OKW* that unfavorable weather conditions in concert with Russian numerical superiority would make an airlift doubtful,[13] Hitler received Göring's assurance that the *Luftwaffe* could supply the encircled forces. When the army's Chief of Staff, Kurt Zeitzler, objected, Göring would not knuckle under and reported that his staff knew Sixth Army's needs and believed the *Luftwaffe* could meet them.[14] Göring's promise seems to have resulted from a hope of restoring his tattered prestige. The success of the Demyansk and Kholm efforts in the previous winter also bolstered the hope that air supply could maintain Sixth Army.

While Göring was the main culprit, Jeschonnek and the general staff agreed to the airlift with scarcely a comment on its long-range impact on the *Luftwaffe*.[15] On the 24th, Richthofen noted a series of conversations with Zeitzler, Field Marshal Maximilian von Weichs (Army Group B), and Jeschonnek; he urged an immediate breakout by Sixth Army. Weichs as well as Zeitzler agreed. Jeschonnek, however, Richthofen noted, had no opinion.[16] The result of Jeschonnek's silence was that *OKH* received no air staff support in its effort to persuade Hitler to abandon Stalingrad. The *Führer* held his belief that the Sixth Army could hold the banks of the Volga with air supply. The *Luftwaffe* thus received an impossible task.

Moreover, the Russian winter offensive caught the *Luftwaffe* in an exposed and difficult situation. Beginning in late August, a diminution of German air strength in the east in favor of other theaters had taken place. Between mid-August and early November, the eastern front lost four and two-thirds bomber *Gruppen* (approximately 140 bombers) and five and one-third fighter *Gruppen* (160 fighers). The collapse in Egypt and the invasion of French Northwest Africa caused a withdrawal of further three and one-third bomber *Gruppen* (100 bombers) and one and one-third fighter *Gruppen* (40 fighters).[17] Much of the withdrawal came from Richthofen's *Luftflotte* 4, thereby diminishing air support for forces fighting around Stalingrad. Further weakening *Luftflotte* 4 was the fact that the general staff created a needless headquarters, *Luftwaffe* Command Don, to provide an air assignment for one of its favored officers.[18]

The collapse of Sixth Army's flanks enabled the Russians to complete a deep encirclement around Stalingrad. Soviet troops seized the airfields that *Luftflotte* 4 had prepared for winter operations and pushed many support and maintenance personnel into the pocket. As a result, Richthofen's units had to establish themselves on new airfields that were soon overcrowded and did not possess the support needed for the operations now beginning. The arrival of transport and bomber squadrons only exacerbated these difficulties.[19] Moreover, Richthofen's flying units faced intense demands to support hard-pressed ground forces. Appalling weather conditions contributed to the losses and strain on flying squadrons.

On November 23, at Göring's behest, the *Luftwaffe* staff began the task of improvising an air transport force to supply Sixth Army. From the start, it was apparent that only in the best circumstances was an airlift capability of 350 tons per day possible (Sixth Army estimated it needed 600 tons). However, only by stripping training units of all aircraft and by removing transport aircraft assigned to duty in Germany could the *Luftwaffe* reach such a level. An assortment of Ju 52's, Ju 86's, and He 111's (now being assigned to some transport units) moved from the *Reich* to support the airlift.[20] In addition, the first operational *Gruppe* of He 177's and several He 111 bomber *Gruppen* joined the force.[21] The former aircraft proved itself as dangerous to crews in combat as it had proven in testing.

The distance from Berlin to Stalingrad, 2,225 kilometers, exacerbated the problem. To reach forward operating bases, transport crews—many new to flying and few with experience in Russia—had to fly nearly 2,000 kilometers to the front. Crew inexperience, the weather, and marginal airfield conditions caused a high accident rate. Perhaps the only mitigating aspect of such bad weather was that operational ready rates rarely reached 50 percent, with most remaining at the 30 to 40 percent level, thus limiting flying opportunities for inexperienced crews. In some cases, when the weather was particularly atrocious, in-commission rates sank to the 10 to 20 percent range.[22] Landing possibilities in the pocket proved unsatisfactory, because not only did Sixth Army fail to maintain the airfields adequately but also Russian fighters often attacked the transports on landing.

The airlift operation remained under Richthofen's control, but Berlin gave little latitude. While admitting that "an order was an order," Richthofen noted bitterly on November 25 that he was little more than "a highly paid noncommissioned officer."[23] *Luftflotte* 4 received transport reinforcements from Germany at a slow rate; not until December 2 did the number of transports reach 200 aircraft, and it was not until December 8 that aircraft strength reached 300. Thereafter, reinforcements barely prevented a collapse in unit strength.[24] Throughout the airlift, transport squadrons remained well below authorized strength, which undoubtedly distorted Berlin's view of the situation. Richthofen was close to despair over differences between himself and senior commanders removed from the front. On December 18, he noted:

> Important conversations take place at *Luftwaffe* and *OKW* headquarters. One talks about the Duce!—no one is available that I seek. I especially no longer telephone Jeschonnek, since all my recommendations are rejected or, after oral agreement, something else is ordered. Moreover, I now have irrefutable proof that certain things that I have said have been turned around and passed along. I now send only teletype messages, today one four pages long about the situation. In it I ask for orders for the conduct of operations, because recently I received only criticism rather than directives.

Probably, they [the staff in Berlin] were themselves without a sense
of what to do.[25]

Under these conditions, it is not surprising that the airlift failed. On only three days,
(December 7, 21, and 31) did the transports fly over 300 tons into Stalingrad. On
most days, the effort hovered around the 100-ton level; on some days, it sank to no
deliveries at all.[26]

In mid-December, the Germans mounted a relief expedition towards Stalingrad.
The forces were only of corps strength but did surprisingly well. By December 19,
LVII Panzer Corps reached Mishkova, only 35 miles from the pocket. Manstein
urged Hitler to allow a breakout; Hitler refused to make a decision, while Paulus
would not disobey the *Führer*.[27] In response, the Russians launched a major
offensive along the Don. The Soviet's Sixth Army quickly broke through the
Italians, and the deteriorating situation along the Don threatened the entire southern
front. On December 24, the Russian advance overran the forward operating field at
Tatsinskaya and brought the other major airlift field at Morozovskaya under
artillery fire. Göring refused permission to abandon the airfield until under tank fire;
only the flying units barely escaped and many supplies were destroyed.[28] On
December 26, flying units at Morozovskaya broke up Russian tank forces that
approached within 6 kilometers of the airfield. Göring's interference and
minimization of the threat so embittered Manstein and Richthofen that the former
urged Hitler to give the *Reichsmarschall* control of *Luftflotte* 4 and Army Group
Don, "since he always asserts that the situation neither here nor in Stalingrad is as
strained as is reported. Motto: The optimistic leader at the place, over which he is
optimistic!"[29]

By the first week of January 1943, the Germans had lost Morozovskaya, and
transport squadrons were operating from Novocherkassk—350 kilometers from
Stalingrad. Meanwhile, the situation within the pocket was deteriorating. On
January 10, the Russians attacked the encircled defenders. Within two days, the
pocket's major airfield had fallen, and landing supplies became an increasingly
difficult task. Henceforth, the *Luftwaffe* relied almost exclusively on airdrops. By
mid-January, the maintenance situation was desperate. On January 18, less than 7
percent of Ju 52's were in commission, 33 percent of the He 111's, 0 percent of the
Fw 200's, and 35 percent of the He 177's.[30] At this moment, Milch arrived. He
brought some relief to the hard-pressed *Luftflotte* 4, and the field marshal got along
well with Richthofen.[31] His managerial skills raised operational ready rates and
supplies to Stalingrad, but the situation had been hopeless from the beginning. The
final collapse came in late January. On February 2, the last Germans surrendered,
and Paulus, a recently promoted field marshal, was the first German officer of that
rank captured by an enemy. Hitler was more upset over Paulus' capture than the
fate of the 200,000 other Germans killed or captured in the pocket.[32]

In every sense, Stalingrad was a grievous defeat. Beside the boost to Russian
morale and the blow to the German army's strength, it had no less of an impact on
the *Luftwaffe*. The air transport forces suffered devastating losses. By February 3,

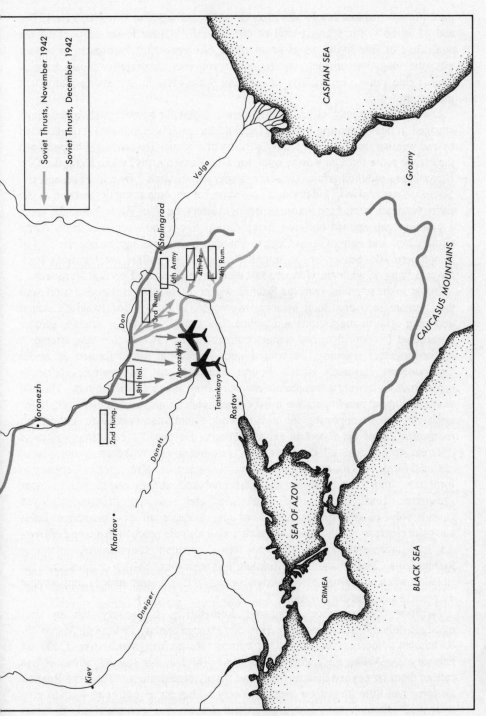

Stalingrad: The Soviet Counterattack

the *Luftwaffe* had lost 269 Ju 52's, 169 He 111's, 9 Fw 200's, 1 Ju 290, 5 He 177's, and 42 Ju 86's, for a grand total of 495 aircraft.[33] These losses represented the equivalent of five flying wings or an entire *Fliegerkorps*.[34] Perhaps as important was the negative impact on training programs, especially those training multiengine pilots. Particularly devastating were crew losses among instrument instructors.

During the resupply effort to Stalingrad, *Luftwaffe* bomber and fighter units engaged in heavy fighting to support ground forces. These missions, compounded by bad weather, resulted in a steady attrition of aircraft. The *Luftwaffe* helped keep the escape route through Rostov open for First Panzer Army, while along the Don the collapse of allied armies caused a desperate situation.[35] By mid-February, the Soviet offensive was in full flood; it now aimed at encompassing destruction of the entire southern front. First Panzer Army held along the Mius River, but to the north a yawning gap opened between Army Group South (now renamed from Army Group Don) and Army Group Center. Russian spearheads approached the city of Dnepropetrovsk; Soviet troops retook Kharkov and pushed the Germans back towards Poltava, while the Germans lost their last hold on the Don near Voronezh.

But as in the previous year, the Russian winter offensive overextended itself, and the Germans recovered their balance. Moreover, Hitler was somewhat chastened and more open to suggestions and advice. As a result, Manstein obtained greater operational freedom than had senior commanders in 1942. Rather than attempt a patched-together response, he waited until substantial forces formed up under Generaloberst Hermann Hoth's Fourth Panzer Army. Meanwhile, *Luftwaffe* capabilities underwent a remarkable recovery from January's difficulties. The end of the Stalingrad relief operation freed considerable bomber and fighter strength for tasks other than supporting the airlift, while Richthofen completed a thorough reorganization of his forces in early February. He ended a confusing welter of different commands, all competing for resources, and withdrew a number of depleted formations for rest and refit. Their flying personnel returned to Germany to form new units, but their support personnel and aircraft transferred to other squadrons. Thus, maintenance capabilities and squadron strength improved considerably. Finally, the Germans were now operating off more permanent fields and were closer to supply depots.[36] Milch's visit also did much to shape up *Luftflotte* 4's rear area organization. Several less competent commanders, including Richthofen's Chief of Staff, von Rohden, lost their jobs.[37] Milch characterized the situation when he warned his subordinates that, "It is a great error to suppose that we possess a ground organization."[38]

Luftflotte 4's capabilities improved dramatically. In Janaury, the air fleet managed only 350 sorties per day. However, from February 20 through March 15, Richthofen's forces averaged 1,000 combat sorties daily with over 1,200 on February 23. Aiding the *Luftwaffe*'s task was the fact that Russian advances had carried them far beyond their airfields and supply organization.[39] Thus, the Russian air force had little impact on operations now taking place; *Luftflotte* 4 could give undivided attention to supporting ground forces. For command of air units supporting the counteroffensive, Richthofen kept long-range bomber units directly under himself; *Fliegerkorps* I, *Fliegerkorps* IV, and *Fliegerdivision* Donetz divided up close air support duties, but Richthofen remained flexible, transferring available assets back and forth between commands as the situation changed.[40]

In the last ten days of February, the German counterattack rolled into high gear. By the end of February, First Panzer Army was driving the Russians in confusion back to the Donets River.[41] *Luftflotte* 4 played a significant role in delaying and softening up Russian armor until ground forces could counterattack.[42] The more important drive came from Hoth's Fourth Panzer Army. This force contained a number of the *Wehrmacht's* best divisions and included *SS* divisions *Das Reich* and *Totenkopf*. Beginning near Dnepropetrovsk, Hoth's forces sliced to the northeast towards Kharkov. By March 14, they had retaken that city; by March 18, the Germans had retaken Belgorad, but the spring thaw ended operations.[43] Richthofen's aircraft substantially aided the advance and managed to destroy large Soviet forces attempting to escape.[44] The counterattack represented a major victory for German arms and restored the highly dangerous situation that had existed at the end of January. It was, however, the *Wehrmacht's* last meaningful victory in the east.

The victory in late winter did not come without cost. In mid-February, aircraft strength in the east had totalled 275 dive bombers, 484 bombers, and 454 fighters.[45] Losses in February and March, mostly in support of the counteroffensive, were 56 dive bombers, 217 bombers, and 163 fighters.[46] As a percentage of the *Luftwaffe's* total strength at the end of January, such losses represented 17.1 percent of available dive bombers, 12.3 percent of fighters, and 17.2 percent of bombers.[47]

Yet, the fighting in southern Russia need not obscure the fact that combat was occurring elsewhere on the eastern front. The results were less spectacular but certainly of importance. For the *Luftwaffe*, this aerial combat, like the daily wastage on the western front in the First World War, imposed a steady and wearing pressure on its capabilities. The battle around Velikiye Luki on the upper Lovat River from November 25 through January 15 indicates this factor. In late November, Russian forces had isolated 7,000 troops in that undistinguished town. By the time that the Germans brought out a few hundred survivors in mid-January,[48] supporting air squadrons had lost 55 aircraft destroyed (including 3 Ju 87's, 8 Bf 109's, and 20 He 111's) and 26 aircraft damaged.[49] The strategic result was virtually nil, but a further attrition had taken place.

For the next three months, ground operations slowed as both sides prepared for the summer. For the *Luftwaffe*, however, the period was anything but quiet. Hitler's inability to tailor strategy to the means at hand forced needless commitments on overstrained air squadrons. The Don collapse in January had finally convinced him to withdraw from the Caucasus; but while First Panzer Army pulled back through Rostov, Seventeenth Army remained on the Kuban Peninsula across from the Crimea. The battle to hold this useless territory, which Hitler hoped would serve as a jumping off point for another offensive into the Caucasus, tied down ground and air forces desperately needed elsewhere and contributed to a heavy attrition rate throughout the period.[50] Elsewhere, fighter sweeps, bomber interdiction missions, and close air support attrited air units despite an absence of major ground operations. From April to June, the *Luftwaffe* lost 256 fighters, 245 bombers, and 115 dive bombers in the east.[51] As a percentage of total air strength (all theaters), these losses represented 18.3 percent of fighters, 17 percent of bombers, and 31.8 percent of dive bombers on hand at the beginning of April.[52] What seems to have happened is that, despite a lower scale of combat and a chance to relieve the pressure on the flying units, the Germans found the urge to use their air assets in insignificant operations irresistible.

The spring thaw raised the question of strategy for the coming summer. Manstein later claimed that he urged a defensive/offensive strategy: The *Wehrmacht* would adapt a defensive posture and allow the Russians the first move. Then using the armored reserves that were rebuilt by rising tank production, the Germans would slam the door shut.[53] Such a strategy was too risky for Hitler and certainly did not appeal to his aggressive instincts. If the Germans were to attack, however, the question was where, when, and with what. On January 23, 1943, armored strength on the eastern front totalled only 495 useable tanks.[54] Considerable resupply took place over the next months, but operations in late winter caused heavy losses. Hitler initially considered three possible spoiling attacks, but by the end of April had settled on "Operation Citadel," aimed at clearing the Kursk salient.[55] Manstein had suggested this possibility as a means of inflicting such heavy losses on the Russians as to prevent a summer offensive. Instead of launching "Citadel" in May, Manstein's suggested date, Hitler postponed it, eventually choosing July 5 in order to strengthen his armored forces in the east.

By June, troops preparing for the offensive had received 900 tanks and 300 self-propelled guns,[56] but by then "Citadel" had raised serious doubts. On June 18, *OKW* staff urged Hitler to cancel the offensive and to establish an operational reserve in Germany to meet any reverse in the *Wehrmacht*'s three theaters.[57] Guderian argued strenuously that the Russians had built up their defenses, and even Hitler admitted that thinking about the pending offensive made him sick to his stomach.[58] But he did not cancel the offensive. Perhaps the rhetoric of his April operational order for "Citadel," announcing that a "victory at Kursk must serve as a beacon for the world," indicates the underlying reason for his decision.[59] He could not publicly admit that the initiative had slipped from his hands.

The pause to build up armored strength allowed the Russians time to prepare. The Central Front, on the northern half of the Kursk bulge, controlled no less than six Russian armies and on the critical northern neck of the salient deployed three armies in two echelons. The Voronezh Front on the southern half of the salient held the line with four Russian armies with a second echelon of two armies behind the neck. Three Soviet armies lay in reserve within the salient, while three more armies lay north of Orel and one to the south of Kursk. In addition, the Russians had dug two or three lines of trenches in the main zone of resistance, and to the rear were second and third zones constructed in the same fashion.[60]

By July, there was no hope of surprise. The greatest land battle of the war opened on July 5; Soviet artillery inflicted heavy casualties on German infantry moving into jumpoff positions. What now occurred was a great battle of attrition.[61] The Germans slowly fought through the first lines of defense; only in the south did they make significant gains, although at great cost. On July 12, the Russians, sure that the raging Kursk battle had entangled German reserves, attacked the northern side of the Orel salient. Their offensive posed an immediate threat to the German northern pincer. That move, combined with the invasion of Sicily on July 10, caused Hitler to shut down "Citadel."[62] Troop withdrawals to both Sicily and to support a desperate situation developing south of Kursk forced an abandonment of the Orel salient. In fact, the most dangerous situation arose in the region south of Kursk. At the beginning of August, Soviet armies went over to the offensive. The cities of Belgorod and Kharkov soon fell, and the entire German position along the Donets unraveled. By the beginning of September, Army Group South was in headlong retreat; its withdrawal carried it to the Dneper by early October.[63]

The *Luftwaffe*'s role in these events was symptomatic of the decline in German power. As with army preparations for "Citadel," the air force gave top priority to rebuilding units scheduled for the offensive. But the effect of high attrition and the drop in training hours for new pilots had an obvious impact on combat effectiveness. A rueful Jeschonnek admitted to Göring that despite high deliveries of aircraft to fighter units, losses due to noncombat causes were severely affecting capabilities.[64] A substantial portion of the *Luftwaffe* strength still remained on the Russian front. Of the total aircraft available at the end of June, 38.7 percent were in the east; more specifically, 84.5 percent of all dive bombers, 27 percent of all fighters, and 33 percent of all bombers were serving in the east.[65] For the offensive, the *Luftwaffe* concentrated nearly all this strength in the two *Luftflotten* deployed near Kursk. In the north, *Luftflotte* 6 possessed 750 aircraft, while *Luftflotte* 4 controlled 1,100 aircraft to support the southern drive.[66]

The air fleets opened the offensive with a massive strike. On the first day, German aircraft flew 3,000 sorties, and some "Stuka" pilots flew up to six missions. Nevertheless, unlike previous years, the *Luftwaffe* did not gain air superiority.[67] If German pilots inflicted heavy losses on Soviet fighters and bombers, their opponents simply put up more aircraft, while German losses inexorably mounted. Soviet "Sturmoviks" struck German ground forces, while Russian bombers hit transportation points. Moreover, the subsequent German failure at Kursk and the Russian summer offensive then forced the *Luftwaffe* to divide its assets to meet the desperate situation on the ground. The retreat from Orel, the Kharkov battle, and a massive Soviet offensive along the lower Donets made extensive demands on *Luftwaffe* resources in three widely separated areas. As a result, the large striking force assembled for "Citadel" now became three small forces engaged in bolstering the situation on the ground. For the remainder of the war, as Russian offensives ripped German defenses to shreds, this was to be the fate of the *Luftwaffe*. With decreasingly skilled pilots but increasing commitments, the eastern *Luftflotten* became the backwater of German efforts in the air.

The losses that *Luftflotten* 4 and 6 suffered in July and August underline the *Luftwaffe*'s overcommitment. In this two-month period, the Germans lost 1,030 aircraft in the east, 16 percent of their total force structure as of June 30, 1943 (351 fighters, 19 percent of all fighters; 273 bombers, 16.4 percent of all bombers; and 202 dive bombers, 38.6 percent of available dive bombers). But the losses should not be viewed in isolation since the air battle in Russia was only one of the three massive commitments that the *Luftwaffe* faced in the summer. While we shall discuss the implications of fighting on three major fronts simultaneously at the end of this chapter, one must note that total losses for all theaters in July and August were 3,213 aircraft (50.6 percent) and 1,313 fighters (71 percent).[68] This was a loss rate that no air force could sustain. Consequently, the *Luftwaffe* had to cut its losses and commitments; to meet the threat at home, it surrendered air superiority on the periphery to Allied air forces.

THE MEDITERRANEAN

In the summer of 1942, Churchill and Roosevelt settled on a Mediterranean strategy. American planners, however, gave heavy emphasis to landings in Morocco, while the British pushed for a landing as far east along the coast of Africa as possible to prevent a German move in Tunisia.[69] The compromise between these views insured that the Allies would gain control of Algeria but could not prevent the Germans from seizing Tunisia.

The *OKW* did not have a clear picture of Allied intentions as the invasion convoy sailed into the Mediterranean. Once, however, the landings occurred, the Germans acted with usual dispatch. Ju 52's flew paratroopers into Tunis; the French governor general collapsed, and the Germans rapidly established control throughout the country. Jodl buttressed Hitler's decision to hold North Africa. At the end of November, he argued that "North Africa is the glacis of Europe and must, therefore, be held under all circumstances."[70] Hitler himself suggested two factors motivating his decision to maintain an Axis presence in Africa: fear that its abandonment would cause an Italian collapse and a desire to keep the Mediterranean closed to Allied shipping.[71] The Germans rushed in paratroopers, *Luftwaffe* field troops, and soldiers from replacement pools, but at the end of November more structured reinforcements began arriving. Tenth Panzer Division was in place by the end of the month; and in early December, Colonel General Jürgen von Arnim assumed command of what was euphemistically called Fifth Panzer Army.[72]

In retrospect, the decision to hold in Africa was a dreadful mistake.[73] At Stalingrad, Russian armies had executed a massive encircling movement to trap Sixth Army. In Tunisia, the Germans were in an equally indefensible position with tenuous supply lines from·Sicily and the mainland. Since the Italian navy was in no position to defend convoys, the *Luftwaffe* had to assume the burden of protecting supplies moving by sea as well as the aerial movement of men and materiel sent into Tunisia. Finally, *Luftflotte* 2 faced increasingly powerful Allied air forces closing in from the east as well as the west. The result, as we shall see, was a thoroughly needless attrition of German air strength. The ground forces and material eventually lost were, arguably, replaceable. Losses in aircraft and pilots were not.

The deteriorating position at El Alamein led to a significant augmentation in *Luftflotte* 2's air strength. In the three months of July, August, and September 1942, Rommel had received 40,000 troops and 4,000 tons of supplies by air. The exhaustion of crews and aircraft, the collapse of sea supply lines to Libya as "Ultra" information allowed the Allies to devastate convoys, and the combination of the Africa Corps' defeat and "Torch" forced the *Luftwaffe* to send 150 Ju 52's to the Mediterranean in early November; and an additional 170 followed at the end of the month. This movement of transport aircraft, combined with the Stalingrad airlift, effectively shut down instrument and bomber transition schools.[74] The development into the Mediterranean also explains why the *Luftwaffe* found it difficult to transfer more transport aircraft to *Luftflotte* 4 and the Stalingrad supply effort. In November and December, transport squadrons flew in 41,768 troops, 8,614.8 tons of equipment and supplies, and 1,472.8 tons of fuel. The cost, however, was prohibitive. The *Luftwaffe* lost no less than 128 Ju 52's in November and December, with an additional 36 destroyed in January (13.9 percent of the *Luftwaffe*'s total transport strength). When combined with those lost at Stalingrad, the Germans had managed to lose 659 transport aircraft (56 percent of the transport force as of November 10) by the end of January.[75]

The German response to "Torch" led to a major transfer of bombers and fighters into the theater. As early as November 4, *Luftflotte* 4 gave up a fighter group to the Mediterranean.[76] Moreover, the North African invasion forced the Germans to shut down attacks on the Murmansk convoys and to send additional antishipping units into the Mediterranean.[77] German bomber and fighter forces operating from Tunisia, Sicily, and Sardinia inflicted considerable damage on Allied shipping and ground forces. The Allies faced two problems in bringing airpower to bear on the bridgehead. The first was one of logistics. Tedder's air forces, still located on Egyptian bases, were too far away to intervene effectively, while the bases that Eighth Army captured in its march along the North African littoral took time to repair and stockpile. Similarly, the air forces in Algeria and Morocco found it difficult to marshal the logistical effort needed in eastern Algeria where it counted. The second problem involved command and control. Anglo-American units in French Northwest Africa operated under different procedures, while Tedder's forces in Middle East Command operated differently. The solution to the first problem was a matter of time. By early January 1943, Allied air forces from Algeria were intervening with greater effectiveness, and Tedder's forces soon joined up.

The second problem was also easily solved. As early as December 19, the Mediterranean naval commander, Sir Andrew Cunningham, cabled London that, "There is one solution and that is to put Tedder in here." Eisenhower brought "Tooey" Spaatz out from England as his deputy, but at Casablanca the Combined Chiefs appointed Tedder as Commander of Allied Mediterranean Air Forces.[78]

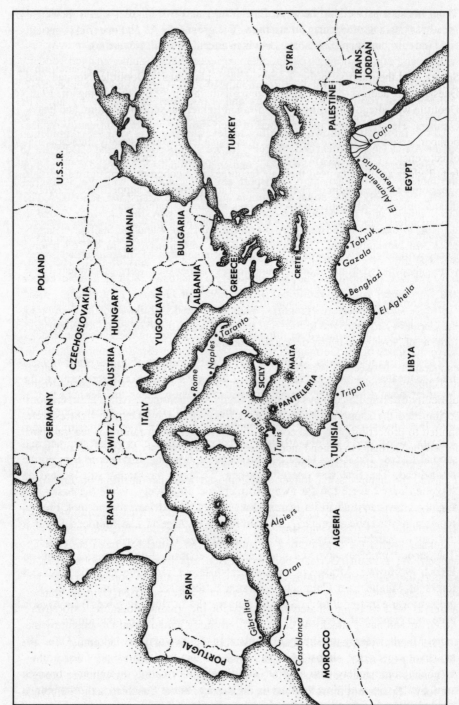

The Mediterranean Theater of Operations

Thus, began a partnership between Eisenhower and two of the premier airmen of the war, Spaatz and Tedder.

Allied air commanders in the Mediterranean proved themselves pragmatic, willing, and eager to draw on battlefield experience. Such attitudes enabled Tedder, Spaatz, and their staffs (in the American case, particularly Doolittle, Norstad, and Quesada) to address critical issues in realistic terms.[79] By the spring of 1943, Doolittle was already pressing for long-range fighters to support medium and heavy bombers. He argued that the presence of such fighters would significantly reduce bomber casualties, while their use "as intruders would greatly increase the effectiveness of our strategic operations."[80] The result of such leadership was soon felt. Tedder and Spaatz used their air resources in a coherent campaign to gain air superiority in the Mediterranean. Their strategy aimed at supporting the overall theater objective of destroying Axis forces in Tunisia rather than a more cavalier "independent" air strategy. As was the case throughout the war, air strategy proved most effective when integrated into an overall strategy in which air, land, and naval forces worked closely together. This does not mean that Mediterranean air forces were subordinated to naval and ground forces, rather they were subordinated to a general strategic framework within which *all* three services worked.

In February, the Germans launched a spoiling attack at Kasserine Pass, but growing pressure around the Tunisian pocket stretched German ground forces to the limit. Allied air units played an important role in disrupting the Kasserine attack, while the shock of the German offensive resulted in considerable improvements in cooperation between American ground and air forces.[81] Meanwhile, Allied antishipping strikes, attacks on harbors, and mine laying operations added to the difficulty of bringing convoys over from Sicily. By February, Allied air operations so impeded the supply situation for Axis forces that most German fighters were limited to protecting ports and convoy routes; this growing failure of sea transport forced the Germans to depend increasingly on aerial resupply.[82] Allied air and naval forces were creating a situation analogous to Stalingrad, except that in the case of Tunisia, the agony lasted longer and imposed a higher attrition on *Luftwaffe* assets.[83]

In March, the German's desperate situation in North Africa became hopeless. The growing quantitative superiority of Allied fighters reduced the survivability of "Stukas," while the deteriorating ground situation resulted in more calls for air support. As a result, German bombers ceased attacks on Allied ports so as to support the hard-pressed troops at the front. This change in bomber strategy not only eased Allied supply troubles but also probably increased German bomber losses as well as being of doubtful utility for the ground situation.[84] Moreover, Allied air and naval attacks on convoys from Sicily halted naval movement by the end of March. Making the supply of Tunisia, in the face of overwhelming Allied air and naval superiority, almost impossible was the fact the "Ultra" provided Anglo-American commanders with accurate and timely information on military convoys from Sicily. So well prepared were Allied air forces that *Fliegerkorps* Tunis concluded in mid-March "that the course for convoys D and C were betrayed to the enemy."[85] The Germans, however, refused to believe to the end of the war that the problem might lie in their electronic communication signals.

There was, then, no other choice for the Germans but to fall back on airlift. This aerial supply of Tunisia in the spring represented the third disaster for the *Luftwaffe*'s transport fleet within a six-month period. In April and the first week of May, as the Tunisian pocket burned itself out, the *Luftwaffe* lost 177 more Ju 52's, along with a number of specialized aircraft such as the Me 323, the "Giant."[86] Particularly noteworthy was the loss of 6 "Giants" and 25 Ju 52's flying to Tunisia ferrying 800 German troops.[87] The third slaughter of German transport aircraft within a six-month period had a wider impact than just on the transport force. As one ranking officer told another after capture: "You cannot imagine how catastrophic the air personnel [situation] is. We have no crews; all the instructor crews were shot down in the Junkers."[88]

The impact of the Tunisian campaign on the *Luftwaffe* far outweighed whatever strategic advantage the Germans gained in closing the Mediterranean for six more months. In the period between November 1942 and May 1943, the Germans lost 2,422 aircraft in the Mediterranean theater (40.5 percent of their total force structure as of November 10, 1942). Table XXXII[89] gives the Mediterranean losses in terms of major aircraft types during the period and suggests their significance for the *Luftwaffe*.

TABLE XXXII

German Aircraft Losses, Mediterranean
Theater—November 1942–May 1943

	Aircraft Losses	Percent of Total Force Structure 10.11.42.
Fighters	888	62.6
Bombers	734	58.3
Twin-Engine Fighters	117	41.1
Dive Bombers	128	35.2
Transports	371	31.5

What makes such losses so appalling is the fact that *Luftwaffe* strength in the Mediterranean varied from 200 to 300 fighters and from 200 to 300 bombers throughout the period.[90] Thus, combat wastage was well over 200 percent of unit strength. Admittedly, some losses were unavoidable. Nevertheless, the impression left by the North African debacle is that had the Germans cut their losses at Libya, they could have defended Sicily with ground forces deployed to Tunisia. In the air, the *Luftwaffe* could have used the strategy it had waged so successfully in western Europe over the past year and a half: fighting only on its own terms or for a decisive strategic object. However, the commitment to Tunisia placed the *Luftwaffe* in a position where it had to fight at great disadvantage with a resulting high rate of attrition.

Germany's troubles in the Mediterranean were not yet over. At Casablanca, Allied statesmen and military commanders had determined that after Tunisia, their forces would invade Sicily and give the Italians a shove that would take them out of the war. For Hitler, the problem was where the blow would come. The Axis collapse in Tunisia destroyed the few good remaining Italian divisions, while the Germans lost heavily enough to prevent establishment of a significant reserve in the Mediterranean. "Citadel" held the priorities, and Allied deception efforts persuaded the *Führer* that the next attack would be in the Balkans.[91] Nevertheless, he did not rule out the possibility that the blow might fall closer to the Italian homeland. Kesselring formed German troops awaiting shipment to Tunisia into three scratch divisions. Despite Mussolini's demand for equipment rather than soldiers, two new panzer grenadier (motorized infantry) and two new panzer divisions moved into the peninsula during June 1943.[92] As all had just received equipment and men, they hardly represented a combat-tested military force. Again the temptation, which proved irresistible, would be to use the *Luftwaffe* to bolster weak ground forces.

While Allied armies rested and trained, Anglo-American air forces attacked German bases in Sicily and Sardinia and raided coastal targets to soften up defenses. Beginning in mid-May, Allied air forces began a bombardment of the Italian island of Pantelleria, located 70 miles southwest of Sicily. After three weeks, Italian forces surrendered before landing operations began; the only casualty was a soldier bitten by a jackass.[93] While Pantelleria provided a base to extend fighter coverage to Sicily, its real value lay in conditions it provided for the study of the effects of aerial bombardment.[94] Allied airmen, using the recommendations of scientists in these air operations, particularly over Sicily and Sardinia, gave no respite to the *Luftwaffe*. Germany's June fighter losses were 131, while a further 72 bombers were lost.[95] July brought the invasion of Sicily and the greatest air battle of the Mediterranean war.

The Tunisian defeat caused a reorganization of German air forces in the south. *Luftflotte* 2 divided in two, with *Luftflotte* South East controlling the Balkans and a new *Luftflotte* 2 controlling Italy, Sardinia, Corsica, and Sicily. A general replacement of commanders also occurred. Richthofen arrived as *Luftflotte* 2 commander, accompanied by a number of staff officers and commanders from the eastern front. Galland, now inspector of fighters, went to Sicily to control fighter operations. Along with these changes, considerable reinforcements arrived in the theater. Fighter bombers transferred from operations against the British Isles, while the number of fighters increased from 190 in mid-May to 450 in early July. Considering the heavy losses in May and June, such transfers were even heavier than the above figures suggest. Close to 40 percent of all fighter production from May 1 through July 15 went to the Mediterranean and two newly formed wings, probably scheduled for Germany's defense, went south.[96] Yet, the movement of fighters to redress Allied superiority achieved nothing more than to cause a rise in German losses—a reflection of how overwhelming the superiority of Allied production had become.

At the end of June, air operations in the Mediterranean heated up. The Germans launched a number of bomber and fighter bomber sorties against Allied shipping. In addition, they attempted to neutralize the air forces building up on Malta and Pantelleria; such efforts required strong fighter support. Facing numerical superiority, German fighters had difficulty in fending off enemy fighters much less protecting bombers and fighter bombers. The air struggle soon turned into a battle for air superiority over Sicily and Sardinia.[97] By the start of Operation "Husky" on July 10, the Allies had achieved general air superiority over the island. German fighters had trouble protecting their own airfields from high and low level attack. Sorties against the invasion achieved little and suffered exorbitant losses. Within a week, much of the *Luftwaffe* had withdrawn to the mainland and used Sicilian bases only as forward operating areas.[98] Losses for the month were heavy. In July, the *Luftwaffe* lost 711 aircraft (10 percent of the German air force at the end of June) of which 246 were fighters (13.3 percent of all fighters) and 237 bombers (14.4 percent of all bombers). In August, Allied air forces, now operating from Sicily, pounded southern Italy and inflicted a further 321 losses.[99] At this point, reinforcements and resupply to units in Italy dried up, while a number of squadrons (with total complement of 210 aircraft) withdrew from Italy after a severe mauling over Sicily. Only one unit returned to the Mediterranean; the rest remained at home to help defend the *Reich*.[100]

Irrationality marked Hitler's conduct of operations during the Tunisian and Sicilian withdrawals. In both cases, he forbade retreat until the last possible moment. As a result, ground crews escaped from Tunisia by the desperate expedient of packing two to three individuals behind the pilot's seat in fighters.[101] In Sicily, ground personnel fled across the straits of Messina by ferry. Nevertheless, the *Führer*'s order that no withdrawal preparations occur forced retreating squadrons to abandon nearly all their maintenance equipment and most spare parts.[102]

These victories in the Mediterranean played a critical role in the winning of the war. They provided American ground forces with an invaluable lesson on the quality and competence of their opponent. Without that experience, bought at high but not exorbitant cost, it is hard to imagine a successful lodgment on the coast of France.[103] Also important for eventual victory was the attrition of *Luftwaffe* strength. Admittedly, the Germans themselves aided and abetted that process by placing their Mediterranean forces in strategically indefensible positions. They thus insured that the *Luftwaffe* would fight at a disadvantage. Much of this failure was directly attributable to Adolf Hitler. Nevertheless, Germany's Mediterranean command deserves its share of responsibility. Kesselring's optimistic reporting throughout the period misled both the *OKW* and Hitler.[104] By the summer of 1943, even the *Führer* seems to have had doubts. He refused to believe "smiling Albert's" assurance that Mussolini's overthrow did not indicate a shift in Italy's attitude towards the war. Nevertheless, Kesselring remained in a position of high responsibility to the end; the fact that Keitel was the only other of the field marshals created in July 1940 still around at the end of the war is ample testimony to Kesselring's integrity and realism. His messages to the hard-pressed air units in the spring campaign summarize his brand of leadership. In March, he threatened "court-martial proceedings owing to the negligence in the escort provided for valuable merchant vessels," while earlier in the campaign he suggested to his aircrews that Japanese fanaticism was an excellent example as to how they should fight.[105] Such attitudes hardly fit most definitions of leadership, but they certainly fit within Hitler's.

THE AIR WAR IN THE WEST: THE COMBINED BOMBER OFFENSIVE

Bomber Command's 1942 performance had at best been spotty. If it had achieved successes in attacking at Lübeck, Rostock, and Cologne, the vulnerability of those cities was due to their location and construction rather than to their overall importance to the war effort. Nevertheless, those successes provided Harris with the time and political clout to turn his command into an effective weapon, although the 1942 campaign bought that time at considerable cost. The command's strength seems to have varied between 400 and 500 aircraft in 1942;[106] losses for the year were 1,404 aircraft shot down and 2,724 damaged. Air raids during 1942 directed against Essen in which British bombers caused no significant damage cost Bomber Command no less than 201 bombers.[107] Of the new four-engine bombers now reaching frontline squadrons, the British wrote off 228 "Stirlings," 249 "Halifaxes," and 202 "Lancasters."[108]

Despite these depressing statistics, Bomber Command entered 1943 on an upswing. Squadrons were receiving four-engine bombers in quantity, and introduction of *Oboe,* a directional aid, *H2S,* a radar target locator, and target marking techniques in the pathfinder force gave British bombers the capability to place bombs in the area of the target under certain conditions. As Harris later noted, the command was "at long last . . . ready and equipped."[109] But he had little intention of integrating its operations with others except on his own terms, an attitude he had displayed since the war's beginning.[110] Harris, by now a firm advocate of "area" bombing, would wage his campaign in 1943 with ruthless determination.

Beginning in March 1943 and for the following three months, Harris' forces battered the Ruhr. As the official historians note, this attack "marked the beginning of a famous Battle in the course of which Bomber Command was to show itself capable of achieving not only an occasional victory, as had previously been the case, but a whole series of consistent and pulverizing blows among which the failures were much rarer than the successes."[111] Nevertheless, while British bombers inflicted serious damage on German cities, mission failures pointed up the limitations on operations. Two separate attacks against the Skoda works (beyond the range of navigational aids) achieved nothing. The first mistook a lunatic asylum for the works, while the second attack in May achieved an excellent bombing concentration in open fields 2 miles to the north.[112]

While the May 1943 raids on the dams in the Ruhr Valley paved the way for subsequent successful operational developments in 1944, Bomber Command overall in 1943 could only act as a bludgeon. It possessed the ability to hit large cities with devastating blows; but with the exception of Essen and a few other cities, German industry lay on the outskirts of major towns. In fact, it is probably an accurate estimate of the command's capabilities to say that it did more collateral damage to industrial targets in the 1943 "area" bombing than would have been the case had it waged a campaign directly aimed at destroying German industry. The dams raids point out a major factor in the failure of bombing to achieve decisive results. Luck eliminated most of the aircraft ordered to take out the critical Sorpe Dam; as a result, only the Möhne and less important Eder Dams received damage. To their surprise, the Germans were able to repair the Möhne Dam by the fall of 1943 with no interference against the vulnerable reconstruction work.[113] Allied air commanders still tended to overestimate raid damage and underestimate German recuperative powers.

Bomber Command pounded Germany in the spring of 1943 at a terrible cost to itself. Losses in the "Battle of the Ruhr" reached the point where Harris' forces flirted with defeat. In 43 major attacks, the RAF lost 872 bombers with 2,126 damaged. Despite these losses, frontline strength rose from 593 crews and aircraft in February to 787 in August—a reflection of the massive production and crew training programs.[114] These heavy losses prompted the British to introduce "Window" (the use of chaff) to confuse German radar. The British official historians have criticized the fact that "Window" was introduced at such a late date; whatever the merits of the case, one can still doubt whether "Window's" use at an earlier date would have equaled the stunning effect that its introduction had in late July 1943.[115]

"Window" enabled Bomber Command to deal the Germans a series of devastating blows at the end of July. The most terrible of these, code-named appropriately "Gomorrah," began on July 24 with an attack on Hamburg. "Window" blinded the entire defense system, and intercept operators of 'Y' Service listened to the rising frustration of German controllers and radar operators, attempting to make sense of radar screens that indicated thousands of bombers.[116] But the destruction of Hamburg came not from any one raid but from the cumulative effect of several raids conducted under perfect weather conditions.[117] On July 25, three American bomb groups attacked the city with the aim of plastering the Blohm and Voss U-boat yard and the Klockner aircraft engine factory. On the following day, another attack by four bomb groups added to the destruction within the city, but both American attacks had difficulty in finding their targets. In the first case, smoke from the still-smoldering fires obscured much of the city; in the second raid, the Germans laid a smoke screen as the bombers began their approach.

On the evening of July 27, the second great RAF attack occurred. This time destruction took place on a wholly different scale from anything in previous experience. Much of the fire-fighting force was on the city's western side to fight smoldering coke and coal fires; this factor, combined with the occurrence of warm, dry weather and the disruption of the water system by the previous bombing, created the right conditions for the start of a massive fire storm. Within 20 minutes

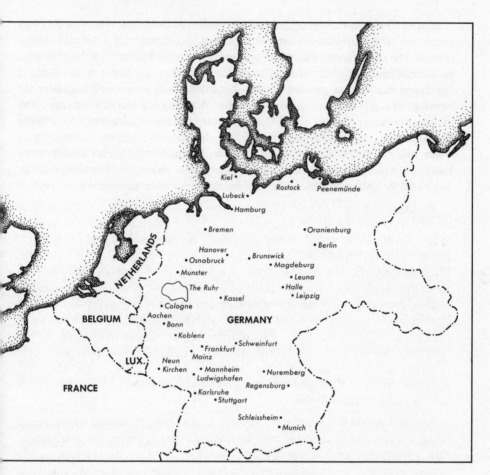

ermany: The Targets

of the raid's start, a growing area—probably centered around a timber yard in the city's center—exploded. Further bombing spread the fire storm to the northeast as the pheonomena of "creep back" occurred (late bombers dumping their loads short of the first bombings). By the next morning, fire had burned an enormous 4-square-mile hole in the city with considerable peripheral damage to areas adjacent to the great fire.[118] Between 30 and 40,000 people perished.[119] Yet, the ordeal was not over. On the evening of July 29, a third great raid occurred. Bomber Command again heavily bombed the city; material damage came close to that of the July 27 raid. Loss of life, however, was considerably less; no fire storm occurred, and the *Gauleiter*—the Nazi Party's official on the scene—had begun a substantial evacuation of the population.[120] One final raid followed early in August, but bad weather spared Hamburg further devastation.

Bomber Command achieved this terrible success at little cost. The missing rates in the four raids on Hamburg were 1.5 percent, 2.2 percent, 3.5 percent, and 4 percent. The rise in losses did reflect a surprisingly quick recovery by the defenses, but aircraft losses were fewer than those suffered during the Battle of the Ruhr.[121] The destruction was the greatest success that Bomber Command would achieve for the next year and a half. It represented "area" bombing in its most devastating and awesome aspects. Out of 122,000 apartments, the raids destroyed or damaged 40,000 and out of 450,000 houses, 250,000. Seventy-five percent of the electric works, 60 percent of the water system, and 90 percent of the gas system were knocked out of commission. The fall off in industrial production was considerable: 40 percent for large firms and 80 percent for medium and small concerns.[122]

The impact on German leadership was considerable. Goebbels could not believe the first reports of the second raid's effects.[123] Speer informed Hitler that six more attacks on this scale would "bring Germany's armaments production to a halt." Hitler, however, replied that Speer would straighten things out.[124] In retrospect, Hitler was correct, not because Speer was wrong in an estimate that six more Hamburgs would halt armament production, but because Hamburg was a unique success, depending on peculiar circumstances: a period of warm, dry weather; the blinding of German defenses; and the location of the city on the Elbe estuary which gave an excellent radar echo. The success, however, was misleading for the conditions rarely reoccurred. For Harris, Hamburg represented the final confirmation that his "area" bombing campaign was on the right track. He would persevere on this course and take his command and crews down a long, dark corridor in the Battle of Berlin.

Bomber Command's subsequent success in smashing the rocket experimental station at Peenemünde indicated both the dangers ahead as well as the possibility of other avenues. For the first time in a major attack on Germany, the command used a "master bomber," who remained over the target throughout the raid and controlled the bombing. A new and improved marker bomb also contributed to the success. Whatever the delay the raid caused the rocket programs, and there is some question on this point,[125] there is no question that the new methods contributed to an accurate, well-placed bomb pattern. However, the German defenses were already on the road to recovery; the raiding force of 597 aircraft lost 40 bombers (6.7 percent) with a further 32 damaged (for a loss and damage rate of 12.1 percent).[126] Thus, at the end of August, Bomber Command was fresh from its great triumphs of high summer, but additional problems and questions arose that required resolution before Harris could be proven correct in his belief that "strategic" bombing would be *the* decisive factor in the war.

While Bomber Command was posing an increasing threat to the security of Germany's cities at night, American daylight "strategic" bombing forces were also building up in England. By late spring 1943, considerably later than Allied planners had hoped, American bombers were ready to try out the theories of precision bombing attacks by self-defending formations in the skies over the *Reich*. The considerable delay in the launching of this offensive resulted from the siphoning off of American air resources to the Mediterranean in November 1942. The forces remaining in England represented a fraction of what American airmen felt they needed to accomplish their campaign. Nevertheless, as suggested earlier, Eaker had seen nothing in the first operations that suggested that daylight, precision, unescorted bombing was not a viable proposition. In fact, Eaker firmly believed that Eighth Air Force could eventually dispense with fighter protection and operate in the depths of the *Reich* in great unescorted formations. In October 1942, he wrote Spaatz that:

> The second phase, which we are about to enter, is the demonstration that day bombing can be economically executed using general fighter support . . . in getting through the German defensive fighter belt and to help our cripples home through this same belt; the third phase will include deeper penetrations into enemy territory, using long-range fighter accompaniment of the P–38 type in general support only and continuing the use of short-range fighters at critical points on a time schedule; the fourth phase will be a demonstration that bombardment in force—a minimum of 300 bombers—can effectively attack any German target and return without excessive or uneconomical losses. This later phase relies upon mass and the great firepower of the large bombardment formations.[127]

With limited numbers of aircraft and beset by maintenance problems, Eighth Air Force launched relatively weak raids onto the continent. Between November 1942 and mid-March 1943, only two attacks numbered more than 100 bombers.[128] Only in May 1943 did its force structure allow Eighth to launch 200 bombers on a regular basis. Nevertheless, in the early spring of 1943, American bombers began more dangerous forays into continental airspace. These first raids quickly indicated the price that German fighter forces could extract. On April 17, 115 aircraft attacked the Focke Wulf factory near Bremen; the Germans shot down 16 bombers (13.9 percent) and damaged 46 (40 percent).[129] The sortie loss rate in May dropped because the targets were less dangerous and because the number of available aircraft climbed faster than losses inflicted by the Germans. Finally, in late spring of 1943, Eaker received reinforcements that raised his dispatchable strength to 300-plus bombers—a level which he and other Eighth Air Force commanders believed would allow daylight, unescorted missions into the heart of the *Reich*. As Eaker had written Spaatz in October 1942, his senior officers were "absolutely convinced that 300 bombers can attack any target in Germany with less than 4 percent losses."[130]

As with the concept of deep penetration, unescorted raids, American target selection showed the imprint of prewar doctrine as well as ongoing war-time experience. In the former case, the size of deep penetration formations showed a great increase over prewar estimates as to what was necessary to insure the survival of bombers. In the latter case, the target priority list laid down by the Combined Bomber Offensive (CBO) Plan was a mixture of doctrine and reality. Because the discussions leading to selection of bombing priorities have received attention elsewhere,[131] an examination of the final list will serve our purposes. The priority list of targets in the final plan was:

(1) Intermediate Objectives:
    German fighter strength.

(2) Primary Objectives:
    German submarine yards and bases.
    The remainder of the German aircraft industry.
    Ball bearings.
    Oil (contingent upon attacks against Ploesti from Mediterranean).

(3) Secondary Objectives:
    Synthetic rubber and tires.
    Military motor transport vehicles.[132]

The placement of German fighter strength at the top of the list was a recognition that the *Luftwaffe*'s fighters represented a critical threat to the daylight bomber. The targeting of U-boat yards and bases reflected the military reality of the Battle of the Atlantic in which Allied sea and air forces were only now beginning to dominate the submarine. Further, the presence of petroleum, synthetic rubber, and ball bearing industries drew directly from prewar theories which had attempted to identify "bottleneck" industries, the destruction of which would cause the failure of the whole economic structure. The ball bearing industry itself was the classic weak link posited by American Air Corps Tactical School thinkers. This is not to say that the selection of ball bearings was entirely an American idea; there were important figures within the Air Ministry who argued persuasively in 1943 that Bomber Command also should attack the ball bearing factories.[133]

In June 1943, Eighth Air Force launched two major raids into German airspace beyond fighter escort range. The first, on June 13, attacked two targets: the main force, Bremen; and a smaller force, Kiel. Of the 228 aircraft dispatched, Eighth lost 26 (a loss rate of 11.4 percent). Nine days later, B–17's and B–24's struck the I.G. Farben synthetic rubber plant at Hüls. While the main and secondary forces lost 20 bombers (6.7 percent), the raid was one of the more successful in the war. It shut down the plant for a full month and reduced rubber stocks to a one-and-a-half month supply. As with the Möhne Dam, Allied bombers did not return and the Germans repaired the damage. In March 1944, Hüls reached peak production for the war.[134]

For most of July, weather conditions prevented Eighth Air Force from attacking Germany. In the month's last week, however, excellent flying conditions occurred and Eaker mounted his most ambitious operations. Eighth attacked Hamburg on July 25 and again on the 26th (along with Hanover). On July 28 and 30th, the American bombers hit Kassel and assorted targets and on the 29th attacked Kiel and Warnemünde. These operations did not come lightly. Ferocious German opposition cost Eighth Air Force 87 bombers.[135] Despite the losses, these operations signalled the arrival of American fighters as a factor in the air battle. On July 28, P–47's, equipped for the first time with drop tanks, caught German fighters attacking B–17 stragglers; on the 30th, escort fighters again caught the Germans and inflicted heavy losses. While these first drop tanks only extended P–47 range by 30-plus miles, the presence of American fighters deeper on the continent portended serious implications for German defenses.[136]

Extensive operations at the end of July exhausted and attrited Eighth's forces so that available strength fell below 300; not until August 12 did the Americans return to skies over the *Reich*. The attack on the Ruhr indicated no weakening of German opposition; 25 bombers out of 330 dispatched fell (a 7.5 percent loss rate).[137] On August 17, Eaker launched his bombers against Schweinfurt and Regensburg in one of the most famous and costly raids of the war. The latter attacks aimed at destroying the Messerschmitt complex—an obvious effort to strike at the source of *Luftwaffe* fighter strength. Within Schweinfurt, three major concerns produced 45 percent of the ball bearings used by German industry (52.5 percent in terms of net

Allied Fighter Range: The Reach into the Reich

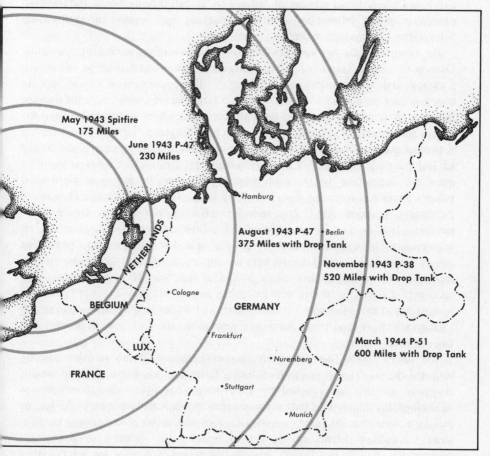

May 1943 Spitfire
175 Miles

June 1943 P–47
230 Miles

• Hamburg

August 1943 P-47
375 Miles with Drop Tank

• Berlin

November 1943 P-38
520 Miles with Drop Tank

NETHERLANDS

• Cologne

BELGIUM

GERMANY

• Frankfurt

LUX.

March 1944 P-51
600 Miles with Drop Tank

• Nuremberg

FRANCE

• Stuttgart

• Munich

worth).[138] The Schweinfurt-Regensburg attack was the most ambitious and deepest penetration by Eighth Air Force thus far in the war. Its results shattered the theory that the German defensive system lacked depth.

Both formations suffered heavy losses. The Regensburg force lost 24 bombers out of 146 dispatched (16.4 percent) and only the fact that they flew on to North Africa, thereby disconcerting German defenses, prevented heavier losses.[139] In fact, the number of aircraft written off was higher than 24, for the Regensburg forces left approximately 20 B-17's in North Africa when they returned to Europe.[140] The second force, attacking Schweinfurt, received no benefit from the first attack because bad weather had delayed its departure. As a result, German fighters savaged it as thoroughly as they had the Regensburg force. Out of 230 bombers, the Schweinfurt groups lost 36 (15.7 percent). The loss of 60 bombers in one day represented the loss of 10.3 percent of the aircraft in Eighth's operational units and 17.5 percent of its crew strength.[141] By themselves these percentages explain why Eighth did not go back to Schweinfurt until the following October. While the attacking force inflicted substantial damage on the ball bearing works, the bombing concentration and the number of aircraft attacking were insufficient to eliminate Schweinfurt as a production center.

The conduct of the Schweinfurt/Regensburg attack raises interesting questions. The size of the attacking force and dual targets reflect an overestimation of both the accuracy and effectiveness of bombing.[142] Thus, there was a tendency to underestimate the aircraft needed to destroy a target and to overestimate the damage inflicted. A second point has to do with the ineffectual cooperation between the British and American strategic bombing forces in England. Despite the friendship between Eaker and Harris, and Eighth Air Force's earlier cooperation in the assault on Hamburg on July 25 and 26th, Bomber Command headquarters showed no interest in supporting the precision bombing offensive by hitting at night what Eaker's forces had hit in the day. It is worth noting that the Air Staff's Director of Bombing Operations, Air Commander S.O. Bufton, was strongly urging in the summer of 1943 that Bomber Command follow up any American attack on Schweinfurt. He suggested that RAF crews be told that history might "prove that tonight's operation, in conjunction with the day attack which is taking place at this moment, will be one of the major battles of this war. If both operations are successful, German resistance may be broken and the war ended sooner than could be possible in any other way."[143] But Harris had set his face against bombing any "panacea" target, and Eight Air Force went down the dark road to Schweinfurt twice in 1943—alone.

The heavy losses that American bombers suffered in the summer directly reflected the insufficient range of escorting fighters. This was a result of Anglo-American attitudes that regarded the use of long-range fighter aircraft not only as technologically impossible but in some cases as not really necessary. As late as mid-June, even after the heavy losses on the Kiel raid, Eaker placed range extension tanks for fighters fourth on his list of priorities. In fairness to Eaker, his conversations with Robert Lovett, Assistant Secretary of War for Air, led the latter to give the long-range fighter escort program strong support when he returned to Washington.[144] Such lassitude and lack of direction marked the drop tank engineering program in the United States that VIII Fighter Command and V Fighter Command, operating in New Guinea, had developed rough and workable tanks before the engineers at Wright-Patterson.[145] The results for the bombers of Eighth Air Force show clearly in Tables XXXIII[146] and XXXIV.[147] As we shall see in the next section, the loss rate for *Luftwaffe* units in the west was equally appalling. The question was who could best stand up to the attrition. In the high summer of 1943, the answer was still in doubt.

While Eighth Air Force mounted increasingly powerful raids, American air forces in the Mediterranean entered the struggle over Europe. On August 1, Ninth Air Force launched five B–24 groups, 177 bombers, against Rumanian oil fields and refineries near Ploesti. Unfortunately, due to errors, the attack suffered from bad timing and alerted the defenses. While damage was considerable, bomber losses were so heavy, 41 due to enemy action (23.2 percent) and 54 overall (30.5 percent), that American air commanders could not intensify the damage with further raids.[148] Thus, the Germans repaired critical areas and utilized capacity not in use. On August 13, these five groups, diminished in strength, struck the Wiener Neustadt aircraft assembly plant in Austria. Catching the defenses by surprise, they inflicted serious damage with the loss of only two aircraft.[149] The Germans were on notice that American aircraft based in the Mediterranean could strike deep onto the continent.[150] The situation would become increasingly serious for the *Reich* as Allied armies invaded the Italian mainland and captured airfields in southern Italy.

THE DEFENSE OF THE *REICH*

The period with which this chapter deals was a time when quite literally the roof over the *Reich* caved in. How Germany's defenses and its leaders responded determined the fate of the *Reich*'s cities and the length of the war. While military events and production decisions taken in the 1940–41 time frame had sealed Nazi Germany's fate, strategic decisions taken in 1943 determined how events would unfold. With the exception of the Battle of Britain, the western air war had remained a peripheral theater, arousing the interest of Hitler and the *Luftwaffe* staff only after a particularly egregious British success such as the May 1942 Cologne raid. However, the threat in the west remained no more than that for the remainder of 1942. There were some who recognized the danger. However, in the fall of 1942, the Germans had accepted battle on the periphery, and as a result the *Luftwaffe* suffered enormous losses on the Mediterranean and Russian fronts. But in the summer of 1943, and for the first time since 1940, aircraft losses in the west reached a sizeable proportion of total losses.

Before examining the conduct of the *Reich*'s air defense, the *Luftwaffe*'s organizational structure in the west deserves attention. That structure did not reflect the strategic needs of 1943 but the bureaucratic growth of the *Luftwaffe* after the French collapse and the invasion of Russia. In 1941, *Luftflotte* 3 remained behind in

Table XXXIII   Aircraft Written Off: Eighth Air Force 1943 (Heavy Bombers)

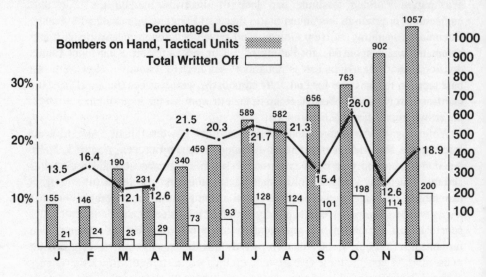

Table XXXIV   Crew Losses Eighth Air Force 1943 (Heavy Bombers)

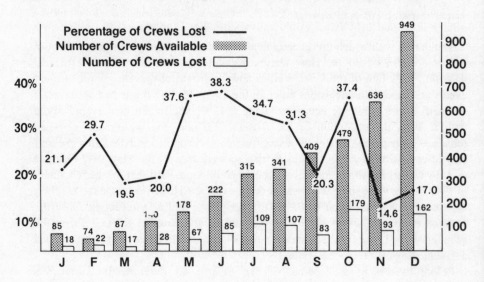

the west to handle the British and to defend the skies over occupied France; it also held responsibility for Belgium and Holland. Meanwhile, in 1941, the Germans established a catch-all organization in northern Germany, whose commander received the lengthy and imposing title *"Luftwaffenbefehlshaber Mitte."*[151] This command was responsible for defending Berlin and controlled the night fighter division and flak divisions throughout northern Germany. However, for bureaucratic reasons the general staff turned two air districts *(Luftgau)* in south Germany over to Field Marshal Hugo Sperrle, Commander of *Luftflotte* 3, in order not to disturb his vanity.[152] From the first, creation of two authorities responsible for air defense in the west proved mistaken. As early as the fall of 1941, Mölders argued for a unified fighter command to defend western Europe.[153] In 1943, Milch urged Göring to unify under one commander all the *Luftwaffe*'s air defense assets, a system which he suggested would possess similarity to the British Fighter Command.[154] Göring, however, refused. As a result, until the collapse in France in August 1944 effectively eliminated *Luftflotte* 3, the *Reich*'s air defense remained split between two competing organizations. While this splitting of responsibility presented serious problems for day fighter operations, it really exacerbated the difficulties of coordinating operations of scarce night fighter forces between two separate commands, adding enormously to the burden of an effective night defense.

While the German high command had ignored Bomber Command's depredations in 1942, it could not do so in 1943. The attacks on the Ruhr in March and April pointed out that Germany faced an extraordinary threat to her cities. Hitler was furious at the *Luftwaffe*'s failure to protect the Ruhr, and Göring's prestige was nearly exhausted, as the *Führer* made clear to Goebbels.[155] The response of many German leaders to the March attacks was that Germany must launch reprisal raids at such a level that the British would call off Bomber Command. Even Milch, who throughout 1943 was the most clear headed on the need for an effective air defense, called in March for reprisal raids. As he told his staff, ''Our entire armaments effort . . . is dependent on whether we can clear our own skies by carrying out the appropriate attacks on the British home base—either on their airfields or on their industry or on their civilians and cities.''[156] Hitler's immediate response to the British attacks was to demand that the *Luftwaffe* drastically strengthen the flak forces despite objections from his air force adjutant.[157] That debate continued throughout the year.

Bomber Command's ability to swamp the night fighter defenses of the tightly controlled Kammhuber line led several *Luftwaffe* officers to suggest radical changes. In late spring, Major Hajo Herrmann, a former bomber pilot, pushed a scheme to concentrate a force of day fighters directly over a target and to use searchlights as well as light reflecting from the bombing to attack the bomber stream. Such a tactic, he suggested, would allow night defenses to throw a concentration of force at the bomber stream at the point where it was most vulnerable to visual interception.[158] In a late June report on fighter defenses in the west, Milch supported Herrmann and suggested that the night fighter corps receive responsibility for the night defense over France.[159] Others argued for a more basic

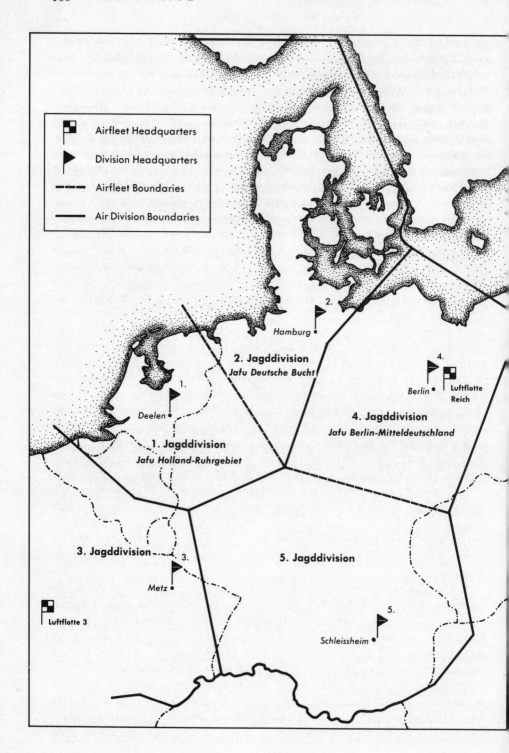

restructuring of the defenses. Shortly before Hamburg, Göring's staff was requesting better radar sets to support a pursuit force that would not be tied directly to GCI sites but would search out and follow the bomber stream.[160]

The use of "Window" over Hamburg forced the Germans to restructure the defense system far more quickly than they would have otherwise. Herrmann already had begun to gather and to train his force before the raids; the collapse of the night defense system caused the *Luftwaffe* to commit his small unit on the night of the fire storm. A number of night fighters also freelanced over the burning city. Unfortunately for the Germans, these forces were not numerous enough to inflict substantial damage on the bomber force, although raid losses did increase from 1.5 percent to 2.2 percent. However, many German night fighters in their boxes to the north and to the south of the inferno were not allowed to freelance despite the fact that they could see bombers.[161]

Substantial reforms were soon in motion. Herrmann's force rapidly increased in size. As early as July 27, a staff paper urged creation of a large night fighter force in Holland that controllers would vector into the bomber stream. It would then fly with the bombers, shooting down British aircraft until it ran out of ammunition or fuel.[162] This tactic, soon known by the code name "Tame Sow," eventually became the keystone of the *Reich*'s defense system. The possibilities of the new system showed clearly in the Peenemünde raid of August 17. Because German controllers fell for an RAF spoof and reported that Berlin was the main target, they vectored the defending forces to the capital. Not until the last minutes of the raid did fighters arrive over the target. Nevertheless, they shot down 24 bombers over Peenemünde and a further 16 elsewhere along the raid's path.[163]

Along with the British night offensive, the Germans now faced an American daylight offensive. Because of a desperate shortage of day fighters, the *Luftwaffe* threw its night fighter force into the battles against Eighth Air Force. The use of the night fighters to meet the American threat typified the short-sighted, short-range calculation of much of the *Luftwaffe*'s effort in the latter period of the war. Night fighter aircraft represented a sizeable investment in terms of equipment, technology, training, and the specialized skills needed by the crews. The commitment of the night force to daylight operations brought with it corresponding high losses. As early as April, an "Ultra" intercept indicated a willingness to use night fighters during daytime when Göring forbade the use of night pilots with more than 20 victories on day operations.[164] Anglo-American attacks on August 17 and 18th caused the loss of 30 night fighters with 35 more damaged. Twenty-one were lost in daylight operations alone, and a senior staff officer remarked that the Bf 110 should not be used in daytime when it might come into contact with British or American fighters—a remark that might have had some uniqueness in the summer of 1940 but seems somewhat out of place in 1943.[165]

Hamburg brought to the fore the question of Germany's response. On July 30, Milch warned his staff in the Air Ministry that Germany could only look forward to an intensification of the enemy's air offensive. "What has happened in Hamburg had never before happened [in air war]." If Germany could not master the threat, she would face a desperate situation. Milch further announced that Hitler had put top priority on air defense and on production of day and night fighters as well as the flak. Fighter productions was to rise to 2,000 aircraft per month by the summer of 1944, and the eastern front would have to make-do until the *Luftwaffe* mastered the air threat.[166] Milch had earlier in the war not found his desire for increased fighter production to the liking of everyone on the Air Staff. He now discovered a less-than-unanimous agreement with his emphasis on the defense of the *Reich*. One colonel suggested that a diversion of Bf 110's from the front to night fighters was "unthinkable." Milch replied that the front would have to make-do—the threat was over Germany.[167]

Milch and other advocates of air defense faced more substantial opposition to their policies from Hitler's natural inclinations. As suggested above, the *Führer* had become increasingly upset in the spring of 1943 over the scale and success of RAF raids. He warned his military aides shortly after the first Hamburg attack: "Terror can only be broken with terror." Attacks on German airfields made no impression on him, he commented, but the smashing of the *Reich*'s cities was another matter. It was the same thing with the enemy. "The German people demanded reprisals."[168] Hitler's attitudes had a disastrous impact on air strategy after August 1943, but his line of argument was already clear. Moreover, efforts to build up the night fighter force were further complicated by Göring's sheer ignorance. It is worth noting that by late August, the *Reichsmarschall* was doubting whether night fighters were worth the considerable expenditures in man-hours and materials.[169] Considering that his staff was wasting them in daylight operations, one can only wonder at the muddle at the top.

As for daylight operations, the Allies—for the first time—placed significant pressure on the *Luftwaffe*. The fighter sweeps of Fighter Command, accompanied by American fighters in large numbers, had combined with Eighth Air Force's bomber operations to make Western Europe the critical theater of air operations by the late summer of 1943. Neither Göring nor many of his more sober commanders had expected this development. In January 1943, the *Reichsmarschall* suggested increases in the day fighter forces but not because of worries over Allied aircraft production, rather the emphasis was on fighters for the fighter bomber mission.[170] Even Galland, who was pushing for a major increase in the fighter force, did not appear to recognize the threat in the west. In January, he predicted that the main weight of the air war would lie in the Mediterranean throughout the year.[171] Thus, the heavy commitment of fighter forces to the defense of Tunisia, Sicily, and Italy received support from the man who later in the year became one of the strongest advocates of beefing up the *Reich*'s defenses. Why Galland held such a position is clear from a remark he made in February that his fighters had solved the problem of fighting four-engine bombers (by day).[172] What the *Luftwaffe* had not yet faced was the problem of dealing with hundreds of bombers that American industry would throw at the *Reich* in the summer of 1943 as well as the thousands in 1944.

In early 1943, the *Luftwaffe* with major commitments in the Mediterranean and on the eastern front left the day defense of the west on the same basis on which it had rested in previous years. Some 250 to 300 fighters, scattered from Holland to Brittany, scrambled in small formations to meet the American thrusts.[173] The resulting lack of fighter concentration made it difficult to dent the "Fortress" formations and put the Germans at considerable disadvantage in fending off Allied fighters. By June, the western fighter defenses were breaking down as *Luftflotte* 3 reported that its fighters were suffering heavy losses in intercepting "Fortress" formations accompanied by numerous fighters.[174] In mid-June, Milch reported after a trip to the west that morale among the fighter pilots was excellent, but the number of available aircraft was "much too weak." He urged that the *Luftwaffe* quadruple fighter forces in the west and that as a minimum a full month's production of Bf 109's and Fw 190's go to units in western Europe.[175]

Fighter losses in the west showed an alarming rise as early as March, and in that month the *Luftwaffe* began to transfer experienced pilots from the east to compensate for its losses in the west. The real pressure arrived in late spring with the first penetrations into German airspace.[176] The rise in fighter losses showed a direct correlation with Eighth Air Force operations. By June, it was clear that the American bombers represented a very different threat to Germany than did Bomber Command. The attack on Hüls suggested that the American bombers were going after specific segments of the German economy. By the end of the month, Jeschonnek recommended that the *Luftwaffe* request an updated list from Speer as to the critical points in the economy needing additional air defense protection.[177]

Eighth Air Force's operations in July and August created a crisis. For July, *Luftflotte* 3 noted that the size and defensive power of bomber formations penetrating into its airspace had reached a level where the only possibility of attack required a timely, massed concentration of German fighter forces.[178] Arguments over exactly how many aircraft B–17 and B–24 gunners shot down in defending themselves have obscured what really occurred in these air battles. First, it is clear bomber crews claimed many more aircraft than in fact they shot down, but the cumulative effect of German fighter losses in these battles was impressive. In July, the *Luftwaffe* lost 335 single-engine fighters in the west.[179] Admittedly, a percentage of these losses was not directly attributable to combat, but the pressure of stepped-up air operations and losses forced the *Luftwaffe* to rely increasingly on partially trained pilots. Thus, noncombat losses reflected the pressures of combat attrition. July's losses in the west represented 18.1 percent of all single-engine fighter strength on July 1, reflecting not only the impact of the heavy daytime raids but also the fact that drop tanks on the P–47's had extended escort range. With new range capability, American fighters could catch German pilots deeper within the *Reich*'s airspace. This escalation in the level of fighting over German airspace had an effect on all theaters. By the end of July, the *Luftwaffe* had put limitations on the employment of fighter aircraft on tasks other than defense of the *Reich*, while it pulled Bf 110 squadrons out of Brittany and the Battle of the Atlantic to return to Germany.[180]

July's efforts placed a great strain on Eighth's capabilities, and in August the aircraft dispatched to targets in Germany showed a significant drop.[181] Losses, depressingly for the crews involved, showed no such decline. The Schweinfurt/Regensburg disaster added measurably to the month's losses, and for the third straight month crew losses were in excess of 30 percent (see Table XXXIV). The German situation was not much better. August 17 cost the Germans no less than 24 single-engine fighters shot down, 12 Bf 110's destroyed, plus an additional 10 single-engine fighters and 2 Bf 110's written off because of battle damage. Thus, the Germans lost no less than 48 fighters destroyed with a further 25 damaged. The German success over Schweinfurt had not come cheaply nor did fighter operations over the course of the month. By the end of August, the Germans had lost 248 single-engine fighters (16.2 percent of their then available total single-engine fighter force) along with 86 twin-engine fighters (11.6 percent of the twin-engine and night fighter force) in air battles in the west.[182] In fact, the whole emphasis in the European air war had shifted radically away from a contest on the periphery to a massive battle of attrition over the *Reich*. Concurrently, Allied fighter forces were feeling their way deeper into the *Reich* and consequently restricting the area over which German fighters could intercept the bombers. Thus, at the end of August, the daylight air war in the west was peaking with each side inflicting serious damage on the other. It still remained an open question as to which air force could last the course.

LOSSES, PRODUCTION, AND STRATEGY

On August 18, 1943, the *Luftwaffe*'s Chief of Staff, Jeschonnek, placed a gun to his temple and blew his brains out. His suicide was the direct result of the two massive blows Allied bombers had launched the previous day and evening (Schweinfurt/Regensburg and Peenemünde). While neither raid represented a decisive blow, together they clearly indicated the bankruptcy of Germany's air strategy. If there were others who deserved a significant share of the blame, and Hitler as well as Göring spring readily to mind, then Jeschonnek's role typified the part that so many of the officer corps had played in Germany's fate. Like too many of his brother officers, Jeschonnek had ignored the industrial, logistical, and technical basis on which modern war between industrialized states since the American Civil War has been fought. That curious blindness which led him in early 1942 to wonder what the *Luftwaffe* would do with 360 fighters had now led his air force and nation into a hopeless situation. The battles on the periphery had quite literally stripped the *Luftwaffe* of whatever chance it had to build up a reserve, and Jeschonnek had accepted those commitments with scarcely a murmur.

In addition, it is worth taking a closer look at the general picture of German losses; they reveal that in this period the *Luftwaffe* had suffered a terrible rate of attrition throughout the force structure. From January through June 1943, the average monthly attrition rate for all aircraft was 13.6 percent. For combat aircraft, the statistics were even more depressing: the bomber attrition rate was 16 percent per month and for fighters it was 19.9 percent.[183] Crew losses were no less significant and more dangerous. While one can replace aircraft, crew replacements and skill level became increasingly difficult to maintain. This was the fourth straight year in which heavy attrition had taken place. It is, therefore, remarkable that the Germans maintained the level of tenacity and competence that they showed throughout the year. While pilot losses for most aircraft types are difficult to determine because crew loss reports included all flying personnel, the situation with regards to single-engine aircraft indicates what was happening to the force structure. For the first three months of 1943, fighter pilot losses ran at a fairly constant rate of between 6 percent and 9 percent per month. However, as a result of heavy fighting in Tunisia, pilot losses climbed to over 12 percent in May and by July were 16 percent. Thus, in the first half of the year, fighter pilot losses equalled 67 percent of the crews present at the beginning of the year.[184] For overall loss trends, see Tables XXXV,[185] XXXVI,[186] XXXVII,[187] and XXXVIII.[188]

This attrition was only a foretaste of what happened in July and August. In those two months, the *Luftwaffe* fought three great air battles and on each one of the three fronts the Germans lost more than 1,000 aircraft.[189] In combat units, the attrition rate reached a level that no military force could long sustain. Fighter losses were 31.2 percent for July and 36 percent for August, while bomber losses were 27.3 percent in July and 32 percent in August.[190] As with the January through June period, only fighter pilot losses are readily attainable. They are clear enough: In July, the Germans lost 16 percent of single-engine fighter pilots available on July 1; in August, they lost 15.6 percent.[191] The impact of the pressure exerted by three different fronts forced the Germans to shut the air war down somewhere. Given the threat posed by the American bombers, there was no other alternative but to defend the *Reich*. Thus, the air war in the east and in the Mediterranean, with one final gasp in September to meet the invasion of Italy, became subsidiary theaters for the *Luftwaffe*. Allied air forces dominated the skies over and behind these two fronts, and the German soldier would see little of his air force for the remainder of the war.

The disastrous rate of attrition was a reflection both of combat losses and numerous aircraft losses through noncombat causes. In fact, the *Luftwaffe* seems to have almost been in a race with its opponents to see who could destroy the most German aircraft. After a fairly respectable showing in 1940, from 1941 through 1944 the *Luftwaffe* lost between 40 percent and 45 percent of its total losses through noncombat causes.[192] The surprising element in such an accident rate is the fact that until the spring of 1944, few in the general staff seem to have been particularly worried about the implication of such a level of noncombat losses. At that point, however, a number of authorities awoke and began to examine the problem in detail.[193] The German safety record, however, deserves no smugness from an American audience. The Army Air Forces managed in 1943 to have no less than 20,389 major accidents in the continental United States with 2,264 pilots and 3,339 other aircrew members killed. The record for 1944 was not much better with 16,128 major accidents (1,936 pilots and 3,037 other aircrew killed).[194] The ability of crews transitioning into B–26's to destroy their aircraft and themselves resulted in a couplet still current among flying crews at MacDill AFB, Florida: "One a day in Tampa Bay."[195]

Table XXXV   German Aircraft Losses 1943 (All Types)

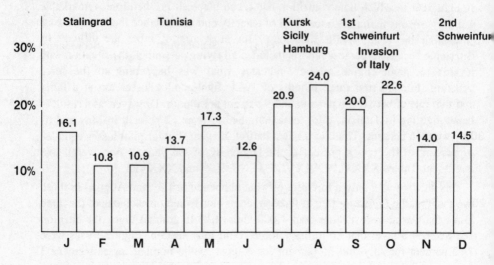

Table XXXVI   German Bomber Losses 1943

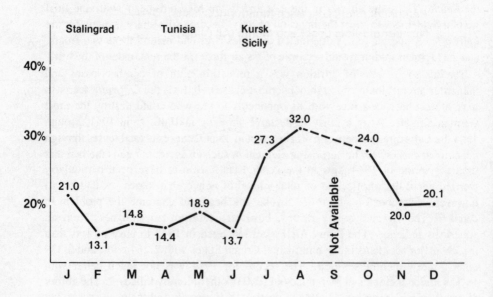

Table XXXVII   German Fighter Losses 1943

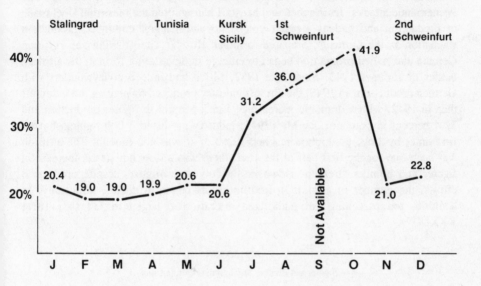

Table XXXVIII   Fighter Pilot Loss January-August 1943

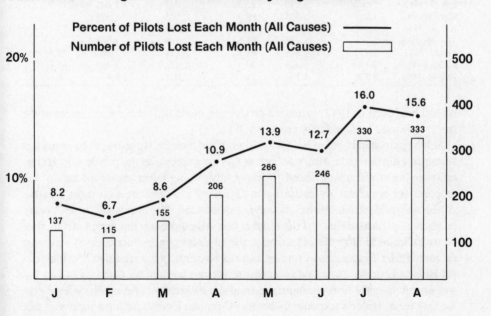

The defeat in the air war represented by the above figures is perhaps a fairer evaluation of Jeschonnek's failure than the Schweinfurt/Regensburg and Peenemünde attacks. Jeschonnek and his staff had ignored the mess that Udet made of production and had as a result voiced no alarm about continued production stagnation as the *Luftwaffe* prepared to attack Russia. The growing gap between German and Allied production began to emerge in devastating form in the attrition battles of summer 1943. Since late 1942, Milch had indeed done wonders with German production. In 1943, the aircraft industry produced 64 percent more aircraft than in 1942, with a dramatic increase of 125.2 percent in fighter production and 31.4 percent in bombers. By May 1943, industry produced 1,000 fighters for the first time; by July, production reached 1,263.[196] It was not enough. The attrition was such that for the first half of the year, there was a slow but steady increase in fighter and bomber strength. However, in July and August, despite production efforts, the number of aircraft in frontline units began to decline noticeably. In addition, the percentage of authorized aircraft also began to fall (see Table XXXIX[197]).

TABLE XXXIX

Fighter and Bomber Strength in Frontline Units

	Fighters Authorized	Present	Percentage	Bombers Authorized	Present	Percentage
Feb 28, 1943	1,660	1,336	80.5	2,025	1,443	71.3
Mar 31, 1943	1,712	1,535	89.7	2,025	1,522	75.2
Apr 30, 1943	1,848	1,582	85.6	2,034	1,574	77.4
May 31, 1943	2,016	1,786	88.6	2,109	1,588	75.3
Jun 30, 1943	2,172	1,849	85.1	2,111	1,663	78.8
Jul 31, 1943	2,172	1,528	70.3	2,122	1,419	66.9
Aug 31, 1943	2,228	1,581	71	2,025	1,134	56

As had happened in 1942, increased production made little difference; losses at the front swallowed what industry produced.

Milch again stands out in his recognition of the danger. He seems to have made a sustained effort to make Hitler as well as Göring understand the problem.[198] Hitler, however, remained unconvinced. In early July, Kammhuber presented him with a proposal for a radical restructuring of Germany's air defenses to meet massive Allied air production. Hitler, however, demanded the origin of these "crazy numbers" and added that "if the numbers on Allied production were correct, then he would have to stop the offensive in the east and concentrate everything on air defense." The figures, however, he assured Kammhuber were false.[199] Milch did get Hitler's approval for an infusion of aircraft into western air defenses in July but was unable to get a firm commitment from the *Führer* to build up air defenses for the long term. Hitler's response to Bomber Command's devastating attacks was that the only way to get the British to cease the destruction of Germany's cities was to pay them back in kind. Thus, any suggestion that industry increase fighter production at the expense of bombers was doomed to failure. Interestingly, there was a recognition for a time on the part of some bomber commanders that their air units might find better employment in defending the *Reich* than in raiding Britain.[200]

Hitler's emphasis on retaliation rather than air superiority led the Germans into another serious error. The army and air forces were both about to produce their own retaliation weapons: the army with the A-4 (later called the V-2) and the *Luftwaffe* with the V-1. The V-2 was a triumph of German engineering but certainly was not a monument to good sense. As a weapon, it represented extremely complex technology, it was expensive, it used scarce raw materials, and its production overloaded the instrument and electrical components industry. However, the V-1, a simpler piece of technology, was inexpensive and did not place a serious strain on German industrial production. In addition, because of its vulnerable launch and flight characteristics, it provided a much greater distraction to British defenders.[201] The last point deserves further elaboration: There was no defense against the V-2. However, the V-1 with its requirement for both a launching ramp and its vulnerable flight path kept a significant portion of Allied air forces busy in 1944 bombing the European continent and chasing V-1's through the skies over Great Britain.

Unfortunately for Germany's cities, the critical production choices that German air strategy faced in the summer and fall of 1943 were made by individuals who did not possess the background to make intelligent decisions. Hitler, while he knew much about army weaponry and the conduct of ground operations, did not understand the technology or conduct of the air war. The fact that he consistently relied on Göring did nothing to enhance his knowledge, for the *Reichsmarschall's* technical expertise was severely lacking. Having once admitted that he did not know how to turn on his radio, he exhibited his scientific knowledge for his staff in discussing German radar sets: ''I have frequently taken a look inside such sets. It does not look all that imposing—just some wires and a few other bits and pieces—and the whole apparatus is remarkably primitive even then. . . .''[202] In another case in February 1943 after Milch urged the inclusion of more women in the production process, Göring suggested that perhaps the best method to include women in the war effort would be to allow them to do the work at home where they would also be able to watch their children. A somewhat flabergasted Milch could only reply that German industry was more advanced than that.[203] The failure to understand modern production and technical problems resulted in a failure to include fully scientists and technicians in the war effort. The services often drafted highly trained and skilled individuals and used them in positions in which their gifts and expertise were minimized.[204] Finally, there was often a failure of designers to talk to production people. The most remarkable example of this was the interaction between the developers of the A-4 rocket and those who were attempting to get it into production.[205] The lack of cooperation between these two groups may, in fact, have been more damaging to the rocket's progress than the raid on Peenemünde.

As this study has suggested at several points, one of the critical elements in modern warfare is the productive capacity of industry and its use. By the summer of 1943, German strategy was already severely hampered by the choices and decisions made in the 1940–41 period that had failed to mobilize the European economy for a great struggle. Now in the summer of 1943, German leaders faced the choice of either radically restructuring the aircraft industry for a massive output of day and night fighters at the expense of other types or facing defeat in the air over the *Reich*. Milch himself had suggested a target of 5,000 fighters per month to Hitler in March.[206] But the top leadership was unwilling to address a military threat with a military response. In fact, the real triumph and impact of Bomber Command's "area" bombing campaign in 1943 was the fundamental distortion it caused in German armaments programs. The anger and desire for a retaliation strategy was particularly clear in the case of Hitler, but even as intelligent and rational an individual as Speer could not resist the attraction of paying the British back in kind. At the end of May 1943, the Armaments Minister suggested to a most enthusiastic and appreciative audience in the Ruhr that while "German mills of retribution may often seem to grind too slowly, they do grind very fine. . . ." Speer had just seen a successful firing of an A–4, and his continued support for the rocket program throughout 1943 and 1944 caused a major diversion of German production capacity and raw materials that would have been far better spent in defending German airspace.[207]

While in a larger sense, the moral questions involved in the "strategic" bombing offensives can never be satisfactorily answered, the question of the military utility of the campaigns is, however, easier to address. By late summer 1943, British "area" bombing attacks and the American precision bombing campaign were having a major impact on the war. In the first case, the real contribution of Bomber Command was indirect, even though it caused more direct damage to the German nation. The problem was the fact that so much of German industry lay on the fringe areas of the cities that the command was blasting into rubble. This distortion that the campaign caused in the German war effort, however, was enormous. Not only did it result in such highly unproductive efforts as the A–4 program but it pushed the Germans into continuing production of bombers for retaliatory raids far too long. Moreover, the A–4 program kept the Germans from ever properly investigating a promising antiaircraft rocket system.[208] Also important was the fact that the growing number of British raids caused a substantial distortion in the manufacturing process for artillery and ammunition. By summer 1943, no less than 89 flak batteries defended Berlin.[209] The growth from 1940 in the number of flak batteries was sizeable. From a level of 791 heavy batteries (88's, 105's, and 128's) in 1940, to 967 in 1941, to 1,148 in 1942, and to 2,132 in 1943, German flak forces represented an enormous investment in equipment and manpower.[210] All of these batteries expended prodigious amounts of ammunition 24 hours a day. Unfortunately for the Germans, the results were more visually spectacular than damaging. The 88mm flak 36 weapon seems to have required an average expenditure of 16,000-plus shells to bring down one aircraft flying at high altitude, and that was the weapon with which most flak batteries were equipped.[211]

As for the Allied effort, American daylight precision bombing had not yet achieved the spectacular results that Bomber Command had thus far caused. In fact, the American campaign had only recently begun and was in serious trouble, considering American losses in deep penetration raids. Nevertheless, Eighth's forces represented a more immediate threat to German armament production as well as a longer range danger to the *Luftwaffe* as an effective military force. In the first case, as the Germans recognized early on, the Americans were going after critical elements within their economic structure. The attack on the rubber factory at Hüls had underscored this intent. Speer found the August attack on Schweinfurt even more dangerous. As he told RAF investigators after the war, a concentrated offensive on the ball bearings industry would have had the following results:

> Armaments production would have been crucially weakened after two months, and after four months would have been brought completely to a standstill. This, to be sure, would have meant:
>
> One: All our ball bearing factories (in Schweinfurt, Steyr, Erkner, Cannstatt, and in France and Italy) had been attacked simultaneously.
>
> Two: These attacks had been repeated three or four times, every two weeks, no matter what the pictures of the target area showed.
>
> Three: Any attempt at rebuilding these factories had been thwarted by further attacks, spaced at two-month intervals.[212]

The difficulty was that no matter what the prospects, Eighth did not have sufficient strength to carry out such an offensive even had it done nothing except bomb ball bearing factories. One Schweinfurt every two months came close to destroying it as an effective force. Another Schweinfurt in this period might have ended Eighth's entire daylight offensive. Thus, the August raid warned the Germans to look for alternative sources of supply; the second attack in October redoubled their efforts at dispersal and substitution. The February 1944 bombing by the RAF did more damage than the American raids but came well after Speer's precautionary measures had taken effect.

The assault on the German aircraft industry was probably in retrospect more damaging to the war effort. The July-August attacks on factories producing aircraft resulted in a fall off in production of approximately 200 fighters. By November, fighter production was 300 under peak production in July.[213] Also important was the attrition that Eighth's attacks were already imposing on the defending fighter forces. If for the short run it was questionable as to who was taking the more severe beating, there was no question that in the long run Eighth Air Force had better prospects. And month by month, American fighters were extending their range to the east.

CONCLUSION

The period between November 1942 and August 1943 was the last opportunity that the *Luftwaffe* had in the war to build up a reserve so that it could maintain air superiority at least over the *Reich*. The unwillingness of Germany's leaders, however, to trade space for time forced the *Luftwaffe* into a battle of attrition on the periphery. The results of those battles bled the German air force white. At the very moment when the air battles in the Mediterranean and in the east peaked, a terrible new danger appeared in the west. While the German war economy could bear the damage that Bomber Command meted out to German cities (except perhaps in psychological terms), the bomber thrusts of Eighth Air Force aimed at the industrial heart. The *Luftwaffe* had no choice but to come up and to fight. In the process, its destruction had already begun.

Notes

1. Michael Howard, *Grand Strategy*, Vol. IV, *August 1942–September 1943* (London, 1972), p. 46.

2. This did not prevent the German high command from contracting for maps and pamphlets in Persian that a German printer was still turning out in 1944—no one had bothered to cancel the order. See Speer, *Inside the Third Reich*, p. 238.

3. BA/MA, RL 2 III/1185–1195, Genst. Gen. Qu. (6.Abt.), "Flugzeugunfälle und Verluste bei den fliegenden Verbänden."

4. Ibid.

5. The origins and conduct of operations around Stalingrad are discussed in a number of significant works; among the best are: Erickson, *The Road to Stalingrad;* Kehrig, *Stalingrad;* Earl F. Ziemke, *Stalingrad to Berlin: The German Defeat in the East* (Washington, 1968).

6. *KTB OKW*, Vol. II, Document #26, Operationsbefehl Nr. 1 vom 14. Oktober 1942 Betr.: Weitere Kampfführung im Osten, p. 130.

7. For the transport and supply problems of Sixth Army, see: Kehrig, *Stalingrad*, pp. 69ff.

8. *KTB OKW*, Vol. II, entry for 3.11.42., pp. 894–96.

9. Walter Warlimont, *Inside Hitler's Headquarters, 1939–1945* (New York, 1964), pp. 270–71. Hitler did regale Speer with comments about what *he* would do were he in command of Allied forces. See Speer, *Inside the Third Reich*, p. 246.

10. The following account of ground operations is drawn from Ziemke, *Stalingrad to Berlin*, pp. 52–55; Erickson, *The Road to Stalingrad*, pp. 464–72; and Kehrig, *Stalingrad*, pp. 131–60. Kehrig's account is particularly enlightening because it is accompanied by an outstanding set of maps.

11. *KTB OKW*, Vol. II, entry for 19.11.42., p. 988.

12. Luftflotte 4 vor Stalingrad: unter Gen. Oberst Frhr, v. Richthofen," notations for 21.11.42. and 22.11.42. with quotation from Richthofen's diary from 21.11.42., AFSHRC: K 113.309–3, v. 9; and Feldgericht des VIII. Fliegerkorps, Br. B. Nr. 7/43, Im Felde, den 26.1.43.; and Abschrift Wolfgang Pickert, Paderborn, 11.1.56., AFSHRC: K 113.309–3, v.9.

13. *KTB OKW*, Vol. II, entry for 25.11.42., p. 1019.

14. "Generaloberst Zeitzler über das Zustandekommen des Entschlusses, Stalingrad aus der Luft zu versorgen," letter from Zeitzler to Professor Suchenwirth, 11.3.55., AFSHRC: K 113.3018–4.

15. Suchenwirth, *Historical Turning Points in the German Air Force War Effort*, pp. 102–03.

16. "Luftflotte 4 vor Stalingrad: unter Gen. Oberst Frhr. v. Richthofen," notation from Richthofen's dairy from 24.11.42., AFSHRC: K 113.309–3, v. 9.

17. *KTB OKW*, vol. II, entries for 17.8.42., 6.11.42., and 21.11.42., pp. 601, 911, and 999. Figures given in these entries list aircraft that were "startbereit." Since operational ready rates were running at approximately 60 percent, the figures somewhat distort total strength, although they do reflect actual capabilities.

18. Suchenwirth, *Historical Turning Points in the German Air Force War Effort*, p. 101.

19. Plocher, *The German Air Force Versus Russia, 1942*, pp. 280–81.

20. Kehrig, *Stalingrad*, p. 219.

21. Russlandkrieg, "Die Luftversorgung Stalingrads," 10.3.56., AFSHRC: K 113.309–3, v. 9.

22. See Kehrig, *Stalingrad*, p. 287; and Plocher, *The German Air Force Versus Russia, 1942*, pp. 320–21.

23. Richthofen diary entry for 25.11.42., quoted in "Luftflotte 4 vor Stalingrad: unter Gen. Oberst Frhr. v. Richthofen," AFSHRC: K 113.309–3, v. 9.

24. For a complete listing of transport aircraft authorized strength, actual strength, and tonnage provided Stalingrad on a day-to-day basis, see: "Luftversorgung der 6. Armee vom 24.11.42. bis 3.2.43.," NARS T–321/18/4758846.

25. Richthofen diary entry for 18.12.42., quoted in "Luftflotte 4 vor Stalingrad: unter Gen. Oberst Frhr. v. Richthofen," AFSHRC: K 113.309–3, v. 9.

26. "Luftversorgung der 6. Armee vom 24.11.42. bis 3.2.43.," NARS T–321/18/4758846.

27. Ziemke, *Stalingrad to Berlin*, pp. 64–65.

28. See particularly "Tagebuch, Generalleutnant Fiebig, Kommandeur VIII. Flieger Korps," entry for 24.12.42., for a description of the wild conditions involved in abandonment of Tatsinskaya, AFSHRC: K 113.309–3, v. 9; see also "Luftflotte 4 vor Stalingrad: unter Gen. Oberst Frhr. von Richthofen," entries for 23. and 24.12.42.

29. "Luftflotte 4 vor Stalingrad: unter Gen. Oberst Frhr. von Richthofen," entry for 26.12.42., AFSHRC: K 113.309–3, v. 9.

30. "Luftversorgung der 6. Armee vom 24.11.42. bis 3.2.43.," NARS T–321/18/4758846.

31. For a somewhat colored account of Milch's activities, see Irving, *The Rise and Fall of the Luftwaffe*, Chapter 13.

32. Ziemke, *Stalingrad to Berlin*, pp. 78–79.

33. "Luftversorgung der 6. Armee vom 24.11.42. bis 3.2.43.," NARS T–321/18/4758846.

34. "Auswirkung der Luftversorgung Stalingrad auf die Luftwaffe," aus einer Ausarbeitung von Gen. a. D. Plocher, AFSHRC: K 113.309–3, v. 9.

35. For the fullest discussion of operations in late winter, see Ziemke, *Stalingrad to Berlin*, Chapter V. See also Erich von Manstein, *Verlorene Siege* (Bonn, 1955).

36. Air Ministry, *The Rise and Fall of the German Air Force*, pp. 227–28.

37. Irving, *The Rise and Fall of the Luftwaffe*, p. 189.

38. Milch was referring to the weather organization, but it is clear that he felt the same way about much of the Luftwaffe's ground support organization in the east: see "Bodenorganisation und Wetterdienst im Osten 1942/1943," aus GL-Besprechung am 16.2.43., AFSHRC: K 113.309–3, v. 13.

39. Air Ministry, *The Rise and Fall of the German Air Force*, p. 231; see also "Ultra, History of the US Strategic Air Force Europe vs German Air Force," June 1945, SRH–013, p. 51, for a message on the number of sorties flown on February 21.

40. Ibid., p. 228.

41. *KTB OKW*, Vol. III, entry for 27.2.43., p. 164.

42. "Das VIII. Flieger-Korps im Osteinsatz 1943," AFSHRC: K 113.309–3, v. 11; "Luftwaffe im Osten 1943, 1.3.43.–13.9.43.," Auzüge aus KTB LFL.4, März-August 1943 als Arbeitsunterlage, AFSHRC: K 113.309–3, v. 12; "Luftflottenkommando 4., Kriegstagebuch und persönliche Aufzeichnungen des Ob. der Luftflotte 4"; and BA/MA, RL 7/487, Lw. Führungsstab Ia Nr. 01130/43, 22.3.43., "Zusätze Chef Luftflotte 4 zum Befehl des Herrn Reichsmarschalls vom 5.3.43."

43. Ziemke, *Stalingrad to Berlin*, pp. 96–97.

44. "Das VIII. Flieger-Korps im Osteinsatz 1943," AFSHRC: K 113.309–3, v. 11; "Luftwaffe im Osten 1943, 1.3.43.–13.9.43.," Auszüge aus KTB LFL.4, März-August 1943 als Arbeitsunterlage, AFSHRC: K 113.309–3, v. 12, "Luftflottenkommando 4., Kriegstagebuch und persönliche Aufzeichnungen des Ob. der Luftflotte 4"; and BA/MA, RL 7/487, Lw. Führungsstab Ia Nr. 01130/43, 22.3.43., "Zusätze Chef Luftflotte 4 zum Befehl des Herrn Reichsmarschalls vom 5.3.43."

45. Zuteilung von fliegenden Verbänden an die Ostfront, Stand 20.2.43., AFSHRC: K 113.309–3, v. 13.

46. Based on loss reports in BA/MA, RL 2 III/1186, 1187, Genst. Gen. Qu. (6.Abt.), "Flugzeugunfälle und Verluste bei den fliegenden Verbänden."

47. Luftwaffe strength on 31.1.43. in Air Historical Branch, "Luftwaffe Strength and Serviceability Table, August 1938–April 1945," Translation No. VII/107.

48. Ziemke, *Stalingrad to Berlin*, pp. 108–09.

49. BA/MA, RL 7/549, Luftwaffenkommando Ost, Führungsabteilung Ia op, 26.3.43., "Gefechtsbericht über die Schlacht um Vel. Luki vom 24.11.42. bis 19.1.43."

50. See Hermann Plocher, *The German Air Force Versus Russia, 1943* (Maxwell AFB, Alabama, 1967), Chapter 2.

51. Based on loss reports in BA/MA, RL 2 III/1188, 1189, 1190, and succeeding volumes, Genst. Gen. Qu. (6.abt.), "Flugzeugunfälle und Verluste bei den fliegenden Verbänden."

52. Luftwaffe strength on 31.3.43. in Air Historical Branch, "Luftwaffe Strength and Serviceability Tables, August 1938–April 1945," Translation No. VII/107.

53. Manstein, *Verlorene Siege*, pp. 480–82.

54. *KTB OKW*, Vol. III, entry for 23.1.43., p. 66.

55. For the most complete account of the Battle of Kursk, see E. Klink, *Das Gesetz des Handelns, 'Zitadelle' 1943* (Stuttgart, 1966).

56. Ziemke, *Stalingrad to Berlin*, p. 131.

57. Warlimont, *Inside Hitler's Headquarters*, p. 333.

58. Guderian, *Panzer Leader*, p. 309.

59. *KTB OKW*, Vol. III, Document #10, "Operationsbefehl Nr. 6 (Zitadelle) vom 15.4.43.," p. 1425.

60. *The Great Patriotic War of the Soviet Union, 1941–1945*, pp. 179–80.

61. For a view of the battle's terrible impact on the frontline infantry (in this case the army's Gross Deutschland division), see: Guy Sager, *The Forgotten Soldier* (New York, 1971).

62. Ziemke, *Stalingrad to Berlin*, p. 137.

63. Ibid., Chapter VIII.

64. "Überlegungen des OKL über den Kräftebedarf für das Unternehmen Zitadelle 1943 an der Ostfront," Auszug aus einer Besprechungsnotiz vom 26.6.43., AFSHRC: K 113.309–3, v. 10.

65. Based on "Einsatz fliegender Verbände der deutschen Luftwaffe an der Ostfront 1943, 30.6.43.," AFSHRC: K 113.309–3, v. 13; and Air Historical Branch, "Luftwaffe Strength and Serviceability Tables, August 1938–April 1945," Translation No. VII/107.

66. Plocher, *The German Air Force Versus Russia, 1943*, pp. 77–79.

67. Air Ministry, *The Rise and Fall of the German Air Force*, pp. 234–35.

68. The above tabulations are based on loss returns for July and August 1943 in BA/MA, RL 2 III/1191, 1192, Genst. Gen. Qu. (6.Abt.), "Flugzeugunfälle und Verluste bei den fliegenden Verbänden"; and Air Historical Branch, "Luftwaffe Strength and Serviceability Tables, August 1938–April 1945," Translation No. VII/107.

69. For a clear, fairminded discussion of the issues involved, see Howard, *Grand Strategy*, Vol. IV, pp. 244ff.

70. See Warlimont, *Inside Hitler's Headquarters*, p. 282; and *KTB OKW*, Vol. II, entry for 1.12.42., p. 1062.

71. Howard, *Grand Strategy*, Vol. IV, p. 355.

72. I. S. O. Playfair, *The Mediterranean and Middle East*, Vol. IV, *The Destruction of Axis Forces in Africa* (London, 1966), pp. 172, 184.

73. For another view, see Howard, *Grand Strategy*, Vol. IV, p. 355; or Kesselring, *A Soldier's Record*, pp. 161–88.

74. Air Ministry, *The Rise and Fall of the German Air Force*, pp. 158–59.

75. Based on the quartermaster general's loss tables for November–December 1942, and January 1943, BA/MA, RL 2 III/1184, 1185, Genst. Gen. Qu. (6.Abt), "Flugzeugunfälle und Verluste bei den fliegenden Verbänden."

76. "Ultra, History of the US Strategic Air Force Europe vs German Air Force," June 1945, SRH–013, pp. 32–33. This is an extremely important source for the Luftwaffe, since it is based on "Ultra" intercepts and quotes many of them at length.

77. See Chapter IV of this book, p. 136.

78. Howard, *Grand Strategy*, Vol. IV, pp. 185–86.

79. See the particularly revealing discussions in Solly Zuckerman, *From Apes to Warlords* (London, 1978), pp. 173–96.

80. Letter from Doolittle, Subject: Escort Fighters; To: Commanding General, US Army Air Forces; Thru: Commanding General, Northwest African Air Forces, 22.5.43., Xerox copy of the letter in possession of the author. For an interesting discussion of the development of fighter escort for bomber formations in the Mediterranean and the early conclusion of Doolittle about the importance of fighter escort, see: Bernard Boylan, "The Development of the Long-Range Escort Fighter," unpublished manuscript (Maxwell AFB, 1955), AFSHRC, pp. 74–76.

81. Craven and Cate, *The Army Air Forces in World War II*, Vol. II, pp. 153–61.

82. Air Historical Branch, "The Luftwaffe in the Battle for Tunis, A Strategical Survey," a study prepared by the 8th Abteilung, 17.10.44., Translation No. VII/v.

83. For the steady attrition of Luftwaffe forces both in combat and through accidents, see the daily reports of F.d.L. Tunis for November, December, and January in BA/MA, RL 7/30, 31, 32.

84. Air Ministry, *The Rise and Fall of the German Air Force*, pp. 252–53.

85. "Ultra, History of the US Strategic Air Force Europe vs German Air Force," June 1945, SRH–013, p. 54.

86. Losses for transports based on the loss tables of the quartermaster general for April and May 1943 in BA/MA, RL 2 III/1188, 1189, Genst. Gen. Qu. (6.Abt.), "Flugzeugunfälle und Verluste bei den fliegenden Verbänden."

87. BA/MA, RL 8/262, Gen. Lt. a.D. Osterkamp, "Vorbemerkungen zum Einsatz des 'Jagdfliegerführer Sizilien'. "

88. "Ultra, History of the US Strategic Air Force Europe vs German Air Force," p. 62.

89. Based on the loss tables of the quartermaster, BA/MA, RL 2 III/1184, 1185, 1186, 1187, 1188, 1189, Genst. Gen. Qu. (6.Abt.), "Flugzeugunfälle und Verluste bei den fliegenden Verbänden"; and Air Historical Branch, "Luftwaffe Strength and Serviceability Tables, August 1938–1945," Translation No. VII/107.

90. See the figures on Luftwaffe strength in "Die deutsche Luftwaffe auf dem Mittelmeer-Kriegsschauplatz," USAF Historical Study #161, AFSHRC.

91. See Ewan Montagu, *The Man Who Never Was* (London, 1953). For the success of these deception efforts, see *KTB OKW*, Vol. III, Doc. #12, p. 1429, OKW/WFST/OP Nr. 661055/93, 12.5.43., which gave priority to the defense of Sardinia and Greece.

92. Warlimont, *Inside Hitler's Headquarters*, pp. 332–33.

93. Craven and Cate, *The Army Air Forces in World War II*, Vol. III, p. 428.

94. See Zuckerman, *From Apes to Warlords*, Chapter 10, and particularly p. 195 for Spaatz's reaction. See also Tedder, *With Prejudice*, pp. 440–44.

95. Based on the loss tables of the quartermaster general (6. Abteilung) for June 1943, BA/MA, RL 2 III/1189, "Flugzeugunfälle und Verluste bei den fliegenden Verbänden."

96. Air Ministry, *The Rise and Fall of the German Air Force*, pp. 257–58.

97. BA/MA, RL 8/262, Gen. Lt. a.D. Osterkamp, "Vorbemerkungen zum Einsatz des 'Jagdfliegerführers Sizilien'."

98. Air Ministry, *The Rise and Fall of the German Air Force*, pp. 260–61; see also "Ultra, History of the US Strategic Air Force Europe vs German Air Force," p. 76.

99. Based on the loss tables of the quartermaster general (6. Abteilung) for July and August 1943, BA/MA, RL 2 III/1190, 1191, "Flugzeugunfälle und Verluste bei den fliegenden Verbänden."

100. Air Ministry, *The Rise and Fall of the German Air Force*, p. 261.

101. BA/MA, RL 8/262, Gen. Lt. a.D. Osterkamp, "Vorbemerkungen zum Einsatz des 'Jagdfliegerführers Sizilien'."

102. Galland, *The First and the Last*, pp. 146–47.

103. See John Grigg, *Invasion 1943: The Invasion that Never Was* (London, 1980), for a restatement of the old but fallacious argument that without the diversion into the Mediterranean, the Allies could have landed in France in 1943.

104. For a critique of Kesselring's leadership, see the study by General von Senger und Etterlin, "Liaison Activities with Italian 6th Army—A Post-War Study," AHB, Translation VII/166; see also Below, *Als Hitlers Adjutant*, p. 333, for Kesselring's optimistic reports, but more sober on the scene analysis.

105. "Ultra, History of US Strategic Air Force Europe vs Geman Air Force," pp. 33, 53–54.

106. Webster and Frankland, *SAOAG*, Vol. IV, Appendix 39, p. 428.

107. Ibid., Vol. II, p. 91.

108. PRO AIR 22/203, War Room Manual of Bomber Command Ops 1939/1945, compiled by Air Ministry War Room (Statistical Section), p. 9.

109. Harris, *Bomber Offensive*, p. 144.

110. In commenting on the plans coming out of Casablanca for a combined bomber offensive, Harris noted in his memoirs that "the new instructions therefore made no difference." Ibid., p. 144.

111. Webster and Frankland, *SAOAG*, Vol. II, p. 108.

112. Ibid., p. 133.

113. Speer, *Inside the Third Reich*, pp. 280–81; see also Max Hastings' *Bomber Command* (New York, 1979), p. 208, for Barnes Wallis' frustration on this point.

114. Webster and Frankland, *SAOAG*, Vol. II, pp. 110–11.

115. Ibid., pp. 143–46. For the arguments about the use of "Window," see in particular Jones, *The Wizard War*, Chapter 33.

116. Clayton, *The Enemy is Listening*, p. 269.

117. For the most complete account of the Hamburg raid, see Martin Middlebrook's excellent study, *The Battle of Hamburg, Allied Bomber Forces Against a German City in 1943* (London, 1980).

118. Ibid., Chapter 15.

119. See among others, Hans Rumpf, *The Bombing of Germany* (London, 1963), pp. 82–83; Middlebrook, *The Battle of Hamburg*, p. 272; and OKW Wehrwirtschaftsstab, "Erfahrungen bei Luftangriffen," von Oberst Luther, WWi D/WK Kdo X, 15.1.44., NARS T–79/81/000641. Milch on 30.7.43. estimated the dead in Hamburg as high as 50,000: "Ansprache Milchs am 30. Juli 1943 über verstärkten Jägereinsatz im Heimatkriegsgebiet," Generalluftzeugmeister-Besprechung, AFSHRC: K 113.312–2 v.3.

120. Middlebrook, *The Battle of Hamburg*, pp. 290–93.

121. Webster and Frankland, *SAOAG*, Vol. II, pp. 155–56.

122. OKW Wehrwirtschaftsstab, "Erfahrungen bei Luftangriffen," von Oberst Luther, WWi O/WK Kdo X, 15.1.44., NARS T–79/81/000641.

123. Goebbels, *The Goebbels Diaries*, p. 419.

124. Speer, *Inside the Third Reich*, p. 284.

125. See Webster and Frankland, *SAOAG*, Vol. II, pp. 282–83.

126. Ibid., p. 159.

127. Letter from Eaker to Spaatz, October 1942, quoted in Fabyanic, "A Critique of United States Air War Planning, 1941–1944," pp. 129–30.

128. Craven and Cate, *The Army Air Forces in World War II*, Vol. II, pp. 842–44. The dates were December 6 and 20.

129. Ibid., p. 330.

130. Quoted by Boyland, "The Development of the Long-Range Escort Fighter," p. 68.

131. See, in particular, Craven and Cate, *The Army Air Forces in World War II*, Chapter II; Webster and Frankland, *SAOAG*, Vol. II, pp. 10–21.

132. Craven and Cate, *The Army Air Forces in World War II*, Vol. II, p. 367.

133. Webster and Frankland, *SAOAG*, Vol. II, pp. 59–64.

134. Craven and Cate, *The Army Air Forces in World War II*, Vol. II, pp. 670–72.

135. Ibid., pp. 846–47.

136. Ibid., pp. 79–81; see also Eighth Air Force, "Tactical Development, August 1942–May 1945," copy in possession of the author.

137. Ibid., p. 847.

138. USSBS, "The German Anti-Friction Bearings Industry," January 1947, p. 18; for a detailed analysis of the German ball bearing industry from a more historical perspective, see particularly Friedhelm Golücke, *Schweinfurt und der strategische Luftkrieg 1943* (Paderborn, 1980), Chapter II.

139. Craven and Cate, *The Army Air Forces in World War II*, Vol. II, p. 848.

140. LeMay, *Mission With LeMay*, p. 296.

141. Percentages based on the losses as established in Craven and Cate, *The Army Air Forces in World War II*, p. 848, and operational and crew strength in "Statistical Summary of Eighth Air Force Operations, European Theater, 17.8.42–8.5.45.," AFSHRC.

142. For a particularly interesting discussion of the problem of evaluating bombing accuracy in the drawing up of plans for the Combined Bomber Offensive, see: Fabyanic, "A Critique of United States Air War Planning."

143. Webster and Frankland, *SAOAG*, Vol. II, p. 62. The British official historians claim that "Eighth Air Force chose a full-moon period to make their first attack on August 19 [*sic*], and, though they carried incendiary bombs in the hopes of lighting the target for a night attack, it must have been obvious that Bomber Command could scarcely carry it out in such circumstances." It is worth noting that on the evening of August 17th when Eighth Air Force bombed Schweinfurt, Bomber Command was over Peenemünde. Even should the moonlit night have been an obstacle to an attack in central Germany, some other date could have been arranged had Harris wished to do so.

144. Boyland, "The Development of the Long-Range Fighter Escort," pp. 90–91, 121.

145. Ibid., p. 30.

146. Based on figures in "Statistical Summary of Eighth Air Force Operations, European Theater, 17.8.42.–8.5.45.," AFSHRC.

147. Ibid.

148. Craven and Cate, *The Army Air Forces in World War II*, Vol. II, pp. 480–83.

149. Ibid., pp. 483–84.

150. For Göring's worries on this, see BA/MA, RL 3/63, Besprechungsnotiz Nr. 85/43, g. Kdos. vom 27.8.43., Jägerhof, p. 7061.

151. Air Ministry, *The Rise and Fall of the German Air Force*, p. 186.
152. For Hitler's care over Sperrle's welfare, see Below, *Als Hitlers Adjutant*, p. 341, for a RM 50,000 gift that the Führer provided the Field Marshal in early July 1943. Sperrle, who had a reputation for a love of good living not short of Göring's, was not to be found at his headquarters but rather vacationing on the Atlantic coast south of Biarritz.
153. Golücke, *Schweinfurt und der strategische Luftkrieg 1943*, pp. 106–07.
154. BA/MA, RL 3/50, Der Staatssekretar der Luftfahrt und Generalinspekteur der Luftwaffe, gst. Nr. 847/43, 29.6.43., "Bericht über Besichtigungsreise 7.6. bis 12.6.43." See also BA/MA, RL 8/88, Generalkommando XII. Fliegerkorps, Ia Nr. 2700/43 Korpsgefechtsstand, 12.9.43. Betr: Tätigkeitsbericht und Erfahrungsbericht des Generalkommandos XII. Fliegerkorps im August 1943, p. 59.
155. Goebbels, *The Goebbels Diary*, entry for 7.3.43., p. 277, and especially entry for 9.3.43., pp. 278–91.
156. Quoted in Irving, *The Rise and Fall of the Luftwaffe*, p. 208.
157. Below, *Als Hitlers Adjutant*, pp. 335–36.
158. Tag-und Nachtjagd, Besprechungsnotiz Nr. 63/43 am 27.6.43., Obersalzberg, AFSHRC: K 113.312–2, v. 3; see also BA/MA, RL 3/45, Der Staatssekretär der Luftfahrt und Generalinspekteur der Luftwaffe, St/GL 490/43 Bericht Nr. 80 über die Amtschefbesprechung am 6.7.43.
159. BA/MA, RL 3/50, Der Staatssekretär der Luftfahrt und Generalinspekteur der Luftwaffe, Gst, Nr. 847/43, "Bericht über Besichtigungsreise 7.6 bis 12.6.43."
160. BA/MA, RL 3/54, Der Reichsminister der Luftfahrt und Oberbefehlshaber der Luftwaffe, Br. 21 Nr. 8731/43, 21.7.43., Betr.: "Sofortmassnahmen für Verfolgungsnachtjagd über grössere Räume."
161. Middlebrook, *The Battle of Hamburg*, pp. 244–48.
162. BA/MA, RL 3/54, "Vorschlag für eine neue Nachtjagdtaktik," 27.7.43.
163. Auszug aus der G.L. Besprechung am 20.8.43. im RLM, "Der erste grosse Einsatz der 'wilden Sau,'" AFSHRC: K 113.312–2, v. 3.
164. "Ultra, History of US Strategic Air Force Europe vs German Air Force," p. 59.
165. Auszug aus der G.L.-Besprechung am 20.8.43. im RLM, "Der erste grosse Einsatz der 'wilden Sau', " AFSHRC: K 113.312–2, v. 3.
166. Generalluftzeugmeister-Besprechung, "Ansprache Milchs am 30.7.43. über verstärkten Jägereinsatz im Heimatkriegsgebiet," AFSHRC: K 113.312–2, v. 3.
167. BA/MA, RL 3/45, Der Staatssekretär der Luftfahrt und Generalinspekteur der Luftwaffe, ST/GI 551/43, Bericht Nr. 83 über die Amtschefbesprechung am 16.7.43.
168. "Hitler zur Frage der Gegenmassnahmen zur Beantwortung der alliierten Luftangriffe," 25.7.43., AFSHRC: K 113.312–2, v. 3.
169. BA/MA, RL 3/63, "Besprechungsnotiz Nr. 85/43 g.Kdos, vom 27.8.43., Jägerhof."
170. BA/MA, RL 3/60, Besprechungsnotiz Nr. 8/43, 25.1.43.
171. Air Ministry, *The Rise and Fall of the German Air Force*, p. 219.
172. Oberst Vorwald, Chef des Technischen Amtes, 19.2.43. "Kurzer Bericht über die Besprechung beim Herrn Reichsmarschall vom 15. bis 17. February 1943."
173. Air Ministry, *The Rise and Fall of the German Air Force*, p. 287.
174. BA/MA, RL 7/112, Luftflottenkommando 3, Führungsabteilung (I) Nr. 8480/43, 12.7.43., "Tätigkeitsbericht der Luftflotte 3 für den Monat Juni 1943."
175. BA/MA, RL 3/50, Der Staatssekretär der Luftfahrt und Generalinspekteur der Luftwaffe, Gst, Nr. 847/43, 29.6.43. "Bericht über Besichtigungsreise 7.6. bis 12.6.43."
176. BA/MA, RL 2 III/1187, 1188, Genst. Gen. Qu. (6.Abt.), "Flugzeugunfälle und Verluste bei den fliegenden Verbänden," March and April 1943 and "Ultra, History of US Strategic Air Force Europe vs German Air Force," March and April 1943.
177. Besprechungsnotiz Nr. 63/43 am 27.6.43. Obersalzberg, AFSHRC: K 113.312–2, v. 3.
178. BA/MA, RL 7/113, Luftflottenkommando 3 Führungsabteilung (I), Ic Nr. 9960/43, 13.8.43. "Tätigkeitsbericht der Luftflotte 3 für den Monat Juli 1943."
179. The following figures are based on my calculations of the loss tables in BA/MA, RL 2 III/1191, 1192, Genst. Gen. Qu. (6.Abt.), "Flugzeugunfälle und Verluste bei den fliegenden Verbänden," July and August 1943.
180. BA/MA, RL 3/61, Generalmajor Galland, 28.7.43., Aktennotiz über Besprechung beim Herrn Reichsmarschall am 26./27.7.43.
181. See the sorties dispatched for July and August in Craven and Cate, *The Army Air Forces in World War II*, Vol. II, pp. 846–48.
182. BA/MA, RL 2 III/1192, 1193, Genst. Gen. Qu. (6.Abt.), "Flugzeugunfälle und Verluste bei den

fliegenden Verbänden," August–September 1943; and AHB, "Luftwaffe Strength and Serviceability Tables, August 1938–April 1945," Translation Nr. VII/107.

183. Based on the figures in BA/MA, RL 2 III/1025, Gen. Qu. 6.Abt. (III A), "Front-Flugzeug-Verluste," January–June 1943.

184. Based on figures of fighter pilot strength and losses in the tables in BA/MA, RL 2 III/722, 723, 724, 725, Gen. Qu. 6. Abt. (I), "Übersicht über Soll, Istbestand, Einsatzbereitschaft, Verluste und Reserven der fliegenden Verbände."

185. BA/MA, RL 2 III, Gen. Qu. 6.Abt. (III A), "Front-Flugzeug-Verluste," January–December 1943.

186. Ibid.

187. Ibid.

188. BA/MA, RL 2 III/722, 723, 724, 725, 726, Gen. Qu. 6. Abt. (I), "Übersicht über Soll, Istbestand, Einsatzbereitschaft, Verluste und Reserven der fliegenden Verbände."

189. Based on the author's tabulation of the losses in BA/MA, RL 2 III/1191, 1192, 1193, Genst. Gen. Qu. (6.Abt.), "Flugzeugunfälle und Verluste bei den fliegenden Verbänden," July, August, September 1943.

190. BA/MA, RL 2 II/1025, Gen. Qu. 6. Abt. (III A), "Front-Flugzeug-Verluste," July –August 1943.

191. Based on figures of fighter pilot strength and losses in the tables in BA/MA, RL 2 III/725, 726, Gen. Qu. 6. Abt. (I), "Übersicht über Soll, Istbestand, Einsatzbereitschaft, Verluste und Reserven der fliegenden Verbände."

192. Based on the figures in BA/MA, RL 2 III/1025, Gen. Qu. 6. Abt. (III A), "Front-Flugzeug-Verluste," 1941–1944. The percentages of noncombat losses work out as follows: Jan–Jun 1941, 44.5 percent; Jul–Dec 1941, 39.5 percent; Jan–Jun 1942, 45 percent; Jul–Dec 1942, 40.9 percent; Jan–Jun 1943, 45 percent; Jul–Dec 1943, 44.6 percent; Jan–Jun 1944, 37.2 percent. The decrease in the last period seems to have been the result of the fact that Allied fighters were shooting down German aircraft faster than their pilots could crash them.

193. Among other items, see: BA/MA, RL 2 II/181, OKL, Führungsstab, Ia/Ausb. Nr. 999/44, 11.4.44., "Herabsetzung von Flugzeugunfällen"; Ia/Ausb., 25.7.44., "Verhütung von Flugzeugverlusten ohne Feindeinwirkung"; OKL Generalquartiermeister, A2 52 b 10 Nr. 1370/44, "Tote und Verletzte der Luftwaffe im Flugbetrieb ohne Feindeinwirkung"; Ia/Ausb. (IIIA), "Studie, Herabsetzung der Flugzeugverluste ohne Feindeinwirkung," 30.9.44.

194. The above figures were provided by the Office of Flying Safety, Norton AFB, California.

195. I am indebted to Colonels Thomas Fabyanic (Ret) and Kenneth Alnwick, USAF, for this item.

196. USSBS, ESBGWE, Appendix Table 102, p. 277. German figures were calculated on a quite different basis than American and British figures. Aircraft that received major battle damage but which were still reparable were counted in production figures after they had been repaired. Nevertheless, an analysis of frontline strength, production figures, and loss tables creates the impression that there was some double bookkeeping going on.

197. Based on figures in BA/MA, RL 2 III/723, 724, 725, and 726, Gen. Qu. 6. Abt. (I). "Übersicht über Soll, Istbestand, Einsatzbereitschaft, Verluste und Reserven der fliegenden Verbände."

198. Irving's account of the Milch-Hitler conversation occurring early in March, The Rise and Fall of the Luftwaffe, pp. 201–03.

199. Golücke, Schweinfurt und der strategische Luftkrieg 1943, p. 115.

200. Irving, The Rise and Fall of the Luftwaffe, p.230. Obviously, the bomber force would provide crews for the night fighter forces, especially the "wild sow" force.

201. For further discussion of these points, see David Irving, The Mare's Nest (Boston, 1964), pp. 229–60.

202. Irving, The Rise and Fall of the Luftwaffe, p. 210.

203. BA/MA, RL 3/60, Stenografische Niederschrift der Besprechung beim Reichsmarschall über Flugzeug-Programm-Entwurf, 22.3.43., p. 66.

204. See in particular BA/MA, RL 3/56, Der Leiter der Fachgliederung Elektrotechnik im Reichsforschungsrat, 23.10.42.

205. See Irving's, The Mare's Nest, pp. 30, 222.

206. Irving, The Rise and Fall of the Luftwaffe, p. 202.

207. Irving, The Mare's Nest, pp. 58–59, 87–90.

208. Golücke, Schweinfurt und der strategische Luftkrieg 1943, p. 157.

209. Irving, The Mare's Nest, p. 109.

210. Golücke, *Schweinfurt und der strategische Luftkrieg 1943*, p. 153.

211. Ibid., p. 156. For other German high altitude cannons, the average ammunition expenditure was as follows: 88mm flak 41: 8,000 shells; 105mm flak 39: 6,000 shells; and the 128mm flak 40: 3,000 shells.

212. Speer, *Inside the Third Reich*, p. 285.

213. Figures are based on the calculations made at Karlsruhe after the war by Germans working for the historical project on the Luftwaffe in World War II: "Alliierte Luftangriffe im Jahre 1943 auf Werke der deutschen Flugzeugindustrie," AFSHRC: K 113–2, v. 3.

VI Attrition over the *Reich:* September 1943–March 1944

Jeschonnek's suicide in August 1943 was symbolic of the collapse of Germany's air strategy. The *Luftwaffe* had committed itself to supporting ground forces deep in Russia and the Mediterranean, and the sustained combat on the periphery had decimated its forces. Meanwhile, the RAF's night offensive and the growing threat of Eighth Air Force represented a direct challenge to Nazi Germany's survival. The homes and lives of the German people became hostage to British bombers, while B–17's and B–24's posed a direct threat to industry. Admittedly, the nature of the American threat was just emerging, but it had already influenced production of fighter aircraft. Thus, the Combined Bomber Offensive represented a danger that the Germans had to meet. The response, however, was in no sense a clear-headed analysis of the *Reich*'s strategic situation. Rather, it was a hodgepodge of expedients to defend Germany's airspace, combined with an effort to find a method of retaliation.

At night, these expedients sufficed to win a tactical victory over Bomber Command by March 1944. However, attrition of the day fighter force, already high in the summer of 1943, continued unabated throughout the year; and then in 1944 as American fighters flew deeper into the *Reich*, it reached a level that literally destroyed the *Luftwaffe*'s fighter forces. As a result, the Americans won air superiority over Europe. For the German fighter pilot, there was no magic number of sorties or hours, the completion of which guaranteed a return home. He was already home, and in the skies over the *Reich* he faced an opponent who enjoyed overwhelming superiority. If he survived the first missions and his skills reached those of his opponents, he would fly until fatigue and strain led to a mistake that was more often than not fatal.

Jeschonnek's death resulted in Günther Korten's appointment as Chief of Staff. He possessed a better grasp of Germany's desperate situation, and his approach aimed at two strategic objectives: building up the air defenses and establishing a "strategic" bombing force to attack critical elements in Russia's economy.[1] The latter strategy would hopefully hinder Soviet armaments production and relieve hard-pressed ground forces in the east. Korten established himself as a man of authority and strength, and Hitler relied increasingly on the Chief of Staff. Göring remained in the background in partial disgrace.[2]

Korten, however, faced an impossible task, for the *Luftwaffe* had already lost its chance for a successful aerial defense of the *Reich*. While Hitler had indicated some interest in defending Germany against Allied bombing, he refused to give top priority to increased fighter production. Hitler's refusal reflected a basic unwillingness, even at this late date, to look at the major reason behind Germany's desperate plight: overwhelming Allied productive superiority. Hitler and Göring dredged up many excuses to explain why Allied bombers were flying deep inside the *Reich*, but one recurring theme was that of the cowardice of Germany's fighter pilots and their refusal to press home attacks on bombers.[3] Korten himself discovered during the winter of 1943–44 that the desperate ground situation in the east as well as the temptation to use the bomber forces for retaliatory attacks on Britain made creation of a "strategic" bombing force totally impractical. Thus, although Korten accomplished a major restructuring of the air staff, he could not alter fundamental misconceptions governing the conduct of the air war.[4]

NIGHT DEFENSE OF THE *REICH*

Bomber Command's efforts continued full scale in the fall of 1943. In September and October, Harris' forces launched a series of devastating attacks on towns and cities in western and northern Germany. On September 5, British bombers achieved a heavy concentration on the Mannheim-Ludwigshafen area and destroyed both towns. On October 4, the command pulverized Frankfurt am Main and on October 8 destroyed most of Hannover's city center. The most damaging attack came on October 22 against Kassel when the pathfinders dropped target indicators so accurately that at least 86 percent of attacking crews bombed within 3 miles of the aiming point. The resulting concentration created a second fire storm within a three-month period. Seven days later, fires still burned.[5] Despite these successes, when weather conditions were bad and pathfinders relied on *H2S* to find and to mark targets in cloud cover, results were less satisfactory. In fact, outside the range of *Oboe,* British bombers found it almost impossible to achieve accurate, concentrated bombing in bad weather.

Nevertheless, despite problems in the fall, Harris embarked on what he regarded as a war winning strategy. The lengthening nights provided his forces with the darkness needed for the long, deep penetrations to Berlin. Harris decided to destroy the German capital and in early November penned a note to Churchill in which he underlined his successes and future strategy. He listed 19 German cities, including Hamburg, Cologne, Essen, Dortmund, Düsseldorf, Hannover, Mannheim, Rostock, and Kassel, as virtually destroyed; 19 cities as seriously damaged; and a further 9 as damaged. "From the above," he minuted, "you will see that the Ruhr is largely 'out,' and that much progress has been made towards the elimination of the remaining essentials of German war power." He concluded:

> I feel certain that Germany must collapse before this programme, which is more than half concluded already, has proceeded much further.
>
> We have not much further to go. But we must get the USAAF to wade in in greater force. If they will only get going according to plan and avoid such disastrous diversions as Ploesti . . ., we can get through with it very quickly.
>
> We can wreck Berlin from end to end if the USAAF will come in on it. It will cost us between 400–500 aircraft. It will cost Germany the war.[6]

Harris was considerably underestimating the cost. As Table XL[7] indicates, bomber losses in 1943 had been very heavy; and with the quick recovery of German night defenses from the effects of "Window," there was little prospect that matters would improve in the coming year.

TABLE XL
Bomber Command Strength and Aircraft Losses—1943

Aircraft Type	Present for Duty in Frontline Squadrons, January 1943	Aircraft Written Off, 1943
Wellington	186	328
Mosquitoe	34	62
Stirling	93	411
Halifax	195	838
Lancaster	256	1,112
TOTAL	764	2,751

Harris' approach raises the question as to his interest in integrating science and analysis into the night bombing effort. He had displayed little interest in the scientific war in 1942, and as one historian of the bomber offensive noted: "The short point is this. When the Bomber Command missing rate started getting into double figures, *then* its chiefs got interested in the scientific war of wits, but not before."[8] By 1943, conditions had forced Harris to use scientists but only on his terms. Solly Zuckerman, one of Britain's leading scientists, relates a remarkable story about meeting Harris in early 1944. Portal sent Zuckerman to High Wycombe, Bomber Command's headquarters, to pass along his scientific work on bombing in the Mediterranean theater. A bizarre evening began with Harris bitterly denouncing Eaker's transfer and characterizing the American as a man who "understood . . . the vital importance of the strategic bombing of Germany, which he thought that Spaatz appreciated not at all." During the entire evening during which reconnaissance photographs of bombed-out German towns appeared, Harris asked not one question about Zuckerman's studies. The next morning, Harris finally brought up the subject of the war in the south.

> He had only one question to put, he said, and he wanted a straight answer, "yes or no—nothing more." "Could heavy bombers be used to bomb coastal defenses?" I paused a second, and then said, "yes." It was clearly not the answer he wanted, and no further word [on the subject] was spoken.[9]

One has the feeling that Harris embarked on the "area" bombing of Berlin as a matter of faith. Science and research were useful only insofar as they supported his campaign and arguments.

In retrospect, it appears that Harris hoped to win the war in the winter of 1943–44 with Bomber Command alone. He told one senior commander at the time that his (Harris') forces would have to show the world.[10] Unfortunately, there comes a point where the maintenance of the objective crosses the fine line between realistic

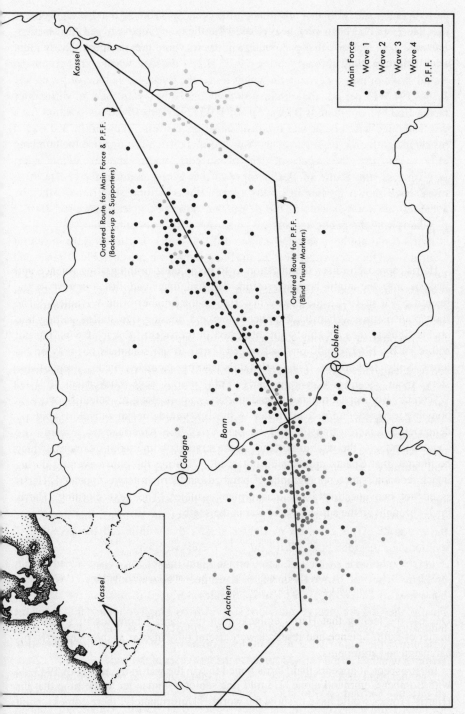

The raid on Kassel: 22/23 Oct. 1943, outward route: position of aircraft at 20:40 hours.

perserverance and stubborn adherence to preconceived ideas.[11] Haig had crossed that line in 1917; Harris now also crossed that line. In fairness to the Air Marshal, one must note that no other commander in the war bore greater strain. Every night from February 1942 through spring 1945, Harris decided whether his command would strike or not, a decision on which rested the lives and welfare of his crews. In the 1942–43 period, that strain was particularly heavy in view of difficulties facing Bomber Command. By the fall of 1943, Harris had held his position for a year and three-quarters; he was tired and under great stress. Thus far, he had waged his campaign for the most part with skill, and it is difficult to imagine the bombing effort achieving the same degree of success under another commander. Nevertheless, the Battle of Berlin suggests that a new commander in late 1943 might have shown greater flexibility (never Harris' strongest attribute), thereby avoiding the worst aspects of the defeat that now took place. However, Harris' popularity with the public and aircrews made his position invulnerable.

Harris could not have selected a more difficult target. Berlin lay deep in central Germany and thus demanded that an attacking force fly a considerable distance and time over hostile territory. On the long run in and out, the bomber stream provided a concentrated target to which German night fighters could react. The fact that Berlin was a great metropolitan center exacerbated the difficulties confronting its attackers. It was easy to bomb within city limits; it was another matter to achieve the concentration on which "area" bombing depended. Moreover, Berlin was beyond most British navigational and target-finding aids, while the city itself was too large and had too few terrain features for *H2S* to be as effective as it had proved in the Hamburg and Peenemünde attacks. Finally, the months of darkness occurred precisely during those months of dreadful weather conditions over central Europe. Thus, the Berlin raids took place during inclement weather that forced the pathfinders to mark and the main force to bomb through heavy overcast. In fact, the cloud cover over Berlin from November 1943, when the offensive began, until mid-February 1944 allowed reconnaissance aircraft to photograph the results only twice.[12] Yet daunting as these difficulties were, the British faced a German night fighter force that was recovering rapidly from the defeat suffered over Hamburg. Thus, Harris embarked on a strategy that was direct and obvious, that maximized the exposure of his bombers to fighter attack, that minimized the potential of evasion, and that took place during the year's worst weather.

On the other side of the hill, the German night fighter forces also faced serious problems. They too had to fly during bad weather. They not only faced "Window" but a host of countermeasures and spoof raids designed to mislead the defenses. Finally, they did not receive undivided support from a high command that found the temptation to use them in daylight operations almost overwhelming. Despite these difficulties, the night fighter force inflicted on its opponent one of the few tactical victories won by German armed forces in the last years of the war.

The inception of the "wild sow" tactic in mid-August did not prove particularly auspicious. German controllers, misled by a "Mosquitoe" feint, concentrated Herrman's force and most of the night fighters over Berlin. Antiaircraft gunners blasted away at the accumulation of aircraft over the capital which they mistook for bombers, while fighters fired off recognition signals at each other. The evening's proceedings ended with a pileup on the Brandenburg-Briest airfield.[13] A few night fighters were not fooled and arrived over Peenemünde to wreak havoc among the last bomber wave.[14] The Peenemünde operation pointed up the limitations under which night forces operated throughout the battle. Without timely information as to the main force's course and target, night fighters could not get at the bomber stream. If the controllers fell for a spoof raid, German night fighters were in for a long, unproductive evening chasing "Mosquitoes," while the main force pounded some unfortunate city. Conditions limited the "wild sow" force of day fighters even more. In single-engine, short-range fighters, they had to receive a vector to the correct city as limited range and lack of radar gave them little chance of intercepting the bomber stream. Almost from the first, the British caught on to the "wild sow" tactics. Their response was twofold. First, they launched more spoof missions to confuse and mislead defenses, and deception tactics became more complicated as the year continued. The second response reduced time over target to a minimum. In October, the British scheduled no raid to last more than 26 minutes over target.[15] As a result, "wild sow" fighters had little time to identify and to attack bombers.

If "wild sow" tactics represented an expedient, the Germans were moving rapidly to redress the balance between bomber and fighter. In particular, they solved the "Window" problem. In the summer, German scientists had been developing a new radar set, the "SN2." It operated on a longer wavelength than older radars; and although it could lock on to targets at a relatively long range, it had the disadvantage of an excessive minimum range. However, "Window" had little effect on its wavelength, and thus it could distinguish targets in the clouds of aluminum strips. The *Luftwaffe* immediately began a crash program to re-equip night fighters.[16] As with all new systems, there were teething troubles with the device, and frontline units squabbled with industry as to who was at fault for initial failures. Nevertheless, by mid-winter, technicians had resolved most defects.[17] In addition, some Ju 88's and He 219's began to appear in the force as replacements for outdated Bf 110's. But the re-equipment program still lagged because night fighters received lower priority than the bomber force. Therefore, despite its limitations, the Bf 110 remained the backbone of night fighters.

One other major equipment change occurred that had a major impact on bomber losses towards the end of the Battle of Berlin. Frontline squadrons developed an upward firing cannon called *schräge Musik*. By aligning himself under and slightly behind the wing of an enemy bomber, a night fighter pilot could destroy the engines and set the fuel tanks on fire. Given the loads of fuel and explosives that British bombers carried and their lack of defensive armor, any attack was dangerous. The only possibility of survival was instantaneous, violent evasion. The new *schräge Musik* allowed fighters to approach bombers unobserved from underneath, as there were no turret gunner on the underside of most British bombers.[18] RAF intelligence remained ignorant of the new tactics since debriefing officers refused to believe the few reports that German fighters were firing upwards while flying underneath the bombers.

One critical factor facing the night fighter force was the level of attrition taking place in frontline units. In October, Kammhuber warned Göring at a meeting of fighter generals that crew losses were approaching unacceptable levels. In June, the night fighter force had lost only 12 crews. From then on, losses had climbed rapidly. In July, it lost 38 crews (6.8 percent), in August 57 (9.8 percent), and in September 53 (7.7 percent).[19] These rising losses among night fighters reflected their use during daytime as well as the pressure of operations against the British homeland. The assembled generals found the losses worrisome, and General Martini commented that the night fighter defenses were eating into their capital. Göring, however, was not upset. He remarked that "today, there is a war on" and that losses were inevitable. Noting the loss of 160 crews in four months (including June's figures and missing the significance of the rise of crew losses), Göring took comfort in the fact that this worked out to only one and one-third crews lost per night. He claimed that this rate was not shocking when compared to the loss of life caused by the British bombardment. As to the efforts to get more equipment for training units, the *Reichsmarschall* lamely suggested that perhaps booty seized in Italy after its surrender might compensate for some of the equipment deficiencies.[20]

At the end of August and beginning of September, lengthening nights allowed Bomber Command to attack Berlin again. The results of three raids and the losses suffered should have served warning for future strategy. Out of 1,179 aircraft claiming to have bombed the capital, only 27 on examination of night camera photographs got within 3 miles of the aiming point. Losses showed a significant rise over the Hamburg raids: The Germans shot down no less than 123 bombers (an overall loss rate of 7.2 percent).[21] By the end of September, Göring felt optimistic enough to congratulate his night fighter commanders and crews for their successful recovery and the losses they were inflicting.[22]

The real offensive against Berlin opened in November with four major raids. The losses in the first stage of the battle were surprisingly low (4 percent of sorties launched on Berlin and 3.6 percent for the overall sortie loss rate). Churchill offered congratulations to Portal and Harris.[23] But loss rates were misleading. November's weather conditions were dreadful; and during some raids, German fighters could not get off the ground. The corollary to the safety advantage that such conditions offered was a corresponding drop in bombing accuracy. Conditions made it impossible to mark or to identify targets, and crews had no choice but to drop their loads higgledy-piggledy over Berlin. Considerable damage was done, but no concentrated bombing on the scale of Hamburg and Kassel took place.

The damage did shake Speer's confidence, however, and Goebbels after a major raid noted that: "The situation has become ever more alarming in that one industrial plant after another has been set on fire. . . . The sky above Berlin is bloody, deep red, and of an awesome beauty. I just can't stand looking at it." Nevertheless, the Propaganda Minister comforted himself in British overestimations of raid damage and forbade any denials in the hope that the "sooner London is convinced that there is nothing left of Berlin, the sooner will they stop their offensive against the *Reich*'s capital."[24] The Germans confined post-bombing damage better than in earlier raids through lessons learned at Hamburg. Goebbels ordered evacuation of nearly 1 million Berliners in August and instituted a massive program throughout the *Reich*'s cities to beef up air raid and fire prevention forces. In Berlin, such efforts helped to hold down casualties and damage.[25]

In December, Bomber Command's losses began to rise. The first raid on Berlin saw 8.7 percent of the attacking force missing with an average loss of 4.8 percent of sorties dispatched for all four attacks on the capital. Disaster struck in January. Harris launched nine major operations against Germany, six against Berlin, and one each against Stettin, Brunswick, and Magdeburg. The loss rates were terrible. The missing rate on six Berlin raids averaged 6.1 percent of sorties dispatched, while attacks on other cities lost 7.2 percent of their aircraft. The least costly raid was on Stettin. Nevertheless, even though the German controller was fooled into believing Berlin was the main attack, the raid still lost 4.2 percent of aircraft dispatched.[26] Total bombers lost for the month came to 316 aircraft, a rate in terms of materiel and manpower that no air force could long support.

These losses reflected the German success in rebuilding the night defenses. New aircraft, new radar sets, and above all a new system of command and control tipped the balance against the bomber. As early as the end of September, General Schmid, now Commander of the I *Jagdkorps* (I Fighter Corps), felt that the "wild sow" tactics had reached their optimum and would not gain any greater success.[27] Herrmann's system depended on a centralized control to give day fighters the location of the attack. During the fall of 1943, that control system evolved into a running commentary by the chief German controller as to the course and progress of the bomber stream. Meanwhile, "wild sow" and "tame sow" radar-equipped fighters scrambled. The controller vectored them to beacons located throughout Germany from which they could then move into the bomber stream. The fighter beacons for "wild sow" aircraft were flashing high-powered lights on the ground, while radio beacons provided concentration points for the twin-engine, radar-equipped fighters. Bad winter weather, however, made it possible to concentrate "wild sow" forces, as Schmid had suspected would be the case.[28]

The "tame sow" aircraft and the controllers became increasingly adept at earlier interception of raids and at feeding night fighters directly into the bomber stream. The development of a number of new devices aided the defense. The first step came with the use of British identification, friend or foe (IFF) transmissions to determine the bomber stream's course. When the British caught on and shut off such signals over the continent, the Germans moved to other transmissions that the bombers made. British scientists developed a device, code-named "Monica," to warn bombers that German airborne radar was scanning them; the Germans captured such a device early on and turned it. With the "Flensburg" apparatus, night fighters homed in directly on bombers using "Monica." In addition, the Germans provided fighters with a device called "Naxos," which homed in on *H2S* transmissions. Not all such measures were German. The British began to use fake controllers, first in England and then airborne in specially built "Lancasters." They confused and gave contradictory information to German fighters.[29] When that no longer worked, the British jammed the frequencies used by German controllers.[30] Nevertheless, the general impression of scientific war in this period is that the defense had the upper hand.

By January, German night fighters were flying out into the North Sea to intercept the bombers.[31] Their successes in that month forced the British to take drastic action. Raid planning became more complex with a number of spoof raids launched with the main effort to deceive defenses. Pathfinders no longer laid route markers to guide the bombers nor could markers indicate course turning points. Such marking devices had pointed out the raid's direction to German fighters and drew them directly into the bomber stream. While such changes helped keep losses down, they decreased bombing accuracy. By January, German commanders had recognized that "tame sow" tactics were proving most effective, although some problems remained with the "SN2" radar.[32]

The German success in January was such that it had virtually won the Battle of Berlin, although Harris did not admit defeat until March. Nevertheless, Bomber Command's operations in February suggest High Wycombe's recognition that Berlin had become a dangerous target. Most of February's attacks were against less dangerous objectives in southern and western Germany. The two missions along the northern route through the heart of the German defenses suffered heavily. The first lost 4.8 percent, while the second lost 9.5 percent of aircraft dispatched. Not until March 24 did a major raid against Berlin recur. Night fighter defenses thus forced the British to deflect the offensive from Berlin to attack what Harris regarded as subsidiary targets.[33] Among these was a heavy raid on Schweinfurt. After great wrangling between the Air Staff's Director of Bomber Operations and Harris, Bomber Command finally attacked the ball bearing plants seven months after the first American raid.[34]

For the first part of March, Bomber Command's efforts centered on attacking targets in southern Germany. Moreover, the commitment to the invasion had already begun to draw attention to targets in France. At the end of the month, however, the British mounted several major deep penetration raids into Germany. They brought a sudden and costly end to the Battle of Berlin. The first on March 24 hit the German capital with one last massive blow. Losses were heavy, 73 bombers were destroyed for a missing rate of 9.1 percent of aircraft dispatched.[35] On the 26th, Bomber Command again devastated Essen in an accurate *Oboe* attack carried out through dense cloud cover. German defenses were off balance, and the British lost only nine bombers.[36] The accurate bombing of Essen, however, underlined again how dependent Bomber Command was on navigational devices to achieve accurate bombing patterns. In one raid against Stuttgart (beyond the range of *Oboe)* earlier in the month, not one aircraft dropped its bombs within city limits.[37]

On March 30, Bomber Command launched its last deep penetration raid for a considerable period of time as preparations for "Overlord" were about to begin.

This was indeed "a curious operation."[38] It reflected serious errors in judgment which, when combined with circumstances such as weather and decisions made by German controllers early in the raid, caused a disaster. In the sense that chance lay largely on Germany's side, the Nuremberg raid was on the opposite end of the spectrum from the Hamburg raids of July and August 1943.

Harris initiated the mission in the early morning hours of March 30. Weather was not favorable and the moon would not set until nearly 0200 hours. However, most dangerous for the bombers' survival was the routing that High Wycombe selected for the attacking force. Turning south of Brussels, the bomber stream would fly a route that 5 Group advocated: a straight in, straight out flight plan with few course alterations. The long leg after the turn south of Brussels would carry the bombers between the Ruhr and Colbenz Flak concentrations. Unfortunately, this gap lay immediately in front of night fighter beacons, "Ida" and "Otto." There was nothing surprising about the bomber stream passing close by such beacons that now existed throughout Germany. What was surprising was the fact that the bombers after their turn south of Brussels flew straight at those beacons for 25 minutes and then continued on the same course for a further 35 minutes. Bennett objected to the route in strong terms.[39] He later suggested that there was a near mutiny among his pathfinder crews when they saw the routing.[40]

At 2322 hours, the bomber stream crossed the coast. Within 20 minutes, the German controller ordered fighters to concentrate at "Ida."[41] Adding to the doom awaiting the bombers were unusual weather conditions. For nearly the entire length of the long leg, the skies remained clear with few clouds. Moreover, strong contrails formed at the bombers' altitude, a rare occurrence considering the relatively low height at which Bomber Command operated.[42] In such conditions, the bombers were in a hopeless position. German fighters, vectored to the "Ida" beacon from the west, found themselves in the bomber stream even before reaching station. Upon arrival at the beacon, fighters from the north and the west were among the bombers. All then flew with the main force to Nuremberg, while more fighters linked up and slaughter of the bombers took place. In Britain, 'Y' Service's listening stations picked up with distressing frequency interception plots and victory calls by German fighter pilots.[43] By the time the bombers turned south on the attack leg, they had lost 61 of their aircraft. By the raid's completion, they had lost a further 47, a total of 108 altogether. The "Halifaxes" of 4 Group had a particularly rough night with 20 aircraft missing and a loss rate of 20.6 percent.[44] As a fitting end to the disaster, not only did the attacking forces fail to achieve a concentration on Nuremberg but many aircraft blown off course bombed Schweinfurt.[45]

Losses over Nuremberg, when combined with those earlier in the week, meant that Bomber Command had lost 190 bombers in seven days (73 in Berlin, 9 in Essen, and 108 in Nuremberg). These were unsupportable losses and reflected not only the recovery of German defenses but also the heavy operations and losses suffered over the past year (see Table XLI[46]).

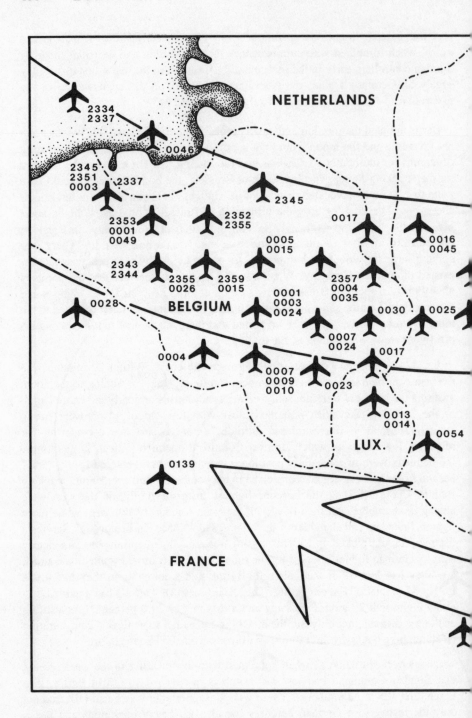

Plots on bombers passed over R/T and W/T to night fighters; raid on Nuremberg 30/31.3. 1944. Symbols indicate aircraft shot down.

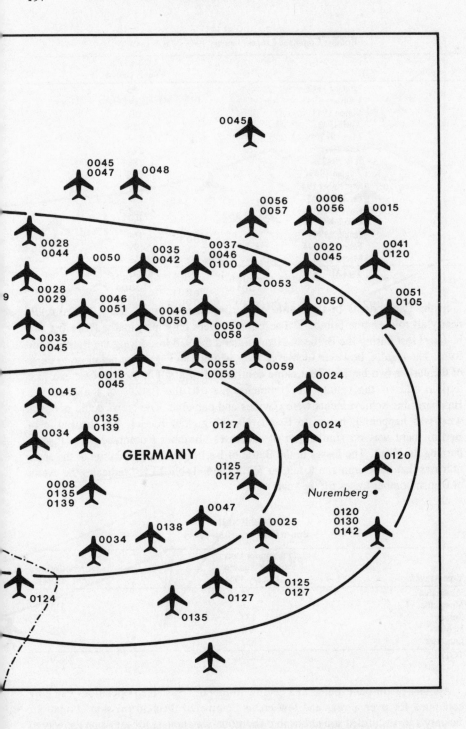

TABLE XLI
Bomber Command Losses, January 1943–March 1944

	Losses, All Causes (Night)
January 1943	86
February 1943	101
March 1943	161
April 1943	253
May 1943	234
June 1943	275
July 1943	188
August 1943	275
September 1943	191
October 1943	159
November 1943	162
December 1943	170
January 1944	314
February 1944	199
March 1944	283
TOTAL	5,881

In the five months of the Battle of Berlin, Harris' forces lost 1,128 aircraft, nearly all four-engine bombers. These losses were only marginally above the 813 bombers lost during the Battle of Hamburg and the 923 lost during the Battle of the Ruhr. The results, however, achieved over winter 1943–44 were not close to those of the earlier two battles. That alone contributed to a fall in morale: One can face terrible odds if the results are commensurate. In the Battles of the Ruhr and Hamburg, the achievements were obvious and palpable. The crews could not miss what was happening below to Essen, Hamburg, and Kassel. For the Battle of Berlin, there was no similar run of successes. Bomber Command was close to burning itself out. The losses in the Battle of Berlin were an indication of the scale of losses that the Command would suffer in 1944. Table XLII[47] indicates the extent of British bomber losses for the year.

TABLE XLII
British Bomber Losses—1944

Type Aircraft	Present for Duty in Frontline Squadrons, January 1944	Aircraft Written Off in 1944
Wellington	15	22
Mosquitoe	116	223
Stirling	134	77
Halifax	307	920
Lancaster	652	1,978
TOTALS	1,224	3,220

Another factor contributed to a decline in morale. Sustained operations had now continued for over a year and few crews completed their 30 mission obligation. January's losses turned squadrons into short one-way houses for crews on the way to their deaths.[48] The drop in morale resulted in more early returns and more aircrew members cashiered for LMF (lacking moral fibre). It also caused some crews to pickle their "cookies" (the 4,000-pound blockbuster) over the North Sea to gain the relative safety of higher altitudes. Air Vice Marshal D.C.T. Bennett, commander of the pathfinders, somewhat uncharitably called such crews "fringe merchants."[49] But Bennett was as hard on himself as he was on his crews. Unlike other group commanders, he had flown a tour on operations and had been shot down over Norway in 1942. He walked out to Sweden. Recently, he observed that one of the great failings in Bomber Command's leadership was that no other senior officer besides himself had any grasp of the operational conditions under which their crews fought, because they had not flown combat missions in this war.[50]

In retrospect, the Battle of Berlin was a mistake—one in which Harris came close to wrecking his command. The objective was obvious and at the outer limits of bomber range. The pathfinder force lost approximately 150 percent of its strength; and as Bennett notes, the battle "had been the worst thing that could have happened to the Command."[51] Thus, at the end of March, Harris had arrived at the same point that Eaker had reached in October 1943. At night, unescorted bomber formations on deep penetrations suffered prohibitive losses. As the official historians suggest: "The implication was equally clear. The German fighter force had interposed itself between Bomber Command and its strategic objective. . . ." For Harris, the message was unambiguous: His forces needed the "provision of night fighter support on a substantial scale."[52] Yet, Bomber Command's defeat may have had a beneficial side effect. Harris, who so often balked at the Air Ministry's directives, followed his orders to the letter when it came to "Overlord," and Bomber Command provided essential support. Whether or not he did so willingly, Harris had no choice. Night raids deep into Germany were no longer possible except at prohibitive cost.

Bomber Command's losses during this period should not obscure the fact that the German night fighters also were having a difficult time. Bad weather, the low level of skill among new crews, and defensive fire from the bombers all took their toll. The worst enemy of night fighter crews seems to have been themselves. In a twelve-day period (March 15 to 26th), *Nachtgeschwader* 6 with two *Gruppen* (a total strength of between 50 and 60 aircraft) lost 6 aircraft that ran out of fuel, had 2 aircraft damaged by belly landings, and had 1 aircraft force-land in Switzerland. Only two aircraft were lost in combat.[53] Crew losses ran at a steady rate, close to 15 percent for the first three months of 1944.[54] While such losses were not light, German crews gained the impression that they were inflicting serious damage on the enemy. Moreover, they were defending German cities from the British bombers, and as a result their loss rate was probably easier to bear. By spring 1944, the night defenses had won a substantial victory over their opponent. They had made the skies over the *Reich* so dangerous that the British could only infrequently risk the losses involved in deep penetration raids. What the Germans were not able to do, however, was to transfer their success to the skies over the occupied western countries. In that region, Bomber Command posed a different threat and would soon show that it could inflict important damage on those Germans preparing to meet the invasion.

THE DAY BATTLE: VICTORY, SEPTEMBER-OCTOBER 1943

We left our account of Eighth Air Force's campaign after the shattering experience of the Schweinfurt/Regensburg attack. Eaker's strength had declined to the point where he had to allow a major lull in operations. In September, only one major raid penetrated deep into German airspace; the results duplicated what had happened over Schweinfurt in August. Forty-five bombers and crews were listed as missing out of 338 aircraft dispatched to attack the bearing and aircraft factories near Stuttgart.[55] For the remainder of the month, Eighth licked its wounds and attacked the occupied districts of western Europe. There, Allied fighters kept bomber losses within tolerable limits. Meanwhile, the flow of aircraft and crews from the States swelled Eighth's groups: Its effective aircraft strength climbed over the 300 mark, while the number of available aircrews went over 400, both for the first time.[56]

In October, the daylight air battle peaked, and American losses in deep penetration, unescorted raids ended illusions that bomber formations could protect themselves. Defeat over Schweinfurt sounded the death of prewar doctrine and the assumptions on which it had been built. Yet if October was a serious setback, the cost paid dividends. By carrying the war to Germany, the daylight bombers forced the *Luftwaffe* to come up and to fight. In the short run, bomber casualties reached unacceptable levels, but German fighter losses, relatively speaking, were even more costly as to their long-term effects. In essence, Eighth's operations imposed a high enough attrition rate to prevent the recovery of Germany's fighter arm after the losses suffered over the summer.

Eighth's October operations began on the 8th with an attack on Bremen and Vegesack. The attacking formations lost 30 bombers with a further 26 receiving major damage. Three-quarters of the 1st Bombardment Division's aircraft received flak damage. This attack initiated a week of heavy operations culminating with a second great attack on Schweinfurt on October 14. On October 9, Eighth's bombers flying over Denmark and the Baltic hit Danzig and Marienburg, and a diversionary force hit the Arado factory at Anklam. Both the Arado works and the Focke Wulf plant in Marienburg received extensive damage, while the depth and extent of the raid surprised German defensive forces. The main force lost only 10 aircraft with 18 more shot down in diversionary attacks.[57] On October 10, Eighth bombed Münster. Relays of German fighters attacked the first task force on the way in and out, and blasted the lead formation flown by the 100th Bombardment Group out of the sky. Not one of the 12 aircraft returned. All told, out of 119 bombers in the first wave, the Germans shot down 29 (24.4 percent).[58] The loss of 1 more aircraft on the second wave brought total losses to 30. So in three days of major operations, Eighth had lost 88 heavy bombers. This represented no less than 18.4 percent of available crews.[59] For the next three days, the command stood down. On the 14th, it went back to Schweinfurt and suffered a terrible mauling. German fighters and flak shot down 60 of its bombers, 17 received major damage, while 121 aircraft were damaged but reparable. The loss rate was 20.7 percent and the damage rate 47.4 percent.[60] Thus for the week, Eighth Air Force had lost 148 bombers in deep penetration raids into Germany. Even by American standards that represented unacceptable attrition.

The Schweinfurt losses caused an outcry in the United States. "Hap" Arnold announced to the American press that "now we have got Schweinfurt." Arnold's assertion, however, could not cover up what Allied economic analysts soon recognized: that more sustained bombing of the ball bearings works was needed almost immediately.[61] Yet, as suggested earlier, the first attack on Schweinfurt had alarmed Speer; but the second raid, with 67 percent of Schweinfurt's production knocked out, was even more disturbing.[62] The Armaments Minister established a crash program to disperse the bearings industry and to substitute alternative roller bearings for ball bearings where possible.[63] But Speer was worried that the bombing would soon recur. However, no matter what the target's value, Eighth Air Force could not return until fighter escort could reach Schweinfurt. Harris, involved in his offensive against Berlin, had no intention of attacking a "panacea" target. By February, those conditions had changed; Eighth possessed fighter protection that could take it all the way to Schweinfurt, while Harris was more amenable to attacking ball bearings after the losses over Berlin. By then, however, the raids had to begin all over again the process of damaging the production of ball bearings.

The disaster at Schweinfurt ended the nonsense about unescorted bomber formations. The losses over the summer had caused a rising chorus of demands for increased fighter range as well as a true long-range escort. The battles in October brought matters to a head. Unfortunately, the development and production of suitable drop tanks involved considerable muddle, particularly in the United States. While some in Washington recognized the importance of range extension tanks, there existed a lack of communication between Eighth and procurement officials at home. American drop tank production had progressed satisfactorily in early 1943, but supply authorities later in the year mistakenly believed that production in Britain could meet Eighth's needs.[64] Meanwhile in England, British industry could not produce the numbers that procurement desired, while Eaker, somewhat as a result of his own emphasis, was left holding a rather empty bag.

On October 14, Eaker wrote Air Marshal Wilfrid Freeman at the Ministry of Aircraft Production to complain of shortfalls in drop tank production. Not yet aware of Schweinfurt's casualties, Eaker suggested that of 30 bombers lost over Münster on the 10th, the availability of drop tanks might have saved as many as 20. Freeman's reply was a model of restraint. He admitted delays but pointed out that current production would cover the shortfall by early November. This deficit, however, in his opinion, was not entirely the fault of the Ministry of Aircraft Production since British industry had not received approval for the required fittings until early October. Freeman pointed to his February warning that British industry, severely overstrained, could not complete a rush order for tanks. Only in June had

Eighth sought large numbers of workable drop tanks.[65] Now after Schweinfurt, everyone pushed the drop tank program, and British production, helped by American efforts, made them available in rising quantities. From November 1943, Eighth felt its way into Germany, but it would go no deeper than its fighter escort could fly; as the escort range rose, the noose tightened.

One other element of the escort program deserves attention: the development of a true long-range escort fighter, the "Mustang." Like the "Mosquitoe," the P–51 was an orphan at birth.[66] North American developed the "Mustang" in a rush to land a contract with the British. The initial variant, with an Allison engine, possessed good low altitude characteristics but lacked power to work at higher elevations. In the summer of 1942, British engineers, after studying the aircraft, decided that with a better engine, the "Mustang" would possess excellent characteristics at higher altitudes. By October, "Merlin" engines had been installed and the first test flights conducted. As things turned out, the Allies had developed the hottest piston engine fighter of the war. The road to production, however, was not easy; there was reluctance to push its development, since it was not entirely a home-grown product. However, tests conducted in the early summer of 1943 indicated the P–51's potential as a combat fighter and suggested that the aircraft did have the capability to provide long-range escort for the bombers.[67] Tests and modification over the summer added an 85-gallon internal tank to the fighter which placed its range without drop tanks at over 400 miles. Problems remained concerning engine modifications and other design changes, but beginning in November 1943 "Mustangs" began to reach the United Kingdom.[68]

Meanwhile, the air battles in July and August forced the Germans to adjust their air strategy. They could no longer support the attrition of those months, while the American threat forced them to cut commitments in the Mediterranean and Russia. Defense of the *Reich* became the top priority, and beginning in July the *Luftwaffe* transferred *Gruppen* from Russia to the west. The process continued throughout late summer as the east and Mediterranean lost their fighter cover. The situation was so critical that transferred units received no time to transition into the western defense system. The III *Gruppe* of the "Udet" *Geschwader* left the eastern front on August 2. Arriving at Münster-Handorf, the unit met its new commander who announced his intention to make them combat-ready as soon as possible. Within four days, the *Gruppe* had flown its first mission and on the following day was declared combat-ready.[69] Fighter strength in Germany rapidly rose. From barely 600 aircraft, fighter numbers rose to 800 by July and nearly 1,000 by early October.[70] In addition, substantial numbers of twin-engine fighters redeployed to the *Reich* so that by mid-October the *Luftwaffe* had nearly 200 of them available in Germany of which 50 percent were "in commission."[71] Finally, German commanders still used night fighters during the day despite the heavy loss of aircraft, radar equipment, and skilled crewmembers.

Along with a redistribution of fighters, substantial changes took place in the defending forces' tactics and weaponry. By September, the Germans had refined the defense system created in the summer to meet the day threat. Twin-engine fighters, equipped with 21cm rocket mortars, flew at the edge of the B-17's defensive armament and fired rockets into the formations to break them up. The Germans had altered the armament of the Bf 109's and Fw190's, and their new heavier armament made them a greater threat to the bombers. The single-engine fighters launched head-on and stern attacks in large groups, their cannon fire dangerous to slow-moving bombers. As for logistics, the *Luftwaffe* stocked a number of bases throughout western and central Germany with ammunition, fuel, and ground crews for quick fighter turnaround, thereby increasing their sortie rate against bomber formations.[72] Interestingly, the Germans were also using drop tanks on their fighters to extend the range and time that the fighters could remain airborne. In October, however, Göring scotched the tactic and suggested that even the Americans would not be so wasteful of material. He suggested that crews not drop tanks when empty but only in combat.[73] An intercepted "Ultra" message on October 12 warned fighter crews that they should only drop tanks in the most desperate circumstances.[74]

This refined and reinforced defense system enabled the *Luftwaffe* to win a series of substantial tactical victories. Warned by radar of an American raid, German fighters scrambled and concentrated. Twin-engine fighters fired rockets into the formations to break up flying cohesion and to hit aircraft. Single-engine fighters individually and in groups attacked from all directions. The aim was to break formation integrity; once German fighters had done that, individual B-17's were easy prey, while damaged aircraft that fell behind were in a hopeless situation. The defensive system proved remarkably effective in October, but it did contain weaknesses. Above all, it depended on the fact that no American fighters were present. Operations in July, when American fighters, using primitive drop tanks, had pushed deeper into the *Reich* and caught German fighters by surprise, underlined this factor. *Luftwaffe* fighters would only engage American bombers out of range of Allied fighter support. Using this rule of engagement, much of western Europe now had targets that were relatively free of *Luftwaffe* coverage. German success in the fall also depended on close cooperation between the single-engine and twin-engine fighters, with the heavier fighters playing a key role in breaking up the integrity of American formations. Without such support, the single-engine fighters faced a much more difficult task, but the Bf 110 had no chance of survival against enemy fighters. Thus defense of the *Reich*'s airspace depended on the continued existence of a zone over which Allied fighters could not operate because of their inadequate range. There were already signs that this situation was breaking down.

German successes in September and October were won, moreover, at a high cost to themselves. The Germans lost 276 fighters in the west in September (17.4 percent of the total fighter force as of September 1) and 284 more in October (17.2 percent).[75] Schweinfurt itself cost the Germans (see Table XLIII[76]) 31 aircraft destroyed, 12 written off, and 34 damaged. As a percentage, this was between 3.5 percent and 4 percent of total fighter aircraft available in the west.

TABLE XLIII
Aircraft Losses, Schweinfurt—October 1943

	100 Percent	60–100 Percent	40–60 Percent	0–40 Percent
Me 410	2			1
Bf 109	24	11	4	17
Bf 110	3			6
Fw 190	2	1	2	4

Luftwaffe records indicate that the Germans lost no less than 41.9 percent of their fighter force (destroyed or written off) in October.[77] Table XLIV[78] indicates the losses among German fighter pilots in late 1943.

The level of attrition for both Germany's fighter forces as well as Eighth Air Force during September and October bordered on the point where both were close to losing cohesion and effectiveness as combat forces. In the long run, considering the massive influx of bombers, fighters, and crews already swelling American bases in England, Eighth held the strategic advantage. It was, of course, difficult for the crews who flew to Schweinfurt to recognize that advantage.

THE DAY BATTLE: THE PAUSE, NOVEMBER-DECEMBER 1943

Historians of airpower, like other military historians, tend to see their topics in terms of decisive battles and clear-cut turning points. The reality, however, is usually more complex. Thus, Schweinfurt often appears as a decisive defeat, followed by a lull in operations until February 1944 when Eighth Air Force's bombers supported by long-range fighters smashed the *Luftwaffe* during "Big Week." Schweinfurt was, of course, a turning point and forced fundamental changes in American doctrine and strategy. For the Germans, however, the pressure eased only marginally after Schweinfurt. Moreover, from the *Luftwaffe*'s perspective, October 14 did not appear as important or decisive as it did for the Americans. The debate within the high command continued unabated, and Göring and Hitler—as they had throughout the summer—proved unwilling to address fundamental strategic questions.

In early November, Galland warned the fighter forces of Göring's dissatisfaction with their October achievements:

> The fighter and heavy formations have not been able to secure decisive success in air defense against American four-engined formations. The introduction of new weapons . . . has not appreciably changed the situation. The main reason for the failure is that the *Kommandeure* and *Kapitane [sic]* do not succeed in securing attacks in close formation up to the shortest ranges. . . .
>
> The *Reichsmarschall* has, therefore, ordered the setting up of an assault *Staffel (Sturmstaffel)*. Its tasks will be to break up the enemy by using more heavily armored fighters in all-out . . . attacks. . . . Then there is no need to discuss here whether this is to be done by shooting down the enemy at the closest range, by employing a new type of weapon, or by ramming.[79]

Table XLIV   Fighter Pilot Losses September-December 1943

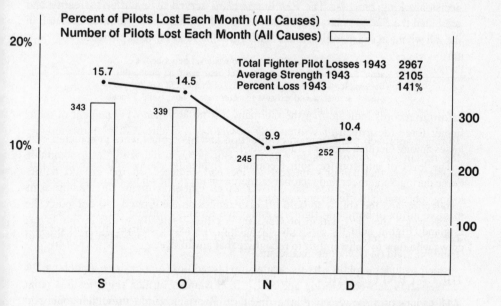

Göring's counsel of despair reflected an essentially negative attitude expressed frequently throughout the period: The day fighters were not doing enough. Speaking to an assemblage of senior officers at Obersalzberg, he announced that the people and frontline soldiers had lost faith in the *Luftwaffe*. They could understand the difficulty of finding British bombers at night, but the sight of American formations flying through Germany's skies was too much.[80] Hitler's bitter reproaches undoubtedly contributed to the *Reichsmarschall*'s disquiet. But misconceptions dotted Göring's speeches. For Göring, the solution for the *Reich*'s defense lay not in increased fighter production or more crews but rather in a fanatical "National Socialist" approach to air defense; supposedly, German spirit and morale could beat superiority in numbers on which the materialistic Anglo-Saxons depended. Such an attitude helps explain Göring's refusal to recognize the danger that the loss of fighter pilots posed.[81] The *Reichsmarschall* expanded his message in a series of conferences throughout the remainder of the year. He was even willing to speak in such terms to his fighter pilots. On November 23, he reproached the day crews of 3rd *Jagddivision* that he had brought them back from the front to defend the *Reich*. They, however, had disappointed him, while the German people could not understand what was happening and were embittered. Intermixed with such remarks were even less tasteful comments about the cowardice of the assembled pilots.[82]

Yet, the real problem lay beyond Göring at the highest level. While Hitler had left the *Luftwaffe* to Göring earlier in the war, he was now enmeshed in its decisionmaking process. The *Reichsmarschall* served as a buffer to reality and presented the *Führer*'s latest demands to his subordinates. He admitted as much in the fall when, in exasperation to his staff's gloomy reports, he exploded:

> I could also go to the *Führer* and to whatever he wished, say: No, *mein Führer*, this can't be done or that can't be done, this is impossible or that is impossible, . . . or that would cost too many losses, or that would exhaust the *Luftwaffe*. Thus, could I speak, [and] I could always contradict what he had proposed.[83]

Göring's approach went in another direction and his replies were punctuated with the refrain of *"Jawohl, mein Führer."* But perhaps the truly insurmountable problem was that Hitler's interest to the end centered on the ground battle. Consequently, he regarded the air war as an embarrassment, threatening arms production and the ability to hold off his enemies on the ground. At one point, he even argued that destruction of Germany's cities "actually works in our favor, because it is creating a body of people with nothing to lose—people who will therefore fight on with utter fanaticism."[84]

Such attitudes explain why the leadership placed little emphasis on air defense. A conversation between Göring and Milch in November further amplifies this point and underscores the dread that a defeat in Russia inspired throughout German society in late 1943. Milch suggested that alongside the life-and-death question of the eastern front, he was equally worried about what the homeland would do when American fighters came in the spring of 1944. Göring replied: "When every city in Germany has been smashed to the ground, the German people would still live. It would certainly be awful, but the nation had lived before there were cities." Milch then suggested that such an occurrence might affect arms production, but Göring was not listening. He asked what was the greater danger, Berlin's destruction or the arrival of the Russians. The latter he noted was the "number one danger."[85]

Thus, interest at the top in air defense was but a fleeting occurrence. One can question whether the *Reich*'s air defense ever received the emphasis promised by Hitler in response to Hamburg. In October, Göring suggested to his staff that the German people did not care whether the *Luftwaffe* attacked British airfields. "All they wished to hear when a hospital or a children's home in Germany is destroyed is that we have destroyed the same in England; then they are satisfied."[86] With Hitler's predilection for retaliation, there was no chance of altering aircraft production in favor of fighters. In fact, conferences between Milch and Göring indicate the *Reichsmarschall*'s definite bias towards bombers. In October, *"der Dicke"* bitterly reproached Milch for placing too much emphasis on the *Reich*'s defense and for robbing production from the bomber forces. Göring could not believe that American production could ever reach estimated levels, because so many men and so much material would be required.[87]

Further conversations in November confirmed the leadership's desire for bomber production. On the 23rd, Göring underlined the importance of using fighters as fighter bombers. When the discussion turned to the distribution of future Ju 388 production between night fighter and bomber forces, he expressed himself in favor of the latter.[88] On the 28th, Göring went even further and decided to hold down future fighter production in favor of bombers. The *Reichsmarschall* commented to Fritz Sauckel, *Gauleiter* and slave labor procurer for the *Reich,* that the *Luftwaffe* had to have bombers.

> Göring: I cannot remain on the defensive; we must also have an offensive. That is the most decisive.

> Sauckel: The only argument that makes an impression on a racial cousin [the British] is that of retaliation.[89]

Two factors were working against the defense. First, Hitler and Göring refused to consider an emergency effort to build fighters. This had particular significance in view of American attacks on aircraft factories. Those raids, beginning in the summer of 1943, had already caused a serious drop in fighter production (see Table XLV[90]).

TABLE XLV
Production of New and Reconditioned Fighter
Aircraft—June-December 1943

	Fighter Production
June 1943	1,134
July 1943	1,263
August 1943	1,135
September 1943	1,072
October 1943	1,181
November 1943	985
December 1943	687

Thus, November's production from factories and repair depots was only 78 percent of July's, while production in December fell to 54.4 percent of the July figure. This decline came at the same time that the *Luftwaffe* was suffering a high rate of attrition. New production was even more affected as a result of Eighth and Ninth Air Forces' efforts against the Messerschmitt and Focke Wulf factories (see Table XLVI[91]).

TABLE XLVI
Production of New Fighters

	Bf 109	Fw 190	Total
June 1943	663	109	772
July 1943	704	169	873
August 1943	515	159	674
September 1943	525	167	682
October 1943	556	127	683
November 1943	472	114	576
December 1943	350	313	663

Now in November 1943, escort support for bomber formations reached deeper into the *Reich*. On the 3rd, despite bad weather, fighters escorted the bombers to Wilhelmshaven. Using radar control *H2X*, an American modification of the *H2S* system, the force bombed through the clouds. Two things were significant about the raid. First, the number of bombers involved, 539, points up how quickly the pipeline of crews and aircraft from the United States had compensated for October's losses; second, escort fighter support kept the bomber losses down to 7 (with only 3 due to enemy fighters).[97] The Germans found the appearance of American fighters at this range most alarming. German losses were so heavy that Galland held a special meeting with I *Jagdkorps'* division commanders on November 4.[98] Contributing to the day fighter losses was the fact that many German fighters did not possess direction finders to locate their bases in bad weather.[99] The Wilhelmshaven raid resulted in several changes. Generaloberst Weise, commander of the central air district *(Befehlshaber Mitte)*, thought that the single-engine fighters must engage protecting fighters so that the heavier fighters (Bf 110's) could close with the bombers. He recognized how dangerous the air environment over central Germany had become and suggested that many heavy fighter squadrons should re-equip with single-engine fighters. Finally, he admitted that the only force available to protect the "Destroyers" (Bf 110's) was Herrmann's single-engine night fighter force (the "wild sow" fighters).[100]

Over the next days, conferences among the leading fighter generals seconded Weise's suggestions. One colonel urged that the entire force possess single-engine fighters. The conclusions, however, were that five light *Gruppen* were adequate to engage enemy fighter forces. General Weise asked whether the lighter fighters could hold off the supporting escorts so that the "Destroyers" could attack the unprotected bombers. General Schmid thought not since there were insufficient fighters.[101] On the next day, the *Jagdkorps I* decided that the "wild sow" force would also have to support the Bf 110's during the day. The decision came immediately before an interesting discussion over the fate of II./JGS which had suffered heavy losses during the preceding week. Colonel von Lutzow suggested that II./JGS be pulled out of the line for rehabilitation. Another officer, however, urged that in view of shortages throughout the western fighter forces, the unit be broken up and its personnel and aircraft divided among other squadrons in the west.[102] Given the German's emphasis on unit cohesion, this represented an important departure in policy and an admission that severe frontline shortages of pilots and aircraft existed. On November 20, Schmid warned his commanders:

> One can estimate that for the foreseeable future, the provision of aircraft will be numerically so small so that for the future our inferiority compared to the British and Americans will remain. It is therefore the responsibility of the commander to act so that with the aircraft on hand . . . every possible loss will be avoided. With enemy attacks, it is important that the 3rd Division carries out timely aerial reconnaissance to report where the enemy formations are flying and whether they are accompanied by fighters. By such action, we will be able to avoid feeding night fighters against enemy day fighters.[103]

The combination of declining production and attrition left Galland with a thin reed with which to defend the *Reich*. While the pressure eased somewhat in November, the Germans still faced a substantial threat. The shadow of American escort fighters and the gradual extension of their range lay over all *Luftwaffe* counterbomber operations. By early October, German intelligence had reported that American fighters were accompanying bombers as far as Hamburg.[92] Eighth's losses in October led the Germans to conclude that during good weather American bombers would have to have fighter escort, and that because of the P–47's limited range the Americans would switch more of their operations to bad weather.[93] A December intelligence evaluation warned that day operations, supported by fighters, were already reaching the middle ranges. The authors suggested, moreover, that the Americans were hard at work developing a true long-distance fighter.[94] In the immediate future, the Germans estimated that Eighth would extend the range of "Lightnings" and "Thunderbolts" by increasing the capacity of their drop tanks. The solution, however, would have to await development of a true long-range fighter.[95]

German intelligence had no idea how close the Americans were to a solution. From the beginning of November, however, P–47's and P–38's, now equipped with better drop tanks, flew deeper into the *Reich*. Göring had no desire to recognize the implications. In early September, American fighters had reached Aachen and Galland reported the occurrence to Hitler. When Göring got wind of Galland's report, he was enraged. Speer recounts the ensuing discussion:

> "What's the idea of telling the *Führer* that American fighters have penetrated into the territory of the *Reich*?" Göring snapped. . . .
>
> "*Herr Reichsmarschall,*" Galland replied with imperturbable calm, "they will soon be flying even deeper."
>
> Göring spoke even more vehemently: "That's nonsense, Galland, what gives you fantasies? That's pure bluff!"
>
> Galland shook his head. "Those are the facts, *Herr Reichsmarschall!* . . . American fighters have been shot down over Aachen. There is no doubt about it!"
>
> Göring obstinately held his ground: "That is simply not true, Galland. It's impossible."
>
> Galland reacted with a touch of mockery: "You might go and check it yourself, sir; the downed planes are there at Aachen." . . .
>
> Göring finally declared: "What must have happened is that they were shot down much farther to the west. I mean, if they were very high when they were shot down they could have glided quite a distance farther before they crashed."
>
> Not a muscle moved in Galland's face. "Glided to the east, sir? If my plane were shot up . . ."[96]

On November 13, Eighth went all the way to Bremen with fighter escort as 345 P-47's and 45 P-38's supported the 143 bombers. The P-47's provided the short-range cover while the P-38's, with two 150-gallon drop tanks, held off German fighters near the target. The attacking bombers lost 16 aircraft but only 2 to German fighters.[104] A more massive attack on Bremen thirteen days later, despite fighter support, cost the attackers 25 bombers; but considering bomber strength, 491 aircraft, losses were only 5.1 percent. That was an attrition rate that Eighth could accept. The November 26 raid is important because for the first time, Eighth dispatched 600 bombers (128 aircraft also attacked Paris). In December, despite the weather, Eighth launched eight major raids against the continent. The size of these raids, in some cases, came close to doubling and, in many cases, actually did double October's attack on Schweinfurt. On December 11, 523 bombers hit Emden; on December 13, 649 bombers attacked a number of targets in Germany; on December 16, 535 hit Bremen; on December 20, 472 attacked Bremen again; on December 22, Eighth hit Osnabrück and Münster; and finally on the 30th, 650 bombers hit Ludwigshafen. The losses in these raids (162) approached those of October (179), but Eighth with fighter escorts and with the influx of new aircraft and crews could stand such attrition much better.[105]

This activity shows that the pressure on the *Luftwaffe* in the last two months of 1943 had eased only marginally. While much of Germany still lay beyond escort range, American operations reaching further to the east caused the Germans serious embarrassment and heavy losses. The December 13 mission against Kiel and Hamburg suggests the increasing complexity and success of the fighter range extension program. Six hundred forty-eight heavy bombers flew the mission with 394 fighter escorts, 41 of which were P-51's. Flying in relays that met contact points along the route, the fighters provided continuous and effective support; Eighth lost only five bombers.[106] German fighter formations refused to tangle with bomber formations supported by large numbers of fighters.

At the end of December, Galland and the staff of *Jagdkorps* I concluded that their new tactics against supported bomber formations had failed. The causes were "(a) the weather, (b) the considerable inferiority of German strength, (c) the impossibility of gathering sufficient strength in an area because of time and distance limitations; result: weak and dispersed fighter attacks."[107] Moreover, German fighter losses, although dropping from October's high point, were still high enough to cause considerable worry. In November, the Germans had to write off 21 percent of their fighter aircraft because of battle damage and noncombat causes. In December, that percentage rose to 22.8 percent.[108] In normal times, such losses would have been catastrophic. Compared with October and the summer, this loss rate did provide some relief to the fighter force. Nevertheless, this continued expenditure, combined with declining production, explains why there was no numerical recovery of the day fighter force at year's end (see Table LXVII[109]).

Losses of fighter pilots in November and December also showed a decline from the high point reached in the July-October period. They, however, remained at a level which under other conditions would have represented a crippling drain. In

TABLE LXVII
Frontline Strength and Operational Ready Rate, Fighter Force—
August-December 1943

	Fighters Authorized	Actually Present	Percent	Operationally Ready	Operationally Ready, Percent
August 31, 1943	2,228	1,581	71.0	1,019	64.4
September 30, 1943	2,228	1,646	73.9	1,080	65.6
October 31, 1943	2,288	1,721	75.2	1,193	69.3
November 30, 1943	2,244	1,789	79.7	1,140	63.7
December 31, 1943	2,244	1,561	69.6	1,095	70.1

November, nearly 10 percent of the fighter pilots were lost, and in December there was a slight rise to 10.4 percent. That increase reflected American pressure and heralded the attrition that would occur in coming months.[110] In 1943, the fighter force had averaged 2,105 full and partially operational ready pilots present for duty each month. Over the year, a total of 2,967 fighter pilots were killed, wounded, or missing in action.[111] The fighter force's weaknesses at the turn of the year and its defeat in the spring of 1944 can only be understood in the context of past attrition rates. Table XLVIII[112] suggests what these losses meant for a frontline unit.

TABLE XLVIII
Losses in *Jagdgeschwader* 26

	Pilots Killed
1939	2
1940	51
1941	64
1942	69
1943	149
1944	249
1945	110
TOTAL	694

DEFEAT: JANUARY-MARCH 1944

In January 1944, the tempo of operations picked up. American production now swamped Germany's defenders. The growth in Eighth's combat strength for both bombers and fighters was phenomenal (see Tables XLIX[113] and L[114]).

In addition to Eighth's fighters, there were so many tactical fighters and intermediate-range bombers in England that a new air force, the Ninth, was established. Finally, RAF Fighter Command offered substantial support over the occupied countries so that Eighth's long-range escorts only had to cover bomber formations deep in German airspace. Earlier in the war, America's announced production plans had met either derision from the *Reich*'s propaganda service or amused disdain from military leaders. Now in early 1944, the Germans discovered what Americans meant by a *real* battle of materiel.

At year's end, America's European air forces underwent major command changes. At Eisenhower's insistence, Spaatz and Doolittle arrived in England from

TABLE XLIX
Bomber and Fighter Strength, Eighth Air Force

Heavy Bombers

Date	AIRCRAFT			CREWS		
	Assigned to Air Force	On Hand Oper Tactical Units	Fully Operational Tactical Units	Assigned	Available	Effective Combat Strength
Sep 1943	881	656	461	661	409	373
Oct 1943	1,000	763	535	820	479	417
Nov 1943	1,254	902	705	1,085	636	578
Dec 1943	1,503	1,057	752	1,556	949	723
Jan 1944	1,630	1,082	842	1,644	1,113	822
Feb 1944	1,852	1,481	1,046	1,683	1,155	981
Mar 1944	1,872	1,497	1,094	1,639	1,063	960
Apr 1944	1,952	1,661	1,323	1,776	1,148	1,049
May 1944	2,507	2,070	1,655	2,180	1,430	1,304
Jun 1944	2,755	2,547	2,123	2,863	2,034	1,855

Fighters

Date	AIRCRAFT			CREWS		
	Assigned to Air Force	On Hand Oper Tactical Units	Fully Operational Tactical Units	Assigned	Available	Effective Combat Strength
Sep 1943		372	274	533	398	274
Oct 1943		559	426	749	591	426
Nov 1943		635	478	771	631	478
Dec 1943		725	565	865	664	565
Jan 1944	1,163	909	707	1,028	810	707
Feb 1944	1,138	883	678	1,177	888	678
Mar 1944	1,197	1,016	720	1,252	998	720
Apr 1944	1,305	1,060	784	1,279	953	775
May 1944	1,465	1,174	882	1,449	1,053	856
Jun 1944	1,243	1,112	906	1,703	1,230	885

the Mediterranean, the latter as Eaker's replacement. Eaker, disappointed at leaving an Eighth receiving massive reinforcements, took over command of Allied Mediterranean air forces. His responsibilities included the newly formed Fifteenth Air Force that would launch "strategic" bombing attacks on Germany from the south. Eaker's replacement may have reflected dissatisfaction with his conduct of the campaign. It is more probable that the close relationship between Eisenhower, Tedder, Spaatz, and Doolittle played a major role in the command changes.

January's weather did not cooperate with American commanders who had hoped to launch their air forces against the *Reich* to win air superiority. Arnold made clear in a Christmas message what he expected to be accomplished in 1944. The overriding aim was destruction of the *Luftwaffe*: "*Destroy the enemy air force wherever you find them, in the air, on the ground, and in the factories* [emphasis in original]."[115] Nevertheless, conditions were sufficient to allow the Germans a glimpse of what they could expect. As early as the start of 1944, *Luftwaffe* intelligence gave a clear picture of the pattern of upcoming day raids. They noted

Table L   Aircraft Written Off: Eighth Air Force 1944 (Heavy Bombers)

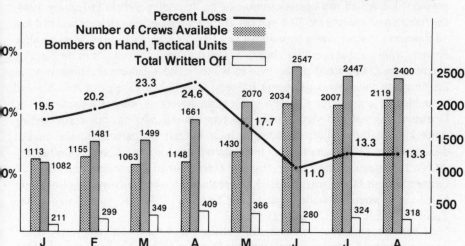

the following characteristics. First, fighter bombers and twin-engine aircraft, such as "Mosquitoes," "Mitchells," and "Marauders," would attack targets throughout France and the Low Countries. Concurrently, four-engine bomber formations would sweep into Germany while clouds of fighters, upwards of 1,000, would accompany the raids. Finally, the B–17 and B–24 formations would attack a number of targets to divide and to confuse the defenders.[116]

Because of bad weather, nearly all of the day raids in January used radar for bombing. In mid-month, conditions cleared for a short period, and Eighth dispatched its forces deep into Germany against the aircraft industry. Although only one-third of the 663 bombers dispatched bombed the primary targets, a major air battle did develop. Out of 174 bombers attacking the A.G.O. *Flugzeugwerke* at Oschersleben, the Germans shot down 34. The day's losses reached the level of the attacks on Schweinfurt in 1943—60 bombers. The cause of such losses were two-fold: the masssive *Luftwaffe* opposition and the fact that only one group of P–51's could provide the deep support that such a raid required.[117] The attack again showed the Germans the importance that Eighth Air Force attached to destroying Germany's aircraft industry. A decrypted "Ultra" message noted:

> The attack against Oschersleben carried out beyond the effective
> range of fighter escort, for which the enemy must have counted on
> having heavy losses, again underlies the importance attached to the
> diminution of German fighter aircraft production. . . . The
> crushing of the attack and the very considerable losses will
> presumably limit American daylight activity for some time to the
> range of escort formations.[118]

A sharp rise in *Luftwaffe* aircraft and crew losses immediately reflected the pressure that Allied day operations exerted on defending forces. In January 1944, the fighter forces wrote off 30.3 percent of their single-engine fighters and had lost 16.9 percent of their crews by month's end.[119] This high attrition of pilots resulted not only from combat operations but also from the continued dilution of the force by inexperienced, ill-trained pilots, who in winter's bad weather conditions were as dangerous to themselves as enemy fighters. One fighter *Gruppe* at month's end scrambled 21 aircraft for a second sortie at an American bomber formation. The Germans achieved two victories but had four aircraft missing, one crash landing (pilot killed), three pilots abandoning their aircraft by parachute, one aircraft damaged after a belly landing, and three aircraft crashing on takeoff.[120] On January 29, the III *Gruppe* of the *Jagdgeschwader Udet* claimed 12 bombers, but out of 28 German aircraft taking off, at least 5 and probably 6 were destroyed; 2 pilots were killed and 1 wounded while 3 parachuted to safety.[121] For the overall trends, see Tables LI,[122] LII,[123] LIII,[124] and LIV[125].

At month's end, the Germans still believed that they need not worry about American escort fighters accompanying the bombers to Berlin because they doubted whether escort fighters could go as far as Braunschweig.[126] In fact, their assumption that part of the *Reich* would lie beyond escort fighters' range soon proved false. The delay that January's and February's bad weather imposed on American operations probably worked in favor of the Allies' coming offensive. Before the end of February, a crash program had transitioned a significant number of pilots into P–51's. By mid-month, Eighth possessed 539 P–38J's, 416 P–47D's, and 329 P–51B's.[127] Toward the end of February, the extended period of bad weather broke and the greatest air battle of World War II began. At this point, Doolittle released his fighters from earlier restrictions that had tied escort fighters close to bomber formations.[128] Fighters now attacked German fighters on sight, and Eighth went after the *Luftwaffe* wherever it existed. With drop tanks that would carry P–51's to Berlin, American operations attacked production facilities throughout the *Reich*. The bombing offensive did not, however, succeed in its direct mission to destroy aircraft production. German industry responded to the attack on aircraft factories in such outstanding fashion that fighter production rose dramatically in the coming months, but the nature of the target forced the *Luftwaffe* to come up and to fight. As a result, American fighter escorts decimated the *Luftwaffe*'s fighter force.

What later historians called "Big Week," code-named "Argument," began on February 20 with a multitarget attack on the German aircraft industry. Most objectives lay in the Brunswick-Leipzig area. Over 1,000 bombers, 16 combat wings of B–17's and B–24's, sortied from their bases.[129] All 17 fighter groups in England provided an escort of 835 fighters (668 P–47's, 94 P–38's, and 73 P–51's).[130] German reaction was generally weak, and the attacking force lost only 21 bombers. Operations on the 20th opened a week of intense operations by Eighth and Fifteenth Air Forces. The raids struck the German aircraft industry and its supporting infrastructure repeated blows. After a relatively easy mission on the 21st, opposition stiffened and Eighth lost 41 bombers and Fifteenth lost 14 on the 22nd.[131]

Table LI   German Aircraft Losses January–June 1944 (All Types)

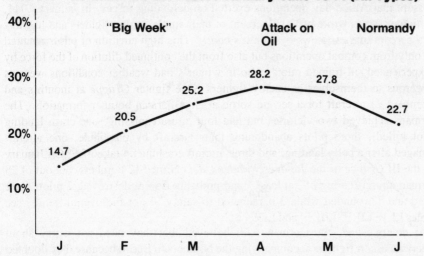

Table LII German Fighter Losses January–June 1944

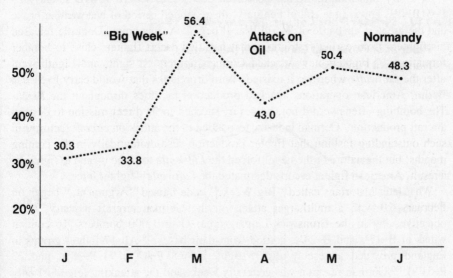

Table LIII German Bomber Losses January-June 1944

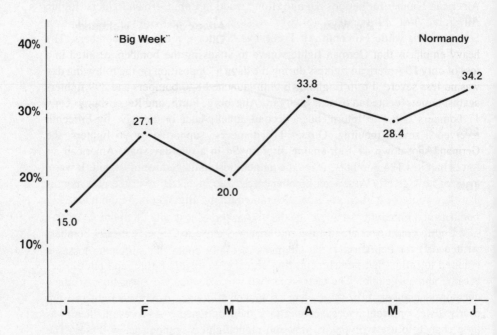

Table LIV Fighter Pilot Losses January-May 1944

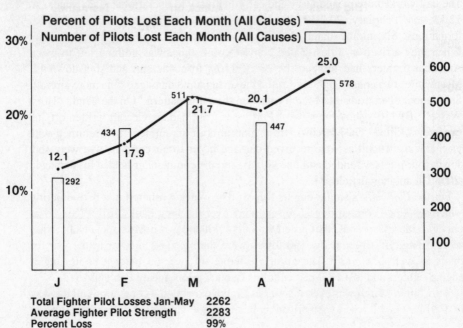

Total Fighter Pilot Losses Jan-May   2262
Average Fighter Pilot Strength   2283
Percent Loss   99%

The final two raids of "Big Week" came on February 24 and 25th. Here again, American bomber formations ran into strong reaction from German fighters. Eighth Air Force lost 49 bombers (5 over Rostock, 33 over Gotha, and 11 over Schweinfurt), while Fifteenth Air Force lost 17, for a total of 66 bombers. The heavy emphasis that German fighters gave to attacking the bombers resulted in a loss of only 10 American fighters during the day.[132] Opposition on the following day was no less severe. From England, Eighth launched 820 bombers and 899 fighters against targets located in or near Stuttgart, Augsburg, Fürth, and Regensburg. Only 17 bombers failed to return; but a second attack, later in the day, by Fifteenth received a severe mauling. Out of 116 bombers, supported by 96 fighters, the Germans shot down 41 four-engine aircraft. So in a two-day span, American air forces had lost 124 bombers, twice the number lost in the Schweinfurt raid. It was a mark of how greatly American bomber forces had increased over the past months that they could bear such attrition. Overall, during "Big Week," Eighth lost 137 bombers and Fifteenth lost 89, while the two air forces lost only 28 fighters.[133]

If Eighth could bear an attrition rate that was close to 20 percent (299 bombers written off) for February,[134] the Germans certainly could not suffer the losses it required to inflict that punishment. In February, *Luftwaffe* fighter and pilot losses became unmanageable. The tactics that had worked when there was time to attack unescorted bomber formations were no longer effective. American fighters were nearly always present and eager to attack their opponent. As a result, there was little chance to use twin-engine day and night fighters without heavy losses. The experiences of *Zerstörergeschwader* "Horst Wessel," a Bf 110 fighter squadron, indicates what happened to twin-engine fighters in the new combat environment. The unit worked up over January and early February to operational ready status. At 12:13, on February 20, 13 Bf 110's scrambled after approaching bomber formations. Six minutes later, three more aircraft took off to join the first group. When they arrived at a designated contact point, there was nothing left to meet. American fighters had jumped the 13 Bf 110's from the sun and shot down 11. Meanwhile, two enemy fighters strafed the airfield and damaged nine more aircraft. Subsequent operations into March followed the same pattern. On the 22nd, "Horst Wessel" Bf 110's shot down two "Fortresses" but had six aircraft written off and two crews killed. On March 6, from nine aircraft scrambled, two returned with mechanical difficulties, one received damage in air-to-air combat, five were shot down (four pilots wounded and one killed), and the commander landed his damaged aircraft at another airfield.[135]

For the *Luftwaffe*'s single-engine force, "Big Week" ushered in a period during which sustained combat devastated its units over the long haul. "Big Week" was only the start of a process that lasted through April and was not the apogee but rather a beginning. Bf 109 and Fw 190 losses were the heaviest thus far in the war for pilots as well as aircraft. The *Luftwaffe* wrote off over 33 percent of its single-engine fighters and lost 17.9 percent of its fighters pilots during February.[136]

Attrition in March was even heavier as Eighth expanded its operations all the way to Berlin. On March 4, American bombers made their first major raid on the

German capital and encountered only light opposition. Two days later, they returned to meet a more tenacious opposition, and the bombers lost 69 of their number while 11 escorting fighters were shot down. The third major raid on Berlin within six days occurred on the 8th; and despite excellent visibility, the attacking formations met relatively light opposition. Eighth's losses remained manageable, 37 bombers and 17 escorts.[137] The appearance of American bombers over Berlin tried the imagination of even Goebbels' Propaganda Ministry. One newspaper suggested that: "If the inhabitants of the capital were surprised that, despite the heavy defenses and heavy losses, isolated enemy formations reached the capital in formation, it must be remembered that this need not be interpreted as a sign of strength at all." The *Völkischer Beobachter*, however, won the prize for biased reporting when it claimed that: "If occasionally they fly in clear sky without at the moment being pursued by the dreaded German fighters, only the layman is fooled, and then only for a few moments. . . . In their case, the closed drill formations is not a sign of strength."[138]

The attrition of German fighter pilots and aircraft reached a new high point in March. *Luftwaffe* units wrote off 56.4 percent of single-engine fighters available on March 1, while crew losses reached nearly 22 percent of pilots present on February 29.[139] Nevertheless, the Germans did impose severe attrition on Eighth's bombers. Eighth wrote off 349 bombers in March. Not until May did a significant decrease in bomber attrition begin, reflecting the continued arrival of new crews and aircraft as well as the final collapse of the *Luftwaffe*'s fighter force (see Table XLIX[140]).

The rising German losses in March reflected several factors. The most obvious was the tempo of operations. Although bad weather prevented the occurrence of another "Big Week," Eighth kept up an unremitting pressure on the defenses. The bombing raids forced the Germans to fight and imposed a continuing battle of attrition on their fighters. During the month, the Americans were active over Germany on twenty-three days, thirteen of which involved an all-out effort.[141] Although the bomb damage may not have been as effective as during "Big Week," aerial combat results, including the achievement of air superiority over the continent, were of critical importance.

The second factor working against the Germans was the growing strength of the escort forces. By March, they had reached a point where American fighters, having accomplished their primary escort mission, dropped to low altitudes and attacked targets of opportunity, particularly airfields.[142] For the Germans, this was a dangerous development that strained not only the fighter force but its supporting infrastructure as well. As an intercepted "Ultra" message on March 8 revealed:

> The enemy has recognized our own tactics of taking off and getting
> away from the airfield with all serviceable aircraft before attacks on
> our ground organization. In the west, he has recently put aside a
> part of the escorting force to attack these aircraft and has achieved
> successes in this connection.[143]

A message on March 24 indicated how widespread the threat had become. *Luftflotte Reich* reported:

> During flights into the home war zone, enemy fighters have
> repeatedly carried out attacks on aircraft which were landing or on
> the airfields themselves. In doing so, they imitate the landing
> procedure of German fighters or effect surprise by approaching the
> airfield in fast and level flight. The difficulty in distinguishing
> friend from foe often makes it impossible for the flak artillery to fire
> on them. [144]

One must note here "Ultra's" impact in indicating to Allied air commanders the effectiveness of their tactics and the severe difficulties the *Luftwaffe* was facing. Intercepted messages did not always reveal what the Allies wished to know (such as bomb damage), but operational intercepts undoubtedly helped keep the pressure where it hurt the Germans the most.

One can glimpse what this pressure meant in the war diaries and messages of the fighter squadrons. The 2nd *Gruppe* of *Jagdgeschwader* II scrambled 16 aircraft on March 13. Returning pilots claimed two "Mustangs" as certain and two as probable, but one German aircraft crashed on return (pilot killed), two aircraft were missing, a fourth was lost when its pilot bailed out, and a fifth crashed near Lübeck. On the 6th, this same group launched 15 aircraft against a Berlin raid: one pilot was killed, one missing, and one wounded when he jumped from his aircraft. [145] The war diary of the 3rd *Gruppe* of *Jagdgeschwader Udet* makes similarly depressing reading. On March 15, the *Gruppe* launched 20 aircraft; 2 pilots were killed (aircraft destroyed), 2 pilots had to parachute to safety, and 2 crash landings took place. On the next day, nine aircraft scrambled; two pilots were killed, four pilots were wounded (one severely), and one pilot parachuted to safety unhurt. On the next day, operations cost the unit one killed and two more pilots wounded (one badly). Thus, in a three-day span, a unit with about 25 pilots had lost 5 killed and 6 wounded (2 severely). [146]

Fighter pilot losses were not confined to the inexperienced. Given the overwhelming odds, the law of averages began to catch up with Germany's leading aces. In March, two *Geschwader* commanders with 102 kills and 161 kills were killed on operations. [147] In mid-March, shortages of skilled pilots caused Galland to send the following message asking for volunteers:

> The strained manpower situation in units operating in defense of the
> *Reich* demands urgently the further bringing up of experienced
> flying personnel from other arms of the service, in particular for the
> maintenance of fighting power to the air arm, tried pilots of the
> ground attack and bomber units, especially officers suitable as
> formation leaders, will now also have to be drawn on. [148]

The loss of aircraft was as serious a problem. Bombing attacks on industry had retarded production at the same time that the fighter force was suffering catastrophic losses in air-to-air combat and through the strafing of airfields. An "Ultra" message at the end of March indicated the severity of aircraft shortages.

> The extraordinarily difficult situation in the air defense of the
> homeland requires with all emphasis: (1) The speedy salvage of all
> fighter and heavy fighter aircraft and their immediate return for

repairs. (2) The unrestricted employment of salvage personnel for salvage tasks. Subordinate units are expressly forbidden to employ them for any other purpose. (3)' That spare parts be acquired by repair and salvage units by removal from aircraft worth salvaging only in case of absolute necessity. (4) That repair of aircraft in your area be energetically speeded up in order to increase serviceability and to relieve supply.[149]

By the end of March, the daylight "strategic" bombing offensive had put the *Luftwaffe* on the ropes. It had retarded, although only for a short period, the expansion of fighter production. More importantly, it had caused an attrition that one can only describe as devastating. American forces were to continue that unrelenting pressure in the coming months. Thus, there was no hope of a recovery for Germany's daylight fighter forces, and the Allies were close to winning air superiority over all of Europe. *Oberst* Hannes Trautloft, serving as inspector of fighters and as a member of the "fighter staff" to increase aircraft production, told a group of factory workers:

The opponent now seeks to fix our fighter forces, the fighters, the "Destroyers," and the night fighters, and to destroy the factories. You know that he has partially succeeded. That has come about . . . because we do not have enough aircraft. We need aircraft. . . . I speak also your language because the language of the workers and the language of the front is the same. We must succeed—and I am convinced we will succeed when the new measures are in effect—in producing more aircraft in the near future.[150]

Unfortunately for Trautloft and Germany's cities, there was no method that could produce enough machines or pilots; the battle for air superiority was lost because the battle of production had been lost in 1940, 1941, and 1942—not 1944.

WAR IN THE EAST, THE MEDITERRANEAN , AND OVER BRITAIN

As cited previously, the *Luftwaffe*'s heavy commitments to the defense of the *Reich* had forced it to scale back commitments elsewhere. Nevertheless, German air operations at the front did continue, although on a much reduced scale. Russia attracted most of the attention because of the deteriorating ground situation, while in Italy the Germans managed to stabilize the front north of Naples. Despite the Allied landing at Anzio in January 1944, the Germans held the Allies south of Rome with little support. In addition to the Mediterranean and Russian theaters, the *Luftwaffe* opened a night offensive against Britain to retaliate for the devastation of the *Reich*'s cities. The diversion of bomber strength from other threaters was considerable, the results meager.

The new Chief of Staff, Korten, had supported two strategies upon assuming office: the defense of the *Reich* and a "strategic" bombing policy on the eastern front. We have catalogued the course of the first strategy; the second element in Korten's policy is worth examining both for its assumptions and its failure. This reorientation in the *Luftwaffe*'s employment began before Jeschonnek's death. In June 1943, *Luftflotte* 6, controlling aircraft on the central part of the eastern front, proposed a bombing offensive against Russia's armament industries. Its staff, while overestimating prospects for the summer, argued that the *Wehrmacht* could not achieve a decisive success with "Citadel." The Russians with their immense production would recover and go over to the offensive in winter. To prevent another winter attack, *Luftflotte* 6 argued that if it possessed sufficient strength, it could successfully attack targets such as the Gorki tank production center. An effective "strategic" bombing offensive, it argued, would injure Russian morale and production to such an extent that the disasters of the previous winters would not recur.[151] Several days later, Jeschonnek himself echoed these points in a conversation with a staff officer. The Chief of Staff suggested that a systematic attack on the armaments factories of the Volga would weaken Russia's ability to launch a "great breakthrough offensive." It would, at least, force Russia's Allies to transfer material from other fronts to make up Soviet shortages. Jeschonnek found the possibility of terror attacks by 20 to 30 aircraft on population centers as a particularly enticing way to injure Russian morale. Nevertheless, his attention for most of the meeting centered on the ground battle.[152]

The growing interest in "strategic" bombing reflected a variety of factors. The most obvious was the general failure of German strategy in Russia. The Germans now had a tiger by the tail, and the tiger was showing signs of an ability to eat his attacker. Thus, there was every reason to look for a new strategy. A second factor, which had greatly contributed to Soviet successes, was the mobilization of Russia's immense economic and industrial resources. Not only on the ground but in the air, Soviet production was playing an important role. Aircraft production had grown from 9,780 in 1941, to 25,436 in 1942, and to 34,900 in 1943.[153] In addition, deliveries from America and Britain added to the total number of aircraft available to the Russians. Soviet aircraft had played an important part at certain critical moments, most notably at Moscow in 1941 and in the fall of 1942. However, not until 1943 at Kursk did the Soviet air force show itself able to intervene in the air and ground battle in a sustained fashion. Despite a concentrated effort in support of "Citadel," the *Luftwaffe* had not been able to win air superiority over the battlefield.

Korten did not find sentiment unanimously in favor of "strategic" bombing. The army with its enormous commitments in the east was loath to lose the air support that the *Luftwaffe* provided its troops.[154] Conversely, Speer added his prestige to those urging creation of a force to attack Russian industry. On June 23, he formed a committee to look for vulnerable points in the Soviet economy. Because of the limited number of bombers available, the committee urged the use of precision bombing by small groups of aircraft. Like the Air Corps Tactical School theorists of the thirties at Maxwell Field, they selected the electric industry as a choke point. According to Speer, one electric plant on the upper Volga supplied Moscow's power, while the destruction of several powerplants in the Urals would halt much of Russia's steel, tank, and munitions production.[155]

Armed with Speer's support, Korten persuaded Hitler and Göring that "strategic" bombing could materially aid the war effort. A November study set forth the arguments. The cover letter admitted that the new approach was a poor man's strategy. It argued that the *Luftwaffe*'s extensive support of ground operations had allowed the Russians to build up their armaments industry undisturbed, and thereby given the Soviets a vast numerical superiority in weapons. Despite an admission that the Red Air Force could defend Russia in depth, the paper optimistically suggested that even with its relatively weak forces, the *Luftwaffe* could launch precision bombing attacks that would have great impact. There was one premise on which such an offensive rested. The *Luftwaffe* must withdraw its bomber strength in the east from the close support mission and train it for a "strategic" bombing offensive against Soviet industry. The study itself examined in detail the structure of Soviet armament industries and gave special emphasis to the electric industry as the structure's weak link.[156]

These arguments convinced Göring and, for a short time, Hitler. On November 21, the *Reichsmarschall* signed a directive to *Luftflotten* 4 and 6 indicating his intention to launch a "strategic" bombing offensive against Soviet industry. He suggested that such a strategy offered better support for the ground forces than the present close support mission. Bomber units would pull back to rear echelon airfields as soon as possible and spend four to six weeks training for the deep penetration, precision bombing missions.[157] Korten thus received authorization to pull bomber units out of the line and to establish a special pathfinder unit for the "strategic" bombing force. The general staff scheduled early February for the start of its "strategic" bombing effort.[158] Nevertheless, the offensive only halfheartedly began in April. There were two reasons for the failure to meet the proposed schedule: First, the ground battle in the east deteriorated, and the Germans found it a virtual necessity to draw on bomber strength to aid hard-pressed troops. The second factor resulted from the diversion of bomber strength to the "Baby Blitz" retaliation attacks on London.

The Russian summer offensive had rolled into high gear after the victory at Kursk, and Soviet forces battered German infantry back to the Dneper. Hitler's consistent refusal to authorize timely withdrawals or the preparation of defensive positions in rear areas placed the *Wehrmacht* at a severe disadvantage. The tendencies that had marked late summer battles continued into the fall. Pushing across the Dneper in early October, Soviet forces drove on Krivoi Roy in the Ukraine and threatened to split the southern front in half. Using forces released from the west, Manstein possessed enough reserves to stem this Russian thrust.[159] The defense of Krivoi Roy was successful not only because of ground reinforcements but because of substantial air support. On this front, the *Luftwaffe* concentrated all twin-engine bombers in the east along with a substantial proportion of ground attack units. By flying 1,200 sorties per day over a five-day period, the *Luftwaffe* aided Manstein's forces in halting the Russian offensive.[160]

The front's stabilization north of Krivoi Roy only brought momentary relief. In the south, a massive Soviet offensive engulfed Sixth Army, captured the city of

Melitopol (near the northwest shore of the Sea of Azov), drove straight across to the northwestern shores of the Black Sea, and isolated the Seventeenth Army in the Crimea. Hitler refused requests to withdraw, and the Russians trapped one German division and seven Rumanian divisions. At the beginning of November, Soviet forces broke out from their bridgehead on the western bank of the Dneper near Kiev. The fighting that developed in this region threatened the entire southern front. Manstein's magic could only patch together inadequate solutions to the crises. All the while a terrible attrition of ground forces took place. First Panzer Army warned that its infantry strength had sunk to desperate straits; its divisions under heavy attack were losing a battalion a day.[161]

The fall disasters were a prelude to what would happen in the winter. In the south, Russian forces kept the pressure on and forced the Germans back from Kiev and the Dneper almost to the Bug River in the western Ukraine. They also cleared the Germans out of Nikopol in the east central Ukraine and finally captured Krivoi Roy. Hitler's refusal to allow any withdrawals until the last moment enabled the Russians to encircle four divisions near Cherkassy, located 100 miles southeast of Kiev; the *Luftwaffe* supplied the pocket from the air. In the first five days of aerial supply, its squadrons lost 44 aircraft to accidents and Russian fighters.[162]

While Army Group South received a severe battering, the Red Army launched a general offensive against the north. Between mid-January and the end of March, it drove the *Wehrmacht* entirely away from Leningrad and the positions that the Germans had held for two years. By spring, the Russians had advanced to Lake Peipus in eastern Estonia and had almost reached the Baltic countries. The final act in the catalogue of disasters befalling the *Wehrmacht* came in the winter when the Russians launched an early spring offensive against Army Group South. The Soviets drove the Germans from their last hold on the Dneper, cleaned the *Wehrmacht* from its hold on the western Ukraine, and finally came to rest on the foothills of the Carpathians and the Dnester—in other words, on the frontier of Rumania and Hungary.[163]

These defeats made the establishment of a "strategic" bombing force to attack Russia's armament industries virtually impossible. Throughout the winter, the Germans faced events on the ground that threatened destruction of not merely divisions and corps but armies and army groups. Only the most desperate expedients allowed the *Wehrmacht* to escape complete destruction. There was no choice except to use what was at hand, and the bomber forces were readily available. The location of the fighting in the south placed the *Luftwaffe* far from centers of supply, and difficulties in maintaining and supplying its forces there— especially after Army Group South and Army Group Center lost contact with each other—were considerable. Hitler's refusal to countenance withdrawals intensified the already considerable burdens on air units. His demand that the Crimea be held forced the *Luftwaffe* to maintain a considerable airlift by Ju 52's and He 111's, including some bomber units. The use of bomber units against Russian spearheads was at times successful and given the desperate situation on the ground, unavoidable. It was certainly not cost-effective.[164] By this time, the Russians were conversant with *Luftwaffe* operations, and they not only possessed aircraft in large numbers but their troops were equipped with ample antiaircraft support. Thus, German air operations tended to be decreasingly effective and more costly. By mid-December, *Luftflotte* 6 reported that Russian air strength was such that the enemy was launching 3,200 sorties a day to support ground operations.[165] Even more depressing for German ground forces was the fact that the Russians had noted the disappearance of German fighters and had therefore re-equipped many fighter units with ground attack aircraft. Those could now range over the battle areas with minimal fear of *Luftwaffe* fighters.[166]

The decrease in German aircraft strength in the east resulted in the remaining units being used as fire brigades, rushed from one frontline spot to another. A log book of an He 111 pilot on the eastern front during the 1943–44 period articulates this point. In his first 25 missions between August 8 and September 6, 1943, he did not fly a single mission lasting more than 10 minutes over enemy territory. In his next 25 missions between September 7 and 22nd, he flew only two missions lasting more than 10 minutes over enemy territory—one of 15 minutes and one of 2 hours duration. In his next 50 missions, he flew only three that lasted more than 10 minutes over enemy territory. For his second 100 missions, 32 lasted longer than 10 minutes, but many of these were weather reconnaissance flights over the Black Sea or supply missions into the Crimea.[167] The *Luftwaffe*'s specialized antitank forces, rushed from one section of the front to another, found it difficult to maintain their operational ready rates and suffered the cumulative effects of constant commitment to combat. One *Luftwaffe* pilot in an antitank squadron in Russia recalls that his unit lost as many aircraft as the number of tanks that it destroyed—hardly, he notes, a cost-effective employment of aircraft.[168]

The result of the defeats in Russia were twofold. First, there was an understandable reluctance to pull bomber units out of the line when ground forces were in trouble. Second, those forces that had pulled back from the front to begin special training programs soon found themselves asked to attack supply lines. For instance, in February when the Germans were in particularly bad trouble, Hitler used these specialized squadrons to bomb railroad tracks. These operations cost the attacking forces heavy losses with no commensurate lessening of pressures on the front.[169] Consequently, the special units did not complete training on schedule, and it was not until late March that the first attacks on Russian industrial targets began. By that time, however, Russian advances in the north had captured the forward operating fields from which the Germans had hoped to launch their air offensive. Gorki now lay entirely outside the range of German aircraft. Finally, hopes for the "strategic" bombing attacks had rested on the idle hope that the He 177 would finally arrive in the winter of 1943–44 in substantial numbers to augment the bomber squadrons. It did not, probably luckily for the crews, as Heinkel still had not solved the engine problems. By the time that the first He 177's (outside of the Stalingrad disaster) arrived on the eastern front in the summer of 1944, lack of fuel precluded sustained use of the aircraft.[170]

Meanwhile in the west, Hitler's decisions sealed the fate of the "strategic" bombing scheme. For the Nazi leadership, the terrible pounding that Bomber Command was inflicting on Germany's cities had reached intolerable levels. Goebbels sprinkled his diary and speeches with the hope that Germany would soon retaliate. In November 1943, Hitler, believing that his revenge weapons were ready, announced to the assembled Nazi faithful in Munich that, "Our hour of revenge is nigh!. . . . Even if for the present we cannot reach America, thank God that at least one country is close enough to tackle."[171] The unfortunate truth for Hitler, however, was that none of the retaliatory weapons were close to being ready. Both the V-1 and V-2 were encountering difficulties in production, and final tests indicated distressing design problems. Tests of the V-2 carrying its payload for the first time failed completely. Through March 1944, of 57 rockets tested, only 26 got off the ground; of the latter, only 4 reached the target area. The others blew up on re-entry or simply disappeared.[172]

Troubles with the rocket program helped turn the Germans to a more conventional means of retaliation: the bomber. The continued emphasis on bomber production and preference for that aircraft type over fighters reflected a human desire to strike back at Germany's tormentors. In October, Göring passed on Hitler's demand that the *Luftwaffe* attack one of the major Italian towns occupied by the British (either Brindisium or Taranto) before the establishment of night fighter defenses. The *Führer*'s purpose was not only to pay back the Italians for their betrayal but also to give neutrals and especially Germany's "rotten" allies an object lesson.[173]

In late November, Göring ordered the young bomber expert, Dietrich Peltz, to prepare for a retaliation offensive against London. He promised that units detailed for these attacks would receive a full complement of crews and aircraft. In conclusion, the *Reichsmarschall* asked Peltz whether he would accept Do 217's in the bombing force; Peltz replied that he would welcome anything that would carry a bomb.[174] That was precisely what he got. Over December and early January, the Germans accumulated a conglomeration of 550 aircraft on the airfields of France for the offensive: Ju 88's, Ju 188's, Do 217's, Me 410's, Fw 200's, and even 35 brand new He 177's. The widely differing capabilities of these aircraft and the limited navigational and flying skills of the crews lead Peltz to make the attack as simple as possible. Specially trained pathfinders, equipped with various marking devices, would locate and mark the target; the other bombers would hopefully bomb on these markers.[175]

Göring opened the offensive on January 21 with a typical gesture. He left Berlin to assume personal command of the operation. He might have saved himself the trouble as the offensive got off to a bad start. The *Luftwaffe* launched 447 bombers in two waves at the British capital. Navigation was poor, the pathfinder system broke down, and out of 268 tons of bombs dropped over England, only 32 tons landed in London.[176] For the following four months, the Germans continued attacking with less than spectacular results. The next two attacks were dismal failures; on February 18th, the bombers managed to drop 175 tons within London's confines. Thereafter, the Germans managed to get 50 percent of bomb loads within the target area, but the decreasing size of the force gave better accuracy less significance.[177] The scale of these attacks was miniscule compared to what Bomber Command was doing to German cities. The losses suffered, however, were not infinitesimal. In the "Baby Blitz" attacks, the Germans lost 329 bombers—a loss that was virtually irreplaceable. From 695 operational ready bombers in northern France at the end of December 1943, bomber strength had sunk to 144 by May 1944.[178] The Germans could not replace these losses because American attacks on aircraft production had forced them to concentrate their industrial effort on building fighters. While it is arguable whether the bomber forces could have had a significant impact on Russia's armament production, there is no doubt that these bombers would have been a useful addition to German strength when D-day occurred.

The other major theater in which the *Wehrmacht* was locked in combat was the Mediterranean. Here, after a strong response by German fighter bombers to the invasion of Italy and a few solid shots at the Italians bailing out of the war, the Germans withdrew most of their air strength. This move had few repercussions for the troops on the ground. The mountainous nature of Italian geography and the German's skill in defensive warfare allowed the *Wehrmacht* to wage a protracted campaign. The Germans inflicted heavy casualties on their opponents and tied up considerable Allied resources. Allied efforts in using airpower to strangle the lines of communications caused some difficulty, but the restricted nature of the theater enabled the Germans to evade the full impact of these air interdiction efforts and to maintain a stable defensive system. That very stability minimized the requirements for fuel and other bulk items that would have complicated supply problems.

PRODUCTION AND TRAINING

This chapter has included a general discussion of major production issues along with operational matters. There are, however, several aspects of the production program best left to this last section. Milch's continued efforts to increase efficiency throughout the aircraft industry was generally successful. However, for the first time in the war, Allied bombing seriously hurt aircraft and particularly fighter production. Milch had by now recognized the desperate need for more fighters to meet the American threat. The choice was either to meet the daylight offensive with enough fighters or lose air superiority over the European continent. Neither Hitler and Göring nor more sober military men like Korten were willing to recognize that they faced an either/or situation. Thus, emphasis remained on a bomber/fighter program until late winter 1944. By then, it was too late; while the aircraft industry under Speer's direction drove up fighter production, no coherent program existed to provide the pilots or fuel that they would require. The point of no return had come by the early fall of 1943; thereafter, it was too late.

One element of German aircraft production and development that has consistently appeared in historical discussions is the development of the Me 262. That fighter was a design and engineering marvel for its time. However, it is doubtful whether its impact on the war could have been much different than what it was. As with most new concepts, word of the aircraft's potential percolated slowly up the chain of command only after its initial flights. Galland flew the aircraft in May 1943 and became an enthusiastic supporter of the aircraft as the savior of the fighter force.[179] What Galland's enthusiasm could not recognize was the difficulty involved in transferring a design model into production, especially since the Me 262 was not its designer's highest priority. Willi Messerschmitt had involved himself in a running battle with Milch from 1942 on and was particularly upset at cancellation of the Me 209 in favor of his new jet.[180] Moreover, there were serious problems with the engines, which is not surprising considering the fact that they represented a quantum leap forward in technology. Not surprisingly, as with all new weapon systems, the Germans found it difficult to get the Me 262 into series production because they were still making design changes at the same time they were working up production lines.

Hitler's interest in the jet became apparent in September 1943 when Messerschmitt suggested that it could also serve as a fast bomber to attack Britain.[181] An aircraft demonstration at the end of the year and some casual remarks that the jet could serve as a fighter bomber put the *Führer* completely on the wrong track.[182] From that point, he considered the Me 262 as the answer to Allied air superiority over the invasion beaches in the coming spring. In late December, he exclaimed:

> Every month that passes makes it more and more probable that we will get at least one squadron of jet aircraft: The more important thing is that they [the enemy] get some bombs on top of them just as they try to invade. That will force them to take cover . . . and in this way they will waste hour after hour! But after half a day our reserves will already be on the way.[183]

The real explosion did not come until the end of May when Hitler discovered that the *Luftwaffe* was manufacturing the Me 262 as a fighter that could not carry bombs. He drastically intervened and ordered major design changes in the aircraft.[184] It is doubtful, however, whether this decision had much impact on the war's final outcome. The engineers had only worked the flaws out of the production line by March with the first models appearing in that month. Output for April was 16 Me 262's, rising to 28 in June, and 59 in July.[185] Even under the best of circumstances, it is unlikely that a massive output of Me 262's could have occurred in 1944. By the time its production began, Allied escorts had already savaged the German fighter forces, and the Germans had irrevocably lost air superiority over the continent. The losses in experienced pilots during the spring make it especially doubtful whether the *Luftwaffe* could have manned an Me 262 force with effective, skilled crews.

American bombing attacks on German aircraft production had begun in the summer of 1943. The target selection represented a direct threat to the *Luftwaffe*'s production base and faced the Germans with a serious dilemma. The most effective use of resources and manpower to produce aircraft calls for a concentration of industrial effort to mass produce the items. The Ford Willow Run plant and the many other great industrial plants then operating in the United States underline this point. Milch, from early 1942, had pushed the German aircraft industry in the same direction. The problem was that such a concentration maximizing production was particularly vulnerable to bombing, especially the type that the Americans were waging.

The threat posed by the American bombing in the summer of 1943 caused the Germans to begin dispersing their aircraft industry to less vulnerable areas. Efforts, however, to scatter its industry to occupied or allied countries foundered on several difficulties. First, German occupation policies had robbed most foreign firms of workers and machines.[186] In addition, bureaucratic squabbling within the Third *Reich* directly affected dispersal plans to occupied territories. At the same time the *Luftwaffe* was desperately trying to move production outside Germany, Sauckel was robbing occupied territories of the skilled workers such a dispersed production would require.[187]

The dispersal effort received added impetus from the great attacks made on the aircraft industry in the winter and spring of 1944. Critics of the "strategic" bombing campaign have often cited the growth of German fighter production in 1944 as evidence of the campaign's failure. In fact, attacks on German industry were effective in keeping production within tolerable limits and in helping to maintain Allied superiority. The mere act of dispersal reduced production efficiency. German industry's vaunted production of 36,000 aircraft in 1944 was only 8,000 above what the Japanese produced that year.[188] The numerical increase in 1944 over 1943, consisting almost entirely of fighters (a percentage rise of 55.9 percent), hides the fact that German production rose only 23.9 percent in terms of airframe weight.[189] Unhindered by Allied bombing, German production would have risen far higher and far faster. The target of 80,000-plus aircraft in production plans for 1945 gives an indication of the direction in which Milch and his planners were pushing.[190]

When all is said and done, however, the German achievement in increasing fighter production in 1944 was remarkable. "Big Week" had proven that the Americans aimed at nothing less than the destruction of Germany's aircraft industry. The German response was to create a special group, the "Fighter Staff," to take control of all aircraft manufacturing in order to maintain and to increase production. The proposal for such a group came from Milch, and the Field Marshal's suggestion that Speer's assistant, Karl-Otto Sauer, head the staff, shrewdly insured that fighter production received maximum support from the Armaments Ministry. Under the battering of American bombers, the aircraft industry was in dangerous shape. Bombing attacks had obliterated factories, machines, roofs, and walls. Moreover, morale had sunk to such low levels that workers scurried for shelter at the mere appearance of fighters.[191] Also, the attacks had destroyed much finished production still awaiting shipment to the front.[192] The "Fighter Staff" began a desperate struggle to bring order in the wake of American raids. A circular from Speer's ministry warned that the fighter defenses were the only means to protect the armament industry from Allied air attacks.[193] Frontline pilots called desperately for replacements for those aircraft that American escorts were so rapidly shooting out of the air. Galland, reporting that he had had only 250 fighters the day before to meet the American onslaught, pleaded for "fighters, fighters, nothing but fighters" from industrialists and managers.[194] The "Fighter Staff" performed an extraordinary job in restoring order and dispersing production to less vulnerable locations. Where Milch and Sauer ran into bureaucratic red tape and recalcitrance, they hustled offending individuals off to the Berlin SS offices of Ernst Kaltenbrunner.[195] German fighter production, even under the attack, began a dramatic rise.[196] One must, nevertheless, interject a word of caution, for production figures in the Strategic Bombing Survey included aircraft that industry repaired after they had received major damage. Given the tempo of Allied air operations, the Germans had large numbers of aircraft to repair.

Concurrent with production problems went the difficulty of finding pilots to fill cockpits. Up to the summer of 1942, the training program had run on a peacetime leisurely basis, with dancing classes and skiing holidays for future pilots.[197] Thereafter, the training program ran into difficulties. Fuel shortages and demands from the front for more pilots led to reductions in training hours. Air transport commitments to Tunisia and Stalingrad curtailed instrument and bomber training programs. In 1943, more fuel was available; and through better management, the Germans doubled the number of new fighter pilots coming out of training schools. The rise from 1,662 new fighter pilots in 1942 to 3,276 in 1943 was barely enough, however, to cover wastage at the front (2,870).[198] In fact, training schools produced barely enough pilots to keep up with losses. Thus, there was virtually no opportunity to build up a pilot reserve. More dangerous for the future of the fighter force was the fact that flying hours in schools for German pilots were less than half of what British and American pilots received. Production shortages meant that German pilots received their training almost entirely in obsolete aircraft. Ironically, the massive production program of spring 1944 finally solved that problem in late summer. However, by that time there was no fuel left for training.

The result of these training weaknesses and the attrition taking place in early 1944 was that the experience and the skill level of German fighter pilots spiraled downward. In July 1944, *Luftflotte* 3 discovered that with few exceptions, only *Gruppen* and *Staffelen* commanders had more than six months' operational fighter experience. A small number of other pilots had up to three months' experience, while the bulk of available pilots had only between eight and thirty days' combat service.[199] All of these factors by 1944 had become mutually reinforcing. The declining skill of German fighter pilots pushed up the level of attrition taking place, which increased the demand that the training establishment turn out more pilots. The viciousness of the circle received its final impetus and the *Luftwaffe* its death blow when the May attacks on German petroleum sources robbed the training program of the fuel needed to produce new pilots.

CONCLUSION

All of the factors that had worked against the *Luftwaffe* in the early periods of the war and that had slowly worn away its strength came together to destroy it as an effective force in the period from September 1943 through March 1944. By refusing to recognize the full nature of the threat, the Germans placed their air force in a hopeless situation. The *Luftwaffe* did manage to make a remarkable recovery in its ability to defend Germany from night attack, but that tactical victory did little to change the war's course. However, despite such tactical victories, the steady, wearing, and growing pressure of the daytime American bomber and fighter offensive destroyed the German fighter force. There were no decisive moments or clear-cut victories. Rather, the American pressure put the German fighters in a meat grinder battle of attrition both in terms of pilots and of material. It was the cumulative effect of that intense pressure that in the final analysis enabled the Western Powers to gain air superiority over Europe; that achievement must be counted among the decisive victories of World War II.

Notes

1. Air Ministry, *The Rise and Fall of the German Air Force*, p. 239.

2. Below, *Als Hitlers Adjutant*, pp. 350–51.

3. Among a whole host of evidence, one might consult in particular Göring's remarks on October 7, 1943: "Heimatverteidigungsprogramm 1943, Besprechung beim Reichsmarschall am 7.10.43. Obersalzberg," AFSHRC: K 113.312–2, v. 3.

4. Air Ministry, *The Rise and Fall of the German Air Force*, pp. 239–40.

5. Webster and Frankland, *SAOAG*, Vol. II, pp. 160–61.

6. Arthur Harris to Winston Churchill, 3.11.43., PRO/PREM/3/14/1.

7. PRO AIR 22/203, "War Room Manual of Bomber Command Ops 1939/1945," compiled by Air Ministry War Room (Statistical Section).

8. Verrier, *The Bomber Offensive*, p. 148.

9. Zuckermann, *From Apes to Warlords*, pp. 218–19.

10. Interview with Air Marshal D. C. T. Bennett, RAF Staff College Library, Bracknell.

11. Hansell, *The Air Plan that Defeated Hitler*, p. 136.

12. Webster and Frankland, *SAOAG*, Vol. II, p. 264.

13. For Milch's reaction to the less than distinguished effort, see: "Der erste grosse Einsatz der 'Wilden Sau', Auszug aus der G. L.-Besprechung am 20.8.43. im RLM," AFSHRC: K 113.312–2, v. 3.

14. Irving, *The Mare's Nest*, p. 113.

15. Webster and Frankland, *SAOAG*, Vol. II, p. 203.

16. Bill Gunston, *Night Fighters* (New York, 1976), pp. 103–04.

17. BA/MA, RL 8/93, I Jagdkorps, "Niederschrift über die Divisionskommand eur-besprechung am 29.12.43.," p. 38; Air Ministry, *The Defeat of the German Air Force*, pp. 278–79.

18. See particularly the clear discussion of the schräge Musik tactics in Martin Middlebrook's admirable work, *The Nuremberg Raid* (New York, 1974), pp. 70–73.

19. "Heimatverteidigungsprogramm, 1943," Besprechung beim Reichsmarschall am 8.10.43., Obersalzberg, AFSHRC: K 113.312–2, v. 3; percentage losses presented on the basis of crews present at the beginning of each month in BA/MA, RL 2 III/725, 726, Genst. Gen. Qu. 6.Abt. (I), "Übersicht über Soll, Istbestand, Einsatzbereitschaft, Verluste und Reserven der fliegenden Verbände," July, August, September 1943.

20. "Heimatverteidigungsprogramm, 1943," Besprechung beim Reichsmarschall am 8.10.43, Obersalzberg, AFSHRC: K 113.312–2, v. 3, p. 57.

21. Webster and Frankland, *SAOAG*, Vol. II, p. 163.

22. "Besprechung über Tag-und Nachtjagd 1943 beim R. M. Göring am 25. und 26.9.43.," AFSHRC: K 113.312–2, v. 3.

23. Webster and Frankland, *SAOAG*, Vol. II, p. 203–04.

24. Goebbels, *The Goebbels Diaries*, pp. 532–35.

25. Hans Rumpf, *The Bombing of Germany* (New York, 1961), pp. 132–35.

26. Webster and Frankland, *SAOAG*, Vol. II, pp. 204–05.

27. BA/MA, RL 8/91, I Jagdkorps, "Kommandeurbesprechung am 29.9.43. im Zeist."

28. Ibid.

29. Air Ministry, *The Rise and Fall of the German Air Force*, pp. 278–79.

30. Middlebrook, *The Nuremberg Raid*, pp. 32–33.

31. Air Ministry, *The Rise and Fall of the German Air Force*, p. 200.

32. BA/MA, RL 8/93, I Jagdkorps, "Niederschrift über die Divisionkommandeur-Besprechung am 25.1.44. um 12.30 Uhr in De Breul."

33. Webster and Frankland, *SAOAG*, Vol. II, pp. 205–06.

34. PRO AIR/20.5815. See in particular the draft reply for CAS signature to a Harris letter arguing about the tactical difficulties which mitigated against an attack on Schweinfurt, 24.1.44.

35. Webster and Frankland, *SAOAG*, Vol. II, p. 207; and Middlebrook, *The Nuremberg Raid*, p. 86.

36. Webster and Frankland, *SAOAG*, Vol. II, p. 206.

37. Middlebrook, *The Nuremberg Raid*, pp. 80–81. The bomb plots for the attacks on Stuttgart on March 15 and Berlin on March 24, on page 81, are most instructive on the limitations under which Bomber Command was still operating.

38. Webster and Frankland, *SAOAG*, Vol. II, p. 207; for the most thorough description of the disaster, see Middlebrook's excellent *The Nuremberg Raid*.

39. Middlebrook, *The Nuremberg Raid*, pp. 88–91.

40. Interview with D. C. T. Bennett, RAF Staff College Library, Bracknell.

41. PRO AIR 14/3489, Probable Reconstruction of German Night Fighter Reaction, Raid on Nuremberg 30/31.3.44.

42. Middlebrook, *The Nuremberg Raid*, p. 140.

43. PRO AIR 14/3489, Plots on Bombers Passed Over R/T and W/T to Night Fighters, Raid on Nuremberg, 30/31.3.44.

44. Middlebrook, *The Nuremberg Raid*, pp. 161, 277, 330.

45. Ibid., pp. 204–07.

46. Webster and Frankland, *SAOAG*, Vol. IV, pp. 431–32.

47. PRO AIR 22/203, War Room Manual of Bomber Command Ops, 1939–1945, Air Ministry War Room (Statitical Section).

48. For a clear picture of what it was like to serve as a crewmember during this period, see Max Hastings, *Bomber Command* (New York, 1979), particularly Chapters VIII and XII.

49. See particularly Bennett's memorandum to Bomber Command, 3.11.44., quoted extensively by Webster and Frankland, *SAOAG*, Vol. II, pp. 195–96; see also Middlebrook, *The Nuremberg Raid*, p. 30.

50. Interview with D. C. T. Bennett, RAF Staff College Library, Bracknell. Bennett further suggests that all senior commanders be required to fly in wartime and that for every Air Vice Marshal lost on operations, Bomber Command would have saved 200 crews.

51. Ibid.

52. Webster and Frankland, *SAOAG*, Vol. II, P. 193.

53. Alfred Price, *Pictorial History of the Luftwaffe, 1933–1945* (New York, 1969), pp. 52–53.

54. Based on the author's tabulations of figures in BA/MA, RL 2 III/728, 729, Genst. Gen. Qu. 6. Abt. (I), "Übersicht über Soll, Istbestand, Einsatzbereitschaft, Verluste und Reserven der fliegenden Verbände."

55. Craven and Cate, *The Army Air Forces in World War II*, Vol. II, p. 688.

56. "Statistical Summary of Eighth Air Force Operations, European Theater, 17 August 1942–8 May 1945," p. 14, AFSHRC.

57. Craven and Cate, *The Army Air Forces in World War II*, Vol. II, pp. 696–97.

58. Ibid., pp. 698–99.

59. "Statistical Summary of Eighth Air Force Operations, European Theater, 17 August 1942–8 May 1945," p. 14, AFSHRC.

60. Craven and Cate, *The Army Air Forces in World War II*, Vol. II, pp. 703–04, 850. For the most

thorough, scholarly study of the second Schweinfurt attack from both sides, see Golücke, *Schweinfurt und der strategische Luftkrieg, 1943*.

61. Ibid., pp. 704–05.

62. Speer, *Inside the Third Reich*, p. 286.

63. For the most comprehensive examination of this process, see Golücke, *Schweinfurt und der strategische Luftkrieg, 1943*, pp. 351–80.

64. Boylan, "The Development of the Long-Range Escort Fighter," p. 129.

65. Ibid., p. 127.

66. For an excellent, concise description, see Boylan, "The Development of the Long-Range Escort Fighter," pp.146–61.

67. Emerson, "Operation Pointblank," pp. 32–34.

68. Boylan, "The Development of the Long-Range Escort Fighter," pp. 155–59.

69. BA/MA, RL 10/639, "Notizen zur Traditionsgeschichte der III. Gruppe des Jagdgeschwaders Udet, (Quellen: Kriegstagebücher der III./e)."

70. Air Ministry, *The Rise and Fall of the German Air Force*, pp. 289–90.

71. Golücke, *Schweinfurt und der strategische Luftkrieg 1943*, p. 198.

72. Air Ministry, *The Rise and Fall of the German Air Force*, pp. 290–91.

73. "Heimatverteidigungsprogramm, 1943, Besprechung beim Reichsmarschall am 7.10.43., Obersalzberg," p. 16, AFSHRC: K 113.312–2, v. 3.

74. "Ultra, History of US Strategic Air Force Europe Versus German Air Force," p. 106. Date of the message was October 12, and it was obviously the result of discussions on October 7.

75. Based on the figures in BA/MA, RL 2 III/1193, 1194, 1195, Genst. Gen. Qu. (6. Abt.), "Flugzeugunfälle und Verluste bei den fliegenden Verbänden."

76. BA/MA, RL 2 III/1194, Genst. Gen. Qu. (6. Abt), "Flugzeugunfälle und Verluste bei den fliegenden Verbänden."

77. BA/MA, RL 2 III/1025, Genst. 6. Abt., "Front-Flugzeug-Verluste im Oktober 1943." Part of the confusion undoubtedly lies in exactly how German records were compiled and for what purposes.

78. Based on the figures of fighter pilot strength and losses in the tables in BA/MA, RL 2 III/722, 723, 724, 725, Genst. Gen. Qu.6. Abt. (I). "Übersicht über Soll, Istbestand, Einsatzbereitschaft, Verluste und Reserven der fliegenden Verbände."

79. "Ultra, History of US Strategic Air Force Europe Versus German Air Force," pp. 112–13.

80. "Heimatverteidigungsprogramm 1943, Besprechung beim Reichsmarschall am 7.10.43., Obersalzberg," AFSHRC: K 113.312–2, v. 3.

81. Ibid., Fortsetzung, p. 9.

82. BA/MA, RL 3/61, "Stenographische Niederschrift der Ansprache des Reichsmarschalls am 23.11.43. vor den fliegenden Besatzungen Tagjagd der 3. Jagddivision in der Halle des Flugplatzes Deelen"; see also Göring's comments in the war diary of the III. Gruppe des Jagdgeschwaders Udet, entry 12.10.43.

83. "Heimatverteidigungsprogramm 1943, Besprechung beim Reichsmarschall am 7.10.43, Fortsetzung," AFSHRC: K 113.312–2, v. 3.

84. David Irving, *Hitler's War* (New York, 1977), pp. 574–75.

85. BA/MA, RL 3/61, "Stenographische Niederschrift der Besprechung beim Reichsmarschall am 28.11.44. in Karinhall," pp. 94–95.

86. "Heimatverteidigungsprogramm 1943, Besprechung beim Reichsmarschall am 7.10.43., Obersalzberg, Fortsetzung," AFSHRC: K 113.312–2, v. 3; one must also note that not until the fall of 1943 did fighter production receive the same priority as U-boat production.

87. BA/MA, RL 3/61, "Stenographische Niederschrift der Besprechung des Reichsmarschalls mit GL und Industrierat am 14.10.43. in der neuen Reichskanzlei, Berchtesgaden."

88. BA/MA, RL 3/62, "Stenographische Niederschrift der Besprechung beim Reichsmarschall am 23.11.43. in Karinhall."

89. BA/MA, RL 3/61, "Stenographische Niederschrift der Besprechung beim Reichsmarschall am 28.11.43. in Karinhall," p. 88.

90. USSBS, *ESBGWE*, Appendix Table 102, p. 277.

91. "Alliierte Luftangriffe im Jahre 1943 auf Werke der deutschen Flugzeugindustrie," AFSHRC: K 113.312–2, v. 3.

92. BA/MA, RL 2 II/365, Der Oberbefehlshaber der Luftwaffe, Führungsstab Ic, Nr. 32487/43, 5.10.43., "Luftlagebericht West, Stand: 1. Oktober 1943."

93. BA/MA, RL 2 II/365, Der Oberbefehlshaber der Luftwaffe, Führungsstab Ic, Nr. 4222/43, 2.11.43, "Luftlagebericht West, Stand: 1. November 1943."

94. BA/MA, RL 2 II/365, Der Oberbefehlshaber der Luftwaffe, Führungsstab Ic., Nr 4611/43, 3.12.43., "Luftlagebericht West, Stand: 1.12.1943."

95. BA/MA, RL 2 II/320, "USA Fliegertruppe, die schweren amerikanischen Kampfverbände, Stand: Dezember 1943," Luftwaffenführungsstab, Ic/Fremde Luftwaffen West.

96. Speer, *Inside the Third Reich*, p. 290. For Göring's own admission after the war that even in the spring of 1944 he could not believe American escort fighters went as far as Liege, see "Reichsmarschall Herman Göring—I," Air Ministry Weekly Intelligence Summary, issued by Air Ministry A.C.A.S. (1) (A.I.I.), No. 315, 17.9.45.

97. Craven and Cate, *The Army Air Forces in World War II*, Vol. III, pp. 15–17.

98. BA/MA, RL 8/92, "Niederschrift über Divisionkommandeur-Besprechung am 4.11.43., 14.00 Uhr in De Breul."

99. BA/MA, RL 8/92, "Besprechung beim Bef. Mitte am 6.11.43., 15.00 Uhr in Berlin-Dahlem."

100. BA/MA, RL 8/92, "Besprechung beim Bef. Mitte am 6.11.43. 17.45 Uhr in Berlin-Dahlem."

101. BA/MA, RL 8/92, "Besprechung beim Bef. Mitte am 7.11.43. 10.30 Uhr in Berlin, Reichssportfeld."

102. BA/MA, RL 8/92, "Besprechung am 8.11.43. 13.00 Uhr auf dem Gefechtsstand De Beul."

103. BA/MA, RL 8/92, "Besprechung in Stade am 16.11.43."

104. Boylan, "The Development of the Long-Range Escort Fighter," p. 107.

105. Craven and Cate, *The Army Air Forces in World War II*, Vol. II, pp. 848–52.

106. Boylan, "The Development of the Long-Range Escort Fighter," p. 108.

107. BA/MA, RL 8/93, "Niederschrift über die Divisionskommandeur-Besprechung am 29.12.1943."

108. BA/MA, RL 2 III/1025, Genst. 6. Abt. (III A), Front-Flugzeug-Verluste, reports for November and December.

109. BA/MA, RL 2 III/726, 727, 728, Gen. Qu. 6.Abt. (I), "Übersicht" über Soll, Istbestand, Einsatzbereitschaft, Verluste und Reserven der fliegenden Verbände.

110. Ibid.

111. These figures are based on the tables in BA/MA, RL 2 III/722, 723, 724, 725, 726, 727, 728, Gen. Qu. 6. Abt. (I)., "Übersicht" über Soll, Istbestand, Einsatzbereitschaft, Verluste und Reserven der fliegenden Verbände.

112. Golücke, *Schweinfurt und der strategische Luftkrieg 1943*, p. 217.

113. "Statistical Summary of Eighth Air Force Operations, European Theater, 17 August 1942–8 May 1945," AFSHRC.

114. Ibid.

115. Futrell, *Ideas, Concepts, Doctrine: A History of Basic Thinking in the United States Air Force*, p. 139.

116. BA/MA, RL 2 II/329, Luftwaffenführungsstab Ic Nr 13/44 (III A), 2.1.44., "Luftlage West Nr. 1 vom 31.12 und Nacht zum 1.1.44."

117. Craven and Cate, *The Army Air Forces in World War II*, Vol. III, pp. 23–24.

118. "Ultra, History of US Strategic Air Force Europe vs German Air Force," p. 136.

119. Based on loss tables in BA/MA, RL 2 III/1025, Genst. 6. Abt. (III A), Front-Flugzeug-Verluste; and BA/MA, RL 2 II/728, Gen. Qu. 6.Abt. (I), Übersicht über Soll, Istbestand, Einsatzbereitschaft, Verluste und Reserven der fliegenden Verbände.

120. "Ultra, History of US Strategic Air Force Europe vs German Air Force," p. 141.

121. BA/MA, RL 10/639, "Notizen zur Traditionsgeschichte der III. Gruppe des Jagdgeschwaders Udet (Quellen: Kriegstagebucher der III./e)."

122. BA/MA, RL 2 III/1025, Genst. 6. Abt. (III A), Front-Flugzeug-Verluste, January-June 1944.

123. Ibid.

124. BA/MA, RL 2 III/728–731, Gen. Qu. 6. Abt. (I), Übersicht über Soll, Istbestand, Einsatzbereitschaft, Verluste und Reserven der fliegenden Verbände.

125. BA/MA, RL 2 III/1025, Genst. 6. Abt. (III A), Front-Flugzeug-Verluste, January-June 1944.

126. BA/MA, RL 8/93, I Jagdkorps, "Niederschrift über die Divisionskommandeur-Besprechung am 25.1.44. um 12.30 Uhr in De Breul."

127. Boylan, "The Development of the Long-Range Escort Fighter," p. 167.

128. Ibid, p. 168.

129. Craven and Cate, *The Army Air Forces in World War II*, Vol. III, p. 33.

130. Boylan, "The Development of the Long-Range Escort Fighter," p. 168.

131. Craven and Cate, *The Army Air Forces in World War II*, Vol. III, pp. 37–38.

132. This total is drawn from Craven and Cate, *The Army Air Forces in World War II*, Vol. III, p. 39;

and Boylan, "The Development of the Long-Range Escort Fighter," p. 172.

133. Boylan, "The Development of Long-Range Fighter Escort," p. 175.

134. Based on the tables in "Statistical Summary of Eighth Air Force Operations, European Theater, 17 August 1942–8 May 1945," AFSHRC.

135. BA/MA, RL 10/257, Kriegstagebuch Nr. 8 des Zerstörergeschwaders "Horst Wessel" Nr 26 vom 1.1.—30.9.44.

136. Based on loss tables in BA/MA, RL 2 III/1025, Genst. 6.Abt. (III A), Front-Flugzeug-Verluste; and BA/MA, RL 2 III/728, 729, Übersicht über Soll, Istbestand, Einsatzbereitschaft, Verluste und Reserven der fliegenden Verbände.

137. Craven and Cate, *The Army Air Forces in World War II*, Vol. III, pp. 51–53.

138. Ibid., p. 53.

139. Based on loss tables in BA/MA, RL 2 III/1025, Genst. 6. Abt. (III A), Front-Flugzeug-Verluste, and RL 2 III/729, Übersicht über Soll, Istbestand, Einsatzbereitschaft, Verluste und Reserven der fliegenden Verbände.

140. Figures based on aircraft written off and combat strength in "Statistical Summary of Eighth Air Force Operations, European Theater, 17 August 1942–8 May 1945," AFSHRC.

141. Craven and Cate, *The Army Air Forces in World War II*, Vol. III, p. 54.

142. BA/MA, RL 2 II/329, Luftwaffenführungsstab Ic, Fremde Luftwaffen West, Nr 1193/44, 18.3.44. "Luftlage West Nr. 32."

143. "Ultra, History of US Strategic Air Force Europe vs German Air Force," p. 153.

144. Ibid., p. 156.

145. Ibid., pp. 153–54.

146. BA/MA, RL 10/639, Notizen zur Traditionsgeschichte der III. Gruppe des Jagdgeschwaders Udet.

147. Golücke, *Schweinfurt und der strategische Luftkrieg 1943*, p. 218.

148. "Ultra, History of US Strategic Air Force Europe vs German Air Force," p. 155.

149. Ibid., p. 157.

150. "Der Einsatz der Jäger in der Reichsverteidigung 1944, Ansprache des Oberst Trautloff vor Rüstungsarbeitern bei den Junkerswerken in Dessau am 15.3.44.," AFSHRC: K 113.312–2, v. 6, 1944.

151. BA/MA, RL 7/51, Der Chef der Luftflotte 6, Br. B. Nr. 241/43, 12.6.43., Betr. Bekämpfung der sow. russ. Kriegswirtschaft.

152. BA/MA, RL 7/521, Besprechungspunkte Oberst i. G. Kless am 17.6.43. in Robinson 4 mit Generaloberst Jeschonnek.

153. Olaf Groehler, *Geschichte des Luftkrieges 1910 bis 1970* (Berlin, 1973), p. 345.

154. Air Ministry, *The Rise and Fall of the German Air Force*, p. 236.

155. Speer, *Inside the Third Reich*, p. 282.

156. BA/MA, RL 2 II/5, Luftwaffenführungsstab, Ia op Nr. 8865/43, 9.11.43., Anlage: "Kurze Studie: Kampf gegen die russische Rüstungsindustrie."

157. BA/MA, RL 2 II/5, Reichsmarschall, 21.11.43., An Lft. Kdo, 4, Chef d. Genst., Lft. Kdo, 6, Genst. Gen. d. Kampffl, Generalmajor Peltz.

158. Air Ministry, *The Rise and Fall of the German Air Force*, p. 240.

159. Ziemke, *Stalingrad to Berlin*, pp. 174–84.

160. Air Ministry, *The Rise and Fall of the German Air Force*, p. 241.

161. Ziemke, *Stalingrad to Berlin*, pp. 176–88.

162. Ibid., pp. 229–31.

163. Ibid., Chapters XII and XIII.

164. Air Ministry, *The Rise and Fall of the German Air Force*, pp. 242–43.

165. "Ultra, History of US Strategic Air Force Europe vs German Air Force," p. 123.

166. Ibid., p. 126.

167. BA/MA, RL 10/544, Leistungsbuch, Leutnant Elmar Boersch, 3./K.G. General Wever. Boersch survived the war with 311 combat missions to his credit.

168. Letter from Oberst Walther Krause in possession of the author.

169. Speer, *Inside the Third Reich*, pp. 282–83.

170. Air Ministry,*The Rise and Fall of the German Air Force*, pp. 242–43.

171. Irving, *The Mare's Nest*, pp. 177, 181. Hitler was assuring Goebbels in September that a "great reprisal campaign by rockets" would begin in January or February; Goebbels, *The Goebbels Diary*, p. 467.

172. Ibid., pp. 220–21.

173. "Heimatverteidigungsprogramm 1943, Besprechung beim Reichsmarschall am 8.10.43., Obersalzberg, Fortsetzung," AFSHRC: K 113.312–2, v. 3.

174. BA/MA, RL 3/62, "Stenographische Niederschrift über Besprechung unter dem Vorsitz des Reichsmarschalls am 28.11.43. in Neuenhazen bei Berlin."

175. Air Ministry, *The Rise and Fall of the German Air Force*, p. 321.

176. Groehler, *Geschichte des Luftkrieges*, p. 396.

177. Air Ministry, *The Rise and Fall of the German Air Force*, p. 322.

178. Groehler, *Geschichte des Luftkrieges*, p. 396.

179. Galland, *The First and the Last*, p. 253.

180. See Irving's interesting discussion, *The Rise and Fall of the Luftwaffe*, pp. 217–18.

181. Ibid., p. 237.

182. Air Ministry, *The Rise and Fall of the German Air Force*, p. 313.

183. Irving, *The Rise and Fall of the Luftwaffe*, p. 266.

184. Ibid., p. 281.

185. Air Ministry, *The Rise and Fall of the German Air Force*, p. 313.

186. For further amplification of this point, see the excellent discussion of this point in Overy, "The Luftwaffe and the European Economy, 1939–1945," pp. 66–67.

187. See the discussion of this point in Speer, *Inside the Third Reich*, pp. 310–11.

188. Richard Overy, *The Air War, 1939–1945* (London, 1980), p. 123.

189. USSBS, *ESBGWE*, Appendix Tables 101 and 102.

190. Overy, *The Air War, 1939–1945*, p. 123.

191. See particularly the discussion of what had happened to the factories at Braunschweig: BA/MA, RL 3/1, "Stenographischer Bericht über die Jägerstabs-Besprechung am 4. Marz 1944 im RLM," p. 47.

192. Irving, *The Rise and Fall of the Luftwaffe*, p. 270.

193. "Sicherung der Jäger und Zerstörerfabrikation gegen Luftangriffe," 16.3.44., Imperial War Museum FD 4352/45. See also Milch's speech in BA/MA, RL 3/1, VI Besprechung in Allach-München, 10.3.44.

194. BA/MA, RL 3/1, "Stenografische Niederschrift der Besprechungen während des 'Unternehmens Hubertus' v. F.–11.3.44.," p. 21.

195. See particularly the interesting exchange between Milch and Sauer on the one hand and an offending official on the other in BA/MA, RL 3/1, "Messerschmitt-Regensburg," Vorbesprechung im Sonderzug, 10.3.44.–0.30 Uhr, p. 178. Milch was also to suggest that if French workers gave trouble when the invasion came, 50 percent should be shot and if that did not work then the rest. Groehler, *Geschichte des Luftkrieges 1910 bis 1970*, p. 414. See also the discussion about getting recalcitrant workers back into the factories in BA/MA, RL 3/1, V. "Messerschmitt-Regensburg," Vorbesprechung im Sonderzug, 10.3.44–0:30 Uhr.

196. USSBS, *ESBGWE*, Appendix Table 102. See also Sauer's discussion of the "Fighter Staff's" success by the end of March in BA/MA, RL 3/3, "Stenographischer Bericht über die Jägerstabs-Besprechung am 25.3.44, 10 Uhr im Reichsluftfahrtministerium."

197. Letter from Oberst Walter Krause, May 25, 1981, in possession of the author.

198. Air Ministry, *The Rise and Fall of the German Air Force*, p. 314; and BA/MA, RL 2 III/722, 723, 724, 725, 726, 727, 728, Gen. Qu. 6.Abt. (I) Übersicht über Soll, Istbestand, Einsatzbereitschaft, Verluste und Reserven der fliegenden Verbände.

199. Air Ministry, *The Rise and Fall of the German Air Force*, pp. 316–17.

VII Defeat: April–September 1944

The air battles of February and March had gone far towards establishing air supremacy over the continent. The basic issue now was how the Allies could best utilize that advantage. At this point, however, the air commanders could no longer claim that only their air forces could strike Nazi Germany. Victory in the Atlantic had enabled Britain and the United States to build up the land and naval power required to make an opposed landing on the coast of France a viable possibility. Debate centered on how the air forces, particularly the "strategic" bombers, could support overall strategy. The results of that debate in effect determined the success of D-day and led to the destruction of Germany's strategic position in western Europe.

On the German side, spring boded ill for the Third *Reich*. In Russia, its forces were in disarray; and in the Ukraine, Soviet armies were reaching towards Rumania and Hungary. Russian advances posed a direct threat to Germany's major source of crude oil and to the entire Balkan region, the raw materials of which were critical to the continued functioning of armaments production. Everywhere in Europe—from Russia to France, from Norway to Greece—resistance movements harried the German occupier. In France, the Germans faced an imminent invasion with little prospect of support from the *Luftwaffe*.

Hitler understood that a successful invasion of France would spell the doom of his regime. In a directive to the *Wehrmacht*, he claimed that Germany could lose territory in the east without such losses having a decisive impact on the war. In the west, however, the situation was different:

> Should the enemy succeed in breaking our defenses on a wide front here, the immediate consequences would be unpredictable. Everything indicates that the enemy will launch an offensive against the western front of Europe, at the latest in the spring, perhaps even earlier. I can, therefore, no longer take responsibility for [the] further weakening of the west in favor of other theaters of [the] war.[1]

For defense of the west, Hitler relied on two of his foremost generals—Rundstedt and Rommel. The former, acclaimed as a master strategist, argued for a mobile defense of France that would trade territory for time and inflict heavy casualties on the attacker. Rommel, often criticized as having little grasp of strategic issues, argued that the *Wehrmacht* must defeat the invasion on the beaches before the Allies could consolidate a foothold. He warned, correctly as events turned out, that if the *Wehrmacht* could not hold the coast, air superiority would allow the Allies to build up their forces more quickly than a defender, harried by strikes against his transportation networks.[2] Hitler by vacillating between these two clear-cut strategies and by controlling the mobile reserves himself, in effect, hamstrung both strategies.

In the air, American fighters and bombers were close to breaking Germany's fighter forces. Bomber Command, however, had lost the initiative over the *Reich*. The night fighters had made the skies over central Europe so dangerous that the British could only risk their bombers on deep penetration raids in unusual circumstances. However, Bomber Command in western Europe was a most effective force. Although flying at night, it was capable of a precision that its commander denied it possessed and which was, in some respects, more accurate than the daylight "precision" attacks of American bombers within the range of navigational aids.[3]

"OVERLORD" AND "STRATEGIC" BOMBING

On January 12, Air Marshal Arthur Harris fired the opening salvo in a prolonged debate over the role of "strategic" bombers in the coming invasion. "Overlord," Harris announced, "must now presumably be regarded as an inescapable commitment." He then pointed out that the "heavy bomber force has been developed as an independent strategic weapon" whose task was "the destruction of the enemy's industrial centers." He claimed that its specialized equipment and training allowed it to attack targets with efficiency and economy. After describing the limitations and navigational problems besetting his force, Harris laid out what his force could not do:

> 17. Consequently, anything like a planned schedule of bomber operations designed to give immediate assistance . . . to ground forces engaged in effecting a landing or operating in the field would be extremely unreliable and almost wholly futile. . . . In no circumstances could it be relied upon to destroy gun emplacements or cause noticeable casualties to defenders in slit trenches. . . . Nor is the heavy bomber force suitable for cutting railway communications at definite points. Indeed in Western Germany, France and the Low Countries, owing to the multiplication of roads and railways and the impossibility of maintaining the requisite continuity of action in the prevailing weather conditions, such a policy is probably impracticable with any type of bomber force. . . .

> 21. There could be no greater relief afforded Germany than the cessation or any ponderable reduction of the bombing of Germany proper. The entire country would go wild with a sense of relief and reborne hope. . . .

> 22. It is thus clear that the best and indeed the only efficient support which Bomber Command can give to OVERLORD is the intensification of attacks on suitable industrial centres in Germany as and when the opportunity offers. If we attempt to substitute for this process attacks on gun emplacements, beach defenses, communications or [ammunition] dumps in occupied territory, we shall commit the irremediable error of diverting our best weapons from the military function, for which it

has been equipped and trained, to tasks which it cannot effectively
carry out. Though this might give a specious appearance of
"supporting" the Army, in reality it would be the greatest
disservice we could do to them.[4]

Harris, never known for understatement, was attempting to minimize the
commitment of his command to "Overload." His strongest argument was that his
forces with their training and doctrine could not effectively help the ground forces.
Harris, however, already had evidence that heavy bombers could destroy gun
emplacements (see Chapter VI). In the end, he did throw his forces into the
campaign against the French transportation system. The reasons for his eventual
acceptance of using Bomber Command in support of "Overlord," a course of
action that he regarded with considerable distaste, were several. On one hand, his
command had suffered terrible losses during the winter, and he seems to have been
more amenable to Air Staff direction in the spring. The second factor pushing
Harris towards compliance was an excellent political sense—he undoubtedly
realized that "Overlord" represented a venture that either he supported or he risked
losing his position.

The final element pushing Bomber Command towards support for the invasion
was the fact that Harris' argument that his bombers could not attack precision
targets in France was incorrect. The initial invasion plan had envisioned an
extensive campaign against the transportation system of northern France, with the
main target being railroad marshalling yards. The claims that Bomber Command
was suitable only for "area" bombing had alarmed Churchill. If Harris were
correct, those French living near the target areas were in great danger. As a result,
in March, British bombers carried out test raids on six French towns. Using *Oboe*
and new marking techniques, the raids succeeded beyond anyone's expectations.[5]
An attack on Vaires not only destroyed the railroad yards but occurred while troop
trains of the *Waffen* SS division *"Frundsberg"* lay on sidings intermingled with
several carloads of mines. The Germans collected nearly 1,200 identity disks from
the *Waffen* SS dead.[6] French casualties were minimal.

Establishment of a command system to control air assets in support of the
invasion was a tortuous process. In 1943, Air Marshal Sir Trefford Leigh-Mallory
received appointment as Commander, Allied Expeditionary Air Force. However,
neither Spaatz nor Harris wished to subordinate their "strategic" bombers to a man
possessing experience only with "tactical" aircraft. Eisenhower then appointed
Tedder as his chief deputy, and Churchill's suggestion that the latter command all
air assets in Britain might have removed some ambiguities in command
relationships. As the official historians note: Had Churchill's suggestion been
adopted, "orders and not ambassadors could have been sent to the strategic air
forces."[7] Churchill's proposal met strong resistance and an eventual compromise
gave Tedder limited control over the bomber commands. He was to form the air
plan in consultation with Harris and Spaatz, while Leigh-Mallory under Tedder's
guidance would draw up the "tactical" air plans for "Overlord." Then Portal and
Eisenhower, acting through the Chiefs of Staff, would see that the heavy bomber

assets required to support the invasion would be available.[8] The command arrangements took a period of time to settle down and, although somewhat clumsy, the good sense of Allied commanders made them function.

Two considerable arguments occurred in the months before the invasion. The first was Churchill's continuing worry that tens of thousands of Frenchmen would die in attacks on the transportation system. Such casualties would have serious implications for future Anglo-French relations. While extensive arguments took place between Churchill and those favoring a bombing campaign against transportation targets, Bomber Command's accurate and precise destruction of French rail yards eventually alleviated the Prime Minister's doubts.[9]

The second argument was between advocates of the transportation plan and Spaatz's adherence to "Pointblank" objectives. The American commander, however, interjected a new element into the "strategic" bombing offensive by pushing Germany's oil industry to the top of his priority list. The tendency among some historians to see a clear delineation between the oil and transportation plans distorts what actually occurred. The plans were not contradictory, although the debate at the time tended to pose them as such. In fact, events proved the plans complementary. Spaatz, one of the more flexible and imaginative commanders in the war, had no serious qualms with the railroad plan. He noted in late February that he would have no quarrel with bombing railway targets if such attacks were to stimulate "the *Luftwaffe* to fight."[10] He did, however, disagree with Leigh-Mallory's contention that the decisive air battle would be won over the beaches. Rather, he felt that Eighth Air Force's attacks on German aircraft plants had already helped establish air supremacy and that his oil plan would continue the process of attacking targets that forced the *Luftwaffe* to fight. His plan had one additional advantage. By destroying Germany's fuel sources, the Allies would eliminate Germany's ability to train the replacement pilots that spiraling attrition rates demanded.

The transportation plan owed its origins to the close work between Zuckerman and Leigh-Mallory. Zuckerman's initial conception was that Allied air forces operating from England would devote themselves, for extended time periods, to the destruction of the railroad system from the German frontier westward:

> An essential preliminary to enable Operation "OVERLORD" to take place is the accomplishment of certain vital tasks by the Strategical and Tactical Air Forces. Unless these are completed by D-day, the success of the Operation will be jeopardized, not only because our naval and ground forces would then have to contend with a highly unfavorable situation but also because the air would not be in any position to lend full support to the actual assault or to deal with the subsequent activities of the enemy. Subject to a satisfactory air situation, the main object of the preliminary air operations is to paralyze the railways from Western Germany to the assault area to such an extent that major reinforcement by rail would be virtually impossible.[11]

Zuckerman's plan did recognize that Allied air forces would have to maintain pressure on the *Luftwaffe* through attacks on its production base.

On March 5, Spaatz suggested that his forces attack the *Reich*'s oil supplies and refineries instead of Western Europe's transportation system. Such an offensive would, he claimed, cause a 50 percent reduction in gasoline supplies within six months.[12] The upshot was a compromise. While Tedder and Eisenhower backed Leigh-Mallory's emphasis on the transportation plan, Spaatz placed active *Luftwaffe* units as well as the German aircraft industry at the top of Eighth's priority list. Nevertheless, he agreed to use his heavy bombers to attack the transportation network as a "secondary objective."[13] Although the directive to the bomber commands said nothing about oil, the *Luftwaffe*'s designation as the main objective allowed Spaatz sufficient latitude to go after the synthetic fuel industry in mid-May. Out of the 80 most important transportation targets, Bomber Command attacked 39, Eighth Air Force 23, and Allied Tactical Air Forces in Britain 18. Thus, Spaatz's forces played an important role in the offensive against enemy transportation systems.[14]

In fact, there was sufficient Allied airpower in Britain to allow the simultaneous execution of a dual strategy that was consistent with the objectives of "Pointblank" and "Overlord." Leigh-Mallory and Zuckerman believed that the only effective method for severely damaging the railway network of western Europe was a sustained offensive against the whole system. Bomber Command would provide its support at night, while during the day Eighth and Allied Tactical Air Forces would attack the network. Critics of the plan had claimed that the Germans would escape the serious consequences of such an offensive by shutting down civilian traffic; they would then be able to continue full military traffic. That did not happen, because in some areas the Allies virtually closed down the railroads.

Bomber Command's shift from targets in Germany to railways in northern France was a tribute to Harris' obedience to his instructions. In March, the command devoted 70 percent of its effort to targets in Germany. In April, the British dropped 34,000 tons of bombs, only 14,000 tons in Germany. In May, three-quarters of the sorties and more than 28,000 tons of bombs were against French targets; while in June, approximately 52,000 tons of bombs were dropped on France.[15]

Allied air forces did not make this effort at a light cost. Between early April and June 5, they lost nearly 2,000 aircraft and some 12,000 officers and men.[16] In mid-March, a precipitous fall in French railway traffic began. By July, the volume of traffic on French railroads had fallen to 10 percent of January's totals. Those who had suggested that the Germans would close down civilian traffic at the expense of military shipments were initially correct. However, the sustained nature of Allied air attacks was such that after March transportation support for the *Wehrmacht* also declined. The May attacks by fighter bombers on the Seine River bridges and on running trains further accelerated the decline.[17] (See Tables LV,[18] LVI,[19] and LVII.[20])

In the last weeks before D-day, the Allies intensified efforts to disrupt rail and road traffic. On May 21, tactical air units began sweeps aimed at destroying stationary and running locomotives. Nearly 800 "Spitfires," "Thunderbolts," and "Typhoons" operated at low level over northern France.[21] In the period between

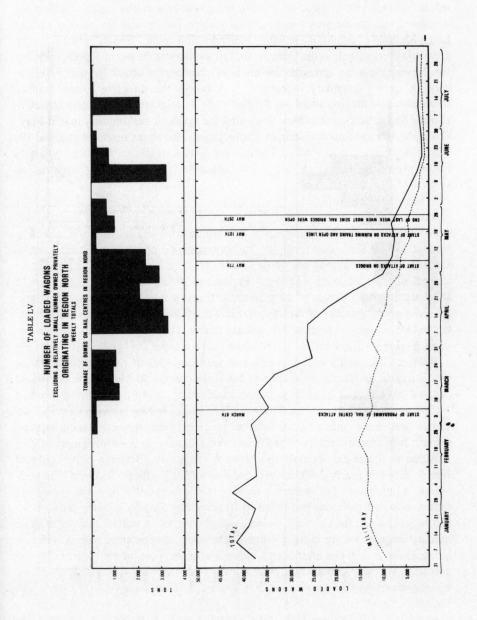

TABLE LV

NUMBER OF LOADED WAGONS
EXCLUDING A RELATIVELY SMALL NUMBER OWNED PRIVATELY
ORIGINATING IN REGION NORTH
WEEKLY TOTALS

TONNAGE OF BOMBS ON RAIL CENTRES IN REGION NORD

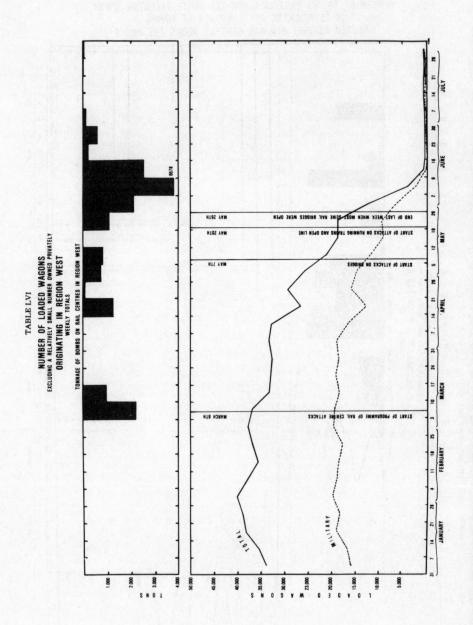

TABLE LVI

NUMBER OF LOADED WAGONS
EXCLUDING A RELATIVELY SMALL NUMBER OWNED PRIVATELY
ORIGINATING IN REGION WEST
WEEKLY TOTALS

TONNAGE OF BOMBS ON RAIL CENTRES IN REGION WEST

TONS

LOADED WAGONS

TOTAL

MILITARY

MARCH 6TH   START OF PROGRAMME OF RAIL CENTRE ATTACKS

MAY 7TH   START OF ATTACKS ON BRIDGES

MAY 20TH   START OF ATTACKS ON RUNNING TRAINS AND OPEN LINE

MAY 26TH   END OF LAST WEEK WHEN MOST SEINE RAIL BRIDGES WERE OPEN

JANUARY   FEBRUARY   MARCH   APRIL   MAY   JUNE   JULY

TABLE LVII

NUMBER OF TRAINS PASSING ALONG THE ROUTE VALENTON-JUVISY
IN RELATION TO THE TONNAGES OF BOMBS
DIRECTED AGAINST RAILWAY CENTRES ALONG THE ROUTE

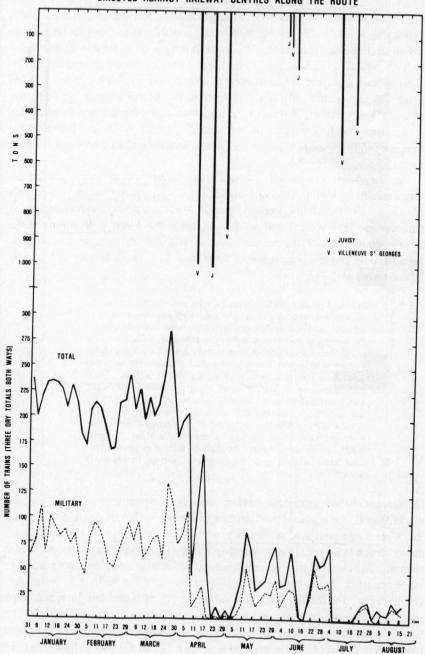

May 20 and 28th, Allied air attacks damaged 500 locomotives.[22] Normally, quick repair of damaged locomotives was not a difficult task, but destruction of repair centers as well as bridges, marshalling yards, and switching points made it extremely difficult.[23] By late May, just before attacks on the Seine bridges, overall rail traffic was down to 55 percent of January's levels. Destruction of those bridges reduced traffic levels to 30 percent by June 6, and thereafter the level of railway utilization declined to 10 percent. Attacks on the system in western France were particularly effective, and by mid-June it had virtually ceased to operate.[24] The effect on military transport was as marked as on other types of travel. In June, in the west, the Germans could only run 7 percent of the March tonnage; in July, the figure was slightly higher, 9 percent. In the north along the Belgian frontier, the figures for June and July were 27 percent and 23 percent, while for all France the movement of military trains through the system in June and July dropped from 56 percent to 35 percent of the March total.[25]

As the campaign progressed, "Ultra" intercepts and decrypts played an important role in providing Allied air commanders with a picture of the campaign's effectiveness on the transportation system.[26] A mid-May appreciation by Commander in Chief West (Rundstedt) warned that the Allies were aiming at the systematic destruction of the railway system and that the attacks had already hampered supply and troop movements.[27] On June 3, a report dealing with attacks on the railroads concluded:

> In Zone 1 [France and Belgium], the systematic destruction that has been carried out since March of all important junctions of the entire network—not only of the main lines—has most seriously crippled the whole transport system (railway installations, including rolling stock). Similarly, Paris has been systematically cut off from long-distance traffic, and the most important bridges over the lower Seine have been destroyed one after another. As a result . . . it is only by exerting the greatest efforts that purely military traffic and goods essential to the war effort . . . can be kept moving. . . The rail network is to be completely wrecked. Local and through traffic is to be made impossible, and all efforts to restore the services are to be prevented. This aim has so successfully been achieved—locally at any rate—that the *Reichsbahn* authorities are seriously considering whether it is not useless to attempt further repair work.[28]

The success of these interdiction efforts was a major contribution to the winning of World War II, for it placed the Germans in an impossible situation. Since much of the *Wehrmacht* consisted of infantry whose equipment was horse-drawn, the Germans depended on railroads for movement of reserves and supplies to the battlefront. Removal of that support made it difficult to redeploy forces once an invasion occurred. Thus, the Germans lost the battle of the buildup in Normandy before it began. Unlike the battle in Italy, the Allies were able to move large numbers of divisions into the invasion area and place heavy pressure on the defenses. The resulting ground battle demanded enormous expenditures of men and material. Destruction of the transportation system forced German infantry to fight

The cost: B-17 straggler under the guns of an Fw 190 (*official USAF photo*)

Air superiority: American fighters over B-17 formation (*official USAF photo*)

Two views of the 'Wonder Bomber', the Ju 88

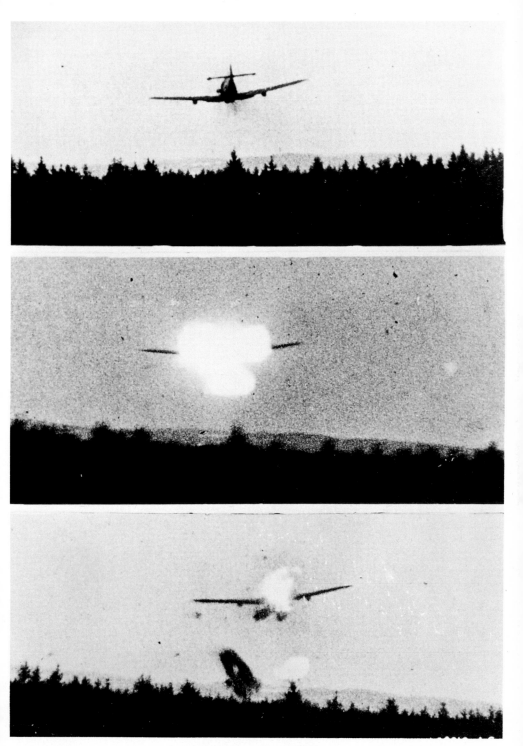

A Bf 109 goes down, 1944

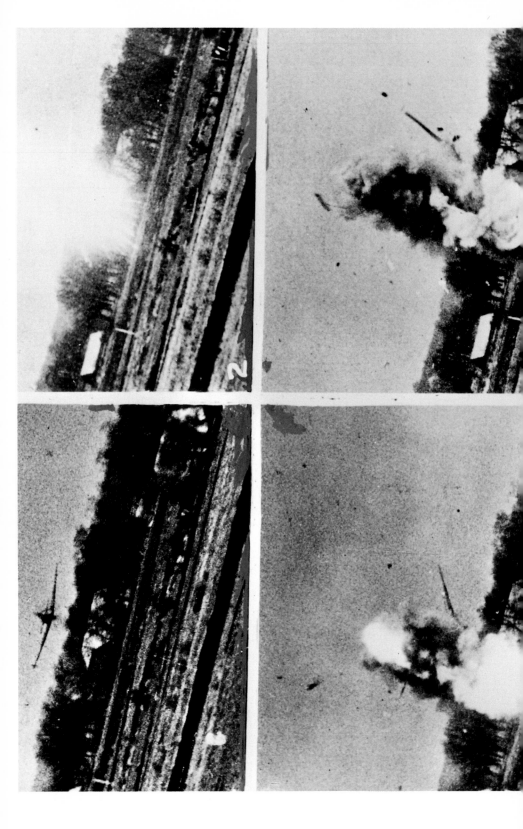

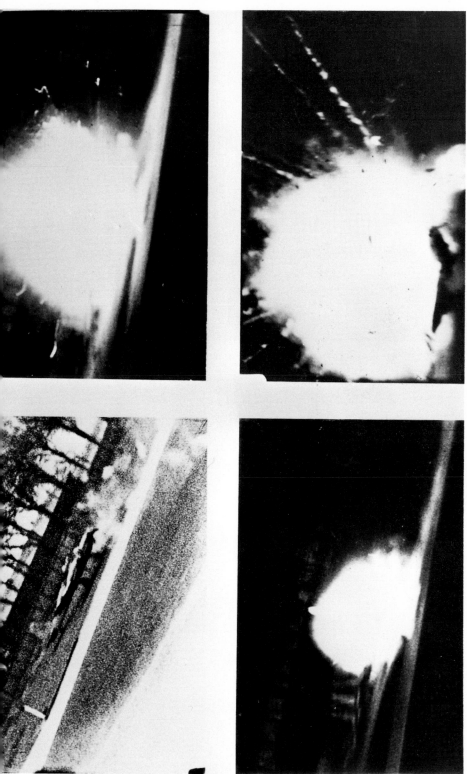

Top: Attrition: destruction of a **Bf**109 (*official USAF photo*)
Bottom: Allied low level attack, 1944

Air superiority: He 177s under strafing attack (*official USAF photo*)

The cost: A B-27 goes down

Defeat: occupied German airfield, 1945 (*official USAF photo*)

Göring in defeat: The *Reichsmarschall* removes his medals for his American captors
(*Courtesy of Colonel Max van Rossum Daum, USAF retired*)

Der Führer greets a favourite before the war (AFSHRC)

without adequate artillery support, and even infantry ammunition was in short supply. Moreover, damage to the transportation system made it difficult for motorized and mechanized units to pick their way past broken bridges at night.[29] For obvious reasons, day movement was virtually impossible.

Eighth Air Force provided substantial help in the attack on transportation targets. Its most important contributions, however, involved continuing pressure on Germany's aircraft industry and, in May, the start of attacks on synthetic fuel plants. Those who have seen the oil and transportation plans as contradictory have ignored the fact that the oil offensive robbed the Germans of their road and air mobility, just as the transportation plan robbed them of their rail mobility. For the invasion, that latter mobility proved more important as movement of most *Wehrmacht* ground troops (including tank units) and the shipment of bulk supplies like food, fuel, and ammunition to fight the invasion depended on railroads. Because the Germans had fuel reserves available, the attack on oil took considerable time to reach full impact. This had led Eisenhower to adopt most of Zuckerman's transportation plan despite gloomy forecasts by some intelligence experts. As the historians of Bomber Command note: "The communication [transportation] plan was adopted more in a spirit of desperation than of optimism."[30] The gloomy forecasts, however, proved mostly wrong.

Since the early days of the war, the Germans had worried about their petroleum supplies.[31] In September 1940, Hitler remarked to Hungarian representatives that British efforts to sabotage Rumanian oil fields had occasioned some anxiety and added that there were two vital raw materials Nazi Germany needed: Swedish iron ore and Rumanian petroleum.[32] He might have added that Germany's own great synthetic fuel plants were also of critical importance. From 1940 on, fuel shortages bedeviled German strategy. The 1942 campaign aimed to capture the Caucasian oil fields in Russia to relieve fuel shortages that were plaguing prosecution of the war. In 1943, there was marginal improvement in the situation as Italy ceased to be a drain and Germany's synthetic fuel industry reached a productive high point.[33] From 1940 to 1943, production from natural wells (mainly in Austria) and from synthetic fuel plants rose from 4,506,000 to 6,985,000 tons per year. Nevertheless, Germany still imported the same percentage of oil in 1943 that she had in 1940, while in tonnage the Germans imported nearly 700,000 tons more than in the war's first year.[34]

Unexpectedly high stocks captured in Italy in 1943 also helped in early 1944.[35] In fact, over the winter of 1943–44, the Germans built up aircraft fuel reserves for the first time since 1941. From a reserve of 33,786 tons in November 1943, the special reserve had grown to 119,738 tons by May 1944. Its existence provided a substantial cushion in meeting the fuel crisis of the early summer.[36] The Germans had found the failure of Allied bombing to strike the synthetic oil industry inexplicable. Writing to Speer in March 1944, Keitel's staff thought it possible that enemy air forces would attack the oil industry to achieve a quick end to the war.[37] In April, a *Luftwaffe* staff officer was more direct. Considering that the major German refineries and fuel plants lay within "the zone threatened by air attack," he found it extraordinary that enemy airpower had not struck the oil industry—a target that would jeopardize the *Reich's* entire war effort.[38]

On May 12, 1944, Spaatz released Doolittle's Eighth Air Force from invasion preparations to attack oil targets. From England, 935 B–17's and B–24's sortied against synthetic oil plants at Zwickau, Merseburg-Leuna, Brux, Lutzkendorf, Bohlen, Zeitz, and Chemnitz.[39] Allied bombers and escorting fighters encountered severe fighter opposition and a moderate response from flak batteries. Eighth lost 46 bombers (43 B–17's and 3 B–24's) and 12 fighters (5 P–47's and 7 P–51's). German losses were also heavy. Twenty-eight German pilots died with 26 injured.[40] The results, while encouraging from the Allied perspective, were not decisive. The great Leuna plant, although damaged, lost only 18 percent of preattack capacity. Speer, nevertheless, was enormously worried and warned Hitler:

> The enemy has struck us at one of our weakest points. If they persist at it this time, we will soon no longer have any fuel production worth mentioning. Our one hope is that the other side has an air force general staff as scatterbrained as ours![41]

What Speer did not know and what has only recently come out is the role of "Ultra" decrypts in keeping American "strategic" bombers attacking the oil plants. The intelligence officer who handled "Ultra" messages at Eighth Air Force headquarters later claimed that intercepts, indicating that shortages were general and not local, convinced "all concerned that the air offensive had uncovered a weak spot in the German economy and led to exploitation of this weakness to the fullest extent."[42] The first intercept, underlining German vulnerability, came almost immediately. On May 16, Bletchley Park forwarded a May 14 message cancelling a general staff order that *Luftflotten* 1 and 6 surrender to *Luftflotte* 3 five heavy and four light or medium flak batteries each. These battteries were to be reassigned to *Luftflotte Reich* to protect the hydrogenation plant at Troglitz. In addition, four heavy flak batteries from Oschersleben, four from Wiener-Neustadt, and two from Leipzig-Erla (defending aircraft production plants) were to move to other synthetic fuel plants.[43] On the 21st, another intercept from an unspecified source ordered that:

> Consumption of mineral oil in every form . . . be substantially reduced . . . in view of effects of Allied action in Rumania and on German hydrogenation plants; extensive failures in mineral oil production and a considerable reduction in the June allocation of fuel oil, etc., were to be expected.[44]

After feverish efforts to repair damage, production had almost returned to preattack levels by the end of the month.[45] On May 28, Eighth Air Force struck again with only half the force used in the first attack. Supported by fighters, 400-plus bombers attacked the synthetic fuel plants. Again fighter opposition was heavy, and 32 bombers were lost (nearly 10 percent of the force). On the next day, Eighth again attacked the fuel plants, while Fifteenth Air Force hit aircraft factories in Austria. Bomber losses were 52, making a total of 84 heavy bombers lost in two days. Attrition of German pilots was also severe. On May 28, day fighter squadrons lost 18 pilots killed and 13 wounded; on the 29th, the Germans lost 21 single-engine pilots killed and 8 wounded. Twin-engine fighters lost 23 crewmembers killed and 10 wounded.[46] Spaatz had been correct that attacks on the oil industry would force the *Luftwaffe* to fight, thereby imposing further severe attrition on its forces. These two attacks, combined with raids that Fifteenth launched against Ploesti, reduced German oil production by 50 percent.[47] The impact of the new raids became almost immediately apparent to air commanders. On June 6, Bletchley Park passed along the following decrypt:

> Following according to *OKL* on Fifth. As a result of renewed interference with production of aircraft fuel by Allied action, most essential requirements for training and carrying out production plans can scarcely be covered by quantities of aircraft fuel available. Baker four allocations only possible to air officers for bombers, fighters and ground attack, and director general of supply. No other quota holders can be considered in June. To assume defense of *Reich* and to prevent gradual collapse of readiness for defense of German Air Force in east, it has been necessary to break into *OKW* reserves. Extending, therefore, existing regulations ordered that all units to arrange operations so as to manage at least until the beginning of July with present stocks or small allocation which may be possible. Date of arrival and quantities of July quota still undecided. Only very small quantities available for adjustments, provided Allied situation remains unchanged. In no circumstances can greater allocations be made. Attention again drawn to existing orders for most extreme economy measures and strict supervision of consumption, especially for transport, personal and communications flights.[48]

May's attacks were a prelude to the devastating raids that followed in succeeding months. After a two-week pause during which most of the aircraft supported the invasion, the Americans staged new raids that knocked out 90 percent of aviation fuel production so that production sank to 632 tons. By mid-July, the Germans had repaired the facilities sufficiently to quadruple production. More American raids and Bomber Command's first intervention on the 22nd lowered production to 120 tons per day. By the end of July, the offensive had knocked out 98 percent of Germany's capacity to produce aircraft fuel.[49] Success did not come without cost. The raids on June 20 cost Eighth Air Force 49 bombers and 12 fighters, while the raid on the 21st cost 24 aircraft shot down by fighters, 20 bombers destroyed by flak, and 44 destroyed on the ground at Poltava.[50] For the remainder of the war, the American "strategic" bombing force concentrated much of its effort against German fuel plants and refineries. In July, Leuna produced only 70 percent of its normal production, while other major production centers dropped to between 43 percent and 58 percent of estimated capacity. Only Ludwigshafen reached full production. Continued attacks would keep a firm lid on German fuel production (see Table LVIII[51]).

TABLE LVIII

German Fuel Production

	Percent of Fuel Capacity Produced	Percent of Aviation Fuel Capacity Produced
August 1944	46	65
September 1944	48	30
October 1944	43	37
November 1944	60	65
December 1944	59	56
January 1945	51	33
February 1945	40	5

The implications were not hard to see. After the June attacks, Speer warned Hitler that he would need six to eight weeks to restore production. Should the *Führer* not provide defensive support for oil production centers, the enemy would soon recognize recovery efforts and destroy the repair work.[52] Speer alluded directly to the fact that Hitler had promised in May to hold the fighter force in Germany to defend synthetic fuel plants. However, he had then turned around in June and thrown it against the invasion where Allied fighters could destroy it.[53] Speer pointed out to Hitler in July that the number of day fighters available in the *Reich* to defend synthetic plants was substantially under what had been present in early June (see Table LIX[54]).

TABLE LIX

Fighter Forces Available, *Luftflotte Reich*

	Single-Engine Fighters	Operationally Ready	Twin-Engine Fighters	Operationally Ready
1 June 1944	788	472	203	83
1 July 1944	388	242	156	64
27 July 1944	460	273	94	42

He noted that the number of fighters in frontline units had remained the same and that the diversion of recent production to the front had only resulted in the wastage of more aircraft to little effect. If Hitler refused to protect the fuel plants, Speer warned, there would not be adequate fuel for the *Luftwaffe*.[55]

By mid-summer, as fighter production reached its wartime high, the Germans were approaching the situation where the hundreds of aircraft their industry turned out had neither fuel to fly nor pilots. Pilot training schools were already shutting down for lack of fuel. The circumstances recall a somewhat ironic remark that Göring made in early 1943:

> . . . furthermore I am of the opinion that the building of our aircraft
> should not depend in any way on the fuel programme. I would
> rather have a mass of aircraft standing around unable to fly owing to
> a lack of petrol than not have any at all.[56]

In fact, the Germans were able to produce a minimum amount of fuel to keep some aircraft and some tanks moving, but throughout this particular period the general impression is of a steady decline in *Luftwaffe* and army capabilities due to fuel shortages. Loss of fuel needed to continue adequate training programs further accelerated the decline in pilot quality and ended the chance that the Germans might rebuild their shattered fighter forces. The decline in maneuverability in the motorized and mechanized forces showed up most clearly in the December Ardennes offensive. There, the Germans launched their attack without fuel to carry it past the Meuse with the hope that its spearheads could capture enough fuel in American dumps to reach strategic objectives.

In the final analysis, Tedder's and Zuckerman's transportation plan and Spaatz's fuel plan were entirely complementary.[57] Their execution placed German troops on the "Atlantic Wall" in a difficult position when the invasion came and insured that, when the collapse occurred, the *Wehrmacht* could not make a fighting withdrawal in France. Destruction of the transportation system prevented the Germans from moving reinforcements up with sufficient speed to match the Allied buildup. Thus, when the contest in the *bocage* country turned into a battle of attrition, the Germans could only bring up enough supplies and reserves to hang on. That their ill-supplied and outnumbered forces held out for so long was a tribute to the skill and tenacity of the German soldier, but certainly not to the political and military leadership that had placed him again in a hopeless situation. Conversely, Spaatz's oil attacks achieved two major goals. First, it continued the decimation of the *Luftwaffe* and it hindered the training program from regenerating pilot strength. Second, it robbed the *Wehrmacht* of its motorized mobility.

The conduct of these operations raises an interesting point concerning the personalities and capabilities of Tedder and Spaatz. Tedder, as he had in the Mediterranean, designed an air strategy that placed Anglo-American air forces firmly within the context of overall Allied strategy. He did not deny the air forces an independent mission but rather insured that the air campaign would make the greatest contribution to the whole effort. The same can be said of Spaatz, who possessed a thorough understanding of how to gain and to maintain air superiority. From January, he attacked targets that forced the Germans to fight, again allowing American escorts to devastate the *Luftwaffe*'s battle strength. Spaatz's push for an offensive against oil revealed his understanding of the need to continue an air superiority strategy as well as his sense that oil might be the weak link in Germany's economic structure. He realized that the destruction of the synthetic fuel plants would not only eliminate the *Luftwaffe* but finish the German army. Thus, Spaatz and Tedder, unlike so many of their contemporaries, grasped the meaning of strategy in the largest sense rather than in the narrow, confusing definition that Douhet and Trenchard had given "strategic" bombing. Only in their personalities was there significant difference between the men. With his quiet, intellectual approach, Tedder did not dominate men or events; his success depended on the cooperation and support of others. In the arguments and debates during the spring of 1944, he relied on Eisenhower's friendship, support, and prestige. Spaatz was more his own man and was, as a result, the premier airman and one of the great generals of the war.

DEFENSE OF THE FRONTIERS: THE *LUFTWAFFE*, APRIL-SEPTEMBER 1944

April witnessed Allied air forces continuing the unrelenting pressure on German defenses that had marked previous months. While the tempo of operations over Germany declined, air attacks against the transportation system and airfields in France kept the wastage of German fighters and pilots close to March's high rate. The *Luftwaffe* wrote off 43 percent of frontline fighters and lost over 20 percent of fighter pilots present at the beginning of April.[58] By mid-month, the Germans were admitting that defending forces over the *Reich* were severely strained. Nevertheless, they still made a sizeable dent in the attacking forces; American bomber units in England wrote off the largest percentage of aircraft thus far in 1944, 24.6 percent of aircraft in tactical units.[59]

But the *Luftwaffe* had reached the breaking point. In April, Eighth Air Force lost the most bombers that it would lose in any month of the war (409 four-engine bombers); thereafter, bomber losses dropped off (See Table L and Appendix 4). Similarly from this point forward, the percentage of operational sorties lost began a significant drop from the steady level of close to 4 percent that Eighth suffered from November 1943 through April 1944.[60] There were, of course, several factors affecting loss rates. The climb in Eighth's frontline strength continued through June and finally began to drive down the sortie loss rate. Operations over western Europe to attack the transportation system also reduced casualties, but the most important factor seems to have been a break in *Luftwaffe* fighter capabilities. From May on, German fighters inflicted increasingly sporadic damage on attacking formations. If American bomber losses dropped in May, German fighter and fighter pilot losses reached a high point in the war. The *Luftwaffe* wrote off 50.4 percent of single-engine fighter aircraft during the month and lost 25 percent of their Bf 109 and Fw 190 pilots.[61] Thus far in the year, its single-engine fighter force had lost 2,262 pilots. On December 31, the *Luftwaffe* had had 2,395 single-engine fighter pilots in frontline units (1,491 fully combat-ready, 291 partially combat-ready, and the rest not combat-ready).[62] Thus, crew losses for the five-month period came close to 100 percent of the entire day fighter force (excluding twin-engine aircraft). The decline in American losses that began in May is therefore explicable in view of these German casualties.

The attrition rate caused a ripple effect throughout the force structure. Pressure to get pilots through training schools was such that German pilots had half the training hours of their Allied counterparts, a point previously mentioned. More costly was the fact that a German fighter pilot received 60 to 80 hours of training in operational aircraft, while his opponent in the RAF or Army Air Forces averaged 225 hours flying time in operational aircraft. Consequently, the product of German training schools was even more inadequate than the ratio between total flying hours suggests.[63] A study by the *Luftwaffe*'s historical section lamely suggested in 1944 that "our pilots must attempt to counterbalance this obvious disadvantage by greater enthusiasm and courage."[64] Extension of American fighter range throughout the *Reich* gave the Germans an additional headache. Training flights, both beginning and advanced, now frequently came under attack from American fighters.[65]

A conference between Galland and Göring in mid-May underlined how enemy air operations were devastating the fighter force. Galland reported that *Luftflotte Reich* had lost 38 percent of its fighter pilots in April, while *Luftflotte* 3 had lost 24 percent of its fighter pilot strength. Altogether, the Germans had lost 489 pilots (100 of whom were officers), Galland reported, while training centers had forwarded only 396 new pilots (including 62 officers).[66] Galland's proposals to meet the shortfall and continued attrition reflected the desperate situation. He urged (1) that all fighter pilots holding short staff positions be transferred immediately to operational units, (2) that qualified night fighter pilots transfer to the day fighter force, (3) that two fighter *Gruppen* transfer from the eastern front as soon as possible, and (4) that the ground attack command release all pilots with more than five victories to the defense of the *Reich*. Finally, Galland reported that flying schools had released 80-plus instructors to fill empty cockpits.[67]

Other evidence suggests a rush to strip commands outside of *Luftflotte Reich* of experienced pilots in order to reconstitute defense forces at the center. *Fliegerkorps* I on the eastern front was ordered to surrender 15 pilots, "including 2 to 4 aces," after it had received a new draft of pilots straight from training school.[68] Galland even suggested that all fighter *Gruppen* in France pull back to Germany to meet the bomber threat. Göring, fearing that an invasion was imminent, refused.[69] As had happened over the past year and a half, the *Luftwaffe* used Russia as a school for inexperienced pilots. There they could build flying and fighting skills before being thrown into the cauldron of western air battles.[70] However, there was less chance to do this now, because there were fewer squadrons in the east and because attrition was so high in the skies over Germany that the *Luftwaffe* had to throw new pilots directly into combat against Allied air forces.

The following two cases show what the scale of combat losses meant to individual fighter *Gruppen*. The III *Gruppe*/JG 53 possessed an average strength of 23 aircraft in April with 16 serviceable. During the month, the *Gruppe* lost nine aircraft in combat with one slightly damaged. Six more were written off due to noncombat causes with one aircraft badly damaged and three slightly damaged. The *Gruppe* suffered five pilots killed and two injured (average crew strength would have approximated the number of aircraft). In the month, its aircraft took part in 38 separate operations on twenty-four days with 431 combat sorties.[71] The tempo of air operations in May showed in the following report of II *Gruppe*/JG 53:

(A) Operations took place on thirteen days. Twenty-one scrambles, 15 of which resulted in air combats. (B) Average aircraft strength, 34; average serviceability, 20. (C) Fifty-three aircraft lost or damaged. Of these: (1) Extent: 34 at 100 percent, 3 over 60 percent, 9 over 35 percent, 7 under 35 percent. (2) Reason: 33 through Allied action, 4 [through] technical faults, 16 owing servicing faults. (D) Repairs: three in *Gruppe*'s workshop, six at GAF station, seven at [the] factory. (E) Personnel Losses—Killed or Injured: seven killed, five missing, three wounded (two bailed out), seven injured (of whom five bailed out). Two more injured not through Allied action. Seventeen parachute jumps, 2 jumped with wounds, 2 jumped twice without injury.[72]

The pressure on the *Luftwaffe* during the spring showed in the diversity of targets that Allied air forces attacked. Not only did fuel, aircraft, and tank industries receive attention but along with the offensive against the transportation system, Allied tactical air forces made a major effort to cripple forward operating bases. Despite the attacks on the fuel plants, the Germans could not divert the protection afforded aircraft production and repair facilities because of the losses frontline units were suffering.[73] At the end of April, an attack on Friedrichshafen revealed the tank industry's vulnerability. Factories in Friedrichshafen produced 40 to 50 percent of the drive gear assemblies for the Pz III, IV, and V tanks; 40 percent of the motors for the Pz IV's; and 65 percent of the motors for Pz V's and VI's. The works, badly damaged by the attack, took at least two to three months to disperse to other factories; thus, there was a production shortfall of at least 30 percent for May and June.[74]

Allied attacks in May against bases in France soon had a decided impact on *Luftflotte* 3's capabilities. "Ultra" intercepts gave Allied intelligence a glimpse into the location and strength of fighter units as well as the effectiveness of attacks carried out by tactical air.[75] They also indicated when the Germans had completed repairs on damaged fields or had decided to abandon permanently operations at particular locations.[76] Armed with this information, the Allies pursued an intensive, well-orchestrated campaign that destroyed the German's base structure near the English Channel and invasion beaches. The scale of these attacks forced the Germans to abandon efforts to prepare bases close to the Channel and to select airfields far to the southeast.[77]

Thus, on the brink of the invasion, the *Luftwaffe* had lost control of its base structure in France. Since December 1943, the Germans had planned to move major aircraft reinforcements into *Luftflotte* 3 when the invasion occurred. That command would then launch a decisive air attack against the landings.[78] Further plans followed in February. Basic premises were that "defense against an invasion [would] be decisive for the successful conclusion to the war" and that "massed intervention of all the flying units in the first hours of a landing would be decisive for the continuation of the whole undertaking."[79] Such platitudes sounded impressive. However, by June, the Allied air offensive had removed all possibility for the Germans to make an effective aerial response. Air battles in Germany had devastated the *Reich*'s fighter forces, German bombing attacks on Britain had eliminated most of the bombers, and Allied attacks on forward operating airfields had destroyed much of the base support.

What is remarkable in examining *Luftflotte* 3's force structure is the fact that it contained few ground support aircraft, as nearly all ground support squadrons were on the eastern front (with 550 aircraft) in anticipation of what the Germans correctly believed would be a major Russian offensive.[80] As a result, fighter aircraft would have to fly most of the attacks on the invasion forces. These fighters would fly in from *Luftflotte Reich,* and their pilots would have received no previous training in fighter bomber tactics. The weight of their bomb loads would put German pilots at an even greater disadvantage against Allied fighters.[81]

On June 5, 1944, *Luftflotte* 3 contained 815 aircraft, of which approximately 600 were in commission.[82] The hope was that fighter forces from *Luftflotte Reich* would build up aerial forces in France to required levels. Unfortunately for the Germans, their forecasters misread the weather for June 6 so that the invasion caught their entire command structure by surprise. (Rommel was in Germany celebrating his wife's birthday.[83]) Through the night and daylight hours of D-day, the Allies enjoyed complete air superiority with Allied air forces flying 14,000 missions in support of the invasion. They lost only 127 aircraft. By the end of the first day, the British had landed 75,215 troops and the Americans 57,500. In addition, some 23,000 airborne troops had dropped behind the invasion beaches.[84] Throughout the day, the *Luftwaffe* was hardly seen. But Field Marshal Sperrle did issue a pompous order of the day to his troops:

> Men of *Luftflotte* 3! The enemy has launched the long-announced invasion. Long have we waited for this moment, long have we prepared ourselves, both inwardly and on the field of battle, by untiring, unending toil. Our task is now to defeat the enemy. I know that each one of you, true to his oath to the colors, will carry out his duties. . . . Great things will be asked of you, and you will show the bravest fighting valor. Salute the *Führer*.[85]

Sperrle's words could not have been further removed from reality. *Luftflotte* 3 launched less than 100 sorties of which approximately 70 were by single-engine fighters. That evening, the bombers and antishipping squadrons mounted 175 more sorties against the invasion fleet.[86] For the day, the Germans lost 39 aircraft with 21 damaged, 8 due to noncombat causes.[87]

The *Luftwaffe* now scrambled desperately to get its fighter forces from Germany to fields in France where they could bring some relief to the pressure being applied by Allied forces. Movement of ground reserves towards the invasion area was extraordinarily difficult. It took five days for the 17th SS Panzer Grenadier Division to cover 200 miles, as Allied air attacks limited its movement to night time and secondary roads. The SS division *Das Reich* set a record for frustration. Tracked elements of the division left Limoges on June 11 and did not arrive on the Normandy front until the end of the month.[88] Frustrated and enraged, SS troops took their anger out on the inhabitants of the village of Oradour sur Glane by herding adults and children into the church and burning it down and machinegunning those who escaped the fire. Movement of divisions immediately adjacent to the beachland was hardly easier. *Panzer Lehr* moved towards the battlefront on five separate roads, and its commander described one of those as a "fighter-bomber race course." On June 6 alone, it lost 80 half-tracks, self-propelled guns, and prime movers.[89]

The buildup of *Luftflotte* 3 strength began with the movement of 200 fighters from Germany to airfields in France within 36 hours of the invasion. An additional 100 had followed by June 10.[90] But the destruction of forward operating bases had forced the *Luftwaffe* to select new and inadequately prepared sites for reinforcements arriving from the *Reich*. But there was confusion even on fields that had been selected early in the spring. A German study written after the defeat in Normandy stated:

> The airfields which had long been earmarked for the emergency day fighter *Geschwader* from the *Reich* in the event of an invasion . . ., were completely inadequate. In almost every case, no H.Q. [headquarters] buildings had been constructed and dispersal points had not been organized; there was a complete lack of splinter screens, trenches, dugouts, shelters, teleprinting and wireless installations, and of ammunition and fuel depots.
>
> To urgent request for the provision of these elementary necessities, the reply received was always that no personnel [were] available for construction purposes and no one for the installation of signals equipment.[91]

"Ultra" intercepts picked up a substantial portion of the move and indicated bases and arrival times for the reinforcing fighters.[92] The *Luftwaffe* was at least able to better the poor showing of June 6. On the nights of June 7-8, the bomber and antishipping aircraft managed to launch 100 sorties, while the day forces flew 500 sorties on the 8th, 400 by single-engine fighters.[93] The *Luftwaffe*, however, could raise the level of sorties only by stripping the *Reich*'s fighter defenses. Losses against swarms of Allied fighters were heavy. On June 8, *Luftflotte* 3 lost 68 aircraft; and in the first week of operations around the beachhead, 362 aircraft. In the second week, the Germans lost another 232 aircraft. Thus, in the two weeks from June 6 to 19th, they lost nearly 75 percent of the aircraft that *Luftflotte* 3 had possessed on June 5.[94] Moreover, by throwing their aircraft into the invasion battle, Hitler and Göring gave Eighth Air Force *carte blanche* to attack the synthetic fuel facilities; and almost as fast as the Germans fed aircraft into the Normandy battle, American and British fighters shot them down.

Allied air superiority led the Germans to vacillate on their tactics, all of which worked to little effect. Initial *Luftwaffe* thrusts consisted mostly of fighter bomber sorties. However, Allied fighters jumped attacking aircraft and forced German pilots to jettison their bombs. Losses were always heavy. "Ultra" often gave Allied commanders advanced warning of German attacks and targets, thus increasing chances of interception.[95] On the 12th, the Germans abandoned the attempt to use the fighter force as fighter bombers and ordered all *Gruppen* to convert back to fighter configuration. The rationale was that as fighters they could drive off their opponents, a thoroughly unrealistic assessment in view of Allied numbers.[96] The change in configuration made little difference, and Allied attacks reduced German fighters to protecting their own airfields. When the Germans managed to assemble 50 to 60 fighters together, they could squeeze 10 to 15 aircraft into Allied territory. These aircraft made a few strafing runs but accomplished little else.[97]

The situation was clearly hopeless and reinforcing the battlefront, in the eyes of a war diarist, was "a race in which conditions inevitably favor the enemy."[98] Allied air superiority was troublesome enough for German ground forces, but when combined with "Ultra" the effects were devastating. "Ultra" intercepts on June 9 and 10th gave Allied intelligence the exact location of Geyr von Schweppenburg's Panzer Group West headquarters. Obligingly, the Germans left their vehicles and radio equipment in the open.[99] The attack not only destroyed most of Panzer Group West's communications equipment but also killed 17 officers, including the chief of staff.[100] The strike effectively removed Panzer Group West as an operating headquarters and robbed the Germans of the only army organization in the west capable of handling large numbers of mobile divisions. On June 14, Bletchly Park decrypted a message from Rundstedt reporting the difficulties involved in conducting a battle when the enemy enjoyed complete air superiority.

> C in C West report morning ninth included: in large-scale operations by thousands of bombers and fighter bombers, Allied air forces stifled German tank attacks and had harassing effect on movements. High losses in wireless equipment by fighter bomber attacks (I SS Corps had, for example, only four wireless troops, and Panzer Group West had lost 75 percent of its wireless equipment) were noticeable in making reporting difficult.[101]

Nevertheless, the Germans were able to hold on, but just barely. A number of factors beside their own military competence played a part. First, the Allied buildup did not proceed as fast as planners hoped. Then, a major June storm almost completely halted the buildup for three days and did severe damage to the artificial harbors established off the beaches to aid in the logistic effort.[102] Moreover, the Normandy terrain, particularly the *bocage* country south of Utah and Omaha beaches, favored the defender. Fighting their way through hedgerows, the Americans slowly bisected the Cotentin Peninsula and captured Cherbourg. They then pushed the Germans south toward St. Lo but were unable to gain the leverage necessary to break loose. Thus, American forces could not use their mobility against an opponent who, because of Allied air superiority, enjoyed little possibility of fighting a battle of maneuver.

On the eastern side of the lodgment, the countryside was more favorable. However, the road system as well as the danger posed by a breakthrough led the Germans to move their armor towards Caen. The accumulation of strength made it difficult for the British to advance, but pressure on the Caen defenses prevented the Germans from massing armor for a counterattack. Instead, panzer divisions moved directly into the line as fast as they came up.[103] Still whatever their ability, German frontline troops were in difficult circumstances. A major in the 77th Infantry Division, captured at SC Sauvern on June 16, told a fellow prisoner:

> I once [remarked] that the *Führer* said that if the invasion came, he would send the whole G.A.F. [German Air Force] into action at the place of the invasion, even if it meant leaving all forces in all the other theaters of war without air cover. That story was over as far as I was concerned after I had seen one single German reconnaissance aircraft in the air between the 6th and the 16th, and apart from that, complete mastery of the air by the Americans. We can bring out whole armies, and they'll smash them completely with their air forces within a week. Above all, we have no petrol at all left. We can no longer move any numbers of troops by means requiring petrol, only by rail or marching on foot.[104]

The performance of Allied air forces during June reflected their overwhelming superiority. From June 6 to the 30th, RAF and American squadrons flew 163,403 sorties over the continent, of which 130,000 supported the invasion. Conversely, *Luftflotte* 3—even with reinforcements—only flew 13,829 sorties. German losses were again devastating. In France, the *Luftwaffe* lost 931 aircraft on operations, with a further 67 lost due to noncombat causes; over *Luftflotte Reich,* the Germans lost an additional 250 aircraft on operations, with 183 more aircraft destroyed due to other than combat causes.[105] Efforts to maintain a high tempo of operations floundered because of combat losses. Depots for replacement aircraft now lay behind the Rhine, as the original replacement centers at Toul and Le Bouget were vulnerable to aerial attack.[106] Ferrying operations were often hazardous affairs that sometimes cost the Germans the aircraft in transit.[107] Thus, the effectiveness of the *Gruppen* fell off rapidly after an initial surge when first on operations. By June 11, the *Luftwaffe* had had to withdraw five *Gruppen* from France because of heavy losses and replace them with units from Germany. The shattered units returned to the *Reich* for new aircraft and new pilots.[108]

At the end of June, the *Luftwaffe*'s strategic position, as well as the *Reich*'s, gave the Germans small cause for optimism. A *Luftwaffe* intelligence report summed up the situation. While Allied air operations over Germany had declined due to the invasion, the authors felt that Allied bombers would soon return to Germany. In France, air attacks had destroyed the transportation system, while bombing attacks in Germany had extensively damaged the fuel industry. Production of aircraft fuel was off by 70 percent, synthetic fuel production was down by 60 percent, and refinery output (including Rumania) had dropped to 70 percent of total capacity. The report noted that aerial attacks on transportation and petroleum industries had provided substantial aid to the ground battle in the west. Particularly worrisome from the German perspective was the possibility that the Allied air forces might do in the Balkans what they had accomplished so successfully in France and Italy; that is, destroy the rail and road system. In conclusion, the report warned that the great danger was a continuation of attacks on the synthetic fuel industry. Thus, the German high command needed to provide adequate support for the great fuel plants.

Attacks on transportation were almost as dangerous, but there was little that could be done because one could not protect an entire rail system.[109]

In July, the Normandy battle swung decisively in favor of the Allies. Hitler, worried by deception plans warning of another seaborne landing at Pas de Calais, held strong forces along that coast.[110] Thus, as had happened in June, German reinforcements were thrown into the line in piecemeal fashion to patch up the defenses. On July 15, two days before being severely wounded, Rommel warned the new commander in chief in the west, Field Marshal Günther von Kluge, that:

> The position in Normandy is becoming daily more difficult and is approaching a serious crisis. Owing to the intensity of the fighting, the exceptionally strong material supplies of the enemy, especially in artillery and armored vehicles, and the operation of their air force, which commands the battlefield unchecked, our own losses are so high that the fighting strength of the divisions is rapidly sinking. Due to the disruption of the railway and the attack carried out on major and minor roads up to 150 km behind the front, only the most essential supplies can be delivered to the troops. Conditions are unlikely to improve in the future, as enemy air activity is likely to become even more intense.[111]

Six days later, Kluge wrote Hitler that his "discussions with field commanders near Caen yesterday have convinced me that in our present position, there is no strategy possible that will counterbalance the annihilating effect of the enemy command of the air."[112] While Montgomery's forces battered past Caen, the Americans pushed southward on the Cotentin Peninsula and created the conditions necessary for a breakout.

The *Luftwaffe*'s situation continued to deteriorate. Loss rates among *Gruppen* and *Geschwader* commanders reached such a level that Göring ordered them to limit their operational sorties to an absolute minimum.[113] Commitments on various fronts, all of which showed signs of collapse, led Göring and Hitler to divide the *Luftwaffe* into a patchwork quilt. Nowhere was there a *Schwerpunkt* (main emphasis). (See Table LX.[114])

TABLE LX

Distribution of German Fighters, End of June 1944

Western Front	425
Norway	40
Defense of the Reich	370
Eastern Front	475
Balkans	65
TOTAL	1,375

In France, the *Luftwaffe* frittered away so much strength in demonstrations that it could rarely support German counterattacks. Periods of sustained effort, under the strain of overwhelming Allied air superiority, resulted in unit exhaustion within two to three days of the start of operations.[115] Meanwhile, Eighth Air Force continued its pounding of the fuel industry. By mid-July, "Ultra" had revealed that fuel shortages were placing the Nazi war effort in desparate straits. A message on July 10 reported that fuel shortages necessitated the limitation of bomber pilot training strictly to replacement crews.[116] By August, a lack of fuel forced a cessation of long-range bomber attacks against Russian targets, as Eighth's attacks had reduced Leuna's production by almost 100 percent.[117]

While Allied air forces and armies battered the *Wehrmacht* in Normandy, the Russians launched their most devastating offensive of the war. The attack came close to destroying an entire army group. On the morning of June 22, 1944, three years after the start of "Barbarossa," Stalin launched his forces against the center of the eastern front. Army Group Center possessed only 38 divisions to cover a 488-mile front, since severe fighting over the past two years in the Ukraine had caused a gradual diminution of strength in the center. By contrast, Army Group North Ukraine had 35 German and 10 Hungarian divisions to cover a 219-mile front. In addition, the two southern army groups possessed 18 panzer and panzer grenadier divisions, while Army Group Center had only 3.[118]

The collapse began at once. The army group commander rigidly adhered to Hitler's instructions that no retreats occur and that the armies maintain a rigid linear defense. By the 28th, the Russians had smashed Ninth Army, destroyed two out of the three corps in Third Panzer Army, and had pierced the front of its one remaining corps in a number of places. Fourth Army was in full retreat. So terrible was the army group's position that its only hope lay in the possibility that the Russians might outrun their supplies. The collapse turned into a rout with German units streaming out of Russia towards Poland. Most did not make it. In the first twelve days of the Soviet offensive, Army Group Center lost 25 divisions, while Fourth Army lost 130,000 men out of its original strength of 165,000 men.[119] In mid-August, the Russian advance finally sputtered to a halt before Warsaw after an advance of over 200 miles. Meanwhile, to the north the Russians also shattered Army Group North and drove it back into the Baltic countries. By early September, German troops held a thin crust from East Prussia through Central Poland. They had little chance of holding their opponent once the Russians had reinforced and resupplied their armies. The Red Army would not, however, resume the offensive on this front for another five months.

As in the west, the *Luftwaffe* played no effective role in this catastrophe. Over the whole eastern front, Soviet air forces enjoyed nearly a 6-to-1 superiority over the Germans and thus could muster a decisive superiority over the *Luftwaffe* on whatever front chosen.[120] The *Luftwaffe*'s forces in the east were as badly skewed in their deployment as were the army's, reflecting the concentration of effort that had gone into defending the Ukraine. In late spring, *Luftflotte* 4 covering the Rumanian-Hungarian frontier possessed 845 aircraft, including 390 ground attack, 160 single-engine fighters, and 45 twin-engine fighters. *Luftflotte* 6 possessed nearly as many aircraft as its neighbor in the south (775), but it had to cover Army Group Center's front with far fewer fighters and ground attack aircraft. It possessed

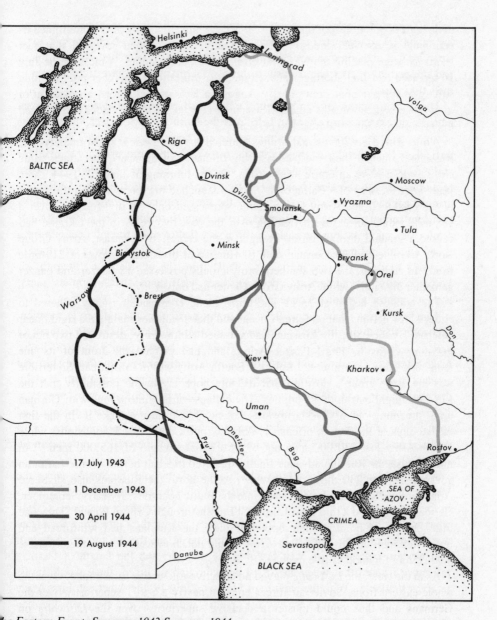

The Eastern Front: Summer 1943-Summer 1944

only 100 ground attack aircraft and 100 single-engine fighters, as its major strength lay in its long-range strike force of 370 bombers.[121] Thus, *Luftflotte* 6's force structure was not suited to meet the offensive the Russians launched. In addition, it had shipped 50 of its fighters early in June to Germany to replace fighters sent to meet the invasion.[122]

The stunning nature of Army Group Center's collapse and the speed of the Soviet advance precluded more effective help from the *Luftwaffe*. Moreover, the Russians soon overran the forward operating fields and forced the *Luftwaffe* back onto airfields in Poland and East Prussia, bases that were neither prepared nor stocked for major operations. Nevertheless, the defeat forced the *Luftwaffe* to rush reinforcements to the east. Nearly 100 fighters moved from Italy, the 50 fighters that had gone to *Luftflotte Reich* returned; the staff stripped *Luftflotten* on the flanks of fighter support; and even 40 fighters arrived from Normandy. Despite substantial reinforcements, losses in the east were so heavy that overall strength declined from 2,085 aircraft in June to 1,760 by the end of July. Virtually no fighters remained in Rumania to defend the refineries and wells from the bombers of Fifteenth Air Force. Finally, loss of forward operating bases, well stocked with supplies, parts, and fuel, caused a serious decline in operational ready rates.[123]

One final aspect of the *Luftwaffe*'s role in this particular defeat deserves mention. *Luftwaffe* flak divisions were extensively involved in the antiaircraft defense of various sectors of Army Group Center. Their after action reports on the collapse make interesting reading and are a fundamental indictment of the leadership and conduct of operations. One report suggested that German propaganda with its claim that the Russians had bled themselves white in the winter and spring offensives of 1943–44 had given German soldiers a false optimism. That overconfidence had soon turned to despair when reality engulfed Army Group Center. As one report summed up the situation, "One can only comment on the measures undertaken [to meet the Russian offensive], 'half measures' and 'too late'."[124]

As Field Marshal Model rebuilt a defensive line to hold the Soviets along the Vistula, disaster broke in the west. Collapse of both the eastern and western fronts in the summer of 1944 showed the insufficiency of Germany's resources to fight what had for the army become a three-front war and for the *Luftwaffe* a four-front war (the eastern front, Normandy, the Mediterranean, and the skies over the *Reich*). The western collapse had been building all summer; and the length of German resistance insured that when an Allied breakthrough occurred, there would be no reserves available. With the capture of St. Lo on July 19, the American First Army had fought its way through the *bocage* country and almost into the open. German reinforcements, however, continued to flow towards the British and Canadian Second Army where Commonwealth forces were placing great pressure south of Caen. On the 24th, a renewed American effort went in; and after heavy fighting, German defenses began to dissolve. Allied tactical air, particularly strikes by Ninth Air Force, contributed to the breakdown. The German Seventh Army, which had hitherto maintained an unbroken front to the coast, fell back away from the ocean in small battle groups facing west instead of north.

By the 30th, American troops had captured Avranches at the juncture between the Breton and Cotentin Peninsulas. The great breakout now began. At the start, American commanders made a serious error. The first divisions through Avranches turned west to capture Brittany rather than east towards Orleans and Paris. This decision pushed the first thrust away from the pocket of German troops already forming in the west. As the American drive spread out from Avranches, first to the west and then finally to the south and east, Hitler reacted. Instead of authorizing a retreat to the Seine to build another line of defense, he demanded that Kluge counterattack the base of the American breakthrough. He assigned XVII Panzer Corps, with a substantial portion of the German armor in the west, the task of cutting off and defeating the Americans.[125] "Ultra" informed Allied commanders of what to expect, and the German counterattack at Mortain ran into a well-prepared reception.[126] German offensive operations made little headway against the ground opposition and heavy tactical air strikes, while Hitler had, in effect, placed his armor deeper in the sack. American forces struck west and captured Le Mans on August 8; both German armies in Normandy were now in danger of being surrounded.

At the same time that Allied operations were destroying Germany's srategic situation in the west, Eisenhower made a number of command changes. Montgomery's Twenty-First Army Group now controlled only the British and Canadian armies. Bradley received equality with Montgomery and command over the Twelfth Army Group, consisting of his First Army and Patton's Third Army. At the end of August, Eisenhower took over control of the land battle himself. With those changes, and in a mood of euphoria, the Allies made the first of a series of mistakes that failed to exploit the rout in France, thereby prolonging the final defeat of the Third *Reich*. British and American forces did not close the pocket forming around Seventh Army. The most obvious responsibility for this error lay at Montgomery's door. However, a portion of the blame also lies at the door of American commanders who were more interested in distant objectives like Paris than with Falaise and with frontline troops who were less than enthusiastic at closing the gap and facing German troops breaking out. In the gap itself, Allied tactical air caused terrible damage to German troops and their equipment attempting escape. Little equipment got through the blasted roads and columns, but thousands of the toughest, most experienced veterans did escape. And in Germany, there was plenty of equipment, through Speer's efforts, to turn those troops back into the formidable formations that had resisted so long and so well in Normandy.

The collapse became complete as the Germans raced for the frontier. On August 17, American and French troops landed in Southern France, and the German position in the west dissolved. Once again, German leaders threw the *Luftwaffe* into battle to mitigate collapse on the ground. The *Luftwaffe* made large numbers of fighter and bomber attacks on rapidly moving Allied columns, but its air operations had little significant impact on the drive towards the German frontier. The *Luftwaffe* suffered heavy losses. By August 14, *Luftflotte* 3 was down to 75 operational ready fighters. The numeric balance was so unfavorable and the enemy advance so dangerous that the *Luftwaffe* high command immediately returned squadrons to the front from *Luftflotte Reich* that had just begun to refit with new pilots and aircraft after July's losses. These units were severely attrited just in moving to airfields in France as Allied fighters once again savaged the refitted squadrons. The haste of the retreat forced the Germans to abandon enormous amounts of material, supplies, and aircraft. By early September, most of *Luftflotte* 3 was back on German airfields in utter disarray. Its new bases did not even have flak protection against Allied fighter sweeps.[127] Losses in the collapse in the west, particularly in aircraft, were high. The II *Gruppe* of *Jagdgeschwader* 53 reported that it had lost 42 aircraft through enemy action, 18 more in noncombat accidents, 20 more abandoned and destroyed on airfields captured by the enemy, and a final 20 through other causes. All told, it had lost approximately 200 percent of its authorized strength in one month.[128] Overall in August 1944, *Luftflotte* 3 lost 482 fighters, while *Luftflotte Reich* lost an additional 375 Bf 109's and Fw 190's. This worked out to loss rates of 24.8 percent and 19.4 percent (total 44.2 percent) of the total fighter force at the beginning of the month.[129]

The Anglo-American advance now struck towards the German frontier. It chewed up whatever resistance the Germans managed to throw together. Unfortunately, the euphoria gripping Allied commanders and troops as they approached the frontier turned into overconfidence and a belief the war was won. Rightly, the Allies sensed that the *Wehrmacht* was teetering on the brink of a final collapse that could cause the end of the *Third Reich*. But that very sixth sense brought with it failure.

As overall commander, Eisenhower held responsibility for that failure—not because his strategy failed but because he was unable to control his subordinates.[130] His personal qualities had enabled him to make the diverse and strong individuals in the Allied high command work together to accomplish the invasion. Those qualities, however, were not the qualities needed to dominate and drive that collection of strong personalities under tight leash, and a very tight leash was required to turn the rout in France into final victory. The failure at Falaise was an initial sign of his inability to control the armies. Now as the rush towards the frontier gathered momentum, Eisenhower held the reins too lightly. Patton diverged towards Metz, the one place where the Germans could put up a creditable resistance. While Third Army entangled itself in that fortress city, the Germans had scarcely a soldier in the Ardennes, an area that would not have significant German forces until the end of September.[131]

In the British drive, Montgomery played a major role in the failure to push the Germans over the brink. The idea of launching one massive narrow front thrust over the Rhine into Nazi Germany fascinated the Field Marshal. The British military historian, Basil Liddell Hart, with justification, suggests that while there were arguments on the side of such an approach as opposed to Eisenhower's broad front strategy, Montgomery was not the person to lead such a thrust.[132] The British Field Marshal's attention as his forces drove towards Antwerp focused on the Rhine. At that moment when he was demanding that Eisenhower shut down Patton's drive and give the British the gasoline and material required to supply his effort, he ignored Antwerp's importance. While Montgomery's attention centered on the Rhine, he allowed the exploitation of Antwerp's capture to slip through his fingers. On September 4, the port fell to the British 11th Armored Division. British tanks had arrived so suddenly that German authorities could not destroy the docks and port facilities. Furthermore, the capture of the port entrapped the German's Fifteenth Army that had recently guarded Pas de Calais and was now in flight up the coast to escape British mechanized forces. At this point, having captured Antwerp, Montgomery showed his greatest failing as a general—his inability to pursue a beaten enemy and reap the full fruits of victory. Lieutenant General Brian Horrocks' XXX Corps was stopped north of Brussels, even though it had few Germans in front of it and possessed enough gasoline to advance another 100 kilometers.[133]

The speed and extent of the pursuit after the German collapse in mid-August now led Montgomery to halt Twenty-First Army Group's operations. As a result, British troops failed to advance beyond Antwerp and cut off the Walcheren Peninsula. Had they pushed on, they would have trapped Fifteenth Army. They did not, and the Germans ferried fleeing troops across the Scheldt. Montgomery paused and regrouped for a great airborne operation, later code-named "Market Garden," to drive to and over the Rhine. Under pressure to use Allied airborne divisions in Britain, Eisenhower agreed, and transport aircraft that had supplied Patton ceased that effort and prepared for a great paratrooper drop.

The pause came at precisely the wrong moment and was sufficiently long for the Germans to recover their equilibrium. In an extraordinary display of organizational ability, as they had so often done in the east, the *Wehrmacht* took the shattered flotsam and jetsam of defeat and reorganized and replenished the beaten men into effective military formations. A number of panzer divisions, including the 9 SS and 10 SS Panzer Divisions, were sent to rework and refit in the Dutch countryside. Two "Ultra" messages on September 5 and 6th indicated that Montgomery's argument for "Market Garden" was faulty even as the planning began. The second message, slightly more explicit, noted:

> Hq and Hq Two SS and SS Panzer Corps subordinated Army Group Baker, to transfer to Eindhoven and Eindhoven to rest and refit in cooperation with General of Panzer Troops West and direct rest and refit of Two and One One six panzer divisions, Nine SS and SS Panzer Divisions and Heavy Assault Gun *Abteilung* Two One Seven. Comment elements these divisions and Ten SS and SS Panzer Divisions not and not operating ordered Fourth to area Venloo and Venloo-Arnheim and Arnheim—Hertogenbosch and Hertogenbosch for refit. . . .[134]

Thus, Allied paratroopers would land among some of the toughest troops in the German armed forces.

Making a difficult task impossible, the Allies selected the inexperienced British 1st Airborne Division to capture the bridge at Arnhem. The division agreed to a drop zone 6 miles from its objective. Having recovered their equilibrium, the Germans prevented British armor from thrusting through to Arnhem and crushed the British paratroopers. As a result, they maintained their hold on the Rhine. Outside of flak units, summer fighting had so shattered the *Luftwaffe* that it made few appearances at Arnhem. On the first day of "Market Garden," the Germans could only launch between 50 and 75 sorties.[135] Nevertheless, despite enemy air superiority, German ground forces, led by the 9th and 10th *Waffen* SS divisions, held the Allies from the Rhine. At this point, logistical reality caught up with Allied armies. Montgomery, having turned his back on Antwerp, faced the grim task of prying the Germans from their hold on the Scheldt. The cost for the Canadians and British Commandos was high. Not until November 28 did the first convoys navigate the Scheldt and unload an Antwerp—a high price for the negligence of late summer.[136]

One other element in the Third *Reich*'s escape from complete defeat in the early fall deserves attention. Stalin, unlike most American political and military leaders, had a deep understanding of Clausewitz's simplest aphorism: "War is a continuation of politics by other means." He recognized that the purpose of Soviet grand strategy should not be the quickest possible defeat of Nazi Germany. Rather, it should be the achievement of maximum political advantage for Soviet Russia. Thus, the Red Army, after defeating Army Group Center in June and July, stood on the defensive for five months along the Vistula River and East Prussian frontier. Meanwhile, Russian armies in the south made a massive onslaught into the Balkans and insured that Rumania, Bulgaria, and Hungary would have regimes in line with Soviet interests. The Yugoslavs also fell initially within the Soviet camp but, unfortunately for Stalin, they made their own revolution and liberated their own territory. Not until January 1945, when the Balkans were well in hand, did the Russians move against German territory.

CONCLUSION

Bereft of fuel, its units ravaged by the summer attrition, the *Luftwaffe* was a force that no longer exercised any influence on the conduct of either air or ground operations. The price that American bombers paid to keep the *Luftwaffe* down was at times high. The attacks on the synthetic fuel factories from September 11 to 13th cost the Americans no less than 91 bombers, but the destruction of fuel capacity, *Luftwaffe* pilots, and aircraft kept the Germans from any substantial recovery.[137] On November 2, 1944, Eighth and Fifteenth Air Forces launched a massive attack on the German fuel industry. Of the 490 fighters that sortied to meet the invading formations, the *Luftwaffe* lost no less than 120 aircraft with 70 pilots killed and wounded. Approximately 40 American bombers fell.[138] Nevertheless, the *Luftwaffe* as a force that could affect the course of the war was through. The Allies had captured the German radar network in France and Belgium. Germany's enemies now based their aircraft in France and Belgium, and even "Spitfires" could range far to the east of the Rhine. For the Allied air forces, the problem was how to turn their air superiority into final victory. At the end of September, control of Allied strategic air forces returned to the air commanders.[139] Like the ground commanders, Harris and Spaatz searched for *their* answer to the question of final victory. Their efforts blasted to bits what little remained of Germany's cities. Nevertheless, contrary to what Douhet and Trenchard had argued, final collapse came only when Allied soldiers moved through the broken wreckage of what had been the Third *Reich*. Then and only then did the structure as well as the fabric of German society collapse.

By April 1944, the task facing the *Luftwaffe* had become manifestly beyond its capabilities. Tedder's and Spaatz's direction of Allied air strategy against Germany's transportation and oil production infrastructures placed Anglo-American air efforts solidly within the framework of overall Allied strategy. The pressure of Allied air and ground forces, landed and supported by their navies, caused the *Wehrmacht*'s entire defensive structure in France to collapse. That collapse threatened to become complete at the beginning of September, but the Allies missed their chance to finish it. The end, however, was no less inevitable. Continued, tenacious German resistance only insured that the *Reich* would suffer even worse physical destruction and mounting casualties for another eight months.

Notes

1. Trevor-Roper, *Blitzkrieg to Defeat,* Directive #51, 3.11.43., p. 149.

2. *KTB OKW,* Vol. IV, pp. 299–300.

3. Webster and Frankland, *SAOAG,* Vol. III, p. 37. This was so, because American bombers were carrying out their missions in great formations; and no matter how accurately the lead bomber might have placed its bombs, the pattern bombing became decreasingly accurate on the fringes of the formations. Bomber Command's aircraft, however, bombed individually on markers placed on the target by the pathfinder forces. If the markers were placed accurately on the target (and within the range of navigational aids reaching into France and the Low Countries, the pathfinders could place their markers with remarkable precision), the individually aimed bombs of the main force could form a very tight pattern.

4. "The Employment of the Night Bomber Force in Connection With the Invasion of the Continent from the United Kingdom," A. T. Harris, 13.1.44., BC/MS.31156/C.-in-C.; copy in the possession of the author.

5. Webster and Frankland, *SAOAG,* Vol. III, p. 27.

6. Middlebrook, *The Nuremberg Raid,* p. 82.

7. Webster and Frankland, *SAOAG,* Vol. III, p. 17.

8. Ibid., p. 19.

9. Zuckerman, *From Apes to Warlords,* Chapter 13.

10. Ibid., p. 234.

11. Ibid., p. 232.

12. Craven and Cate, *The Army Air Forces in World War II,* Vol. II, p. 76.

13. Webster and Frankland, *SAOAG,* Vol. IV, "Directive by the Supreme Commander to USSTAF and Bomber Command for Support of 'Overlord' During the Preparatory Period," 17.4.44., p. 167.

14. Major L. F. Ellis, *Victory in the West,* Vol. I, *The Battle of Normandy* (London, 1962), p. 101.

15. Webster and Frankland, *SAOAG,* Vol. III, p. 39.

16. Ellis, *Victory in the West,* Vol. I, p. 112.

17. PRO AIR 37/1261, Bombing Analysis Units, 4.11.44., B.A.U. Report No. 1, "The Effects of the Overlord Air Plan to Disrupt Enemy Rail Communications." It should be noted that there was some squabbling between Leigh-Mallory and General Louis Brereton who took matters into his own hands and proved that bridges could be destroyed.

18. PRO AIR 37/1261, Bombing Analysis Unit, 4.11.44., B.A.U. Report No. 8, "Changes in the Volume of French Traffic, Expressed in Kilometre Tons, as a Result of Air Attacks, January to July 1944."

19. Ibid.

20. Ibid.

21. Ellis, *Victory in the West*, Vol. I, p. 101.

22. "Die Kämpfe im Westen, I. Teil," based on KTB of Wehrmachtsführungsstab, Die Feindlichen Luftangriffe und die Massnahmen gegen ihre Auswirkungen," NARS, T–77/781/5508003.

23. Zuckerman, *From Apes to Warlords*, p. 232.

24. PRO AIR 37/1261, Bombing Analysis Unit, 4.11.44., B.A.U. Report No. 1, "The Effects of the Overlord Air Plan to Disrupt Enemy Rail Communications."

25. PRO AIR 37/1261, Bombing Analysis Unit, 6.12.44., B.A.U. Report No. 8, "Changes in the Volume of French Traffic, Expressed in Kilometre Tons, as a Result of Air Attacks, January to July 1944."

26. Among many other messages, see PRO DEFE 3/47, KV 3015, 6.5.44., 1316Z; DEFE 3/153, KV 3300, 9.5.44., 2301Z and KV 3292, 9.5.44., 1659Z; DEFE 3/155, KV 3763, 14.5.44., 0412Z; DEFE 3/158, KV 4690, 21.5.44., 0534Z; DEFE 3/161, KV 5446, 27.5.44., 2131Z; DEFE 3/162, KV 5626, 29.5.44., 1107Z; DEFE 3/162, KV 5622, 29.5.44., 0817Z; DEFE 3/163, KV 5825, 31.5.44., 0039Z; DEFE 3/163, KV 5999, 1.6.44., 1516Z.

27. PRO DEFE 3/155, 14.5.44., 0412Z.

28. Air Historical Branch, "Air Attacks Against German Rail Systems During 1944," Luftwaffe Operations Staff/Intelligence, No. 2512/44, "Air Operations Against the German Rail Transport System During March, April, and May 1944," 3.6.44.

29. See, among many others, PRO DEFE 3/58, XL 2299, 16.7.44.; DEFE 3/171, KV 7998, 14.6.44., 0753Z; DEFE 3/179, KV 9976, 28.6.44., 2135Z.

30. Webster and Frankland, *SAOAG*, Vol. III, p. 33.

31. For a fuller discussion of this point, see Murray, "The Change in the European Balance of Power, 1938–1939," Chapter V.

32. *DGFP*, Series D, Vol. XI, Doc. #41, 10.9.40.; see also Hitler's comment to the Rumanians in Hillgruber, *Staatsmänner bei Hitler*, pp. 248–49.

33. For a short account of Germany's petroleum difficulties, see: Der Chef des OKW, Nr. 77986/44, WFST/Qu 3, 25.3.44., An Reichsminister Speer, Imperial War Museum, Speer Collection Reel #27.

34. "Der Beauftragte für den Vierjahresplan 'Mineralöl' Planung für 1940–1945, Planungs-Stand," Dezember 1943, Imperial War Museum, Speer Collection, Reel #35.

35. Der Chef des OKW, Nr. 77986/44, WFST/Qu 3, 25.3.44., An Reichsminister Speer, Imperial War Museum, Reel #27.

36. For the development of the fuel reserve, see: Der Reichsminister der Luftfahrt und Oberbefehlshaber der Luftwaffe, Az 85 Nr. 2995/43, 13.12.43., An das Oberkommando der Wehrmacht, Betr.: "Bildung einer Flugbenzin-Reserve"; and Reichminister der Luftfahrt und Oberbefehlshaber der Luftwaffe, Az. 85 Nr. 1873/44, 15.6.44., An das Oberkommando der Wehrmacht, Betr.: Bildung einer Flugbenzin-Reserve, and assorted other memoranda in NARS, T–77/90/814909–814948.

37. Der Chef des OKW, Nr. 77986/44, WFST/Qu 3, 25.3.44., An Reichsminister Speer, Imperial War Museum, Speer Collection, Reel #27.

38. "Gedanken über die Ausarbeitung des Oberstlt. i.G. Sorze, Die luftstrategische Lage Mitteleuropas," 14.4.44., NARS, T–321/18/4759386.

39. Craven and Cate, *The Army Air Forces in World War II*, Vol. III, p. 176.

40. Wener Girbig, *. . . mit Kurs auf Leuna, Die Luftoffensive gegen die Treibstoffindustrie und deutscher Abwehreinsatz 1944–1945* (Stuttgart, 1980), pp. 28–32.

41. Speer, *Inside the Third Reich*, pp. 346–47.

42. PRO 31/20/16, "The Handling of Ultra Information at Headquarters Eighth Air Force," Ansel E. M. Talbert, Major, US Army Air Corps.

43. PRO DEFE 3/156, KV 4021, 16.5.44., 0558Z.

44. PRO DEFE 3/159, KV 4762, 21.5.44., 2054Z.

45. Speer, *Inside the Third Reich*, p. 348.

46. Girbig, *. . . mit Kurs auf Leuna*, pp. 40, 55.

47. Speer, *Inside the Third Reich*, p. 348.

48. PRO DEFE 3/166, KV 6673, 6.6.44., 2356Z.

49. Speer, *Inside the Third Reich*, p. 350; and Speer's memorandum to Hitler on the fuel situation, 29.7.44., Imperial War Museum, Speer Collection, FD 2690/45 GS, Vol. 3.

50. Girbig, . . . *mit Kurs auf Leuna*, pp. 66, 77.

51. See the papers dealing with fuel production in the 1944–45 period in the Speer Papers, Vol. 7, Imperial War Museum, FD 2690/45.

52. Speer to Hitler, 30.6.44., Speer Papers, Imperial War Museum, FD 2690/45 G.2, Vol. 3.

53. Speer, *Inside the Third Reich*, p. 351.

54. Speer to Hitler, 29.7.44., Imperial War Museum, Speer Collection, FD 2690/45G.2, Vol. 3.

55. Ibid.

56. Report of a conference held by Reichsmarschall Göring on 22.2.43., AHB, Translation No. VII/85.

57. For the German sense that attacks on elements of the transportation system and oil industry were part of a larger plan to destroy the entire transportation system, see the following translation of an OKW Report: "A Report on Enemy Air Attacks on Rumanian and German Centres of Fuel Production, and German Counter Measures, August 1943–June 6, 1944: A Study Issued by the Operations Staff of OKW," Air Historical Branch, Translation No. VII/77.

58. Based on the loss tables in BA/MA, RL 2 III/1025, Genst. 6. Abt. (III A), Front-Flugzeug-Verluste; and BA/MA, RL 2 III/729, 730, Übersicht über Soll, Istbestand, Einsatzbereitschaft, Verluste und Reserven der Fliegenden Verbände.

59. "Statistical Summary of Eighth Air Force Operations, European Theater, 17 Aug 1942–8 May 1945," AFSHRC.

60. Ibid.

61. Based on the loss tables in BA/MA, RL 2 III/1025, Genst, Qu. Gen. 6. Abt. (III A), Front-Flugzeug-Verluste; and BA/MA, RL 2 III/730, Übersicht über Soll, Istbestand, Einsatzbereitschaft, Verluste und Reserven der fliegenden Verbände.

62. BA/MA, RL 2 III/728, Genst. Qu. Gen. 6. Abt. (III A), Übersicht über Soll, Istbestand, Einsatzbereitschaft, Verluste und Reserven der fliegenden Verbände.

63. "The Problems of German Air Defense in 1944," A study prepared by the German Air Historical Branch (8. Abteilung), 5.11.44., Air Historical Branch, Translation No. VII/22.

64. Ibid.

65. BA/MA, RL 2 II/127, Oberkommando der Luftwaffe, Lw Führungsstab, Nr. 1640/44 (Ia/Ausb), "Taktischer Einzelhinweis Nr. 19, Sicherung des Flugbetriebes gegen feindliche Jagdangriffe."

66. This figure is slightly different from my figure of pilot losses for April calculated on the basis of the quartermaster report in BA/MA, RL 2 III/729, but the discrepancy is not major and is explicable in terms of a differing method of calculation. Galland's figure probably is based on *actual* losses, while the quartermaster's table is based on the losses *reported* during the month of April.

67. "Notes on Discussions with Reichsmarschall Göring, Held on May 15–16, 1944, on the Subject of Fighters and Fighter Personnel," Air Historical Branch, Translation No. VII/71.

68. "Ultra, History of US Strategic Air force Europe vs German Air Force," p. 169.

69. "Notes on Discussion with Reichsmarschall Göring, Held on May 15–16, 1944, on the Subject of Fighters and Fighter Personnel," Air Historical Branch, Translation No. VII/71.

70. See the "Ultra" message in DEFE 3/178, KV 9684, 26.6.44., 1528Z, for confirmation on the continuation of this practice.

71. PRO DEFE 3/46, KV 2850, 4.5.44., 2257Z; and DEFE 3/47, KV 3174, 8.5.44., 0759Z.

72. DEFE 3/165, KV 6476, 5.6.44., 1210Z.

73. BA/MA, RL 7/553, see: Der Chef der Luftflotte 6, 0.Qu. Nr. 1402/444, Betr.: "Jägerhilfsaktion."

74. Organisationsabteilung III, Nr. 91 520/44, 1.5.44., Betr.: "Auswirkung der Fliegerschäden Friedrichshafen auf Panzer-Fertigung." Stand 29.4. Abends., NARS, T–78/414/6382263.

75. Among many messages, see PRO DEFE 3/154, KV 3525, 11.5.44., 2032Z; DEFE 3/153, KV 3417, 10.5.44., 2033Z; DEFE 3/153, KV 3327, 9.5.44., 0845Z; DEFE 3/160, KV 5141, 25.5.44., 1020Z; DEFE 3/159, KV 4944, 23.5.44., 2054Z; and DEFE 3/168, KV 7135, 9.6.44., 1648Z.

76. See, among others, PRO DEFE 3/155, KV 3863, 14.5.44., 2020Z; and DEFE 3/153, KV 3430, 10.5.44., 2129Z.

77. PRO DEFE 3/163, KV 5762, 30.5.44., 1440Z.

78. BA/MA, RL 2 II/5, Der Reichsmarschall des Grossdeutschen Reiches und Oberbefehlshaber der Luftwaffe, Nr. 8947/43, 6.12.43., Betr.: "Drohende Gefahr West."

79. BA/MA, RL 2 II/5, Der Reichsmarschall des Grossdeutschen Reiches und Oberbefehlshaber der

Luftwaffe, Nr. 9221/44, 27.2.44., Betr.: "Drohende Gefahr West." See also BA/MA, RL 2 II/127, Oberkommando der Luftwaffe, Führungsstab, Ia/Ausb. Nr. 70/44, 13.5.44., Taktischer Einzelhinweis Nr. 4, "Richtlinien für die Ausbildung von Jagdverbänden im Schlachtfliegereinsatz," for a thoroughly unrealistic appreciation of the possibilities open to the Luftwaffe to meet the invasion.

80. Air Ministry, *The Rise and Fall of the German Air Force*, p. 329.

81. BA/MA, RL 2 II/127, see Oberkommando der Luftwaffe, Führungsstab, 13.5.44., "Taktischer Einzelhinweis Nr. 4, Richtlinien für die Ausbildung von Jagdverbänden im Schlachtfliegereinsatz."

82. Air Ministry, *The Rise and Fall of the German Air Force*, p. 329.

83. Ellis, *Victory in the West*, Vol. I, p. 130.

84. Ibid., p. 223.

85. "Ultra, History of US Strategic Air Force Europe vs German Air Force," p. 196.

86. Air Ministry, *The Rise and Fall of the German Air Force*, pp. 329–30.

87. Air Historical Branch, "Luftwaffe Losses on the Western Front (Luftflotte 3), June 1944," Translation No. VII/136.

88. Craven and Cate, *The Army Air Forces in World War II*, p. 221.

89. Headquarters Air P/W Interrogation Detachment, Military Intelligence Service, A.P.W.I.U. (North Air Force) 63/1945, 29.5.45., "A Crack German Panzer Division and What Allied Air Power Did to It Between D-day and V-day."

90. Air Ministry, *The Rise and Fall of the German Air Force*, p. 330.

91. "Some Aspects of the German Fighter Effort During the Initial Stages of the Invasion of N. W. Europe," 18.11.44., Oberst Mettig, Air Historical Branch, Translation No. VI/19.

92. Among others, see PRO DEFE 3/166, KV 6675, KV 6699, KV 6694, KV 6749, and KV 6735; see also "Ultra, History of US Strategic Air Force Europe vs German Air Force," p. 196.

93. Air Ministry, *The Rise and Fall of the German Air Force*, p. 330.

94. Based on figures in "Luftwaffe Losses on the Western Front (Luftflotte 3), June 1944," Air Historical Branch, Translation No. VII/136.

95. "Ultra, History of US Strategic Air Force Europe vs German Air Force," p. 197.

96. PRO DEFE 3/171, KV 7815, 13.6.44., 0715Z.

97. PRO DEFE 3/176, KV 9416, 24.6.44., 2151Z.

98. Ellis, *Victory in the West*, Vol. I, p. 238.

99. Ralph Bennett, *Ultra in the West, The Normandy Campaign 1944–45* (New York, 1979), p. 68. This is a thoroughly admirable book by an author who has taken the trouble to read the "Ultra" files and has, therefore, been able to indicate among other things that claims that there was no "Ultra" information on the Battle of the Bulge are entirely false. A recent book about Eisenhower and his generals has continued this claim. Astonishingly, the author of that work, who makes all sorts of claims for "Ultra's" impact on the war, does not appear to have read the files. The messages on the location of Panzer Group West are in PRO DEFE 3/168, KV 7171, 9.6.44., 2044Z; and KV 7225, 10.6.44., 0439Z.

100. Ellis, *Victory in the West*, Vol. I, p. 258.

101. PRO DEFE 3/171, KV 7998, 14.6.44., 0753Z.

102. Ellis, *Victory in the West*, Vol. I, pp. 271–74.

103. Russell Weigley in his *Eisenhower's Lieutenants* (Bloomington, 1981), pp. 50–53, suggests that had the Americans been on the left flank at Normandy instead of the right flank, they would have better utilized the open country around Caen. This is an interesting thesis, but on the whole untenable given the nature of the resistance that the Germans established. 1 SS, 2 SS, 12 SS, 21 Panzer Division, 2 Panzer Division, and 116 Panzer Division were not the sort of units that one broke through easily.

104. "Ultra, History of US Strategic Air Force Europe vs German Air Force," pp. 210–11.

105. Based on the figures in "Luftwaffe Losses on the Western Front (Luftflotte 3), June 1944," Air Historical Branch, Translation No. VII/136; and "Luftwaffe Losses in the Area of Luftflotte Reich, June 1944," Air Historical Branch, Translation No. VII/139.

106. Air Ministry, *The Rise and Fall of the German Air Force*, p. 332.

107. "Ultra, History of US Strategic Air Force Europe vs German Air Force," p. 199.

108. Air Ministry, *The Rise and Fall of the German Air Force*, p. 332.

109. Oberkommando der Luftwaffe, Führungsstab Ic, Nr. 3080/44, 16.7.44., Betr.: "Britisch-nordamerikanische Luftkriegsführung gegen Deutschland," Imperial War Museum, Speer Collection, Roll #21, FD 3046/49.

110. J. C. Masterman, *The Double Cross System* (New Haven, 1972), pp. 157–58.

111. "The Effects of Air Power," Air Historical Branch, Translation No. VII/40.

112. Ibid.

113. "Ultra, History of US Strategic Air Force Europe vs German Air Force," p. 216.

114. Air Ministry, *The Rise and Fall of the German Air Force*, p. 333.

115. Ibid.

116. "Ultra, History of US Strategic Air Forces Europe vs German Air Force," p. 217.

117. Ibid., pp. 224–25, 234.

118. Ziemke, *Stalingrad to Berlin*, p. 319.

119. Ibid., pp. 323–25.

120. Air Ministry, *The Rise and Fall of the German Air Force*, p. 363.

121. Ibid., p. 357.

122. Ibid., p. 358.

123. Ibid., pp. 357–59.

124. See the reports of the three flak divisions involved in the collapse of Army Group Center in BA/MA, RL 7/522, 12. Flakdivision (mot), Kommandeur, Br. B. Nr. 167/44, 24.8.44., An Luftwaffenkommando 6; 23. Flakdivision (mot), Kommandeur, Br. B. Nr. 3/44, 25.8.44., Betr.: Stellungnahme zum Zusammenbruch der Verteidigungsfront im Abschnitt der Heeresgruppe Mitte; Flakdivision (mot.), Kommandeur, 26.8.44.,"Der Zusammenbruch der Heeresgruppe Mitte im Sommer 1944."

125. *OKW KTB*, Vol. IV, p. 338.

126. Bennett, *Ultra in the West*, pp. 114–16.

127. Air Ministry, *The Rise and Fall of the German Air Force*, pp. 335–39.

128. "Ultra, History of US Strategic Air Force Europe vs German Air Force," p.251.

129. Based on figures in "Luftwaffe Losses on the Western Front (Luftflotte 3), 1 July–31 August 1944," Air Historical Branch, Translation No. VIII/144; "Luftwaffe Losses in the Area of Luftflotte Reich, July-September 1944," AHB, Translation No. VII/142; and "Luftflotte Strength and Serviceability Tables, August 1938–April 1945," AHB, Translation No. VII/107.

130. The following account is based on Ellis, *Victory in the West*, Vol. I; R. W. Thompson, *The Eighty-Five Days* (New York, 1957); Weigley, *Eisenhower's Lieutenants;* Martin Blumenson, *Breakout and Pursuit* (Washington, 1961); Liddell Hart, *History of the Second World War*.

131. OKW situation maps on the western front, August and September 1944, NARS, Captured German Records Division, Washington, D.C.

132. Liddell Hart, *History of the Second World War*, pp. 364–67.

133. J. L. Moulton, *Battle for Antwerp, The Liberation of the City and the Opening of the Scheldt, 1944* (London, 1978), pp. 52–53.

134. PRO DEFE 3/127/XL 9188, 5.9.44., 1152Z; and DEFE 3/128, XL 9245, 6.9.44., 0103Z.

135. Air Ministry, *The Rise and Fall of the German Air Force*, p. 339.

136. See particularly Thompson, *The Eighty-Five Days*, p. 19, and Parts 3 and 4.

137. Girbing, . . . *mit Kurs auf Leuna*, p. 139.

138. Ibid., pp. 154–55.

139. PRO AIR 2/8699, 25.9.44., CMS/608/DCAS, Air Ministry.

VIII Conclusion

THE RESULTS

The apostles of airpower in the interwar period argued strongly and seemingly persuasively that the airplane would be the decisive weapon of the next war and would relegate armies and navies at best to the role of policemen and at worst make them irrelevant to the final outcome. In effect, they were stating a belief that airpower had negated the general principles of war and that the experience of the past was of no consequence. However, the war that did come on September 1, 1939, resulted in a conflict quite different from what anyone, including the airmen, had expected. The air war was not independent. It was dependent on all the strategic, logistical, economic, social, and productive variables that had governed military operations since the beginning of time. As one historian of the bombing offensive has noted:

> Thus we are left with one clear reminder of a painful truth: The laws of war applied as much to the strategic air offensive waged over Europe's skies through five-and-a-half bitter years as they did to the sailors and soldiers on the distant seas or in the mud and sand below. Occasionally, the airman may have felt himself living and fighting in a new dimension, just as the air force commander may have sometimes felt he enjoyed a freedom of manoeuvre denied to admirals and generals. But the airman died, and the air force commander was defeated and stalemated unless the laws were kept. When they were kept, success came; until they could be kept, hope was kept alive by courage alone.[1]

When one strips aside the layers of myth and legend from those dark days over Europe when "strategic" bombing ground Germany's cities into dust, there is no doubt that airpower played *a* decisive role in the winning or losing of the war. But that decisive role was no greater than the victory in the Atlantic that allowed America to bring its industrial and military power to bear or the victories of the Red Army on the eastern front that slowly but surely wore away the *Wehrmacht*'s fighting edge. Although the air war was only a part of an enormous conflict that swept over Europe, it did prove decisive in helping the Allies achieve victory since it played an indispensable role, without which the Anglo-American lodgment on the continent and the final defeat of the Third *Reich* is inconceivable.

In 1945, the deserts that had once been cities bore mute testimony to what American and British bombing had wrought in the course of the war. The question posed then, and with increasing frequency since, is what did that terrible destruction contribute to the winning of the war? Bomber Command's achievements through the spring of 1944 were largely indirect, even though the destruction of population centers was obvious and extensive, and the damage to industrial production in the spillover of "area" bombing attacks at times important. Yet, the night bombing campaign's greatest contribution to the winning of the war was precisely what Harris claimed and what the conventional wisdom has so often discounted: The "area" bombing attacks did have a direct and palpable effect on the morale of the German population, and the German leadership, in response to that impact, seriously skewed Germany's strategy. Recent scholarship in the Federal Republic indicates that as early as the summer of 1942, the night bombing campaign was affecting German attitudes.[2] In 1943, the heavy bombing caused a dramatic fall off in popular morale. Knowledge of what had happened at Hamburg spread throughout Germany; and in south Germany, the attacks on Nuremburg, Munich, and Augsburg made the population restive, angry, and bitter. The *SD* (*Sicherheitsdienst,* Secret Police) reports on what the population was saying (reports widely read in the highest levels of Nazi leadership) noted that people no longer exchanged the Nazi salute, reviled the party as the author of their trouble, regarded Goebbels as an outright liar and cheat, wore party badges less and less, and were depressed and embittered at the course of the war. The population singled out the *Luftwaffe* particularly for their reproaches, and as early as the "Lancaster" attack on the MAN works in Augsburg in April 1942 wondered why such an important location had not received sufficient protection. Even more alarming to Germany's leaders were comments by women "of the lower classes" that even 1918 was not as bad as this.

These *SD* reports clarify several aspects of Nazi political and strategic behavior in the last years of the war. Initially, the constant repetitive theme in Nazi propaganda that Germany would never suffer another November 1918 reflected real worries, reinforced by the *SD* reports, in the highest levels of government concerning the impact of bombing on popular support and morale. These reports help explain why the regime was unwilling to embark on a scheme of "total" mobilization of the *Reich*'s economic and human resources until after the July 20, 1944 attempt on Hitler's life. Until that point, reports on popular dissatisfaction and lowered morale due to the bombing made Hitler leery of squeezing the German population as hard as Germany's World War I government had done, and thus running the risk of another popular explosion similar to October and November 1918.

There is another aspect of popular reaction that also had serious impact on the leadership in 1943. In one of those quirks of human nature, at the same time that the Germans were depressed and gloomy over the bombing, they were also extraordinarily angry at their tormentors and were demanding retaliation against Britain for the damage inflicted on their homes. The *SD* reports, reflecting the popular mood, explain the leadership's demand for retaliation weapons (the V–1 and V–2), its willingness to waste the *Luftwaffe*'s bomber fleet over the winter of 1944 even though faced by the threat of an Allied invasion, and its refusal to provide the necessary support needed to the fighter forces until military defeat was obvious and inescapable. Moreover, the distortion in military production as a result of demands for the V–1 and V–2 retaliation weapons was enormous. The strategic bombing survey estimates that the industrial effort and resources expended for these weapons in the last year and a half of the war alone equalled the production of 24,000 fighter aircraft.[3] Here the regime was reacting to popular pressures, and the resulting decisions responded to political factors rather than to strategic and military realities. Thus, just in terms of the retaliatory weapons policy, the distortion that the bombing achieved in the German war effort was of real consequence to the war's outcome.

The American daylight bombing campaign reinforced these trends. Throughout the last half of 1943, Göring bitterly reproached his fighter pilots despite their efforts and sacrifices. His comments that the German people could not understand how American bomber formations flew untouched over the *Reich* shows that the *Reichsmarschall* was reading the *SD* reports as well as receiving bitter comments from Hitler and other Nazi leaders. References drawn from popular disquiet over the daylight bombing sprinkled Göring's speeches to his generals as well as pilots.[4] But the contribution of the American air forces to the war effort was more direct in 1943 and 1944 than Bomber Command's skewing of Germany's production efforts. From late spring 1943, American "strategic" bombing attacks against German industry imposed a wasting attrition on the *Luftwaffe*'s fighter forces. The severe fighting over the *Reich* in the summer and fall coupled with decimation of air units fighting on the periphery placed a rising and, in the long run, intolerable burden on the *Luftwaffe*. Moreover, production of new fighters fell off substantially due to American bombing. Nevertheless, American air commanders were forced to suspend daylight, unescorted bombing missions in October. The respite was short indeed. In February 1944, the American bombing forces returned to the *Reich,* this time accompanied by fighter support. In the air battles that followed, American air forces broke the back of the *Luftwaffe* and assured complete Allied air superiority over the continent for the invasion.

The achievement of that air superiority allowed the Allies to launch a true "strategic" bombing effort in which the air effort was closely integrated into overall strategy. Bomber Command's specialized marking capabilities and navigational aids allowed it to destroy marshalling yards throughout northern France, while Eighth Air Force and the Allied Tactical Air Force contributed to a creeping transportation paralysis throughout western Europe. German movement was substantially hindered, and the transportation of reserves to the battlefront in Normandy became most difficult. Meanwhile, Eighth's attacks on oil production insured that the immobility of the rail system spread to motorized movement as well. They also ended permanently what small chance the *Luftwaffe* had for a comeback. Thus, the efforts of the Allied air forces, "strategic" and "tactical," played a critical role in the winning of World War II. Airpower had shown that it worked to greatest effect when its strategy was integrated and was connected with efforts on the ground and at sea; and that while airpower had not changed the rules of the game, it had become a critically important element in the overall equation.

THE OTHER SIDE OF THE HILL

One can argue with justification that the Germans lost World War II in the late summer of 1940 and that their future defeats on the ground and in the air sprang from their unwillingness at that time to identify and to face the real strategic situation. In the euphoria of victory over France, the political and military leadership refused to acknowledge that it had won only the first round of a long struggle. Even defeat in the Battle of Britain failed to shake a remarkable mood of optimism. Hence, the force structure and organization with which the *Wehrmacht* embarked on "Barbarossa" was in no fashion suitable to the demands of a continental war. Conversely, the British and Americans drew certain lessons from the Battle of Britain that determined the course of the air war three years later. Overestimating the *Luftwaffe*'s actual size, Anglo-American planners organized their nation's economic effort for an enormous increase in aircraft production.

What is almost incomprehensible is the fact that the Germans paid so little attention to the attrition that had occurred in France and over Britain. Not until the *Wehrmacht* was deep in the Soviet Union did Göring finally authorize Milch to bring order to the aircraft industry. By that time, it was too late. British production programs had a two-year head start, while the American programs were at least a year ahead. If that handicap were not enough, Milch faced a constant, uphill battle to persuade the general staff to accept as a necessity the production increases that he proposed. That failure to gear German aircraft production to a worst case analysis of what Anglo-American industry might turn out cost the *Luftwaffe* the air war in 1943 and 1944. One cannot stress enough that administrative, strategic, and productive decisions in the 1940 to 1941 time frame insured the permanent inferiority of Germany's air effort throughout the remainder of the war. The basis of those decisions lay in an overestimation of the *Reich*'s strength and a contemptuous arrogance that dismissed the Russians as subhumans and the Americans as capable of building only radios and refrigerators. Disdainful of their enemies and proud of their victories, the Germans were sure that their technological expertise and military competence could master any threat.

In addition to production and mobilization issues is the question of attrition. There is an irony here, for airpower thinkers before the war, like the ground theorists, were sure that their doctrine would provide a means to return to the era of quick, cheap wars. According to them, aircraft would enable the nations equipped with air fleets to escape the killing of Passchendaele, the Somme, and Verdun. The terrible reality was that war in the air was even deadlier for those who flew from 1939 to 1945 than the war in the trenches. Martin Middlebrook in his book, *The Nuremberg Raid,* presents the survival prospects for aircrews who served in Bomber Command long enough to have a chance of completing a tour on operations (see Table LXI[5]).

German pilots had no such thing as a tour on operations. For fighters, the attrition of German pilots over the war was probably well into the 90th percentile. The statistic

TABLE LXI

Aircrew Survival Rate, Bomber Command—1939–1945

	Percent
Killed on Operations	51
Killed in Crashes in England	9
Seriously Injured in Crashes	3
Prisoners of War (Some Injured)	12
Shot Down But Evaded Capture	1
Survived Unharmed	24

mentioned in the last chapter on the average length of service of line pilots (between eight and thirty days) is an indication of the fate awaiting those who flew fighters for the *Luftwaffe*. The statistics for bomber, night fighter, or "Stuka" pilots could not have been much better.

The statistics available on the *Luftwaffe* point out in unambiguous terms precisely how attrition affected its force structure and capabilities (see Tables LXII,[6] LXIII,[7] and LXIV[8]). Through the first two years of the war (1940–41), the loss rates for aircraft had been alarming, even though the Germans had for the most part enjoyed qualitative superiority over their opponents. Thereafter, however, the impact of swelling enemy production and the commitment of the *Wehrmacht* to hold the distant perimeter of the expanded *Reich* steadily increased the attrition rate. Increases in German aircraft production, no matter how impressive graphically, were ineffective since, in relation to Allied industrial efforts, the Germans were falling further and further behind. In fact, the impact of the air war on the German force structure was such that rising attrition cancelled out increasing production so that there was remarkably little change in the *Luftwaffe*'s total frontline strength from 1940 through 1944, particularly in the combat categories of fighter and bomber aircraft (see Tables LXV[9] and LXVI[10]). A comparison of the figures for May 1940 and January 1944 are most instructive; at the start of the French campaign, the *Luftwaffe* possessed 1,369 fighters and 1,758 bombers; over three and one-half years later, the Germans possessed only 1,561 fighters and 1,604 bombers (see Tables LXV and LXVI). In fact, the loss rate was such that increasing German production was never able to sustain frontline squadrons at their full authorized strength (see Table LXVII[11]). While there were, of course, fluctuations in the percentages of authorized strength on hand in frontline units, the trend from 1942 on was unmistakenly downwards.

The loss of aircraft was only one indicator among many as to what was happening to the *Luftwaffe*. The attrition of pilots and skilled aircrews was perhaps the most important factor in the destruction of the *Luftwaffe* as an effective fighting force. The rise in the attrition rate for pilots resulted in a steady reduction in the skills and experience of those flying German aircraft. While the losses among the fighter pilots (see Table LXVIII[12]) may have been somewhat heavier than for other categories, they undoubtedly reflected what was happening throughout the force structure. The increasing attrition of pilots forced the Germans to curtail training

Table LXII   German Aircraft Losses 6 Month Periods

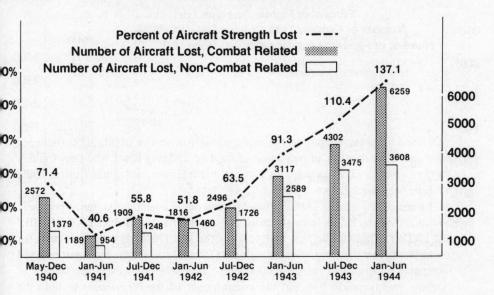

Table LXIII   Bomber Losses 6 Month Periods

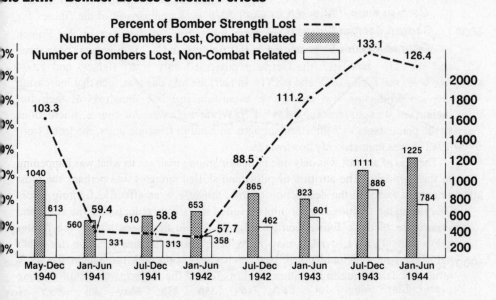

Table LXIV   Fighter Losses 6 Month Periods

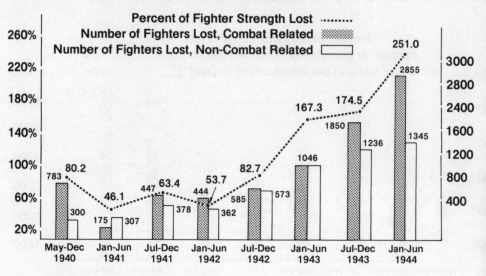

Table LXV

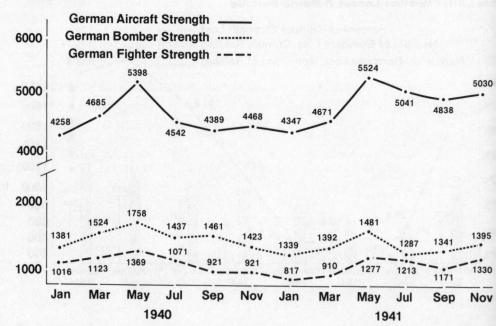

ble LXVI

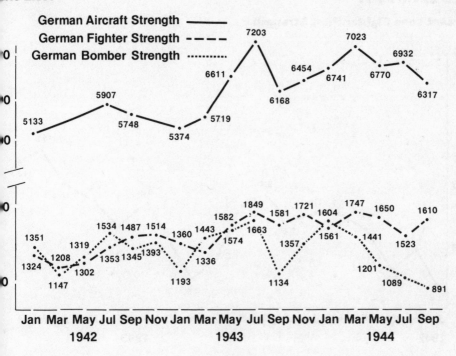

ble LXVII   Percent of Aircraft Authorized Strength

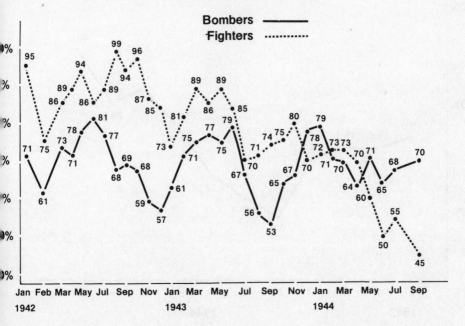

Table LXVIII Part I

Percent Loss Fighter Pilot Strength

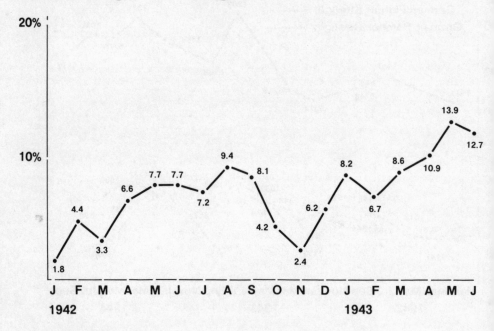

Table LXVIII Part II

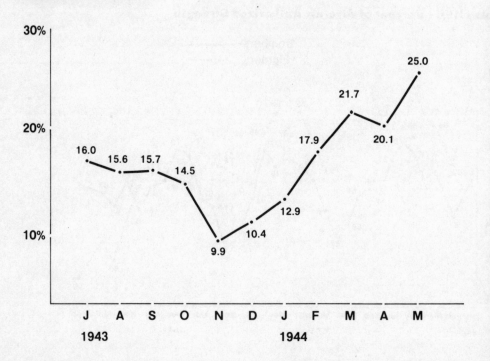

programs to fill empty combat cockpits. As a result, new pilots with less skill than their predecessors were lost at a faster rate. The increasing losses, in turn, forced the training establishments to produce pilots even more rapidly. Once they had begun this vicious cycle, the Germans found no escape. One of the surest indicators of the declining skill of German pilots after the 1940 air battles was the rising level of noncombat losses (see Tables LXII through LXIV). By the first half of 1943, they had reached the point where the fighter force suffered as many losses due to noncombat causes as it did to the efforts of its opponents. Thereafter, the percentage of noncombat losses began to drop. The probable cause of this was due less to an awakening on the part of the *Luftwaffe* to the need for better flying safety than to the probability that Allied flyers, in their overwhelming numbers, were shooting down German pilots before they could crash their aircraft.

By the beginning of 1942, the Germans had lost the equivalent of two entire air forces. The result was that the Germans had to curtail their training programs to meet the demands of the front for new pilots. By January 1942, of the pilots available for duty in the fighter force, only 60 percent were fully operational, while the number in the bomber force was down to 47 percent (see Table LXIX[13]). For the remainder of the war, the percentage of fully operational fighter and bomber pilots available, with few exceptions, remained below, and at many times substantially below, the 70 percent level. Further exacerbating this situation was the fact that the Germans were forced to lower their standards for a fully operational pilot as the war continued. There was, one must note, no decisive moment in this decline in expertise. Rather, as Winston Churchill has suggested in another context, the *Luftwaffe* had entered the descent from 1940 "incontinently, fecklessly. . . . It is a fine broad stairway at the beginning but after a bit the carpet ends. A little further on, there are only flagstones; and a little further on, these break beneath your feet."[14] The graph for the number of training hours for new pilots clearly reflected such a course (see Table LXX[15]). In the period through the late summer of 1942, German pilots were receiving at least as many training hours as their opponents in the RAF. By 1943, that statistic had begun a gradual shift against the Germans until the last half of the year when *Luftwaffe* pilots were receiving barely one-half of the training hours given to enemy pilots. In terms of flying training in operational aircraft, the disparity had become even more pronounced: one-third of the RAF total and one-fifth of the American total. But those *Luftwaffe* pilots who had survived the attrition of the first air battles of the war had little difficulty defeating new Allied pilots no matter how many training hours the latter had flown. In fact, the ratio of kills-to-sorties climbed as those *Luftwaffe* pilots who survived built up experience (see Table LXXI[16]). However, few German pilots survived the attrition of the first war years, and thus the *Luftwaffe* became, in fact, two distinct forces: the few great aces—the Hartmanns, Gallands, and Waldmanns—and the great mass of pilots who faced great difficulty in landing their aircraft, much less surviving combat. Only 8 of Germany's 107 aces to score more than 100 victories joined their squadrons after mid-1942.[17]

Table LXIX Percent of Crews Operationally Ready (Fully)

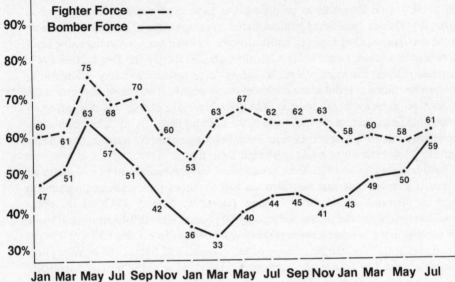

Table LXX Flying Hours in British, American and German Training

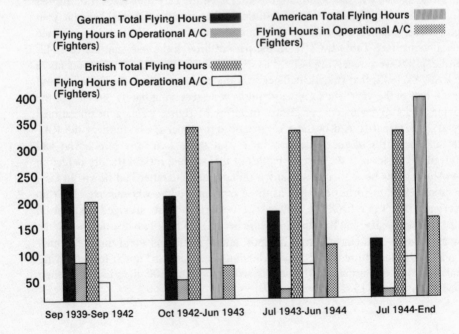

Table LXXI   Number of Victories Achieved Each 50 Missions Flown: Four German Aces

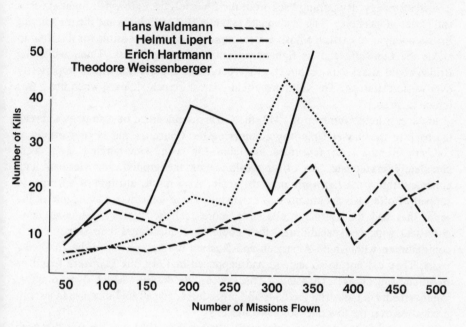

The Germans had embarked in the spring of 1940 on their campaign against Scandinavia, France, and the Low Countries. The military machine that made those conquests had been trained by some of the finest tactical and operational military minds in the history of warfare. Yet, even in the French campaign, a serious attrition of Germany's air and mechanized forces took place. For the next year and a quarter, the *Wehrmacht* went on a rampage that saw it conquer the Balkans, drive into Egypt, and win devastating victories in the Soviet Union. Nevertheless, despite the facade of glittering success, the ruthless, incontrovertible laws of attrition were at work. By the end of 1941, the Germans had lost the sharp edge on the ground as well as in the air.

Having spent two years on the offensive, Hitler was unwilling to forgo the initiative, and German ground and air forces once again went over to the offensive in the summer of 1942. It is worth noting that several different types of attrition occurred during the war: "offensive," "reactive," and "imposed." In the summer of 1942, as in the previous two years, the attrition of aircraft and pilots resulted from offensive operations. Had the Germans not launched the major offensive in the east, little attrition of the *Wehrmacht*'s strength would have taken place. Having established an equilibrium in the east in the spring of 1942 after the winter defeats, the Germans were in a position to fight on the strategic defensive. Had they done so, they could have substantially rebuilt and refitted both their ground and air forces. Their air strategy in 1941 and 1942 in the west suggested the possibilities involved in such a strategy. By pulling back from the Channel, the *Luftwaffe* fought at times and places of its choice. The inadequate range of British fighters and the inability of British bombers to exist in a hostile environment made it impossible for the RAF to tackle the *Luftwaffe* and its fighters except on German terms. Thus, while the British could attack coastal targets, they could not and did not win air superiority over western Europe. The Germans could contest French airspace when there was reason to do so.

In the east in the summer of 1942, the Germans embarked on a strategy to break the back of the Soviet Union by conquering the Caucasus and large portions of southern Russia. The resources available for such wide-ranging aims were completely inadequate. To offset weakness on the ground, the German high command threw the *Luftwaffe* onto the scale. As a result, attrition of air units in support of offensive operations was extensive. These losses were avoidable in the sense that had the Germans chosen a more realistic strategy that was more consistent with their capabilities, they could have husbanded their strength for a confrontation with Anglo-American and Russian military power in the following years. They did not do so and, as had happened in 1941, the *Luftwaffe* found its frontline squadrons exhausted. This occurred despite Milch's substantive improvements in industrial methods and procedures, and a rapid increase in aircraft production over the low rates for 1940 and 1941.

The second factor that was different in 1942 than in 1941 was the fact that both the Soviet Union and the Western Powers were able to reap the first benefits of their industrial mobilizations. Accordingly, they challenged Nazi Germany on the periphery far from German sources of power. In the Mediterranean, the British at El Alamein and the Anglo-American effort against Algeria and Morocco attacked the entire Axis position in Africa. Unwilling to recognize how much the balance had swung against Germany, Hitler, supported by the *OKW*, responded to that challenge. The attrition that resulted was what one might term a "response" attrition. The Germans, reacting to moves in the Mediterranean, determined to stand and fight despite the disadvantage of vulnerable lines of communications from Sicily to Tunisia. At the same time, the Russians launched their counterattack at Stalingrad. Responding to a strategic move by his Soviet opponent, Hitler ordered Sixth Army to stand and fight along the Volga. Here again, the attrition was a "response" attrition, losses that the Germans could have avoided had they traded space for time.

The resulting erosion in the Mediterranean and on the Russian front pushed the *Luftwaffe*'s loss rates for the end of 1942 and the first half of 1943 towards a level of 20 percent per month. Meanwhile, a new danger appeared. In the west, British night raids had become an increasing threat to the safety of Germany's cities; and in the spring of 1943, the appearance of American daylight formations over the *Reich* represented a direct threat to the *Luftwaffe* and its sources of supply—the aircraft industry. Without new aircraft, the *Luftwaffe* could not meet its growing responsibilities and the increasing losses at the front. Unlike 1941 and 1942 when the *Luftwaffe* could fight on its own terms, it now had to meet the American bombers. The attrition that took place over the *Reich,* we might call "imposed" attrition, for Eighth Air Force forced the *Luftwaffe* to fight. However, as the Americans discovered, attrition is a two-way street. Even with the successes of American industrial and training programs, no organization can sustain a constant monthly attrition of 30 percent in manpower without consequences. The second raid on Schweinfurt produced so many aircraft and crew losses that Americans had to rethink their operational and tactical approach.

The *Luftwaffe* losses in the summer and early fall likewise forced the Germans to rethink their strategy. The threat to the armament industries, particularly the aircraft industry, and the extent of losses in the Mediterranean, on the eastern front, and over the *Reich,* gave the Germans no choice but to reorder their priorities. They had to cut air commitments in the Mediterranean and in the east to provide more fighters for defense of the homeland. But Hitler was unwilling in 1943 to reorder his production priorities completely and to give unqualified emphasis to building fighters. This undoubtedly made the task of the American strategic air forces easier when the Eighth returned to the offensive. The great air battle was not a painless struggle as bomber losses through April 1944 indicate. But the combination of long-range escorts, with an overwhelming productive advantage, enabled Eighth to swamp Germany's defenders. The Americans, with their sustained pressure, shattered the *Luftwaffe*'s fighter force to the point where they were no longer a serious factor in the air war. By the time of the Normandy invasion, the Americans had won general air superiority over Europe, while attacks on the synthetic fuel industry insured that the *Luftwaffe* would not recover. Not only did it no longer have the necessary fuel but there was no hope to train new pilots in the numbers needed to meet the daylight threat.

The *Luftwaffe* attrition rate over the last three years of the war was extraordinarily high. Its impact on the German air force only began to become apparent in the summer of 1943 when it was arguably too late for the Germans to reverse trends that put them at an increasing disadvantage. There was some slight hope that a massive influx of resources might redress the balance between the fighter force and the enemy's growing air superiority. But even at this desperate moment, the *Reich*'s leaders were unwilling to support such a program.

The warning signs had been apparent earlier. The Americans especially had made no secret of their production plans. As the Germans fell behind in the production race, their losses mounted and attrition levels reached new highs, but they coped for a time. They coped until the gap between their production and Allied production reached such an extent that the *Luftwaffe* was effectively destroyed by numbers as well as quality. In the first years of the war, the Germans had confidently expected that their technological expertise and qualitative superiority would permit them to handle the numbers of aircraft that their Soviet and Western enemies produced. The rate of attrition was such that bit by bit the Germans lost their technological superiority. Moreover, the quickened pace of attrition forced the Germans to produce aircraft that were qualitatively inferior in a desperate attempt to keep up with the enemy's growing numerical advantage. On the pilot side, the wastage forced the Germans to settle for pilots whose training was manifestly inferior to those of Allied air forces. Even against the Russians, the qualitative difference between the pilots of the opposing sides narrowed after 1942; and by 1943, the Soviets also enjoyed overwhelming numerical superiority.

In retrospect, it is difficult to understand how the Germans were able to get individuals to fly against such overwhelming odds. Several factors undoubtedly came into play. The most obvious is the fact that from the summer of 1943, German fighter pilots were desperately struggling to save their homeland from Allied bombing. In such circumstances and considering their ideological indoctrination, it is not surprising that German pilots continued to fly in the face of terrible odds. There are several other factors. The most important of these was the outstanding quality of middle-level leadership. The explanation for how squadron and flight commanders kept their organizations together lay in a rigid refusal by the Germans to lower the standards in the officers corps. "Better no officer than a bad officer" might be a characterization of how the Germans viewed recruiting for the officer corps.

There was one additional element in the Germans' ability to continue the fight. Like the army, the *Luftwaffe* until almost the end prized unit cohesion. Units were not left in the frontline for interminable periods of time, with replacements arriving one or two at a time. Rather, when units had been badly shattered by heavy losses, they were pulled out of the line to be physically rebuilt with new crews and new aircraft. The Germans were thus able to renew the bonds between those who would fly and fight together and who would depend on each other for survival.

The failure of the *Luftwaffe* was symbolic of the fate of the Third *Reich*. Germany's leaders held goals that were manifestly beyond the nation's capabilities. The devastating nature of their success in the first years of the war should not disguise the dilettantism among those who conducted the *Reich*'s grand strategy. Thus, intermixed with an exceedingly high level of competence on the tactical and operational side was a complete inability to see a relationship between means and ends on the level of grand strategy. With the exception of the foundering that occurred between the fall of France and the onset of "Barbarossa," one can doubt whether Hitler ever had a grand strategy. Defeat in Russia led to the swift removal of those who might have raised questions about Germany's strategy; and the Germans, led by a *Führer* who based his approach to war on intuition, went to their inevitable doom. To the end, they waged that struggle with operational and tactical competence, but the tenacity of their defense only insured that their final defeat would be all the more terrible.

Notes

1. Verrier, *The Bomber Offensive*, p. 327.
2. The following discussion is based on a very interesting section of a major work on the establishment of the Hitler myth in Germany. The author has based his study on the SD reports on attitudes in the population; and as those reports were widely read in the upper levels of the Nazi Government, certain aspects of German strategy on the last war years now become clear: Ian Kershaw, *Volksmeinung und Propaganda im Dritten Reich* (Stuttgart, 1980), pp. 176–86.
3. USSBS, "V-Weapons (Crossbow) Campaign," Military Analysis Division, Report #60, January 1947.
4. See particularly: "Heimatverteidigungsprogramm 1943, Besprechung beim Reichsmarschall am 7.10.43.," AFSHRC, K 113.312–2, v. 3.
5. Middlebrook, *The Nuremberg Raid*, p. 275.
6. BA/MA, RL 2 III/1025, "Front-Flugzeug-Verluste," Genst. 6. Abt. (III A), May 1940–Jun 1944.
7. Ibid.
8. Ibid.
9. "Luftwaffe Strength and Serviceability Tables, August 1938–April 1945," Air Historical Branch, Translation No. VII/107.
10. Ibid.
11. BA/MA, RL 2 III/717–732, "Übersicht über Soll, Istbestand, Einsatzbereitschaft, Verluste und Reserven der fliegenden Verbände," 1942–1944.
12. Ibid.
13. BA/MA, RL 2 III/717–732, "Übersicht über Soll, Istbestand, Einsatzbereitschaft, Verluste und Reserven der fliegenden Verbände," 1942–1944.
14. Martin Gilbert, *Winston Churchill*, Vol. V, *1922–1939* (London, 1976), p. 927.
15. USSBS, "Overall Report (European War)," September 30, 1945, p. 21.
16. I am indebted to Benjamin Rand of Yale University for the information on which this table is based.
17. Ernest Obermaier, *Die Ritterkreuzträger der Luftwaffe*, Vol. I (Mainz, 1970), p. 21. I am indebted to Benjamin Rand of Yale University for pointing this out to me.

Appendix 1

The Prewar Development of British and American Doctrine and Airpower

The discussion of Chapters I through VII has concentrated on the development of the *Luftwaffe* and on its conduct of operations during the Second World War. For the benefit of the general reader not familiar with the prewar development of doctrine and force structure in Britain and the United States, the following discussion is included. One must note that while the theme of ''strategic'' bombing would play a major role in these developments, the Royal Air Force and the American Army Air Corps (later the Army Air Forces) came to have substantially different doctrinal emphases in their approach and attitudes towards the coming war. Those differences, in fact, go far in explaining the directions along which the Americans and the British traveled during the conduct of the ''strategic'' bombing campaign.

THE ROYAL AIR FORCE

The Royal Air Force was the first independent air force. It owed its creation in World War I less to the strategic and military requirements of the hour than to the hue and outcry in the British press and public over the bombing of London by German aircraft based in Belgium. Both the army and navy acquiesced in the surrender of their air forces with scarcely a murmur. However, not all airmen were enthusiastic about a new service. Some in France feared that creation of the RAF might detract from the support that the Royal Flying Corps provided Haig's plodding offensive in Flanders. ''Boom'' Trenchard, the first Chief of Staff, argued strenuously against standing air patrols to defend London (the only possible means of air defense in 1917) and opposed the transfer of fighter units from France to defend Great Britain.[1] Trenchard's first tenure as Chief of the Air Staff (CAS) proved less than auspicious, and in 1918 the Cabinet moved him to a relatively less important position. He assumed command of the independent bomber force in France that showed, whatever its promise, little performance in the remaining months of war.[2]

The last years of the war saw a crystallization of certain patterns in strategic thinking that would dominate the Royal Air Force throughout the interwar period. The political response to the Zeppelin raids had been, in many cases, to see air warfare in apocalyptic terms.[3] However, Trenchard, soon to be closely identified with the concept of ''strategic'' bombing, was dubious at first about the establishment of a bombing force to attack targets within Germany.[4] His attitude mostly reflected a deep sympathy for Haig and a desire to concentrate maximum forces in support of the western front.[5] However, already by the spring of 1917, some in the Royal Flying Corps were emphasizing the impact on morale of air attacks:

> The moral[e] effect of a successful cavalry action is very great; equally so is that of successful fighting in the air. . . . The moral[e] effect produced by an aeroplane is . . . out of all proportion to the material damage which it can inflict, which in itself is considerable, and the mere presence of a hostile machine above them inspires those on the ground with exaggerated forebodings of what it is capable of doing.[6]

Establishment of the Royal Air Force as an independent service reinforced this tendency to accentuate the importance of the airplane in attacking morale. The political rationale behind the RAF's creation seems more to have been the launching of reprisal raids on Germany than the defense of British territory. As one recent commentator has noted: "Indeed, an essential continuing characteristic of the RAF was established in its very creation; it was an offensive service arm which was created to deal with defensive needs."[7] Trenchard, himself, once he had returned to France to command the independent bombing force became a convert to the concept of attacks on German industries and cities. This formative period determined his attitude towards airpower for the remainder of his life.

By the summer of 1918, the British were strong advocates of the creation of an independent "strategic" bombing force drawn from Allied air forces. In response to a French position paper asking whether or not it was desirable to establish a coordinated plan for attacking targets within the *Reich,* the RAF replied with an emphatic yes. British representatives to the Inter-Allied Aviation Committee suggested that "strategic" bombing "must be conducted in pursuance of a carefully conceived policy and with a thorough elaboration of detail." Attacks on enemy railroads and airfields in the vicinity of the battlefield should be the task of units assigned to cooperate with ground forces. The "special long-range striking force" would have a more important task: "the dislocation of the enemy's key industries." They argued that "a general inter-Allied plan for bombardment of military, industrial, and morale objectives in Germany by an Allied strategic striking force should be formulated without delay." The launching of attacks by the pooled resources of Allied air forces would force the Germans to divert significant resources from the western front to home defense and to exacerbate further Germany's strategic difficulties. In conclusion, they noted:

> . . . that the alternative to such diversion would be that the German government would be forced to face very considerable and constantly increasing civil pressure which might result in political disintegration. In this connection, if the Allies are to reap the full benefit of the reaction in Germany due to the failure of the German effort in 1918, it is essential that no time shall be lost in developing coordinated and widespread strategic air attacks to synchronize with a period of acute popular depression.[8]

This emphasis on the results that "strategic" bombing would have on German morale is contained in an October 1918 Air Ministry paper on both the morale and material impact of air raids against Germany. This document suggested: "In the period August-October, evidence has accumulated as to the immense moral[e] effect of our air raids into Germany." The deduction drawn was that the enemy's fighting capacity decreased

> as the number of raids increased. . . . Though material damage is as yet slight when compared with moral[e] effect, it is certain that the destruction of "morale" will start before the destruction of factories and, consequently, loss of production will precede material damage.[9]

Trenchard, directed by the Supreme War Council in Versailles to draw up a detailed plan for the proposed "strategic" bombing force, began his work with a statement of his philosophical approach to the problem:

> There are two factors—moral[e] effect and material effect—the object being to obtain the maximum of each. The best means to this end is to attack the industrial centres where you:
>
> a. Do military and vital damage by striking at the centres of supply of war material.
>
> b. Achieve the maximum of effect on the morale by striking at the most sensitive part of the German population—namely, the working class.[10]

The actual conduct of operations, however, pointed out most of the considerable problems that Bomber Command would face in the Second World War. Aircrew training, lack of aircraft, and serviceability, as well as weather and navigational difficulties, all combined to keep Trenchard's bomber force at a rather limited stage of effectiveness.[11] Some of these problems, including even the thorny problem of nighttime navigation, were examined at least in conception, if not in detail, by elements within the Royal Navy Air Service in the years before creation of the Royal Air Force.[12] Nevertheless, the full complexity of the problem of accurately placing bombs on targets unfortunately remained obscure to many post-war commanders.

With the coming of peace, the British government made wholesale cuts in military expenditures. For all intents and purposes, by 1933 the British had disarmed almost as thoroughly as the Treaty of Versailles had disarmed the Germans (the Royal Navy was, of course, an exception). Trenchard, once again as Chief of Air Staff, confronted a dwindling establishment of squadrons and personnel due to decreased military funding. With relatively few resources, RAF commanders justifiably feared that loss of aircraft or crews to the navy (for aircraft carriers) or army (for close air support missions) would threaten the existence of their service.[13] Army and navy leaders may well have persisted in demands for the return of such aircraft precisely to remove one of the hungry mouths at the treasury's increasingly spare dinner table.

The RAF was saved from a quick death at the end of World War I when Lloyd George had entertained the idea of ending the independence of the air service. The choice of Churchill to hold both the War Office and the Air Ministry did not appear fortuitous in December 1918; however, not only did Churchill defend the new service but he also was instrumental in bringing Trenchard back as Chief of Staff.[14] And Trenchard, through the sheer force of his personality as well as his skillful political maneuvering, insured the continued existence of the fledgling service. Among other devices, Trenchard expanded the emerging trends in strategic thinking that were present in the Royal Air Force at the end of the war into a full-fledged doctrine of "strategic" bombing. Outside influences seem to have played almost no role in this development. Harris claims never to have heard of Douhet before the war, while Slessor admits in his memoirs that not only had he never read Douhet but had never even heard of him before the war.[15] Trenchard's doctrine postulated that airpower alone could defend Britain and that its massive striking power could destroy England's enemies at the onset of war. In the 1920's, there was some difficulty in persuading the politicians of the efficacy of such a view, although for a short time France appeared as a putative enemy, perhaps because it was the only serious military power within range of British aircraft. Unfortunately for the British, by the end of the decade, Trenchard's doctrine had become dogma within the halls of an Air Staff and organization that down to the outbreak of the war defined airpower almost exclusively in terms of "strategic" bombing.

In conference with leading members of his staff in July 1923, Trenchard underscored his faith in "strategic" bombing and his belief that the British people would exhibit greater staying power in a bombing exchange. Trenchard argued:

> I would like to make this point again. I feel that although there would be an outcry, the French in a bombing duel would probably squeal before we did. That was really the first thing. The nation that would stand being bombed longest would win in the end.

Trenchard said that he strongly disagreed with the view that it would be better to add four fighter squadrons to defend Great Britain than four bomber squadrons to hit the French. He suggested that 48 more bombing aircraft would exercise a strong impact on French morale, while the downing of a few bombers "would have very little effect." One senior officer objected that if a French squadron came over Britain with 12 aircraft and returned with 4, it would adversely affect their morale. Trenchard agreed that this would have a greater effect on the morale of the

> French pilots than it would on ours. Casualties affected the French more than they did the British. That would have to be taken into consideration too, but the policy of hitting the French nation and making them squeal before we did was a vital one—more vital than anything else.[16]

In March 1924, the Air Staff presented its case in a memorandum on the proper objectives of an air offensive. It argued that the forces employed in attacking an enemy nation

> can either bomb military objectives in populated areas from the
> beginning of the war, with the objective of obtaining a decision by
> moral[e] effect which such attacks will produce, and by the serious
> dislocation of the normal life of the country, or, alternatively, they
> can be used in the first instance to attack enemy aerodromes with a
> view to gaining some measure of air superiority and, when this has
> been gained, can be changed over to the direct attack on the nation.
> The latter alternative is the method which the lessons of military
> history seem to recommend, but the Air Staff are convinced that the
> former is the correct one.

For the conduct of the air offensive against an enemy power (the belligerent countries, not named, would be "separated by 20 or 30 miles of sea"), the Air Staff suggested that fighters would play almost no role. The distances involved would make it impossible to build a fighter that would have sufficient range and efficiency. Thus, the Air Staff could state "as a principle that the bombing squadrons should be as numerous as possible and the fighters as few as popular opinion and the necessity for defending vital objectives will permit."[17]

In May 1928, Trenchard further elaborated for the benefit of his fellow chiefs of Staff the view expressed in the above memorandum that air forces could alter "the lessons of military history." The CAS claimed that it would not be necessary for an air force, as with the other services, to defeat the enemy's armed forces in order to defeat his nation. "Airpower can dispense with that immediate step. . . ." While Trenchard admitted that it would be wrong and "contrary to the dictates of humanity" to conduct "indiscriminate bombing of a city for the sole pupose of terrorizing the civilian population," he argued that it was an entirely different matter "to terrorize munition workers (men and women) into absenting themselves from work or stevedores into abandoning the loading of a ship with munitions through fear of attack. . . ."[18]

If Trenchard can be accused of taking a too single-minded approach to the question of airpower, his accomplishment in defending the independence of the Royal Air Force was his greatest monument. Moreover, he identified and supported such strong personalities as Dowding, Tedder, Portal, and Slessor, among others. They and their service would be Trenchard's contribution towards the winning of the Second World War. One should also note that throughout the 1920's when Trenchard and the Air Staff were creating their doctrine of "strategic" bombing, RAF officers serving in the world of colonial pacification, police actions, and border skirmishes were actively engaged in air operations that had little to do with "strategic" bombing. Their experience and the flexibility of mind that such tasks demanded proved of vital importance once the war began.

By and large, however, such experience had little impact on the higher levels of the Air Staff. Trenchard's persuasive influence endured long after he had relinquished his position. Even the work of Slessor, usually a perceptive thinker on airpower and later Chief of Coastal Command in the war, showed the heavy imprint of official thought. Slessor's position as the Chief of Plans on the Air Staff in the late thirties makes his views, aired publicly in 1936, of particular significance.[19] While he was more willing to recognize the potential of modern mechanized warfare than most of his army contemporaries, Trenchard's influence was unmistakable in Slessor's discussions of air war. He argued that the coming war would be nearly all air combat and that Britain could only gain and maintain air superiority through a "resolute bombing offensive" against enemy cities and industries. Such a strategy would force the enemy to use his air strength in a defensive, not offensive, role, thereby diverting strength away from the primary task of "strategic" bombing, which alone would be decisive. Aerial bombardment would help intimidate the poorer and more unreliable segments of the population and would force the enemy to divert further strength from his strategic effort. Ground operations would rarely occur, and armies would mostly serve as frontier guards while the bombers flew overhead.[20] Slessor reasoned that

> it is difficult to resist at least the conclusion that air bombardment on anything approaching an intensive scale, if it can be maintained even at irregular intervals for any length of time, can today restrict the output from war industry to a degree which would make it quite impossible to meet the immense requirements of an army on the 1918 model, in weapons, ammunition, and warlike stores of almost every kind.[21]

Considering that "strategic" bombing represented the *raison d'être* for the Royal Air Force, it is surprising that so little was done to prepare for this task. Prewar doctrine called for trained aircrews to precede the bomber force and to mark the targets for following aircraft. In the late 1920's, when asked how trained aircrews would find their targets, Tedder replied, "You tell me!"[22] Unfortunately, the RAF would not really face up to this problem until 1941 when analysis of mission photography revealed that half of the bombs dropped on Germany were landing in the countryside.[23]

Admittedly in the late 1930's, there was no clear conception of the parameters involved in the coming air war in terms of weapons or tactics. There was considerable difficulty in estimating capabilities with so little prior experience. In 1938, the Joint Planning Committee conceded:

> In considering air attack, we are faced with the difficulty that we lack the guidance of past experience in almost all the factors which affect it, and consequently the detailed methods of application and their effects are almost a matter for conjecture. We do not know the degree of intensity at which a German air offensive could be sustained in the face of heavy casualties. We do not know the extent to which the civilian population will stand up to continued heavy losses of life and property.[24]

However, evidence did exist on the difficulty of locating and damaging targets. In May 1938, the Assistant Chief of Air Staff admitted that

it remains true, however, that in the home defense exercise last
year, bombing accuracy was very poor indeed. Investigation into
this matter indicates that this was probably due very largely to [the]
failure to identify targets rather than to fatigue.[25]

A 1937 experiment underlined the extent of the accuracy problem. The RAF
placed 30 obsolete aircraft within the circumference of a circle possessing a 1,000-
yard diameter. For one week, Bomber Command attacked the stationary aircraft
from high and low level. At the test's completion, the effort had destroyed only 2
aircraft, had damaged 11 beyond repair, had left 6 damaged but reparable, and had
missed 11 entirely.[26] The First World War had already indicated that night bombing
represented an even more complex challenge than daylight operations. In
September 1917, Lieutenant Commander Lord Tiverton of the Royal Naval Air
Service reported to the Air Board that "experience has shown that it is quite easy
for five squadrons to set out to bomb a particular target and for only one of those
five ever to reach the objective; while the other four, in the honest belief that they
had done so, have bombed four different villages which bore little, if any,
resemblance to the one they desired to attack."[27]

These difficulties in finding and then hitting targets whether by day or by night
plagued British airmen and scientists despite the immense resources that were
available to them throughout the Second World War. The poor bombing capability
in the 1930's, given the available assets, is not particularly surprising.
Nevertheless, where the Air Staff is vulnerable to criticism lies in its unwarranted
confidence that no substantial problems existed and, therefore, its general
unwillingness to initiate an effort to address these difficulties.

This emphasis on "strategic" bombing as *the* doctrine seriously affected the
development of other aspects of airpower in Britain during the interwar period.
Even air defense, which would win the Battle of Britain in the summer of 1940,
received little recognition from the Air Staff during the early 1930's. The RAF's
position was that air defense had little prospect of blunting an enemy bombing
offensive and, therefore, represented a waste of aircraft and resources. Sir Warren
Fischer of the Treasury reflected bitterly over the course of the rearmament debates
in a letter to the Prime Minister in October 1938. He recalled that:

When I insisted on the insertion in the report of passages such as
these on the need to build up Britain's air defense system, the
representative of the Air Staff acquiesced with a shrug of his
shoulders. The Air Staff proposals were, of course, again quite
insufficient.[28]

In February 1937, the RAF set forth its estimates on the air threat from Germany
over the coming two years. Among other things, it argued that Germany's bombing
capacity would increase 600 percent in 1937 and that a German air offensive in
1939 would do ten times more damage than an attack in 1937. The underlying
assumption was that air defense could play little role in counteracting this massive

German buildup. Among the Chiefs of Staff, only the Chief of Naval Staff, Lord Chatfield, cast doubts on the Air Staff's pessimistic estimates. Referring to the resources that the government had allocated to defensive measures, Chatfield felt that it was illogical to estimate German capability at such a high level.[29] Ironically, it was the Chamberlain government, which for the most part had an abysmal record in rearmament, and Prime Minister Neville Chamberlain, in particular, that forced an unwilling Air Ministry to invest substantial resources in air defense.

The Air Staff itself pushed the development of the two-seater as the fighter of the future.[30] A memorandum generated during the late spring of 1938 argued that:

> The speed of modern bombers is so great that it is only worthwhile to attack them under conditions which allow no relative motion between the fighter and its target. The fixed-gun fighter with guns firing ahead can only realize these conditions by attacking the bomber from dead astern. The duties of a fighter engaged in "air superiority" fighting will be the destruction of opposing fighters. . . . For these purposes, it requires an armament that can be used defensively as well as offensively in order to enable it to penetrate into enemy territory and withdraw at will. The fixed-gun fighter cannot do this.[31]

Slessor, from the planning staff in the Air Ministry, had suggested in 1936 that the RAF needed only a few single seaters for air defense since the two-seater offered better prospects of employment.[32] It was only because of Dowding's spirited objections to the two-seater "Defiant" in June 1938 that the British maintained a high level of "Spitfire" and "Hurricane" production.[33]

It is worth emphasizing that the creation of Fighter Command as an effective defense force and the articulation and conception of an air defense system was due almost entirely to Dowding. As the Air Member for Supply and Research in the early thirties, he provided critical support for the development of radar as well as for the single-seater fighter. As the Commander of Fighter Command in the late thirties, he waged a lonely fight with the Air Staff to build up an integrated air defense system based on the "Spitfire" and "Hurricane."[34] He then conducted and won the Battle of Britain with the force and strategy that he had created—surely as great a conceptual triumph as the creation of the German panzer force.

Dowding was helped considerably by Chamberlain's refusal to buy a big bomber air force. As was the case with so many defense decisions made in the thirties, the preference for fighters over bombers stemmed from the fact that fighters were cheaper rather than from any firm belief in the efficacy of air defense. In this case, given the enormous cost of a bomber program and the scarcity of resources available for repairing Britain's military unpreparedness, feelings that Britain could only afford a major fighter program seem quite reasonable.[35] Unfortunately, even here shortsightedness dominated; after the Munich Conference of September 1938, the Cabinet addressed the obvious weaknesses of the air defense system through the dubious expedient of increasing the numbers of fighters on order by extending the number of months in each contract without increasing the number of fighters produced each month. Thus, there was *no* effort to increase substantively fighter production after Munich. The fact that "Spitfire" and "Hurricane" production was marginally exceeding production targets throughout the post-Munich period suggests that production might have increased almost immediately and certainly within six months.[36] It was not.

The record of the Air Staff concerning other aspects of airpower was scarcely better than its record on fighters; furthermore, it was in no way mitigated by interference from the Chamberlain government. The RAF resolutely rejected close air support as one of its missions. After a 1939 combined exercise, General Sir Archibald Wavell commented that the RAF had obviously given no thought to supporting ground operations, and thus its pilots were incapable of performing that mission.[37] He was substantially correct. In a 1937 Chiefs of Staff meeting, the army minister, Leslie Hore-Belisha, suggested that the Spanish Civil War indicated the value of close air support. The CAS immediately asserted that this was a gross misuse of airpower. Air Ministry reports, he added, disclosed that the Italians had been so impressed with low flying support missions that they had diverted 50 percent of their aircraft to that mission. He hoped that such reports were true but doubted whether the Italians would be so stupid.[38]

As late as November 1939, Air Staff doctrine on close air support ran along the following lines:

> Briefly the Air Staff view—which is based on a close study of the subject over many years—is as follows: The true function of bomber aircraft in support of an army is to isolate the battlefield from reinforcement and supply, to block or delay the movement of reserves, and generally to create disorganization and confusion behind the enemy front. . . . But neither in attack nor in defense should bombers be used on the battlefield itself, save in exceptional circumstances. . . . All experience of war proves that such action is not only very costly in casualties but is normally uneconomical and ineffective compared with the results of the correct employment of aircraft on the lines above.[39]

The above is indeed a somewhat surprising document when one considers that the Polish campaign had just ended. In France in 1940, requests by the First Armored Division for close air support met with objections that such calls were impracticable and unnecessary.[40] Moreover, in July 1938, the Chiefs of Staff dismissed the employment of parachute troops with the argument that such a task would divert aircraft from more useful employment as bombers.[41] The result of such attitudes was that the RAF neither possessed the aircraft nor the training to carry out interdiction, close air support, or transport missions at the outbreak of war in 1939. Only at a great cost in aircraft and crews would the RAF develop these capabilities in North Africa.[42]

In 1936, Harris—working in the Plans Division of the Air Staff—claimed that reconnaissance of enemy bases was the only way to locate naval forces and that the employment of aircraft over the ocean would be a waste of effort. In addition, Harris told the Joint Planning Committee that the Air Staff reserved the right, at any time, to withdraw aircraft from subsidiary missions (i.e., naval support or reconnaissance) for use in the primary mission of "strategic" bombing.[43] Not until late 1937 did the CAS unwillingly concede that aircraft allocated for convoy protection could only be transferred by the Air Staff to other functions with the approval of the Chiefs of Staff and War Cabinet.[44]

RAF attitudes provided substantial support to the appeasement of Germany. The belief in RAF circles that the *Luftwaffe* was preparing to launch a "bolt from the blue" played a major role in framing the gloomy prognostications that Chamberlain used to such effect in persuading his Cabinet to support his policies.[45] Symptomatic of the atmosphere created by fear of an air war was the December 1938 warning issued by the Emergency Reconstruction Committee of the CID (Committee of Imperial Defense):

> On the assumption that the enemy may make his maximum effort at the beginning of the war, the estimate accepted by the CID is that the weight of bombs dropped might be 6,000 tons during the first week and 7,000 during the next fortnight. It had been in this connection estimated that a 500-lb bomb dropped on a built-up area like London would on the average destroy 8 and damage 92 homes. If, therefore, every bomb found a previously undamaged target in a closely built-up area, then in the first three weeks 465,000 would be totally destroyed and 5,375,000 damaged out of some 14 million houses in the country.[46]

Even this Committee found such an assumption "extravagant," but the damage had been done. The conclusion by the Air Ministry in September 1938 that, in the final analysis, fear of a German "bolt from the blue" was unwarranted could not counteract the impression that many appeasers had gained from the Air Staff's apocalyptic estimates. As Sir Samuel Hoare argued to his colleagues in the Cabinet over an army report on a possible land commitment to the continent:

> The impression made upon him by the report was that it did not envisage the kind of war that seemed most probable. In a war against Germany, our own home defences would be the defensive position behind the Maginot Line. . . . The problem was to win the war over London. . . . We should need in the initial stages all our available troops to assist in the defense of this country.[47]

In summation, the myopia of the Air Staff hindered the development of a broadly based conception of airpower in Great Britain. Admittedly, Trenchard's devotion to his service and his advocacy of airpower saved the Royal Air Force as an independent service. Moreover, one must admit that the evidence from World War I did not provide clear, unambiguous evidence on the impact of airpower. But when all is said and done, too many of those in the higher positions of the Royal Air Staff between the wars allowed doctrine to become dogma and failed to examine the assumptions on which they based their air strategy in the light of current capability and the difficulties that emerged just in peacetime flying. The result was that outside of air defense—and the Air Staff's role there was somewhat ambiguous—

the RAF had prepared only for "strategic" bombing; in all the other aspects of airpower (close air support, interdiction, airborne operations, long-range reconniassance, and maritime operations), the Royal Air Force had done far too little in anticipating the requirements of the coming war.

THE DEVELOPMENT OF AIRPOWER IN THE UNITED STATES

The peculiar position of the United States, isolated geographically from European centers of power, had a decided impact on the development and articulation of American airpower both before and during the Second World War. The nature of the American continent, relatively secure from the direct threat of enemy attack, enabled the United States to maximize her reserves of manpower and industrial plant. If that security allowed the United States to build up its military potential undisturbed, it also made it exceedingly difficult to bring that military potential to bear: The distance from America to the centers of enemy power required a logistical structure reaching out from America across several thousand miles of ocean. Throughout the prewar period, that very geographic isolation had the predictable effect of encouraging American politicians to believe that the United States was immune from the diseases of war and power politics that beset the rest of the world.

The naiveté that characterized the debate over foreign policy spilled over into discussions of national security. As in Britain, there was little money available for the services: In this case, only two—the army and the navy. Locked within the body of an unsympathetic army, air enthusiasts increasingly advocated a theory of airpower as an independent strategic force capable of deciding the next war by itself. This line of argumentation undoubtedly served a similar political purpose to that of Trenchard and the Air Ministry in Britain. In the case of the latter, the "strategic" bombing argument provided a *raison d'être* for the continued independence of the RAF, while in the former arguments for "strategic" bombing suggested an independent role for the Air Corps and eventual independence from the army. The evolution of American "strategic" bombing theory, however, differed considerably from British doctrine. Whereas the British became enamoured with a direct assault on an enemy's population to break his morale, Army Air Corps thinkers turned to a more sophisticated, surgical approach to "strategic" bombing. Instead of attacking an enemy's morale directly, they suggested that precision bombing could take out a critical element of an enemy's economic structure with a relatively few aircraft. This approach would minimize civilian casualties, destroy the enemy's economy, and cause a general collapse of morale. The elements in this theory were not necessarily unique to American thinkers,[48] but American attitudes in this period made the theory particularly attractive. It appealed to a growing American enthrallment with technology, and it reflected an idealistic intellectualism that would have been appalled at a direct assault on the enemy's population.

American "strategic" bombing theory did not immediately emerge from World

War I. It took longer to evolve into its final form of the late 1930's and drew from a wider variety of sources than had British thought. The development of American airpower theories grew out of collective experiences of World War I, especially among those American flyers assigned to fight in France. "Billy" Mitchell, whose argumentative personality dominated the early history of American airpower, was influenced not only by aerial combat but also by meeting British air officers, especially Trenchard.[49]

If Mitchell's stridency set the tone for the debate in the United States, his view on airpower differed substantially from Trenchard's or Douhet's. Mitchell remained a firm believer in the importance of gaining and of maintaining air superiority. Unlike many British or his successors in the Air Corps Tactical School, Mitchell argued strongly for pursuit aviation as well as bombers. In his first book, he suggested that the proper ratio of aircraft within the Air Corps should be 60 percent pursuit, 20 percent bombardment, and 20 percent observation. For him, the first task in air war would be the defeat of the enemy air force; not until that mission had been achieved could effective bombardment take place. While Mitchell did rate the defensive possibility of bombers quite highly, he regarded enemy pursuit forces as the most serious threat to successful bombing operations. Thus, the task of American pursuit was not necessarily to escort bomber formations but to seek out and to attack enemy fighters.[50]

In the early 1920's, the thrust of teaching at what was eventually the Air Corps Tactical School followed Mitchell's arguments closely. The instructions on air tactics drew heavily on the lessons and experience of the First World War; and based on that experience, pursuit aviation received pride of place. The school emphasized aerial "barrage" as a technique to protect ground forces. Because close protection of the bomber or observer aircraft in World War I had proven costly, a more flexible and aggressive use of fighter formations was advocated. Since pursuit aircraft had been largely responsible for achieving air supremacy, the school argued that pursuit aviation was the Air Service's chief arm.[51] One tactics course went so far as to claim that, "Pursuit in this relation to the Air Service . . . may be compared to the infantry in its relation to the other branches of the army. Without pursuit, the successful employment of the other air branches is impossible."[52]

Nevertheless, if pursuit aviation received pride of place at first, certain factors pushed the school's doctrine in another direction. The goal of air superiority seemed to serve a largely negative function: Its achievement had little impact unless one could utilize it to accomplish further tasks. In the mid-1920's, American thinkers turned increasingly to bombardment as the exclusive mission for aircraft. Here the lessons of the last war were moot. There had not ever been sufficient bombing capability in the war to have a decisive impact on events. With little historical evidence available, the theorists (as in Italy and Britain) thought in terms of future potential rather than past experience. The tendency, quite naturally, was to cast that potential by referring to aircraft not yet on the drawing boards. Even in the early 1920's, those interested in bombardment argued that defensive machineguns and "compact formations" could protect bombers sufficiently against enemy fighters. Altitude and speed would also help. The actual mission of bombardment aircraft would be to attack enemy airbases, thereby assisting fighters in the destruction of enemy forces. There does not seem to have been much target analysis beyond enemy air forces.[53]

At the mid-point in the 1920's, a significant shift away from pursuit aviation towards bombardment took place. Where early training manuals had discussed the potential of aerial bombardment, the manual for the 1925–26 academic year emphasized more forcefully the role of bombardment in air warfare.[54] Moreover, where previous texts had pointed at the enemy's air forces as the chief target, Air Corps thinkers now suggested that independent strategic operations could achieve a decisive impact by destroying the enemy's will to resist. By 1926, training manuals argued that bombardment might "have a direct, although not . . . immediate effect . . . by attacking the enemy's aircraft industry." The destruction of that target system would lead to the collapse of the enemy's air force. The possibility of attacking the enemy's aircraft industry was only one among many, but the critical point was the suggestion that the enemy's economy possessed "vital parts" or "sensitive points," the destruction of which would bring an entire section of economic life to a halt.[55] It would not take a great intellectual jump for Air Corps thinkers to argue that the destruction of a vital portion of the enemy's industrial potential would cause the collapse of this entire economic structure and, therefore, his will to resist further.

This change in thinking from a position that emphasized a balance between pursuit, attack and bombardment to a heavy emphasis on bombardment was the result of several factors. First, the advocates of a more balanced approach left the school to be replaced by individuals who favored bombardment.[56] The second was probably due to the influence of Douhet, whose writings were now available in translation, as well as Mitchell's increasingly strident advocacy of airpower, especially the value of bombardment.[57] While, as suggested earlier, Mitchell never lost interest in pursuit, his publicity campaign for airpower, contributing directly to his court-martial, emphasized the potential of attacking industrial centers and the possibility for directly destroying war-making potential.[58] Those at the Air Corps Tactical School found it relatively easy to emphasize the latter while ignoring the former aspects of Mitchell's arguments. Finally, certain technical changes, such as heavier bomb weights and more capable bombers, suggested a greater capability for bombing than had hitherto been possible. The result was that, while earlier instructors at the Air Corps Tactical School had recognized that combat experience in the last war indicated that bombers would suffer unnecessarily high losses when not protected by fighters, the emphasis on bombardment at the school became increasingly an emphasis on bombing unprotected by pursuit aviation.[59]

These developments in targeting doctrine and theory occurring in the middle 1920's were decisive for future formulations. The changes that took place from this point on represented refinements rather than changes in basic philosophy. For obvious reasons, daylight operations would simplify the problems of navigation and bombing accuracy; as was to be the case in Britain, the first advances in design that moved aircraft capabilities beyond those of the last war came in bomber design. Thus, the new bomber aircraft that the Air Corps possessed through the thirties enjoyed superiority over most fighter aircraft in nearly every performance characteristic. Combined with the enhanced flying capabilities were new increased defensive armament. Furthermore, since there was little combat experience on which to draw, Air Corps thinkers emphasized the defensive potential of daylight bomber formations. As early as 1930, one text used at the Air Corps Tactical School suggested that:

> Bombardment formations may suffer defeat at the hands of hostile pursuit; but with a properly constituted formation, efficiently flown, these defeats will be the exception rather than the rule. Losses must be expected, but these losses will be minimized by proper defensive tactics.[60]

The combination of easier operating conditions, the assumed defensive capacity of bomber formations, and the small differential between bomber and fighter capabilities led the Air Corps School doctrine towards the assumption that daylight, unprotected bomber raids could be conducted without serious difficulty. As one instructor put it in the early thirties: "A well-planned and well-conducted bombardment attack, once launched, cannot be stopped."[61]

By 1935, the bombardment advocates were arguing that even if enemy pursuit possessed "overwhelming superiority in all factors influencing air combat, . . . escorting fighters will neither be provided nor requested unless experience proves that bombardment is unable to penetrate such resistance alone."[62] There were, of course, factors that gave such a position greater validity in 1935 than in 1940: Without radar, air defense forces were at considerable disadvantage in finding and attacking bomber formations. Nevertheless, the line of argument within the school clearly implied that even *should* enemy fighters discover the attacking formations, the bombers could fight their way through to the target. It was not so much that bomber advocates rejected the concept of long-range fighter support for their formations, they simply assumed that such aircraft were not necessary and could not be built. In the late 1920's, there was some interest in such aircraft among pursuit supporters who suggested that with drop tanks and extended range, fighters could support bombers in deep penetration raids.[63] Nevertheless, in all fairness, one must note that in the 1930's, the few advocates of pursuit aviation were not enthusiastic about using fighters to escort bombers. One veteran of the school recalled that the foremost pursuit expert, the future General Claire Chennault, showed little interest in using fighters to escort bombers.[64]

America's geographic isolation also reinforced the direction of Air Corps thinking. It was hard to imagine an enemy bomber force acquiring bases from which it could attack the United States. Thus, air defense never had the significance that it came to have in Britain. Moreover, bomber-pursuit exercises heavily favored the former, thus furthering the impression of bomber invulnerability.[65] Arguments between navy and Air Corps pioneers like Mitchell had centered on the issue of which was more suitable for the defense of America:

bombers or battleships. In its first taste of interservice squabbling, the early Air Service articulated a position that bombers could protect the United States from an enemy at less cost and with greater effectiveness than could the navy.[66] That argument remained alive until World War II.[67]

For using airpower to attack and destroy an enemy's will, American geography similarly favored the bomber. Although the United States had suffered relatively few casualties in the First World War compared to European nations, American popular opinion had reacted almost as violently in the post-World War I era to the terrible bloodletting in the trenches as public opinion in France and Britain. As with the RAF, American airpower theorists argued that by attacking the enemy directly through aerial bombardment, the Air Corps could destroy his economy and break his will to resist—all at little cost and few casualties. The fundamental assumption was that airpower offered an escape from the trenches and horror of the last war. As Harold George suggested in a lecture: "Airpower has given to the world a means whereby the heart of a nation can be attacked at once without first having to wage an exhausting war at the nation's frontier."[68] Moreover, bombers could deploy from the United States to overseas far more quickly than a great army.

While early arguments had centered on attacking the enemy's aircraft industry as a means of defeating his air force, instructors at the school now looked for specific industries, the destruction of which would handicap not merely an industry but perhaps the entire economy. Interestingly, the 1932–33 manual suggested that destruction of the enemy's fuel industry would render an opponent's air forces harmless and make further attacks on engine and aircraft factories, or airfields unnecessary.[69]

Acquisition of the B–17 and Norden bombsights in the mid-thirties gave the Air Corps an aircraft capability to fulfill what had hitherto only been theory. In the last half of the 1930's, the general theory that targeting an attack on the enemy's industrial base could prove decisive went one step further and became a specific argument that sought to identify targets within an industry or within the economy. The destruction of these targets would so dislocate or disorganize the enemy that his economy could no longer function. Again, George noted: "It appears that nations are susceptible to defeat by the interruption of this economic web. It is possible that the morale collapse brought about by the breakup of this closely knit web would be sufficient, but connected therewith is the industrial fabric which is absolutely essential for modern war."[70] Contributing further to the elaboration of this theory of precise, exact targeting was the Army Air Corps' force structure in the late thirties. Neither for the present nor for the immediate future was it realistic to forecast a large bomber fleet. Thus, a target doctrine in which a small number of bomber aircraft using precision bombing could break the back of the enemy's economic system obviously possessed great appeal for the theorists. They argued, for example, that the destruction of 49 selected electric plants in the northeastern United States should prove sufficient to strain the economic capacity of the nation to the breaking point.[71]

By the end of the 1930's, airpower theorists in the Army Air Corps had evolved a theory of air warfare that was a precisely thoughtout body of interconnected assumptions. They based their argument on the belief that a well-led, disciplined bomber formation could fight its way through enemy controlled airspace unsupported by fighter escort. Once the bomber force had made its high altitude, deep penetration, it could, through precision bombing aided by the technological means provided by the Norden bombsight, place an adequate number of bombs on the selected target to assure destruction. That target would represent a section in the enemy's economic web, and its destruction would result in wide dislocation within his economy. The full impact of these dislocations would eventually destroy both the means and the will of the enemy to resist. The theory was undoubtedly the most carefully conceived of all the theories and strategies that airpower enthusiasts hammered out between the wars. Considering that *little* information was available based on actual combat experience, its evolution represented a triumph of human ingenuity and imagination.

Given the many unknowns, the planners had to work with a body of assumptions. What they were unwilling to see was the fact that the relationship between these assumptions was geometric rather than arithemetic. There was then an accumulation of risk that made the theory unrealistic and unworkable. As one commentator on the development of doctrine in the Air Corps Tactical School has noted:

> By accepting a concept based upon nonaccumulation of risks or problems, the school admitted its inability to recognize that in the realm of force application, a single factor or condition cannot be changed without affecting all other factors. The school ignored what seemingly was obvious: that each premise, supported by assumptions, contained inherent weaknesses. Taken individually, the shortcomings were not serious; if taken collectively, they might have undermined the entire concept.[72]

What needs emphasis is not the supposed faults in the doctrine evolved by these Air Corps theorists but rather the difficulty in peacetime in calculating on the basis of existing information, the nature of a future war. In fact, the real lesson may be that when one embarks upon a military campaign after a long period of peace, one *must* recognize that much of peacetime doctrine, training, and preparation will prove faulty. The truly effective military organization is one that recognizes and adapts to real conditions on the battlefield and absorbs its combat experience into its doctrine and training. The serious questions that one can raise against those who led the air war against Germany does not deal with the evolution of doctrine and theory through 1939 but rather whether the leaders adapted their tactics, equipment, and strategy to the conditions of air war in Europe from 1939–43, or whether they allowed preconceived judgments to filter out reality until "Black Thursday" over Schweinfurt faced them with defeat.

Notes

1. Powers, *Strategy Without Slide-Rule*, pp. 64–65.
2. Gavin Lyall, "Trenchard," *The War Lords, Military Commanders of the Twentieth Century*, ed. by Field Marshal Sir Michael Carver (Boston, 1976), pp. 182–83.
3. See, in particular, the speech by Pemberton Billing quoted in Powers, *Strategy Without Slide-Rule*, p. 16.
4. Ibid., p. 103.
5. Andrew Boyle, *Trenchard* (London, 1962), p. 228.
6. "Fighting in the Air," issued by the General Staff, March 1917, p. 1, Trenchard Papers, RAF Staff College, Bracknell, D–33.
7. Powers, *Strategy Without Slide-Rule*, p. 100.
8. Supreme War Council, Annexure to Process Verbal, Third Session 1–A, Aviation Committee. "Remarks by the British Representative for the Third Sessions of the Inter-Allied Aviation Committee held at Versailles, 21st and 22nd July 1918." Trenchard Papers, RAF Staff College, Bracknell.
9. Air Ministry, "Results of Air Raids on Germany Carried Out By British Aircraft, January 1st-September 30th, 1918," D.A.I., No. 5 (A.IIB, October 1918), Trenchard Papers, RAF Staff College, Bracknell, D–4.
10. Quoted by Group Captain R. A. Mason in "The British Dimension," *Airpower and Warfare*, ed. by Alfred F. Hurley and Robert C. Ehrhard (Washington, 1979), p. 32.
11. See, in particular, Trenchard's report on the operation of his force, June 1918, "Report of Operations Carried Out by the Independent Force During June 1918," Trenchard Papers, RAF Staff College, Bracknell.
12. Mason, "The British Dimension," pp. 30–31.
13. See D. C. Watt's discussion of this point in his article: "The Air Force View of History," *Quarterly Review* (October 1962).
14. Powers, *Strategy Without Slide-Rule*, pp. 163–64.
15. Interview with Arthur T. Harris, RAF Staff College Library, Bracknell; Sir John Slessor, *The Central Blue* (London, 1956), p. 41.
16. Webster and Frankland, *SAOAG*, Vol. IV, Appendix 1, Minutes of a Conference Held in the Room of the Chief of the Air Staff, Air Ministry, on 19 July 1923.
17. Public Record Office, Air 20/40, Air Staff Memorandum No. 11A, March 1924.
18. Webster and Frankland, *SAOAG*, Vol. IV, Appendix 2, Memorandum by the Chief of Air Staff and Comments by His Colleagues, May 1928.
19. Sir John Slessor, *Airpower and Armies* (London, 1936).
20. Ibid., pp. 15, 65, 68, 80.
21. Ibid., pp. 214–15.
22. Guy Hartcup, *The Challenge of War* (London, 1967), p. 126.
23. See particularly the report of Mr. Butt to RAF Bomber Command, "Examination of Night Photographs, 15 August 1941," Webster and Frankland, *SAOAG*, Vol. IV, p. 205.
24. PRO CAB 53/40, COS 747 (JP), 15.7.38., CID, COS Committee, "Appreciation of the Situation in the Event of War Against Germany in April 1939," p. 47.
25. PRO AIR 2/2598, Air Ministry File, #541137 (1938).
26. Basil Collier, *The Leader of the Few* (London, 1957), p. 170.
27. Quoted in Mason, "The British Dimension," pp. 30–31.
28. PRO CAB 21/902, Letter from Sir Warren Fischer to Neville Chamberlain, 1.10.38., p. 4.
29. PRO CAB 53/7, COS/198th Mtg, 18.2.37., CID, COS Committee Minutes, p. 31.
30. The Luftwaffe faced the basic same choice, between a two-seater (the Me 110) and a single-seater (the Me 109). It did, however, opt proportionately for considerably more Me 110's than the RAF opted for Boulton Paul "Defiants." This is probably a result of Dowding's strong objections to the two-seater program.
31. PRO AIR 2/2964, 17.6.38., Air Staff Note on the Employment of Two-seater and Single-seater Fighters in a Home Defence War; see also Air 2/2964, 20.6.38., Minutes by DDops (Home).
32. Slessor, *Air Power and Armies*, p. 51.
33. PRO AIR 2/2964, Headquarters Fighter Command RAF Stanmore, Middlesex, 25.6.38.

34. See, in particular, Mason, *Battle of Britain* pp. 82–92, 99–102.

35. See, in particular, G. C. Penden, *British Rearmament and the Treasury* (Edinburg, 1979); and to a lesser extent, Robert Paul Shay, Jr., *British Rearmament in the Thirties* (Princeton, 1977), for discussion of the financial limitations on British rearmament.

36. See particularly: PRO CAB/143, DPR 285, 14.10.38., CID, 24th Progress Report: "Week Ending 1.10.38.," DPR 291, 14.12.38., 25th Progress Report; DPR 297, 26th Progress Report; PRO CAB 16/144, DPR 305, 27th Progress Report, 18.4.39.; DPR 312, 28th Progress Report, 14.6.39.

37. John Connell, *Wavell, Scholar and Soldier* (New York, 1964), p. 204.

38. PRO CAB 53/8, COS/219th Meeting, 19.10.37., CID, COS Subcommittee Minutes, p. 149.

39. PRO CAB 21/903, 18.11.39., "Bomber Support for the Army," memorandum by the Air Staff; see also the letter from Admiral Lord Chatfield to Chamberlain, 15.11.39., on the air force arguments against the provision of special units for the close support of the army.

40. Major General Evans, "The First Armored Division in France," *Army Quarterly*, May 1943, pp. 57–58.

41. PRO CAB 53/40, COS 747 (JP), 15.7.38., CID, COS Subcommittee, "Appreciation of the Situation in the Event of War Against Germany in April 1939," Joint Planning Committee Appreciation.

42. See the outstanding discussion of the air war in North Africa by Tedder, *With Prejudice*.

43. PRO CAB 55/2, JP/127th Mtg., 3.12.36., CID, Joint Planning Committee of the COS Committee, p. 5; see also the argument between Admiral Lord Chatfield and Ellington on the provision of aircraft to protect trade routes: CAB 53/6, COS/190th Mtg., 21.12.36., CID, COS Subcommittee Minutes, pp. 240–43.

44. PRO CAB 53/8, COS/221st Mtg., 4.11.37., CID, COS Subcommittee Minutes, p. 12.

45. In particular, see Chapter II in my dissertation; "The Change in the European Balance of Power, 1938–1939."

46. PRO CAB 4/29, 1499.B, 16.12.38., CID, Subcommittee on Emergency Reconstruction Report, p. 85.

47. PRO CAB 24/276, CP 94(38), "Staff Conversations with France and Belgium, Annex II," CID: Extract from Draft Minutes of the 319th Meeting, 11.4.38., p. 157.

48. See, in particular, the arguments advanced by Professor Dr.-Ing. Steinman, Min.-Rat im RLM, Az. 67c. Tgb. Nr. 50/40, Berlin, 27.5.40., BA/MA, RL 7/56.

49. Craven and Cate, *The Army Air Forces in World War II*, Vol. I. pp. 12–13.

50. Alfred F. Hurley, *Billy Mitchell* (New York, 1964), pp. 63–83.

51. Thomas H. Greer, *The Development of Air Doctrine in the Army Air Arm, 1917–1941* (Air University, 1955), pp. 8–9.

52. Quoted in the outstanding dissertation on prewar planning: Thomas A. Fabyanic, "A Critique of United States Air War Planning, 1941–44," St. Louis University, 1973.

53. Ibid., pp. 9–10.

54. "Employment of Combined Air Force" (Langley Field, Virginia, 1925–26), AFSHRC.

55. "Bombardment Text" (Langley Field, Virginia, 1926–27), pp. 62–65, AFSHRC.

56. Fabyanic, "A Critique of United States Air War Planning," pp. 16–19.

57. For the availability of Douhet's writings in translation, see Robert F. Futrell, *Ideas, Concepts, and Doctrine*, Vol I (Air University, June 1971), p. 38.

58. Hurley, *Billy Mitchell*, p. 93.

59. Fabyanic, "A Critique of United States Air War Planning," pp. 18–19.

60. "Bombardment Aviation" (Air Corps Tactical School, Langley Field, Virginia, 1930), p. 109, AFSHRC.

61. Haywood S. Hansell, Jr., *The Air Plan That Defeated Hitler* (Atlanta, 1972), p. 15.

62. "Bombardment Text" (Air Corps Tactical School, Maxwell Field, Alabama, 1935), p. 140, AFSHRC.

63. "Pursuit Text" (Air Corps Tactical School, Langley Field, Virginia, 1929), Vol. II, Chapter III, pp. 109, 137, AFSHRC.

64. Hansell, *The Air Plan That Defeated Hitler*, p. 19.

65. For Chennault's description of such exercises, see Fabyanic, "A Critique of United States Air War Planning," p. 29.

66. For a full discussion of Mitchell's views on the utility of the United States Navy, see Hurley's *Billy Mitchell*.

67. For the arguments and exercises in the 1930's, see Curtis E. LeMay with MacKinlay Kantor, *Mission With LeMay* (New York, 1965), pp. 139–52.

68. Hansell, *The Air Plan That Defeated Hitler*, p. 34.

69. "Air Force" (Air Corps Tactical School, Maxwell Field, Alabama, 1932–1933), p. 8, AFSHRC.

70. Hansell, *The Air Plan That Defeated Hitler*, p. 33.

71. "Air Force: National Economic Structure" (Air Corps Tactical School, Maxwell Field, Alabama, 1938–1939), p. 24, AFSHRC.

72. Fabyanic, "A Critique of United States Air War Planning," p. 47.

Appendix 2

Effect on a 10,000-Aircraft Force Structure of a 3.6-Percent Loss Rate

Mission 1	10,000	Mission 11	6,931
Loss	360	Loss	250
Mission 2	9,640	Mission 12	6,681
Loss	347	Loss	241
Mission 3	9,293	Mission 13	6,440
Loss	335	Loss	232
Mission 4	8,958	Mission 14	6,218
Loss	322	Loss	224
Mission 5	8,636	Mission 15	5,994
Loss	311	Loss	216
Mission 6	8,325	Mission 16	5,778
Loss	300	Loss	208
Mission 7	8,025	Mission 17	5,570
Loss	289	Loss	201
Mission 8	7,736	Mission 18	5,369
Loss	278	Loss	193
Mission 9	7,458	Mission 19	5,176
Loss	268	Loss	186
Mission 10	7,190	Mission 20	4,990
Loss	259	Loss	180
			4,810

Appendix 3

Aircraft Written Off,
Bomber Command—1941-1944

Type Aircraft	No. of Aircraft Present for Duty, Frontline Squadrons— Jan 1941	No. of Aircraft Written Off, 1941	No. of Aircraft Present for Duty, Frontline Squadrons— Jan 1942	No. of Aircraft Written Off, 1942
Wellington	275	463	374	743
Mosquitoe	0	0	5	30
Sterling	7	51	52	228
Halifax	3	38	46	249
Lancaster	0	0	20	202
Total All Types Bomber Command	601	1,326	928	1,789

Type Aircraft	No. of Aircraft Present for Duty, Frontline Squadrons— Jan 1943	No. of Aircraft Written Off, 1943	No. of Aircraft Present for Duty, Frontline Squadrons— Jan 1944	No. of Aircraft Written Off, 1944
Wellington	186	328	15	22
Mosquitoe	34	62	116	223
Sterling	93	411	134	77
Halifax	195	838	307	902
Lancaster	256	1,112	652	1,978
Total All Types Bomber Command	882	2,823	1,093	3,238

[1] Based on tables in PRO AIR 22/203, War Room Manual of Bomber Commands Ops 1939–45, compiled by Air Ministry War Room (Statistical Section).

Appendix 4

Eighth Air Force, Percentage Sortie Loss Rate (Heavy Bombers)

Year	Loss Rate as Percent of Credit Sorties Bombers	Fighters
Aug 1942	0%	.9%
Sep 1942	1.9%	0%
Oct 1942	4.5%	.5%
Nov 1942	2.9%	.5%
Dec 1942	5.8%	0%
Average, 1942	3.5%	.5%
Jan 1943	7.5%	1.7%
Feb 1943	8.1%	1.1%
Mar 1943	3.2%	.8%
Apr 1943	7.8%	1.2%
May 1943	5.4%	.6%
Jun 1943	6.4%	.5%
Jul 1943	5.5%	.6%
Aug 1943	6.0%	.5%
Sep 1943	3.9%	.5%
Oct 1943	9.2%	.5%
Nov 1943	3.9%	1.6%
Dec 1943	3.6%	.8%
Average, 1943	5.1%	.8%
Jan 1944	3.8%	1.1%
Feb 1944	3.5%	1.1%
Mar 1944	3.3%	1.6%
Apr 1944	3.6%	1.3%
May 1944	2.2%	1.4%
Jun 1944	1.1%	1.0%
Jul 1944	1.5%	.9%
Aug 1944	1.5%	1.5%
Sep 1944	2.2%	1.9%
Oct 1944	1.1%	1.0%
Nov 1944	2.2%	1.8%
Dec 1944	1.2%	1.2%
Average, 1944	1.9%	1.3%

[1] Based on tables in "Statistical Summary of Eighth Air Force Operations, European Theater, 17 Aug 1942–8 May 1945."

Bibliography

UNPUBLISHED SOURCES

The documentary sources available for the researcher working in *Luftwaffe* history are generally spotty since so many air force records were damaged, destroyed, or lost either during the war or in its chaotic aftermath. Nevertheless, considerable materials do remain that shed light on strategy, tactics, supply, losses, and specific campaigns in which the *Luftwaffe* fought. The most thorough collection of documentary material, now that the British and Americans have returned the records captured at the end of the war, exists in the *Bundesarchiv/Militärarchiv*, Freiburg, Federal Republic of Germany. This material is well catalogued, and the services provided to the researcher by the staff are very helpful. Most important to this study were the Milch papers, which contain a wide range of material on aspects of the *Luftwaffe* in which the field marshal was involved, and the records of the Quartermaster General on the *Luftwaffe*'s losses, force strength, maintenance performance, and crew strength. As nearly all the operational records of the *Luftwaffe* were destroyed, the Quartermaster General's reports on aircraft and crew losses are the only available source that can give a picture of the impact of losses on the *Luftwaffe*. One must note that these records are based on when aircraft and crews were reported lost rather than when they were actually lost. Thus, there is at least a week's time lag. Nevertheless, the trends that these records indicate are unmistakable.

In the United States, two sources duplicate a portion of the records available in Germany. At Maxwell AFB, Alabama, the Albert F. Simpson Historical Research Center (AFSHRC) possesses a duplicate set (the other set is in Freiburg) of the historical and documentary material collected for the American Air Force's historical project on the *Luftwaffe*. This set contains post-war written reports on aspects of the *Luftwaffe*'s history by various senior officers as well as a sizable collection of typed extracts from archival material. It is apparent that some of the historians working on this project had access to the von Rohden collection as well as other material that the British had captured at the end of the war and which in the 1950's was located in the Air Historical Branch, London. The National Archives and Record Service (NARS) in Washington, D.C., possesses a microfilm set of the small section of *Luftwaffe* archival materials captured by American forces at the end of the war. More importantly, they also possess a full microfilm set of the von Rohden collection, which represents the holdings of the *Luftwaffe* general staff's historical section. This is an important and useful collection; its holdings are duplicated in Freiburg.

The somewhat spotty documentary material can and should be supplemented with a variety of other materials available to the researcher. The "Ultra" decrypts available in the Public Record Office (PRO), London, England, give a useful look at the operational message traffic of the German armed forces. The messages themselves range from critical pieces of information to reports on venereal disease cases on individual ships. These messages are also of use in evaluating what was available to Allied intelligence sources. In the PRO, the DEFE series contains the messages pertaining to German army and air force matters. It is useful for evaluating the actual German situations as well as establishing when Allied commanders were informed about German strategic moves. Thus, from these records one can establish what was known and when. It is worth noting that only one historical work has examined this material with consistency. Ralph Bennett's *Ultra in the West* (London, 1980) is an invaluable study of the impact of "Ultra" on the western campaign from 1944 forward. The ADM series covers the naval intercepts and is critical for an understanding of the war in the Atlantic. Obviously, it had less importance for this study than the DEFE series. Complementing this source is a valuable history of "Ultra" and its impact on American air operations that was written at the conclusion of the war: "Ultra, History of US Strategic Air Force Europe Versus German Air Force," June 1945, SRH–013. It contains many direct quotes from "Ultra" decrypts and is available in the NARS. The above material on "Ultra" is particularly important for a study of the *Luftwaffe,* since so much of the operational record was destroyed at the end of the war. Also of use are the 'Y' Service intercepts and reconstruction of the response of the German night fighter force to British night raids. That material is available in the PRO.

The records of Bomber Command in the PRO are useful in reconstructing the debates on British bombing policy within the Air Ministry. On the losses suffered by Allied bomber fleets, there are two particularly useful compilations: "War Room Manual of Bomber Command Operations 1939–1945," compiled by the Air Ministry War Room (Statistical Section) and located in the PRO; and "Statistical Summary of Eighth Air Force Operations, European Theater, 17.8.42.–8.5.45.," located in the AFSHRC.

On the American and British side, I have also made some use of the extensive records available on the development of doctrine and the course of the air campaigns in Europe. These records are available in Britain at the PRO and at the RAF Staff College, Bracknell; and in the United States, at the AFSHRC. At the latter archives, the records and texts of the Air Corps Tactical School are particularly interesting and important for the development of American prewar doctrine.

PUBLISHED DOCUMENTARY SOURCES

There are a number of published documentary sources available that have bearing on the study of German military and *Luftwaffe* history. The published volumes of documents collected for the prosecution of the major war criminals (International

Military Tribunal, *The Trial of Major War Criminals*) contain some useful information on the *Luftwaffe* and are important sources for German strategy in general. The collections of German diplomatic papers, published both in the original and in translation *(Akten zur deutschen auswärtigen Politik* and *Documents on German Foreign Policy),* provide an excellent guide to the evolution of German diplomacy and include some of the more important military documents. Karl-Heinz Völker, *Dokumente und Dokumentarfotos zur Geschichte der Deutschen Luftwaffe* (Stuttgart, 1968), has important documents on the prewar development of the German air force. H. R. Trevor Roper's *Blitzkrieg to Defeat, Hitler's War Directives* (New York, 1965) is a useful collection of the directives that Hitler issued through the *OKW* headquarters. The war diary of that headquarters is available in a multivolume set edited by a number of Germany's leading military historians *(Kriegstagebuch des Oberkommandos der Wehrmacht).* This series has important information on the *Luftwaffe;* but given the emphasis on the conduct of ground operations, its coverage is somewhat uneven on the air war. It is very useful on German strategy. Franz Halder's diary, *Kriegstagebuch,* edited by Hans Adolf Jacobsen (Stuttgart, 1964), is an important source on German strategy in the first three years of the war. It does touch tangentially on air force matters. There are a number of other diaries that are also of interest but of less immediate concern to the historian of the *Luftwaffe.* Joseph Goebbels, *Diaries, 1942–1943,* edited by Louis Lochner (New York, 1948), is interesting and informative on the opinions of one of Germany's most important political leaders. The various volumes of the "strategic" bombing survey carried out by American economists immediately at the end of the Second World War contain much important statistical information as well as useful analyses of the impact of the "strategic" bombing campaign on the German war economy. The final volume of the survey, *The Effects of Strategic Bombing on the German War Economy* (Washington, 1945), has a particularly important set of summary charts on German armaments production. In this same area, the final volume of Sir Charles Webster's and Nobel Frankland's *The Strategic Air Offensive Against Germany,* Vol. IV (London, 1961), has an interesting collection of documents on the British side of the "strategic" bombing offensive as well as several useful tables. Hans-Adolf Jacobsen, *Dokumente zur Vorgeschichte des Westfeldzuges, 1939–1940* (Göttingen, 1956), is useful on the 1940 campaign.

MEMOIRS

There is, of course, an immense literature of fighter pilot memoirs from the war. This study has relied on a minimum of such works and only on those which shed particular light on aspects of the war's general conduct. Walter Warlimont's *Inside Hitler's Headquarters* (New York, 1964) provides some insight into the workings of the *OKW.* Nicholaus von Below's *Als Hitlers Adjutant 1937–1945* (Mainz, 1980) has recently appeared and provides an interesting look into Hitler's relationship with his military aides. It also has important information on the air war and air strategy as Below was Hitler's *Luftwaffe* adjutant. Albert Kesselring's *A Soldier's Record* (New York, 1953) is not particularly informative and leaves many important issues undiscussed. Adolf Galland's *The First and the Last* (New York, 1954) has much of the flavor of most fighter pilot memoirs but also has interesting material on his relationship with Göring. As for bomber pilots, see Werner Baumbach's *The Life and Death of the Luftwaffe* (New York, 1960). Concerning the German economy, there are two important memoirs that one should consult: Albert Speer's *Inside the Third Reich* (New York, 1970) provides the reader with an important insight into the functioning of the war economy from 1942 on and also a sense of the ambiance of life at the highest levels of the Third *Reich;* conversely, Georg Thomas' *Geschichte der deutschen Wehr- und Rüstungswirtschaft 1918–1943/45* (Boppard am Rhein, 1966) is a valuable source of the prewar and early wartime periods.

The British memoir sources on the air war are extensive and enlightening. Marshal of the Royal Air Forces Lord Tedder's *With Prejudice* (London, 1966) is observant and perceptive, although perhaps somewhat reticent. Arthur Harris' *Bomber Offensive* (New York, 1947) is contentious and argumentative but lively and readable. Sir John Slessor's *The Central Blue* (London, 1956) is a clear, intelligent discussion of the career of one of the more important airmen of the Second World War. Slessor's *Air Power and Armies* (London, 1936) is one of the most realistic books about airpower written in the prewar period. Two important memoirs on the role of British scientists in the winning of the war have appeared in the last several years: R. V. Jones, *The Wizard War* (New York, 1978); and Solly Zuckerman, *From Apes to Warlords* (London, 1978). Aileen Clayton's *The Enemy Is Listening* (London, 1980) provides an interesting insight into how the British 'Y' Service established itself in the first years of the war.

OFFICIAL HISTORIES

The official histories that have come out of the Second World War have been at a consistently higher level than was the case with those of the First World War. The historians of the *Militärgeschichtliches Forschungsamt,* Federal Republic of Germany, have recently produced the first two volumes of what can best be described as a "semiofficial" history of Germany's role in the war. The first volume, Wilhelm Deist, Manfred Messerschmidt, Hans-Erich Volkmann, Wolfram Wette, *Das deutsche Reich und der Zweite Weltkrieg,* Vol. I, *Ursachen und Voraussetzung der deutschen Kriegspolitik* (Stuttgart, 1979), sets the highest possible standards of scholarship and historical objectivity. It examines both the larger questions of German preparation for the war as well as the specific rearmament issues involved with the three services. The second volume, Klaus Maier, Horst Rohde, Bernd Stegmann, and Hans Umbreit, *Das deutsche Reich und der Zweite Weltkrieg,* Vol. II, *Die Errichtung der Hegemonie auf dem Europäischen Kontinent* (Stuttgart, 1979), meets the same standards and contains a groundbreaking discussion of German air doctrine in the prewar period.

One of the most important series of official histories is the *Grand Strategy* series done by the official historians in Great Britain. Of particular use to this study from that series are the following volumes: J. R. M. Butler, *Grand Strategy,* Vol. II, *September 1939–June 1941* (London, 1957); and especially Michael Howard, *Grand Strategy,* Vol. IV, *August 1942–September 1943* (London, 1972). The three-volume set (with one additional volume of appendices) by Sir Charles Webster and Noble Frankland, *The Strategic Air Offensive Against Germany* (London, 1961), is arguably the best work yet done on this aspect of the air war. Basil Collier's *The Defense of the United Kingdom* (London, 1957) contains important information on the air defense of the United Kingdom. The first volume of a new history on the role of British intelligence in the war, F. H. Hinsley, E. E. Thomas, C. F. G. Ransom, R. C. Knight, *British Intelligence in the Second World War,* Vol. I (London, 1979), contains useful information but is disappointing in many respects. Its style is generally undistinguished and its knowledge of what was happening in Germany rather superficial. This study has also consulted a number of other British official histories peripherally: Llewellyn Woodward, *British Foreign Policy in the Second World War* (London, 1962); L. F. Ellis, *The War in France and Flanders, 1939–1940* (London, 1955); I. S. O. Playfair, *The Mediterranean and the Middle East,* Vol. I (London, 1974); and L. F. Ellis, *The War in the West,* Vol. I (London, 1962).

In the United States, the official history of air operations appeared soon after the war was over. Nevertheless, Wesley F. Craven and James L. Cate, *The Army Air Forces in World War II* (Chicago, 1948) still holds up well, although certain issues understandably are not examined in full detail. The Green series, produced in many volumes by the Office of Chief of Military History, are all of high quality but are somewhat tangential to the issues discussed in this work.

GENERAL HISTORIES

One of the most important books on the defeat of the *Luftwaffe* was written by anonymous authors in the British Air Ministry shortly after the war was over. This work never appeared in general print but can be read in a number of archives including the AFSHRC and the AHB: Air Ministry, *The Rise and Fall of the German Air Force* (London, 1948). Perhaps the most provocative and challenging work on the strategic bombing offensive is Anthony Verrier, *The Bomber Offensive* (London, 1968). Read with the official histories (American and British), one can gain deep insights into the nature of the problems faced during the bomber campaign. Noble Frankland has produced a readable, incisive summary of the overall bombing offensive for Ballantine Books: Noble Frankland, *Bomber Offensive, The Devastation of Europe* (New York, 1970). He has also written an excellent summary of British operations, *The Bombing Offensive Against Germany* (London, 1965). Both works are useful departure points. The multivolume set by Dennis Richards, *The Royal Air Force, 1939–1945* (London, 1953), is somewhat dated but still useful. Richard Overy's *The Air War, 1939–1945* (London, 1980) represents a new departure; and while it contains several small errors, it puts the air war into a much larger perspective than most historians have been willing to address. The sections dealing with production questions are particularly important. David Irving's *The Rise and Fall of the Luftwaffe, The Life of Field Marshal Erhard Milch* (Boston, 1973) is uneven but contains some interesting observations. Horst Boog's "High Command and Leadership in the German Luftwaffe, 1935–1945," in *Air Power and Warfare, Proceedings of the Eighth Military History Symposium, USAF Academy,* edited by Colonel Alfred F. Hurley and Major Robert C. Ehrhart (Washington, 1979), is a valuable piece. B. H. Liddell Hart's *History of the Second World War* (New York, 1971) has a particularly insightful chapter dealing with the issues involved in the "strategic" bombing offensive. John Killen's *History of the Luftwaffe* (London, 1966) and Cajus Bekker, *The Luftwaffe War Diaries* (New York, 1968) add little to the subject. Richard Suchenwirth's *Historical Turning Points in the German Air Force War Effort* (USAF Historical Study No. 189, 1968) contains some interesting points as does that author's *Command and Leadership in the German Air Force* (USAF Historical Study No. 174, 1969).

THE PREWAR PERIOD

Several important works exist on the *Luftwaffe* in the period before the war. The best of these in German are Karl-Heinz Völker, "Die Entwicklung der militärischen Luftfahrt in Deutschland, 1920–1933," in *Beitrage zur Militär-und Kriegsgeschichte,* Vol. III (Stuttgart, 1962), and Karl-Heinz Völker, *Die deutsche Luftwaffe, 1933–1939: Aufbau, Führung und Rüstung der Luftwaffe sowie die Entwicklung der deutschen Luftkriegstheorie* (Stuttgart, 1967). Both of these are informative on the creation of the *Luftwaffe* before the war. In English, Edward Homze's *Arming the Luftwaffe, The Reich Air Ministry and the German Aircraft Industry, 1919–1939* (Lincoln, 1976) is excellent concerning German armament production and air rearmament issues. It also contains useful and perceptive comments about the German military's role. For the early developments of the Nazi rearmament effort, see Edward W. Bennett's *German Rearmament and the West, 1932–1933* (Princeton, 1979). Wilhelm Deist's *The Wehrmacht and German Rearmament* (London, 1981) is the most important book on German rearmament in English in the last ten years. It has an excellent discussion on the *Luftwaffe*'s place in Germany's preparation for war. On early strategic thinking in the *Luftwaffe,* see particularly: Bernard Heimann and Joachim Scunke, "Eine geheime Denkschrift zur Luftkriegskonzeption Hitler-Deutschlands vom Mai 1933," *Zeitschrift für Militärgeschichte,* Vol. III (1964). Richard Overy's "The German Pre-War Aircraft Production Plans: November 1936–April 1939," *English Historical Review* (1975) gives an interesting account of the muddle in prewar production. It draws upon his important dissertation: "German Aircraft Production 1939–1942: A Study in the German War Economy," Cambridge University dissertation, 1977. Richard Suchenwirth's *The Development of the German Air Force* is dated and somewhat tendentious but does contain useful information. On the *Luftwaffe*'s involvement in the Spanish Civil War, Klaus Maier's *Guernica* (Freiburg, 1975) is the best work. There are several other works on the *Luftwaffe*'s preparation in the prewar period: Herbert Mason, Jr., *The Rise of the Luftwaffe, 1918–1940* (New York, 1973), and Hanfried Schliephake, *Birth of the Luftwaffe* (Chicago, 1971). The Schliephake work is more careful; the Mason work indicates little research. For an evaluation of the preparedness of air forces to fight in 1938 during the Czech crisis, see my article, "German Air Power and the Munich Crisis," *War and Society*, Vol. II, edited by Brian Bond and Ian Roy (London, 1975). On German foreign policy in the 1930's, Gerhard Weinberg's two-volume set (particularly the first volume), *The Foreign Policy of Hitler's Germany*, Vol. I, *1933–1936*, and Vol. II, *1936–1939* (Chicago, 1970, 1981), is a useful point of departure. For the considerable economic constraints on German rearmament, see *Wirtschaft und Rüstung am Vorabend des Zweiten Weltkrieges*, edited by Friedrich Forstmeier and Hans-Erich Volkmann (Düsseldorf, 1975). For a comparison of the *Luftwaffe* and RAF, see my article "British and German Air Doctrine Between the Wars," *Air University Review* (March-April 1980). For a closer look at German air doctrine, see my article "The Luftwaffe Before the Second World War: A Mission, A Strategy?" in the *Journal of Strategic Studies* (September 1981).

On the development of British doctrine before the Second World War, Barry D. Powers, *Strategy Without Slide-Rule, British Air Strategy, 1914–1939* (London, 1976), is an important work. Group Captain R. A. Mason's "The British Dimension," *Airpower and Warfare*, edited by Alfred F. Hurley and Robert C. Ehrhard (Washington, 1979), gives a new look at the First World War and its air strategy. D. C. Watt's "The Air Force View of History," *Quarterly Review* (October 1962), is sharp and challenging and an important article. Basil Collier's *The Leader of the Few* (London, 1957) is a bit too uncritical but an important source on the career of Dowding. For the influence of the Treasury on British rearmament, two useful works have recently appeared: G. C. Peden, *British Rearmament and the Treasury* (Edinburgh, 1979), and, to a lesser extent, Robert Paul Shay, Jr., *British Rearmament in the Thirties* (Princeton, 1977). On the American side, Alfred F. Hurley's *Billy Mitchell* (New York, 1964) presents a balanced view of the early airpower theorist. Haywood S. Hansell, Jr's. *The Air Plan that Defeated Hitler* (Atlantic, 1972) is a forthright but uncritical examination of the evolution of American doctrine and plans by one of the individuals at the heart of the Air Corps Tactical School. Robert F. Futrell's *Ideas, Concepts, Doctrine: A History of Basic Thinking in the United States Air Force, 1907–1964* (Montgomery, 1971) is a useful jump-off point for an examination of the development of American air doctrine. Thomas A. Fabyanic, "A Critique of United States Air War Planning, 1941–1944," St. Louis University dissertation (1973), is an interesting critique of the planning and doctrinal developments before and during the war. Thomas H. Greer, "The Development of Air Doctrine in the Army Air Arm, 1917–1941" (unpublished manuscript, Air University Library), is also useful.

THE EARLY WAR, 1939–41

Robert M. Kennedy's *The German Campaign in Poland, 1939* (Washington, 1956) is an excellent study of the first battles in that war. For the study of the "phony war," two articles are noteworthy. The first one is mine, "The German Response to Victory in Poland: A Case Study in Professionalism," *Armed Forces and Society* (Winter, 1981); the second is Peter Ludlow's outstanding article, "The Unwinding of Appeasement," in *Das 'Andere Deutschland' im Zweiten Weltkrieg,* edited by L. Kettenacker (Stuttgart, 1977). For difficulties within the German high command, see Harold C. Deutsch, *The Conspiracy Against Hitler in the Twilight War* (Minneapolis, 1968). A number of important works exist on the defeat of France in 1940. Among those worth consulting are Telford Taylor, *The March of Conquest* (New York, 1958); Alistair Horne, *To Lose a Battle, France 1940* (London, 1969); and Hans-Adolf Jacobsen, *Fall Gelb, Der Kampf um den deutschen Operationsplan zur Westoffensive 1940* (Wiesbaden, 1957). For obvious reasons, these works do not concentrate on the air battle and its significant losses but rather on the course of the decisive land conflict. Patrice Buffotot and Jacques Ogier, "L' armée de l'air francaise dans la campagne de France (10 Mai–25 Juin 1940)," *Revue historique des Armées,* Vol. II, No. 3, pp. 88–117, offers a unique look at the problems that the French air force faced in 1940 as well as its contributions.

On the first developments in the intelligence war, see Ronald Lewin, *Ultra Goes to War* (New York, 1978). Brian Johnson's *The Secret War* (London, 1978) looks at the development of the scientific war as well as intelligence. For the best book on the Battle of Britain, see Francis K. Mason, *Battle Over Britain* (New York, 1968). Telford Taylor's *The Breaking Wave* (New York, 1967) is also good on the wider strategic questions as well as the air battles. Basil Collier's *The Battle of Britain* (New York, 1962) is also useful.

Adam Ulam's brilliant work, *Expansion and Coexistence: History of Soviet Foreign Policy, 1917–1967* (New York, 1974), has much to say on the diplomatic background to the Russo-German War. Gerhard Weinberg's *Germany and the Soviet Union, 1939–1941* (Leiden, 1954) still is useful but flawed.

There are a number of important works that treat particular aspects of the 1941 campaigns. Martin van Creveld's *Hitler's Strategy 1940–1941, The Balkan Clue* (Cambridge, 1973) is interesting but perhaps overstated. For the spring battles, George Blau's *The German Campaigns in the Balkans (Spring, 1941)* (Washington, 1953) is an excellent piece of work. Hans-Otto Mühleisen, *Kreta 1941, Das Unternehmen 'Merkur'* (Freiburg, 1968), is a thorough battle study. For the German invasion of Russia, a number of outstanding works exist. For the intelligence background to the invasion, see Barton Whaley, *Codeword Barbarossa* (Cambridge, 1973). The best work on German strategy in the first years of the war is Andreas Hillgruber's monumental *Hitlers Strategie* (Frankfurt, 1965). George E.

Blau's *The German Campaign in Russia—Planning and Operations (1940–1942)* (Washington, 1955) is an excellent summary for the time when it was written. The best account on Barbarossa's failure, though somewhat limited in its span of time, is Klaus Reinhardt, *Die Wende vor Moskau, Das Scheitern der Strategie Hitlers im Winter 1941/42* (Stuttgart, 1972). Herman Plocher's study, *The German Air Force Versus Russia, 1941* (USAF Historical Study No. 154, 1967) has much interesting information but is narrow in scope. Richard Overy's "The Luftwaffe and the German Economy 1939–1945," *Militärgeschichtliche Mitteilungen 2/79*, is a brillant account of why the Germans made such a hash of aircraft production in the war years. On why the campaign turned into such a terrible war of atrocity, see: Jürgen Förster's "Hitler's War Aims Against the Soviet Union and German Military Leaders," *Militärhistorisk Tidskrift* (Stockholm, 1979). For the most thorough study of this subject, see Christian Streit, *Keine Kameraden, Die Wehrmacht und die sowjetischen Kriegsgefangenen 1941–1945* (Stuttgart, 1978). Robert Conquest's *The Great Terror, Stalin's Purge of the Thirties* (London, 1968) gives the political background and results of Stalin's savaging of his military services. The results, the catastrophic collapse of 1941–42, are graphically described by John Erickson, *The Road to Stalingrad* (New York, 1975). For the suffering of Russia's civilians, see Harrison Salisbury's *The 900 Days, The Siege of Leningrad* (New York, 1969). Seweryn Bialer's collection of translated Russian memoirs, *Stalin and His Generals* (New York, 1969), contains many interesting accounts. Albert Seaton's *The Russo German War, 1941–43* (New York, 1971) covers both sides of the war and is interesting in parts but has some major weaknesses. For the Soviet summary in English of their great military history effort on the war, see: *The Great Patriotic War of the Soviet Union 1941–1945, A General Outline* (Moscow, 1974). On the Russian air force, one can consult Walter Schwabedissen, *The Russian Air Force in the Eyes of German Commanders* (USAF Historical Study No. 175, 1960), and Klaus Uebe, *Russian Reaction to German Airpower in World War II* (USAF Historical Study No. 176, 1964). From the Russian point of view, one can consult the translation of the Soviet official history by Leland Fetzer and edited by Ray Wagner, *The Soviet Air Force in World War II* (New York, 1973).

THE LATER WAR YEARS

On the air war in Russia, Herman Plocher's *The German Air Force Versus Russia, 1943* (USAF Historical Study No. 155, 1967) has the same weaknesses of his volumes on 1941 and 1942. There are a number of important works on the German defeats in Russia in the last years of the Second World War. The best work in English is Earl F. Ziemke's excellent *Stalingrad to Berlin: The German Defeat in the East* (Washington, 1968). Not surprisingly, there are a number of works in German. Manfred Kehrig's *Stalingrad, Analyse und Dokumentation einer Schlacht* (Stuttgart, 1974) is as thorough a study of that battle as one could expect. The Battle of Kursk has also received the same sort of attention: see, in particular, E. Klink, *Das Gesetz des Handelns, 'Zitadelle' 1943* (Stuttgart, 1966).

A number of worthwhile pieces have appeared on various aspects of the air war in 1943–44. Martin Middlebrook has written two excellent studies that cover major incidents in those years. The first of those is *The Nuremberg Raid* (New York, 1974). The coverage on Bomber Command's operations was excellent; that of German operations adequate. His more recent work, *The Battle of Hamburg, Allied Bomber Forces Against a German City in 1943* (London, 1980), has the same strengths and weaknesses. From the German viewpoint, Friedhelm Golücke's *Schweinfurt und der strategische Luftkrieg, 1943* (Paderborn, 1980) is thorough on all aspects of the German side but leaves many aspects of the American air offensive untouched. It is an important work. David Irving's *The Mare's Nest* (London, 1964) is arguably his best work and covers the development of German rocket technology and the British response. While Hans Rumpf's *The Bombing of Germany* (New York, 1961) is much weaker than the above works, it does contain some useful statistics. Thomas M. Coffey's *Decision Over Schweinfurt* (New York, 1977) does not compare with Middlebrook's or Golücke's works. Max Hastings' *Bomber Command* (New York, 1979) is a unique mixture of squadron histories and an operational account of the course of the British campaign. It is one of the more interesting books on the air war that have recently appeared. Gordon Musgrove's *Pathfinder Force, A History of 8 Group* (London, 1976) gives a close look at the development and effectiveness of Bennett's force. Werner Girbig's . . . *mit Kurs auf Leuna* (Stuttgart, 1980) is an important account of the "strategic" bombing attacks on Germany's oil industry and the efforts of the *Luftwaffe* to defend its life blood. On German aircraft production during the war, see the outstanding article by R. J. Overy, "The Luftwaffe and the European Economy, 1939–1945," in *Militärgeschichtliche Mitteilungen,* 2/79. Olaf Groehler's "Starke, Verteilung und Verluste der deutschen Luftwaffe im Zweiten Weltkrieg," *Militärgeschichte,* Vol. 17 (1978) presents some interesting tables based on the loss reports of the Quartermaster General. His interpretation, colored by the political atmosphere of the GDR, leaves much to be desired. On the Normandy campaign, Ralph Bennett's *Ultra in the West, The Normandy Campaign, 1944–1945* is the first work to integrate the impact of "Ultra" with supporting evidence directly into an account of ground and air operations.

Index